Rust Blockchain

Rust Blockchain

A Full-Stack Implementation Guide

Building blockchain systems with Tokio, Axum, and modern Rust

Bill Kunyiha

First Edition

Rust Blockchain: A Full-Stack Implementation Guide
First Edition

ISBN-13: 979-8-9954311-1-4 (paperback)
ISBN-13: 979-8-9954311-2-1 (hardcover)
ISBN-13: 979-8-9954311-0-7 (ebook)

Typeset with LaTeX using the memoir document class.

Cover design and illustrations by the author.

Source code and companion materials:
`https://github.com/bkunyiha/rust-blockchain`

To the contributors behind Rust, Bitcoin Core, and the countless

open-source projects that made this work possible.

You proved that trust can be built in code.

Contents

II Deployment & Operations 641

III Language Reference 685

List of Listings

List of Figures

1

Quick Start — See It Run

▷ **What you will learn in this chapter**

- Deploy a multi-node blockchain network with a single command using Docker Compose
- Observe blocks being mined, hashed, and propagated between peers in real time
- Query the blockchain REST API and view the web admin dashboard
- Understand which chapters of the book correspond to each running component

BEFORE writing a single line of Rust, take a look at the finished product. The next chapter introduces the system architecture in detail; for now, let's see it running. In under five minutes, you will have a multi-node blockchain network—like the one Bitcoin runs on—mining blocks on your machine, propagating them to peers, and serving a live web admin dashboard. All you need is Docker and Docker Compose; no Rust installation required.

1.1 Step 1: Clone the Repository

```
git clone
https://github.com/bkunyiha/rust-blockchain.git
cd rust-blockchain
```

1.2 Step 2: Start the Network

```
cd ci/docker-compose/configs
docker compose up --build
```

This builds the Rust node from source (first run takes a few minutes while Cargo (Rust's package manager and build tool) compiles), then starts two containers—lightweight, isolated processes that each run a copy of your node software without affecting your host system—a **miner** node and a **webserver** node.

1.3 Step 3: Watch It Work

Once the build finishes, you will see output like this in your terminal:

```
miner-1      | [INFO] Starting miner on port 8010...
miner-1      | [INFO] Mining block #1 ...
miner-1      | [INFO] Block mined: hash=00a3f2...
height=1  txns=1
webserver-1 | [INFO] Connected to peer miner-1:8010
miner-1      | [INFO] Mining block #2 ...
miner-1      | [INFO] Block mined: hash=0017cb...
height=2  txns=1
webserver-1 | [INFO] Received block #2 from miner-1
```

Blocks are being mined, hashed, and propagated across the network in real time.

1.4 Step 4: Open the Admin Dashboard

While the network is running, open your browser to:

```
http://localhost:8080
```

If the dashboard prompts you to configure an API key, use the default **Admin API key**: `admin-secret` (unless you have overridden it via `BITCOIN_API_ADMIN_KEY`).

▷ Note

API keys (what they are): An API key is a shared secret that restricts access to specific server endpoints. The webserver protects its REST endpoints with such shared secrets passed on each request. In Docker Compose there are two keys:
Admin key (`BITCOIN_API_ADMIN_KEY` , default `admin-secret`): full access to `/api/admin/*` endpoints used by the admin dashboard.
Wallet key (`BITCOIN_API_WALLET_KEY` , default `wallet-secret`): access to wallet-related endpoints.

You will see the Web Admin Interface showing the current chain height, connected peers, recent blocks, and the mempool. This is the same React dashboard we build in Chapter 30.

1.5 Step 5: Query the API

In another terminal, try:

```
curl http://localhost:8080/api/admin/blockchain-info
| python3 -m json.tool
```

You will get a JSON response with the chain height, tip hash, peer count, and mempool size—the same API we build in Chapter 24.

Key Takeaways

- ✓ **Primitives** (Ch 6) — the `Block` and `Transaction` structs that were serialized into each mined block
- ✓ **Cryptography** (Ch 8) — the SHA-256 hashing and ECDSA signing that produced each block hash
- ✓ **Chain validation** (Ch 9–10) — the consensus rules that accepted each block into the canonical chain
- ✓ **Storage** (Ch 11) — the sled database that persisted blocks to disk
- ✓ **Networking** (Ch 12) — the TCP protocol that propagated blocks between the miner and webserver nodes
- ✓ **Node orchestration** (Ch 13) — the coordinator that routed messages between subsystems

- ✓ **Web API** (Ch 15) — the Axum REST API that served the `/api/admin/*` endpoints
- ✓ **Web Admin UI** (Ch 21) — the React dashboard you just opened in your browser
- ✓ **Docker Compose** (Ch 22) — the deployment configuration that wired everything together

1.6 Clean Up

```
docker compose down -v      # Stop containers and
remove volumes
```

Part I

Foundations & Core Implementation

Chapters 2–30 build your blockchain from first principles: cryptographic primitives, the UTXO transaction model, proof-of-work consensus, peer-to-peer networking, and a persistence layer—all implemented in safe, idiomatic Rust.

2

Introduction & Overview

> ▷ **What you will learn in this chapter**
>
> - Understand the project architecture and how every crate in the workspace fits together
> - Identify the role of each system layer, from primitives through networking to user interfaces
> - Trace the data flow from a user action through the REST API, node context, and blockchain state
> - Set up the development environment and run the project for the first time

By the final chapter of this book, a fleet of blockchain nodes will be running on your machine, mining blocks in competition, propagating them peer-to-peer, and serving a web dashboard that shows your wallet balance and transaction history—all written from scratch in Rust. This is a complete, self-contained guide to building a full-stack system following Bitcoin's architecture, walking you through every module, every function, and every design decision in a working implementation—from raw byte serialization and cryptographic primitives all the way up to desktop wallet UIs and containerized deployment. You will not need to clone the repository or read external documentation to understand the system; the book *is* the documentation, and the inline comments inside every code listing are part of that documentation—they explain *why* the code works, not just *what* it does.

The target audience is **intermediate to advanced Rust developers** who want to understand how blockchain works at the implementation level.

We assume you are comfortable with ownership, traits, generics, and async/await. If you need a refresher on any Rust concept, **Chapter 33: Rust Language Guide** at the end of the book serves as a standalone reference—read it before diving into the implementation chapters, or refer to it whenever you encounter unfamiliar syntax.

> ▷ Note
>
> This project runs entirely on **Tokio**, the async runtime that powers most production Rust systems. You will use `async` / `await` throughout: spawning mining tasks, managing peer-to-peer TCP connections, orchestrating node subsystems with channels and `select!`, serving REST endpoints with Axum, and handling IPC commands in Tauri. If you want to learn async Rust through real code rather than toy examples, this book provides that from Chapter 10 onward.

> ⋆ Read the Comments
>
> Every code listing in this book is heavily commented. The comments are not afterthoughts—they are part of the explanation. When you encounter a listing, read the inline comments as carefully as the surrounding prose; they explain design intent, document trade-offs, and call out subtle behavior that would otherwise require a separate paragraph. Skipping the comments means skipping half the teaching.

2.1 How the Book Is Organized

The book follows the same path data takes through a Bitcoin node:

- **Part I (Chapters 2–30)** builds the system from the ground up. We start with the Bitcoin whitepaper (Chapters 3–5) to understand *what* we are building and *why*. Then we implement it in Rust: primitives and byte encodings (7–8), cryptographic identity and authorization (9), blockchain state and consensus (10–19), persistent storage (20), networking (21), node orchestration (22), wallet (23), a REST API (Chapter 24), and multiple frontend interfaces—desktop UIs in Iced and Tauri (Chapters 25–28), an embedded encrypted database (Chapter 29), and a React web admin panel (Chapter 30).
- **Part II (Chapters 31–32)** covers deployment with Docker Compose and Kubernetes.

- **Part III (Chapter 33)** is the Rust language reference.

Each implementation chapter opens by explaining what problem the module solves, shows the complete annotated code, and closes by connecting forward to the next layer. The reading order is designed so that every concept is introduced before it is used. Pay particular attention to the inline comments inside code listings—they carry explanations of design decisions, edge cases, and "why this and not that" reasoning that complements the prose discussion around each listing.

2.2 System Architecture

The diagram below shows how every module in the system connects. Data flows upward from raw bytes to user-facing interfaces. Keep this picture in mind as you read—each chapter builds one layer of this stack.

2.3 What This Book Does Not Cover

This is an educational implementation, not a production Bitcoin client. To keep the book focused and the codebase readable, we deliberately exclude:

— **Production mining difficulty**—our proof-of-work uses a simplified difficulty target. Real Bitcoin's difficulty adjustment algorithm (recalculated every 2,016 blocks—roughly two weeks at one block every ten minutes, since 2,016 $\times$ 10 minutes $\div$ 60 $\div$ 24 $\approx$ 14 days—to keep the average block time near that 10-minute target as total network hash power rises or falls) is not implemented.

— **NAT traversal and peer discovery**—nodes connect via configured addresses. The DNS seeding, UPnP, and NAT hole-punching that production Bitcoin uses for peer discovery are outside our scope.

— **BIP-32 HD wallets**—our wallet generates standalone key pairs. Hierarchical Deterministic key derivation (BIP-32/39/44, a family of Bitcoin Improvement Proposals that let a single seed deterministically produce unlimited keys) is covered in the Further Reading section of the Wallet chapter.

— **Lightning Network**—layer-2 payment channels are an entirely separate protocol built on top of Bitcoin. We focus exclusively on the layer-1 blockchain.

— **Smart contracts and scripting**—Bitcoin's Script language for transaction conditions is not implemented. Our transactions use a simplified signature-based authorization model.

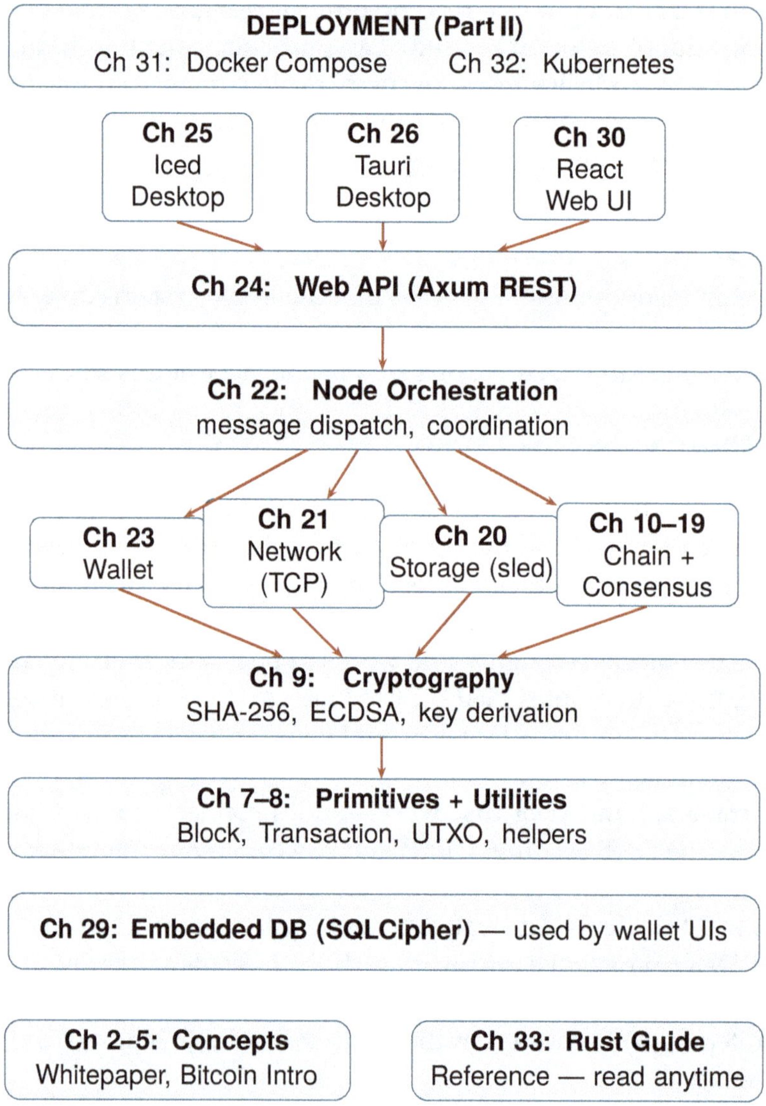

Figure 2.1: System Architecture: Layered Stack from Primitives to User Interfaces

— **Multi-signature wallets**—all transactions require a single signature. Multi-sig (P2SH and P2WSH, the Pay-to-Script-Hash and Pay-to-Witness-Script-Hash output types that let a transaction require M-of-N signatures) is a natural extension but adds complexity beyond our teaching goals.

Each exclusion is a deliberate scope decision. The Further Reading sections at the end of relevant chapters point you to specifications and crates that cover these topics.

With the scope established, let's examine how the codebase organizes these design choices.

2.4 Project Structure

```
blockchain/
+-- bitcoin/
|   +-- src/
|   |   +-- primitives/
|   |   +-- node/
|   |   +-- store/
|   |   +-- web/
|   +-- ...
+-- bitcoin-desktop-ui-iced/
+-- bitcoin-wallet-ui-iced/
+-- bitcoin-web-ui/
+-- ci/
|   +-- docker-compose/
|   +-- kubernetes/
```

Directory	Description
`bitcoin/`	Core blockchain implementation
`bitcoin/src/primitives/`	Transaction, Block, UTXO structures
`bitcoin/src/node/`	Node context and networking
`bitcoin/src/store/`	Blockchain storage (file system, database)
`bitcoin/src/web/`	REST API server (Axum)
`bitcoin-desktop-ui-iced/`	Desktop admin interface (Iced)
`bitcoin-wallet-ui-iced/`	Wallet user interface (Iced)
`bitcoin-web-ui/`	Web admin interface (React/TypeScript)
`ci/docker-compose/`	Docker Compose deployment
`ci/kubernetes/`	Kubernetes deployment

⋆ Tip

If you want to see the system running before reading further, jump to Chapter 1: Quick Start. You can return here afterward for the full architectural picture.

2.5 Technical Stack

Backend (Rust)

- **Tokio**: Async runtime for non-blocking I/O—provides an async runtime for concurrent I/O without blocking.
- **Axum**: Type-safe web framework for building REST APIs—a modern, composable framework designed for building web services.
- **Sled**: Embedded key-value store for blockchain persistence—maintains persistent state for blockchain data on disk.
- **SQLCipher**: Encrypted SQLite database—provides encrypted database storage for wallet security.
- **Serde**: Serialization framework—handles serialization and deserialization of data structures across the codebase.

Desktop UIs (Rust)

- **Iced**: Cross-platform GUI framework (Model-View-Update architecture)
- **Tauri 2**: Desktop framework pairing a Rust backend with a web-technology frontend
- **Desktop Admin Interface**: Admin UI for blockchain management (Iced and Tauri variants)
- **Wallet User Interface**: User-facing wallet application (Iced and Tauri variants)

Web UI (TypeScript/React)

- **React 18**: UI framework
- **TypeScript**: Type-safe JavaScript
- **Vite**: Build tool and dev server

2.6 What to Read Next

If you are reading the book front-to-back, continue to **Chapter 3: Introduction to Blockchain**—it builds the conceptual vocabulary (transactions, blocks, consensus, UTXO) that every implementation chapter depends on.

If you want to brush up on Rust first, jump to **Chapter 33: Rust Language Guide** and return here when you are ready. The **Tokio Runtime Guide** is also useful preparation for the async code that appears from Chapter 21 onward.

2.7 Further Reading

- **The Rust Programming Language**—The official Rust book, covering everything from installation to advanced features. See `https://doc.rust-lang.org/book/`
- **Cargo Reference**—Comprehensive guide to Rust's package manager and build system. See `https://doc.rust-lang.org/cargo/`
- **Bitcoin Developer Guide**—Bitcoin.org's technical documentation for developers. See `https://developer.bitcoin.org/devguide/`

Key Takeaways

- ✓ The full project architecture: a Cargo workspace of specialized crates spanning primitives, cryptography, chain logic, networking, storage, wallet, web API, and multiple UI frontends.
- ✓ Four system layers—core blockchain, API/services, desktop UIs, and deployment—and the data flows connecting them.
- ✓ The technical stack that powers the system: Rust for the backend, Iced and Tauri for desktop UIs, React/TypeScript for the web UI, and Docker Compose and Kubernetes for deployment.
- ✓ Learning paths are established for different readers—first-timers, experienced developers, and operations teams—each guiding them through the material.
- ✓ In the next chapter, the fundamental concepts of Bitcoin and blockchain technology are explored—what they are, why they matter, and the cryptographic building blocks that make them work.

3

Introduction to Blockchain

> ▷ **What you will learn in this chapter**
>
> - Explain what blockchain technology is and why decentralization matters
> - Describe Bitcoin's key innovations: proof-of-work, the UTXO model, and trustless consensus
> - Identify real-world blockchain applications across finance, governance, and supply chain
> - Understand the cryptographic building blocks that secure every transaction

WHEN you spend a digital coin, what stops someone from copying your coin and spending it again?—this is the *double-spend problem*, and solving it without a bank or referee is the core engineering challenge that Bitcoin answers. This chapter builds the technical vocabulary—transactions, blocks, consensus, UTXO, proof-of-work—that every subsequent implementation chapter depends on. We ground these concepts in the problems they solve, then connect them to the whitepaper in Chapters 4 and 5 before translating them into Rust.

> ▷ **Note**
>
> This chapter covers Bitcoin as a technology and protocol. We do not cover cryptocurrency trading, investment, or regulatory considerations—our focus is purely on the engineering.

3.1 What Is Bitcoin?

Bitcoin is a decentralized digital currency and payment system that operates without a central authority or intermediary. It was introduced in 2008 through a whitepaper published by an individual or group using the pseudonym Satoshi Nakamoto. Bitcoin enables peer-to-peer transactions over the internet, allowing users to send and receive value directly without relying on traditional financial institutions.

At its core, Bitcoin is three things:

1. **A Digital Currency**: Bitcoin exists purely in digital form, represented as entries in a distributed ledger. Unlike traditional currencies, there is no physical coin or bill—only cryptographic records.
2. **A Payment Network**: Bitcoin operates as a global payment network that processes transactions 24/7 without borders, bank holidays, or intermediaries. Transactions are verified by network participants and recorded on a public ledger.
3. **A Store of Value**: Many people view Bitcoin as "digital gold"—a scarce asset that can serve as a store of value and hedge against inflation, independent of any government or central bank.

3.2 What Is Blockchain?

Blockchain is the underlying technology that powers Bitcoin and many other cryptocurrencies. At its simplest, a blockchain is a distributed, immutable ledger that records transactions in a secure and verifiable way.

Core Components

Blocks: A blockchain consists of a series of blocks, each containing a collection of transactions. Each block includes:

- A list of transactions
- A reference to the previous block (creating a chain)
- A cryptographic hash that uniquely identifies the block
- A timestamp
- Other metadata depending on the blockchain implementation

Chain Structure: Blocks are linked together sequentially, with each block containing the hash of the previous block. This creates an unbreakable chain—if any block is modified, its hash changes, breaking the chain and making tampering immediately detectable.

Distributed Network: Unlike traditional databases stored in a single location, blockchain data is replicated across many nodes (computers) in a peer-to-peer network. Each node maintains a complete copy of the blockchain, ensuring redundancy and resilience.

Consensus Mechanism: Network participants must agree on which transactions are valid and in what order they occurred. Bitcoin uses a consensus mechanism called Proof of Work (PoW), where miners compete to solve cryptographic puzzles to validate transactions and create new blocks.

Key Characteristics

- **Decentralization**: No single entity controls the network. Power is distributed among all participants.
- **Immutability**: Once recorded, transactions cannot be easily altered or deleted.
- **Transparency**: All transactions are publicly visible (though identities are pseudonymous).
- **Security**: Cryptographic techniques ensure that only authorized parties can spend their funds.
- **Trustlessness**: Participants don't need to trust each other or a central authority—the protocol enforces rules.

3.3 The Origin of Bitcoin and Blockchain

The Pre-Bitcoin Era

The concept of digital cash and cryptographic currencies predates Bitcoin by decades. In the 1980s and 1990s, researchers explored various approaches:

- **David Chaum's DigiCash (1989)**: An early attempt at anonymous digital cash using cryptographic protocols, but it required a central authority.
- **B-Money (1998)**: Wei Dai proposed a distributed electronic cash system, introducing concepts like proof-of-work and decentralized consensus.
- **Bit Gold (1998)**: Nick Szabo's proposal for a decentralized digital currency, though it was never fully implemented.

These early attempts faced two fundamental challenges: the **double-spending problem** (how to prevent someone from spending the same digital coin twice) and the **Byzantine Generals' Problem**. Imagine several army generals surrounding a city: they must all attack at the same time to win, but they can only communicate by messenger, and some generals might be traitors who send false messages. How do the honest generals agree on a plan? This is the core challenge of any distributed system—reaching agreement when some participants might lie or fail. Bitcoin solves it through proof-of-work consensus—computational effort replaces trust in any single participant.

Satoshi Nakamoto's Breakthrough

On October 31, 2008, a paper titled "Bitcoin: A Peer-to-Peer Electronic Cash System" was published to a cryptography mailing list. The author, Satoshi Nakamoto (whose true identity remains unknown), solved the double-spending problem without requiring a trusted third party.

Key Innovations:

1. **Proof of Work**: A mechanism where participants (miners) expend computational resources to validate transactions and create blocks. This makes attacking the network economically unfeasible.
2. **Blockchain Structure**: Linking blocks cryptographically creates an immutable history. Any attempt to modify past transactions requires redoing all subsequent work, making tampering computationally impractical.
3. **Incentive Structure**: Miners are rewarded with newly created bitcoins and transaction fees, aligning their economic interests with network security.
4. **Peer-to-Peer Network**: A distributed network where all nodes participate in validation and consensus, eliminating single points of failure.

The Genesis Block

On January 3, 2009, the first Bitcoin block (the "Genesis Block") was mined by Satoshi Nakamoto. Embedded in this block was a message referencing a headline from *The Times* newspaper: "The Times 03/Jan/2009 Chancellor on brink of second bailout for banks." This message is often interpreted as a commentary on the financial system that Bitcoin was designed to replace or improve upon.

Evolution and Growth

Since 2009, Bitcoin has grown from an experimental system used by cryptography enthusiasts to a global financial asset with:

- A market capitalization in the hundreds of billions of dollars
- Millions of users worldwide
- Acceptance by major corporations and institutions
- Recognition as legal tender in some countries
- A thriving ecosystem of exchanges, wallets, and applications

The blockchain technology underlying Bitcoin has also inspired thousands of other cryptocurrencies and blockchain projects, each exploring different use cases, consensus mechanisms, and technical approaches.

3.4 Bitcoin Whitepaper Summary

Bitcoin started with a paper: Satoshi Nakamoto's *Bitcoin: A Peer-to-Peer Electronic Cash System* (2008).

In the next section, we go through the whitepaper end-to-end, focusing on the core ideas we must preserve when we implement Bitcoin.

Chapter 4 provides a section-by-section summary of the whitepaper, covering the double-spending problem, proof-of-work, network operation, the incentive structure, Merkle trees, and security analysis. Understanding the whitepaper provides the theoretical foundation we use throughout the rest of this project—it helps us separate consensus-critical rules (which must be implemented correctly) from engineering details (which can vary without breaking consensus).

3.5 System Architecture: Centralized vs. Decentralized vs. Distributed

Understanding the architectural differences between centralized, decentralized, and distributed systems is fundamental to grasping how blockchain represents a paradigm shift in system design. These three architectures embody different approaches to organizing computational resources, control, and data storage, each with distinct trade-offs in performance, reliability, and governance.

Centralized Systems

Centralized systems consolidate control, processing, and data storage within a single central server or a tightly coupled cluster of servers. All client requests flow through this central point, which manages all operations, resources, and data. Clients typically possess minimal processing capabilities and depend entirely on the central server for computational tasks.

Centralized architecture offers several advantages: simplified management through a single administrative point, efficient resource utilization through centralized optimization, and straightforward security implementation since all controls exist in one location. However, centralized systems suffer from inherent limitations. They present a single point of failure—if the central server fails, the entire system becomes inoperative. Scalability becomes problematic as the central server becomes a bottleneck under increased load. Adding more clients strains server resources, leading to performance degradation.

Traditional examples include enterprise resource planning (ERP) systems, customer relationship management (CRM) platforms, centralized email servers, and traditional banking systems. These systems excel in environments where centralized control, consistent data management, and simplified administration are priorities.

Decentralized Systems

Decentralized systems distribute control and processing power across multiple independent nodes without a single central authority. Each node operates autonomously while collaborating with others to achieve common system goals. This architecture eliminates single points of failure and distributes control, creating a more resilient and fault-tolerant system.

Decentralized systems have key characteristics: distributed control where no single node has authority over others, enhanced fault tolerance where individual node failures don't compromise the entire system, and improved scalability through independent node addition without overwhelming a central point. However, this architecture introduces complexity: nodes must coordinate and communicate to maintain system integrity and consistency, often requiring sophisticated consensus algorithms and protocols.

Decentralized systems manifest in two primary categories: blockchain-based systems that leverage distributed ledger technology and consensus mechanisms, and non-blockchain systems that achieve decentralization through alternative architectural patterns.

Blockchain-Based Decentralized Systems

Blockchain-based decentralized systems utilize distributed ledger technology (DLT) and consensus mechanisms to operate without central authority. These systems maintain state through cryptographic verification and peer-to-peer coordination.

Cryptocurrencies represent the foundational application of blockchain decentralization. Networks like Bitcoin and Ethereum operate as decentralized payment systems, relying on global node networks to validate transactions and maintain immutable public ledgers. Each node independently verifies transactions against consensus rules, eliminating the need for trusted intermediaries.

Decentralized Finance (DeFi) platforms extend blockchain principles to financial services, offering lending, borrowing, and trading without traditional banking infrastructure. Decentralized exchanges (DEXs) such as Uniswap[1] and PancakeSwap utilize automated smart contracts to facilitate peer-to-peer token swaps, removing order book intermediaries and enabling direct user-to-user transactions.

Decentralized Applications (dApps) operate on blockchain networks rather than centralized servers. Built primarily on Ethereum and similar platforms, dApps execute smart contract logic across distributed nodes. Examples include OpenSea,[2] an NFT marketplace operating without centralized control, and Audius,[3] a music streaming platform that distributes content storage and delivery across network participants.

Decentralized Autonomous Organizations (DAOs) represent community-led entities governed by smart contracts rather than hierarchical management structures. Decision-making occurs through

[1]See https://blog.uniswap.org/what-is-uniswap

[2]See https://opensea.io/

[3]"Blockchain-Based Music Streaming Service Audius Up to 5M Monthly Users," CoinDesk, August 2021. See https://www.coindesk.com/markets/2021/08/05/blockchain-based-music-streaming-service-audius-up-to-5m-monthly-users

token-weighted voting on proposals, with execution enforced by blockchain-based smart contracts. This eliminates traditional corporate governance structures while maintaining organizational functionality.

Supply Chain Management systems leverage blockchain immutability to track goods from origin to consumer. Platforms like De Beers' Tracr system[4] record diamond provenance on distributed ledgers, ensuring transparency and ethical sourcing verification without relying on centralized certification authorities.

Identity Verification platforms utilize blockchain to enable self-sovereign identity management. Systems like Civic[5] allow individuals to cryptographically verify identity attributes without sharing sensitive personal information with centralized authorities, reducing identity theft risk while maintaining privacy.

Non-Blockchain Decentralized Systems

Non-blockchain decentralized systems achieve decentralization through alternative architectural patterns that don't rely on cryptographic chaining of blocks.

Peer-to-Peer (P2P) File Sharing networks enable direct file transfer between users without central servers. Protocols like BitTorrent distribute file segments across participating nodes, with each node serving as both client and server. Gnutella represents an earlier P2P architecture that routes queries through neighbor nodes without centralized indexing.

Mesh Networks create resilient connectivity infrastructure where each participant node relays data for the network. This architecture provides internet connectivity in areas lacking central infrastructure, with nodes dynamically routing traffic through multiple paths to maintain connectivity despite individual node failures.

Distributed Web Protocols reimagine content addressing and storage. The InterPlanetary File System (IPFS) implements content-addressed storage where files are identified by cryptographic hashes rather than location-based URLs. Content retrieval occurs through distributed hash tables (DHTs), enabling censorship-resistant content distribution without centralized hosting.

[4]See `https://www.debeersgroup.com/about-us/case-studies/2024/tracr`

[5]See `https://www.civic.com/`

Communication Protocols like Tor (The Onion Router) create decentralized anonymity networks through volunteer-operated relay nodes. Traffic routing through multiple encrypted layers prevents traffic analysis and enables anonymous communication resistant to surveillance and censorship.

Distributed Ledger Technologies (DLT) Alternatives explore consensus mechanisms beyond traditional blockchain structures. Directed Acyclic Graphs (DAGs), as implemented in IOTA's Tangle, enable faster transaction processing and improved scalability without transaction fees. DAG-based systems allow parallel transaction validation, contrasting with blockchain's sequential block processing model.

Blockchain technology exemplifies decentralized systems through Bitcoin's network architecture, where each node maintains a complete copy of the blockchain, validates transactions independently, and participates in consensus without requiring a central authority. The diversity of decentralized system implementations demonstrates that decentralization represents an architectural principle applicable across multiple domains, not merely a blockchain-specific innovation.

The architectural principle of decentralization depends on three technical foundations—hashing, signatures, and consensus—that make trustless coordination possible.

Distributed Systems

Distributed systems represent a broader category where multiple independent nodes work together as a single coherent system, appearing transparent to end users. These nodes communicate over a network and share resources such as processing power, storage, and data. Unlike decentralized systems, distributed systems may have centralized coordination mechanisms while distributing computational resources geographically.

The architecture emphasizes geographical distribution of nodes across different physical locations, resource sharing for efficient utilization, concurrency through parallel processing across nodes, and transparency that hides system complexity from users. Distributed systems excel at scalability through horizontal expansion, fault tolerance through redundancy and replication, and performance optimization through parallel processing.

Cloud computing platforms like Amazon Web Services (AWS) and Microsoft Azure exemplify distributed systems, as do content delivery networks (CDNs) that distribute content across geographically dispersed servers, distributed databases like Google Spanner and Apache Cassandra, and microservices architectures where applications consist of loosely coupled services.

The Blockchain Approach

Bitcoin and blockchain combine aspects of both decentralized and distributed architectures. Like decentralized systems, blockchain networks have no central authority—each node operates independently and participates in consensus. Like distributed systems, blockchain networks distribute computational resources across geographically dispersed nodes that communicate over networks.

However, blockchain adds unique characteristics: cryptographic verification ensures data integrity without requiring trust in any single node, consensus mechanisms enable agreement on system state without central coordination, and immutability through cryptographic linking creates an auditable, tamper-resistant record. This hybrid approach provides the fault tolerance and censorship resistance of decentralization with the scalability and performance benefits of distribution.

Understanding these architectural distinctions helps explain why blockchain represents such a fundamental shift. Traditional centralized systems require trust in a single authority, decentralized systems distribute control but may sacrifice efficiency, and distributed systems optimize performance but often retain centralized coordination. Blockchain's innovation lies in achieving decentralization while maintaining the performance and reliability characteristics of distributed systems through cryptographic guarantees and consensus mechanisms.

3.6 Technical Foundations

Understanding blockchain requires familiarity with several key technical concepts. While we explore these in detail throughout this book, here's an introduction to the fundamental building blocks.

Cryptographic Hash Functions

Hash functions are mathematical algorithms that take input data of any size and produce a fixed-size output (hash). Key properties:

- **Deterministic**: Same input always produces same output
- **Fast to Compute**: Hash calculation is computationally efficient
- **One-Way**: Cannot reverse-engineer input from hash
- **Avalanche Effect**: Small input changes produce completely different hashes
- **Collision Resistant**: Extremely difficult to find two inputs with same hash

Bitcoin uses SHA-256 (Secure Hash Algorithm 256-bit), which produces 256-bit (32-byte) hashes (since $256 \div 8 = 32$ bytes). These hashes are used for:

- Creating unique transaction IDs
- Linking blocks together
- Proof of Work mining
- Creating addresses

Digital Signatures

Digital signatures provide cryptographic proof that a transaction was authorized by the owner of the funds. The process involves:

1. **Key Pair Generation**: Each user generates a public/private key pair
2. **Signing**: Private key is used to sign transactions
3. **Verification**: Public key is used to verify signatures

Bitcoin uses the Elliptic Curve Digital Signature Algorithm (ECDSA) with the secp256k1 curve. This ensures:

- Only the private key holder can authorize transactions
- Anyone can verify transaction authenticity
- Signatures cannot be forged
- Signatures are tied to specific transaction data

Public Key Cryptography

Bitcoin uses asymmetric cryptography, where:

- **Private Key**: Secret key that must be kept secure. Used to sign transactions.
- **Public Key**: Derived from private key, can be shared publicly. Used to verify signatures.

- **Address**: Derived from public key, used as a destination for payments.

The mathematical relationship ensures that:

- Public keys can be derived from private keys, but not vice versa
- Signatures created with private keys can be verified with corresponding public keys
- Losing a private key means losing access to funds permanently

Merkle Trees

Merkle trees are data structures that enable efficient verification of large datasets. In Bitcoin:

- Each transaction is hashed
- Transaction hashes are paired and hashed together
- If there is an odd number of transactions, the last hash is duplicated before pairing.
- This process continues until a single root hash (Merkle root) is created
- The Merkle root is included in the block header

Benefits:

- **Efficient Verification**: Verify a transaction's inclusion without downloading entire block
- **Tamper Detection**: Any transaction change alters the Merkle root
- **Scalability**: Proof size grows logarithmically with number of transactions

Proof of Work Consensus

Proof of Work (PoW) is Bitcoin's consensus mechanism:

1. Miners collect pending transactions
2. They create a candidate block
3. They repeatedly modify a nonce value and hash the block header
4. They search for a hash below a target difficulty threshold
5. First miner to find valid hash broadcasts block to network
6. Other nodes verify and accept valid blocks

Security Properties:

- Requires significant computational work to create blocks
- Makes attacking the network economically unfeasible
- Aligns miner incentives with network security
- Difficulty adjusts automatically to maintain consistent block times. If blocks arrive faster than the ten-minute target, the difficulty increases; if slower, it decreases.

Energy Considerations: PoW requires substantial energy consumption, which has led to exploration of alternative consensus mechanisms like Proof of Stake (PoS) in other blockchains.

UTXO Model

Bitcoin uses the Unspent Transaction Output (UTXO) model. Instead of tracking a running balance per account, the ledger is a collection of discrete, not-yet-spent outputs; a wallet's "balance" is simply the sum of the outputs it can unlock. This is the key conceptual shift from bank-account thinking, and it enables the parallel validation and privacy properties listed below:

- **Transaction Outputs**: When you receive Bitcoin, you receive UTXOs
- **Transaction Inputs**: When you spend Bitcoin, you reference UTXOs as inputs
- **Balance Calculation**: Your balance is the sum of all UTXOs you can spend
- **No Account Balances**: Unlike traditional banking, there are no account balances—only UTXOs

Advantages:

- Parallel transaction processing
- Better privacy (addresses can be reused or changed)
- Simpler verification logic
- Natural support for complex transaction types

Network Protocol

Bitcoin nodes communicate using a peer-to-peer protocol:

- **Discovery**: Nodes discover peers through DNS seeds or manual connections
- **Handshaking**: Nodes exchange version information
- **Block Propagation**: New blocks are broadcast to all peers
- **Transaction Propagation**: Transactions are broadcast and relayed
- **Synchronization**: New nodes download blockchain history from peers

The protocol is designed to be:

- **Resilient**: No single point of failure
- **Scalable**: Handles network growth
- **Efficient**: Minimizes bandwidth usage
- **Secure**: Validates all received data

3.7 Applications Beyond Cryptocurrency

Blockchain technology extends well beyond digital currency. The core properties—immutability, decentralization, and cryptographic verification—solve real problems in multiple domains.

Finance: Cross-border payments settle in minutes instead of days, bypassing correspondent banking fees. Decentralized Finance (DeFi) platforms recreate lending, borrowing, and exchange services using smart contracts, removing intermediaries entirely. Stablecoins provide programmable money pegged to fiat currencies.

Supply Chain: Immutable ledgers enable end-to-end traceability from raw material to consumer. Walmart uses blockchain for food safety tracking;[6] De Beers uses it for diamond provenance verification. Counterfeit detection and recall efficiency both improve when every handoff is recorded on-chain.

Digital Identity: Self-sovereign identity systems let users control their own credentials and selectively disclose information using zero-knowledge proofs, reducing both identity theft and dependence on centralized identity providers.

Governance: Token-weighted voting in Decentralized Autonomous Organizations (DAOs) provides transparent, auditable decision-making without hierarchical management structures. Several governments have piloted blockchain-based voting systems for elections and referendums.

3.8 Challenges and Limitations

While blockchain offers significant advantages, it's important to understand current limitations:

Scalability

Challenge: Bitcoin processes approximately 7 transactions per second, compared to thousands for traditional payment systems.

[6]"Walmart's Food Safety Solution Using IBM Food Trust Built on the IBM Blockchain Platform," IBM, 2018. See also the Linux Foundation case study at https://www.lfdecentralizedtrust.org/case-studies/walmart-case-study

Solutions Being Explored:
- Layer 2 solutions (Lightning Network for Bitcoin)
- Alternative consensus mechanisms (Proof of Stake)
- Sharding (dividing blockchain into smaller pieces)
- Optimized block structures

Energy Consumption

Challenge: Proof of Work requires substantial energy, raising environmental concerns.
Solutions:
- Transition to Proof of Stake (Ethereum's approach)
- Renewable energy for mining operations
- More efficient consensus algorithms
- Layer 2 solutions reducing on-chain transactions

Regulatory Uncertainty

Challenge: Evolving regulations create uncertainty for businesses and users.
Status:
- Different countries have varying approaches
- Some countries embrace blockchain, others restrict it
- Regulatory clarity improving gradually
- Compliance requirements evolving

User Experience

Challenge: Blockchain applications can be complex for non-technical users.
Improvements:
- Better wallet interfaces
- Simplified transaction processes
- Educational resources
- Integration with familiar applications

Interoperability

Challenge: Different blockchains operate independently, limiting cross-chain functionality.
Solutions:
- Cross-chain bridges
- Interoperability protocols
- Multi-chain platforms
- Standardized protocols

3.9 The Future of Blockchain

Blockchain technology continues to evolve rapidly. Emerging trends include:
- **Improved Scalability**: Solutions enabling thousands of transactions per second
- **Better Privacy**: Zero-knowledge proofs enabling private transactions
- **Interoperability**: Seamless interaction between different blockchains
- **Sustainability**: More energy-efficient consensus mechanisms
- **Regulatory Clarity**: Clearer frameworks enabling broader adoption
- **Enterprise Adoption**: More businesses integrating blockchain solutions
- **Web3**: Decentralized internet built on blockchain foundations

3.10 Conclusion

Bitcoin and blockchain represent a fundamental shift in how we think about trust, value transfer, and digital systems. By eliminating the need for trusted intermediaries and enabling direct peer-to-peer interactions, blockchain opens new possibilities across finance, governance, social media, supply chains, and beyond.

As we progress through this book, we build a complete Bitcoin blockchain implementation, understanding not just what these systems do, but how they work at the deepest technical levels. We explore the cryptographic primitives, data structures, network protocols, and consensus mechanisms that make blockchain possible.

The concepts in this chapter—hashing, signatures, UTXO, consensus—reappear in every implementation module that follows. With this vocabulary established, we move to the whitepaper itself.

3.11 Further Reading

- **Bitcoin Whitepaper**—The original paper by Satoshi Nakamoto that started it all. See `https://bitcoin.org/bitcoin.pdf`
- **Mastering Bitcoin**—Andreas Antonopoulos's comprehensive guide to Bitcoin internals. See `https://github.com/bitcoinbook/bitcoinbook`
- **But How Does Bitcoin Actually Work? (3Blue1Brown)**—An excellent visual explanation of blockchain mechanics. See `https://www.youtube.com/watch?v=bBC-nXj3Ng4`

Key Takeaways

- ✓ Blockchain technology defined: a distributed, append-only ledger secured by cryptographic hashing and consensus mechanisms.
- ✓ Bitcoin's origins and the key innovations—proof-of-work, the UTXO model, and decentralized consensus—emerge as the solutions to the double-spending problem.
- ✓ Real-world blockchain applications span finance, voting, governance, supply chain, and social media, each demonstrating the technology's versatility.
- ✓ The cryptographic building blocks—hash functions, digital signatures, and Merkle trees—provide the security foundation for every transaction in the system.
- ✓ In the next chapter, the focus moves directly to the source: Satoshi Nakamoto's Bitcoin whitepaper, the nine-page document that defined the entire system.

4

The Bitcoin Whitepaper

▷ **What you will learn in this chapter**

- Summarize each of the twelve sections of Satoshi Nakamoto's Bitcoin whitepaper
- Explain how proof-of-work prevents double spending without a trusted third party
- Describe the role of the timestamp server in establishing chronological order
- Understand how the incentive mechanism aligns miner behavior with network security

IN 2008, a nine-page whitepaper titled "Bitcoin: A Peer-to-Peer Electronic Cash System" launched a trillion-dollar asset class and showed how to build trustless money without banks—by combining old cryptographic techniques in a novel way that no one had thought to try before. This chapter provides a **technical summary** of that whitepaper, answering one practical question: **what does Bitcoin actually do, end-to-end, and why does it work?** These foundations are essential for a correct implementation—knowing which rules are consensus-critical and which properties must hold separates engineering choices from non-negotiable invariants.

This chapter presents a comprehensive technical analysis of Satoshi Nakamoto's foundational paper: *Bitcoin: A Peer-to-Peer Electronic Cash System* (2008). The paper introduced blockchain technology as a cryptographic solution to the double-spending problem in digital currency systems, enabling trustless peer-to-peer electronic transactions without requiring a central authority or trusted third party.

> ▷ Note
>
> All quotations in this chapter are from Satoshi Nakamoto, *Bitcoin: A Peer-to-Peer Electronic Cash System* (2008), available at https://bitcoin.org/bitcoin.pdf and reproduced under the MIT License. Section numbers refer to the original paper.

4.1 Historical Context and Significance

The Bitcoin whitepaper represents a fundamental breakthrough in distributed systems and cryptography. Prior to its publication, digital currency systems required trusted third parties to prevent double-spending—the ability to spend the same digital coin multiple times. The paper's key innovation, as stated in its abstract, proposes "a solution to the double-spending problem using a peer-to-peer network. The network timestamps transactions by hashing them into an ongoing chain of hash-based proof-of-work, forming a record that cannot be changed without redoing the proof-of-work."

The whitepaper opens with a problem statement, then develops the solution step by step. To appreciate the solution's elegance, we must first understand the problem it addresses.

This solution combines several existing cryptographic and distributed systems concepts — digital signatures, hash functions, Merkle trees, and proof-of-work—into a novel architecture that achieves Byzantine fault tolerance (the ability to reach agreement even when some participants are adversarial or unreliable) in an open, permissionless network.

4.2 Scope and Organization

This chapter systematically examines each section of the Bitcoin whitepaper, providing technical analysis, formal definitions, and implementation considerations. The material is organized to build understanding progressively, beginning with the problem statement and proceeding through the cryptographic foundations, consensus mechanisms, and security analysis.

Throughout this chapter, citations follow the format *Bitcoin Whitepaper, Section X*, where X denotes the section number in the original paper.

> ▷ **Note**
>
> Cross-References: This chapter serves as foundational material for understanding the implementation details presented in subsequent chapters:
> - Technical Foundations: Blockchain Architecture — Implementation architecture and domain model
> - Cryptography Documentation — Cryptographic primitives and algorithms
> - Transaction ID Format — Transaction representation and encoding
> - Network Layer — Peer-to-peer protocol implementation
> - Node Orchestration — Node coordination and state management

4.3 The Problem: Trust in Electronic Payments

The Trust-Based Model and Its Limitations

The Bitcoin whitepaper begins by analyzing the fundamental limitations of existing electronic payment systems. As stated in Section 1: "Commerce on the Internet has come to rely almost exclusively on financial institutions serving as trusted third parties to process electronic payments. While the system works well enough for most transactions, it still suffers from the inherent weaknesses of the trust based model."

Architectural Dependencies

Traditional electronic payment systems exhibit a centralized architecture where all transactions flow through trusted third parties—typically financial institutions or payment processors. This architecture introduces several fundamental constraints.

A **trusted third party** is an intermediary entity that both transacting parties trust to validate, authorize, and record transactions. The trust model requires that this entity:

- Maintains accurate transaction records
- Prevents double-spending
- Resolves disputes fairly
- Maintains system availability

Inherent Weaknesses

The whitepaper identifies five critical weaknesses in the trust-based model:

1. **Transaction Reversibility**: "Completely non-reversible transactions are not really possible, since financial institutions cannot avoid mediating disputes." This reversibility creates uncertainty for merchants and enables fraudulent chargebacks.
2. **Economic Inefficiency**: "The cost of mediation increases transaction costs, limiting the minimum practical transaction size and cutting off the possibility for small casual transactions." Mediation costs create a lower bound on economically viable transaction sizes.
3. **Trust Propagation**: "With the possibility of reversal, the need for trust spreads. Merchants must be wary of their customers, hassling them for more information than they would otherwise need." The requirement for reversibility necessitates additional verification procedures.
4. **Accepted Fraud Rate**: "A certain percentage of fraud is accepted as unavoidable." The system design inherently tolerates a baseline fraud rate.
5. **Architectural Constraint**: "No mechanism exists to make payments over a communications channel without a trusted party." Direct peer-to-peer electronic payments are architecturally impossible in the current model.

Economic Implications

These limitations have measurable economic consequences. The whitepaper notes: "These costs and payment uncertainties can be avoided in person by using physical currency, but no mechanism exists to make payments over a communications channel without a trusted party." The inability to replicate physical currency's direct transfer properties in digital form represents a fundamental gap in electronic payment systems.

Requirements for a Cryptographic Solution

The whitepaper establishes the requirements for an alternative system: "What is needed is an electronic payment system based on **cryptographic proof** instead of trust, allowing any two willing parties to transact directly with each other without the need for a trusted third party."

> i
>
> Core Requirements The system must use cryptographic mechanisms rather than trust relationships to ensure transaction validity and prevent double-spending. It must enable direct transactions between parties without requiring intermediaries.
>
> - **Irreversibility**: "Transactions that are computationally impractical to reverse would protect sellers from fraud." The computational cost of reversing a transaction must exceed the economic value of doing so.
> - **Buyer Protection**: "Routine escrow mechanisms could easily be implemented to protect buyers." The system architecture must support additional trust mechanisms when needed.

The proposed system aims to achieve:

- Elimination of Mediation Costs — Direct transactions remove intermediary fees
- Microtransaction Support — Enable economically viable small-value transactions
- Reduced Fraud Surface — Cryptographic verification reduces reliance on identity verification
- Peer-to-Peer Architecture — No central point of control or failure

4.4 The Solution: Peer-to-Peer Electronic Cash

Architectural Overview

The Bitcoin whitepaper proposes a solution architecture based on "a peer-to-peer distributed timestamp server to generate computational proof of the chronological order of transactions. The system is secure as long as honest nodes collectively control more CPU power than any cooperating group of attacker nodes."

Core Architectural Principles

- **Peer-to-Peer Architecture**: The system operates as a distributed network of equal peers, eliminating the need for central authority or hierarchical control structures.
- **Distributed Timestamp Server**: Transactions are ordered chronologically through a distributed consensus mechanism that creates cryptographically verifiable timestamps.
- **Computational Proof**: Network security derives from proof-of-work—a computationally expensive operation that demonstrates commitment of resources.
- **Majority Assumption**: System security requires that honest nodes collectively control a majority of computational resources. This assumption forms the basis for Byzantine fault tolerance in an open network.

Security Model

The security model relies on economic and cryptographic mechanisms:

- **Cryptographic Security**: Digital signatures ensure transaction authenticity and authorization
- **Economic Security**: Proof-of-work makes attacks economically unprofitable
- **Distributed Security**: No single point of failure or control
- **Temporal Security**: Chain structure makes historical modifications computationally infeasible

4.5 Transactions: Digital Signatures and Ownership

The Transaction Model

The Bitcoin whitepaper introduces a transaction model based on cryptographic signatures. Section 2 defines an electronic coin as "a chain of digital signatures. Each owner transfers the coin to the next by digitally signing a hash of the previous transaction and the public key of the next owner and adding these to the end of the coin. A payee can verify the signatures to verify the chain of ownership."

Formal Definition

An **electronic coin** is a cryptographically linked sequence of transactions, where each transaction represents a transfer of ownership. The coin's value and ownership history are encoded in this transaction chain.

A **transaction** is a data structure containing:

- Reference to a previous transaction (input)
- Digital signature authorizing the transfer
- Public key of the recipient (output)
- Additional metadata

Transaction Structure and Verification

The transaction model operates as follows:

1. **Input Reference**: Each transaction references a previous transaction where the current owner received the coin. This creates a directed acyclic graph (DAG) structure.
2. **Signature Generation**: The current owner generates a digital signature over a hash of the previous transaction using their private key. This signature proves authorization to transfer the coin.
3. **Output Specification**: The transaction includes the public key of the recipient, establishing the new owner.
4. **Verification Process**: Any party can verify the transaction by checking the digital signature against the previous transaction hash, verifying the signature using the previous owner's public key, and confirming the transaction structure is valid.
5. **Chain Formation**: Transactions form a chain where each link cryptographically proves the transfer of ownership from one party to another.

Cryptographic Properties

Only the holder of the private key corresponding to a transaction output can authorize a transfer from that output. This follows from the unforgeability property of digital signatures.

The chain exhibits these critical properties:

- **Chain Integrity**: Any modification to a transaction in the chain invalidates all subsequent transactions, as their signatures depend on the previous transaction's hash.
- **Public Verifiability**: The chain of ownership is publicly verifiable without requiring trusted third parties. Any party with access to the transaction history can verify the entire chain.
- **Tamper Evidence**: Attempts to modify historical transactions are detectable through signature verification failures, providing tamper-evident properties.

Transaction Chain Example

Consider a transaction chain:

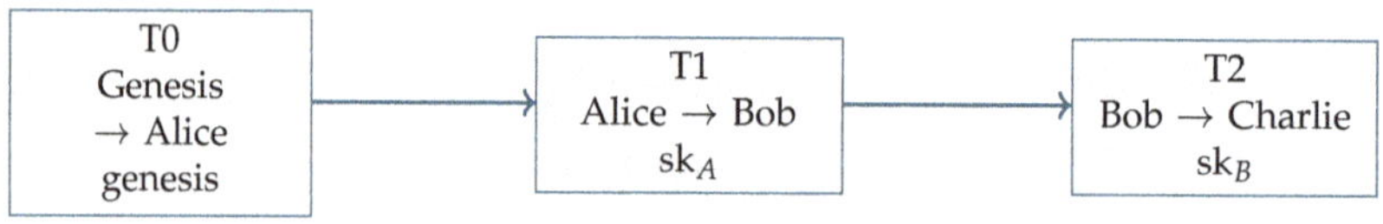

Figure 4.1: Transaction chain example

Each transaction T_i contains the following, where sk denotes an owner's secret (private) key and pk their public key:

- Hash reference to T_{i-1}
- Signature $\sigma_i = \text{Sign}(sk_{i-1}, \text{Hash}(T_{i-1}))$
- Public key pk_i of the recipient

Verification of T_i requires:

- $\text{Verify}(\sigma_i, \text{Hash}(T_{i-1}), pk_{i-1}) = \text{true}$
- T_{i-1} exists and is valid

4.6 The Double-Spending Problem

Problem Statement

The fundamental challenge in digital currency systems is preventing double-spending. As the whitepaper states: "The problem of course is the payee can't verify that one of the owners did not double-spend the coin."

Formal Definition

Double-spending occurs when a party attempts to spend the same digital coin or transaction output multiple times, creating conflicting transactions that reference the same input.

A **double-spending attack** is an attempt by an adversary to create two or more valid transactions that spend the same coin, with the goal of having multiple recipients accept the coin as payment.

The Fundamental Challenge

Unlike physical currency, digital information can be perfectly copied. A digital coin, represented as data, can be duplicated and presented to multiple recipients simultaneously. Without a mechanism to detect and prevent this, a malicious party could:

1. Create transaction T_1 spending coin C to recipient R_1
2. Create transaction T_2 spending the same coin C to recipient R_2
3. Broadcast both transactions simultaneously
4. Potentially have both recipients accept their respective transactions

The problem is that neither recipient can independently verify that the coin hasn't been spent elsewhere.

Traditional Solutions and Their Limitations

The traditional approach introduces "a trusted central authority, or mint, that checks every transaction for double spending." This authority maintains a registry of all transactions and validates each new transaction against this registry.

However, "the problem with this solution is that the fate of the entire money system depends on the company running the mint, with every transaction having to go through them, just like a bank." This creates:

- Single point of failure

- Centralized control
- Dependency on trust in the authority
- Potential for censorship
- Scalability bottlenecks

The Blockchain Solution

Fundamental Insight

The whitepaper establishes a crucial insight: "The only way to confirm the absence of a transaction is to be **aware of all transactions**." This observation forms the theoretical foundation for the blockchain solution.

To prevent double-spending in a distributed system without a trusted authority, all participants must maintain awareness of all transactions. This follows from the need to verify that a transaction input has not been previously spent.

Solution Architecture

The blockchain solution addresses double-spending through four mechanisms:

- **Public Announcement**: "To accomplish this without a trusted party, transactions must be publicly announced." All transactions are broadcast to the network, ensuring all participants can observe transaction attempts.
- **Consensus on Order**: The network must agree on a canonical ordering of transactions. This ordering determines which transaction spending a particular coin is considered valid.
- **Earliest Transaction Rule**: "For our purposes, the earliest transaction is the one that counts, so we don't care about later attempts to double-spend." The consensus mechanism establishes temporal ordering, and the first valid transaction to spend a coin is accepted.
- **Majority Consensus**: "The payee needs proof that at the time of each transaction, the majority of nodes agreed it was the first received." The consensus protocol ensures that a majority of honest nodes agree on transaction ordering.

Comparison with Central Authority Model

In the centralized model: "In the mint based model, the mint was aware of all transactions and decided which arrived first." The blockchain replaces this single authority with a **distributed consensus** mechanism where multiple nodes collectively determine transaction ordering.

4.7 Timestamp Server: Immutable Chronological Records

The Timestamp Server Concept

Section 3 of the whitepaper introduces the **timestamp server** as the foundational mechanism: "The solution we propose begins with a timestamp server. A timestamp server works by taking a **hash of a block of items to be timestamped and widely publishing the hash**, such as in a newspaper or Usenet post."

Formal Definition

A **timestamp server** is a system that creates **cryptographic proof** that certain data existed at a specific point in time by publishing a hash of that data.

A **timestamp** is a cryptographic commitment that proves data existed at or before a specific time. The timestamp is created by publishing a hash of the data, where the publication time serves as the timestamp.

Operational Model

The timestamp server operates according to the following procedure:

1. **Data Collection**: The server collects a set of items to be timestamped into a block.
2. **Hash Computation**: The server computes a cryptographic hash of the block: $H = \text{Hash}(\text{block})$
3. **Publication**: The hash is widely published through a public medium (newspaper, Usenet, etc.), establishing the publication time as the timestamp.
4. **Verification**: The timestamp proves that the data existed at the publication time, as stated: "The timestamp proves that the data must have existed at the time, obviously, in order to get into the hash."

Chain Structure

The whitepaper extends this concept to create a chain: "Each timestamp includes the previous timestamp in its hash, forming a chain, with each additional timestamp reinforcing the ones before it."

A **timestamp chain** is a sequence of timestamps where each timestamp includes the hash of the previous timestamp in its computation, creating a cryptographically linked chain.

This structure exhibits critical properties:

- **Chronological Ordering**: The chain structure establishes an immutable chronological ordering of timestamps, as each timestamp depends on all previous timestamps.
- **Reinforcement**: Each new timestamp cryptographically reinforces all previous timestamps, making modification of historical timestamps computationally infeasible.
- **Verifiability**: Any party can verify the timestamp chain by recomputing hashes and comparing with published values.

4.8 Proof-of-Work: Securing the Network

Distributed Timestamp Server Implementation

To implement a distributed timestamp server on a peer-to-peer basis, the Bitcoin system employs "a proof-of-work system similar to Adam Back's Hashcash." This mechanism replaces the centralized timestamp server with a distributed consensus protocol.

Proof-of-Work Definition

Proof-of-Work is a cryptographic mechanism that requires a prover to demonstrate computational effort by finding a value that, when hashed, produces an output meeting a specified difficulty criterion. Double hashing defends against length-extension attacks—a class of cryptographic vulnerability where knowing $H(x)$ allows an attacker to compute $H(x\|y)$ without knowing x. Hashing twice eliminates this weakness.

Mining is the process of finding a valid proof-of-work for a block of transactions, requiring the miner to solve a computationally expensive cryptographic puzzle.

Algorithm Specification

The whitepaper specifies: "The proof-of-work involves scanning for a value that when hashed, such as with SHA-256, the hash begins with a number of zero bits. The average work required is exponential in the number of zero bits required and can be verified by executing a single hash."

Proof-of-Work Generation:

1. Construct block header containing transactions, previous block hash, timestamp, and nonce (a 32-bit counter the miner can freely vary to change the hash output)
2. Compute $H = \text{SHA-256}(\text{block\_header})$
3. Check if H begins with d zero bits, where d is the difficulty parameter
4. If condition not met, increment nonce and repeat from step 2
5. If condition met, broadcast block with valid proof-of-work

Why "zero bits"? SHA-256 is designed so every output bit is independent and uniformly random: any single bit is 0 or 1 with probability $\frac{1}{2}$. Requiring d leading zero bits is equivalent to demanding d independent coin flips land on zero, so only 1 in 2^d header variations will qualify. Each nonce guess is statistically independent, which is why the expected number of hash operations grows exponentially with the difficulty parameter: $E[\text{operations}] = 2^d$.

Implementation Details

The whitepaper states: "For our timestamp network, we implement the proof-of-work by incrementing a nonce in the block until a value is found that gives the block's hash the required zero bits."

> ▷ **Implementation Note**
>
> Our implementation uses a simplified fixed difficulty target rather than Bitcoin's dynamic difficulty adjustment every 2,016 blocks. This keeps the teaching code clear while preserving the core proof-of-work mechanism.

Once a block satisfies the proof-of-work requirement, modifying the block requires recomputing the proof-of-work. As stated: "Once the CPU effort has been expended to make it satisfy the proof-of-work, the block cannot be changed without redoing the work. As later blocks are chained after it, the work to change the block would include redoing all the blocks after it."

Security Properties

Consensus Mechanism

Proof-of-work is essentially one-CPU-one-vote. The majority decision is represented by the longest chain, which has the greatest proof-of-work effort invested in it.

This property establishes that consensus is determined by computational power rather than node count, preventing Sybil attacks.

Sybil Attack Resistance

Sybil resistance is a network's defense against Sybil attacks, where a single malicious entity creates numerous fake identities (Sybil nodes) to gain disproportionate control, undermining fairness and decentralization. Resistance is achieved by making identity creation costly, typically through resource-intensive Proof-of-Work like Bitcoin.

As the whitepaper notes: "If the majority were based on one-IP-address-one-vote, it could be subverted by anyone able to allocate many IPs." Proof-of-work prevents this by requiring computational resources proportional to voting power.

Attack Resistance

"If a majority of CPU power is controlled by honest nodes, the honest chain will grow the fastest and outpace any competing chains. To modify a past block, an attacker would have to redo the proof-of-work of the block and all blocks after it and then catch up with and surpass the work of the honest nodes."

This property establishes the security guarantee: as long as honest nodes control majority computational power, the honest chain will maintain the longest proof-of-work chain.

Difficulty Adjustment Mechanism

Adaptive Difficulty

The whitepaper specifies: "To compensate for increasing hardware speed and varying interest in running nodes over time, the proof-of-work difficulty is determined by a **moving average targeting an average number of blocks per hour**. If they're generated too fast, the difficulty increases."

Difficulty Adjustment is a mechanism that dynamically modifies the proof-of-work requirement to maintain a target block generation rate, compensating for changes in network hash rate.

Difficulty Adjustment Algorithm:

1. Measure time elapsed for last N blocks (typically 2016 blocks)
2. Calculate target time: target_time $=$ $N \times$ target_block_interval
3. Calculate difficulty multiplier: multiplier $=$ actual_time/target_time
4. Adjust difficulty: new_difficulty $=$ old_difficulty $\times$ multiplier
5. Clamp to reasonable bounds to prevent extreme adjustments

The difficulty adjustment mechanism automatically maintains consistent block generation intervals regardless of network hash rate changes.

4.9 Network Operation: How Nodes Coordinate

Network Protocol Specification

Section 5 of the whitepaper specifies the network operation protocol through six sequential steps:

Network Operation Protocol:

1. **Transaction Propagation**: New transactions are broadcast to all nodes
2. **Block Assembly**: Each node collects new transactions into a block
3. **Proof-of-Work Computation**: Each node works on finding a difficult proof-of-work for its block
4. **Block Propagation**: When a node finds a proof-of-work, it broadcasts the block to all nodes
5. **Block Validation**: Nodes accept the block only if all transactions in it are valid and not already spent
6. **Chain Extension**: Nodes express their acceptance of the block by working on creating the next block in the chain, using the hash of the accepted block as the previous hash

Protocol Properties

- **Asynchronous Operation**: Nodes operate independently and asynchronously, without requiring synchronized clocks or coordinated timing.
- **Best-Effort Delivery**: "Messages are broadcast on a best effort basis," meaning the protocol does not guarantee message delivery but operates probabilistically.
- **Fault Tolerance**: "Block broadcasts are also tolerant of dropped messages. If a node does not receive a block, it will request it when it receives the next block and realizes it missed one."

Chain Selection Rule

Longest Chain Consensus

"Nodes always consider the longest chain to be the correct one and will keep working on extending it."

The length of a chain is measured by the total proof-of-work invested, not merely the number of blocks. The chain with the greatest cumulative proof-of-work is considered the longest.

Under the longest chain rule, if honest nodes control majority computational power, the network will converge to a single canonical chain with probability approaching 1 as time increases.

Fork Resolution

Fork Occurrence

A **fork** occurs when two blocks are mined referencing the same parent block, creating two competing branches in the blockchain.

An **orphan block** is a valid block that is not part of the longest chain, typically resulting from a fork that was later resolved.

Fork Resolution Protocol

The whitepaper specifies: "If two nodes broadcast different versions of the next block simultaneously, some nodes may receive one or the other first. In that case, they work on the first one they received, but save the other branch in case it becomes longer. The tie will be broken when the next proof-of-work is found and one branch becomes longer; the nodes that were working on the other branch will then switch to the longer one."

Fork Resolution Algorithm:

1. **Fork Detection**: Node receives two blocks B_1 and B_2 with same parent
2. **Branch Selection**: Node selects branch based on first-received heuristic
3. **Branch Tracking**: Node maintains both branches in memory
4. **Proof-of-Work Extension**: Node works on extending selected branch
5. **Branch Comparison**: When new block extends either branch, compare chain lengths
6. **Chain Switch**: If alternative branch becomes longer, switch to that branch

The fork resolution protocol ensures eventual convergence to a single chain, with forks resolving probabilistically based on relative hash rates of competing branches.

Network Resilience Properties

Flexible Participation

"Nodes can leave and rejoin the network at will, accepting the longest proof-of-work chain as proof of what happened while they were gone." This property enables nodes to synchronize state after disconnection periods.

Message Loss Tolerance

The protocol recovers from lost messages through block request mechanisms when nodes detect gaps in their chain.

4.10 Incentive Mechanism: Rewarding Honest Behavior

Mining Rewards

"By convention, the first transaction in a block is a special transaction that starts a new coin owned by the creator of the block. This adds an incentive for nodes to support the network, and provides a way to initially distribute coins into circulation, since there is no central authority to issue them."

Understanding Coinbase Transactions

The first transaction in every block is special — it has no inputs and creates new coins from nothing. This is called the **coinbase transaction** and it's the only way new coins enter circulation.

Components:

- **Coinbase Transaction**: Creates new coins as block reward. The whitepaper notes: "The steady addition of a constant of amount of new coins is analogous to gold miners expending resources to add gold to circulation. In our case, it is CPU time and electricity that is expended."
- **Transaction Fees**: "If the output value of a transaction is less than its input value, the difference is a transaction fee that is added to the incentive value of the block containing the transaction."

- **Inflation-Free Future**: "Once a predetermined number of coins have entered circulation, the incentive can transition entirely to transaction fees and be completely inflation free."

Economic Model

The whitepaper's design creates a sustainable economic model:

- **Initial Distribution**: New coins distributed through mining (no central authority needed)
- **Diminishing Rewards**: Block rewards decrease over time (Bitcoin halves every ~4 years)
- **Fee Transition**: Eventually, transaction fees become the primary incentive
- **Fixed Supply**: Total supply is predetermined, preventing inflation

Why does this design work? The whitepaper explains: "This adds an incentive for nodes to support the network." Without rewards, there would be no economic reason for miners to expend computational resources securing the network.

Economic Security

"The incentive may help encourage nodes to stay honest. If a greedy attacker is able to assemble more CPU power than all the honest nodes, he would have to choose between using it to defraud people by stealing back his payments, or using it to generate new coins. He ought to find it more profitable to play by the rules."

Understanding the Security Model

The whitepaper's security model relies on economic incentives, not just cryptography. Even if an attacker could theoretically attack the network, it's economically irrational to do so.

Attack Scenario Analysis

If an attacker controls majority CPU power, they can either:
1. **Attack**: Try to reverse transactions and steal back payments
2. **Mine Honestly**: Generate new coins by following the rules

"He ought to find it more profitable to play by the rules, such rules that favour him with more new coins than everyone else combined, than to undermine the system and the validity of his own wealth."

The economic incentive aligns miner interests with network security, making attacks economically irrational. An attacker would destroy the value of the system they're attacking, making their attack counterproductive.

This design means that as the network grows and becomes more valuable, it becomes more secure because:
- More miners participate (increasing honest CPU power)
- Attack costs increase (need more CPU power to attack)
- Attack becomes less profitable (destroying valuable system is costly)

4.11 Merkle Trees: Efficient Storage and Verification

Disk Space Reclamation

"Once the latest transaction in a coin is buried under enough blocks, the **spent transactions before it can be discarded to save disk space**. To facilitate this without breaking the block's hash, transactions are hashed in a **Merkle Tree**, with only the **root** included in the block's hash."

The Problem

Without Merkle trees, storing the entire blockchain would require keeping every transaction forever, leading to massive storage requirements as the blockchain grows.

The Solution

Merkle trees allow nodes to discard old transaction data while maintaining cryptographic integrity. The whitepaper explains: "Old blocks can then be compacted by stubbing off branches of the tree. The interior hashes do not need to be stored."

How Merkle Trees Work

1. **Transaction Hashing**: Each transaction is hashed
2. **Pairwise Hashing**: Pairs of transaction hashes are hashed together
3. **Recursive Hashing**: Continue hashing pairs until one root hash remains
4. **Root Storage**: Only the Merkle root is stored in the block header
5. **Verification**: Can prove transaction inclusion using only a small "Merkle path"

The bottom-up process starts with raw data (transactions in a blockchain context) and progressively combines their hashes:

- **Leaf Nodes**: Each individual data block (transaction) is hashed to create the leaf nodes.
- **Intermediate Nodes**: Leaf hashes are paired, concatenated, and hashed again to form parent nodes. This repeats recursively up the tree.
- **Merkle Root**: The procedure continues until a single final hash remains at the top—the Merkle root, a unique, secure summary of all underlying data. This root is stored in the block header.

Benefits

The benefits of Merkle trees are substantial:

- **Efficient Storage**: "Old blocks can then be compacted by stubbing off branches of the tree. The interior hashes do not need to be stored."
- **Compact Block Headers**: "A block header with no transactions would be about 80 bytes."
- **Scalability**: The whitepaper calculates: "If we suppose blocks are generated every 10 minutes, 80 bytes $\times$ 6 $\times$ 24 $\times$ 365 = 17 MB per year."

Merkle Tree Properties

- Only the Merkle root is stored in the block header
- Changing any transaction changes the root (tamper detection)
- Enables efficient verification without full block download
- Enables simplified payment verification (SPV)
- Logarithmic proof size: Proving transaction inclusion requires only $\log_2(n)$ hashes

4.12 Simplified Payment Verification

Lightweight Verification

"It is possible to verify payments without running a full network node. A user only needs to keep a **copy of the block headers** of the longest proof-of-work chain, which he can get by querying network nodes until he's convinced he has the longest chain, and obtain the Merkle branch linking the transaction to the block it's timestamped in."

Understanding SPV

SPV (Simplified Payment Verification) allows users to verify their own transactions without downloading the entire blockchain. This is crucial for **mobile wallets** and **lightweight clients**.

How SPV Works

1. **Block Headers Only**: Store only block headers (~80 bytes each), not full blocks
2. **Query Network**: Query multiple nodes to find the longest chain
3. **Merkle Proof**: Obtain a Merkle branch proving your transaction is in a block
4. **Verification**: Verify the Merkle proof links your transaction to the block header
5. **Confirmation**: Check that blocks were added after your transaction (confirmations)

Storage Efficiency

Instead of storing gigabytes of transaction data, SPV clients store only:
- Block headers: ~80 bytes ×~52,560 blocks/year = ~17 MB/year
- Merkle proofs: Small proofs for transactions of interest
- Total: Megabytes instead of gigabytes

SPV Capabilities and Limitations

What SPV Can Verify:
- Transaction exists in a block
- Transaction has confirmations (blocks added after it)
- Transaction is in the longest chain

What SPV Cannot Verify:
- Transaction validity (doesn't check if inputs were spent)
- Full transaction history
- Network consensus state

Security Trade-offs

The whitepaper notes: "The verification is reliable as long as honest nodes control the network, but is more vulnerable if the network is overpowered by an attacker." SPV clients trust that full nodes validated transactions correctly.

One strategy to protect against this: "Accept alerts from network nodes when they detect an invalid block, prompting the user's software to download the full block and alerted transactions to confirm the inconsistency."

Use Cases

The whitepaper notes: "Businesses that receive frequent payments will probably still want to run their own nodes for more independent security and quicker verification." SPV is suitable for:

- Mobile wallets
- Personal wallets
- Low-security use cases

4.13 Combining and Splitting Value

Multiple Inputs and Outputs

"Although it would be possible to handle coins individually, it would be unwieldy to make a separate transaction for every cent in a transfer. To allow value to be split and combined, transactions contain multiple inputs and outputs."

Transaction Structure

- **Multiple Inputs**: "Normally there will be either a single input from a larger previous transaction or multiple inputs combining smaller amounts."
- **Multiple Outputs**: "At most two outputs: one for the payment, and one returning the change, if any, back to the sender."

Why multiple inputs and outputs? The whitepaper explains: "Although it would be possible to handle coins individually, it would be unwieldy to make a separate transaction for every cent in a transfer." This design enables practical, flexible payments.

Real-World Example

Consider a realistic scenario:

Scenario: Alice wants to pay Bob 1.5 BTC, but she only has:

- UTXO 1: 0.8 BTC
- UTXO 2: 0.5 BTC
- UTXO 3: 0.3 BTC

Transaction: Alice creates a transaction with:

- **Inputs**: UTXO 1, UTXO 2, UTXO 3 (total: 1.6 BTC)
- **Outputs**:
  - Output 1: 1.5 BTC to Bob
  - Output 2: 0.1 BTC back to Alice (change)

Benefits

Multiple inputs and outputs provide:

- Enables flexible payment amounts regardless of UTXO sizes
- Combines multiple small UTXOs into larger payments
- Returns change to sender as new UTXO
- Minimizes number of transactions needed
- Efficient use of available funds

Fan-Out Structure

"It should be noted that fan-out, where a transaction depends on several transactions, and those transactions depend on many more, is not a problem here. There is never the need to extract a complete standalone copy of a transaction's history."

A transaction can reference multiple previous transactions (inputs), and each of those can reference multiple previous transactions. This creates a tree-like structure. However, the whitepaper notes that this doesn't cause problems because:

- You only need to verify inputs exist and are unspent
- You don't need the full history of each input
- The UTXO model makes verification efficient

4.14 Privacy in a Public Ledger

Privacy Challenge

"The traditional banking model achieves a level of privacy by limiting access to information to the parties involved and the trusted third party. The necessity to announce all transactions publicly precludes this method."

Privacy Solution

"Privacy can still be maintained by breaking the flow of information in another place: by keeping public keys anonymous. The public can see that someone is sending an amount to someone else, but without information linking the transaction to anyone."

Understanding Pseudonymity

Bitcoin provides pseudonymity, not anonymity. Transactions are public, but identities are represented by public keys (addresses) that aren't directly linked to real-world identities.

This is similar to the level of information released by stock exchanges, where the time and size of individual trades (the "tape") is made public, but without telling who the parties were.

What's Public and Private

What's Public:
- Transaction amounts
- Transaction timestamps
- Public keys (addresses)
- Transaction structure (inputs/outputs)

What's Private:
- Real-world identities behind addresses
- Who controls which addresses
- Transaction purposes

Additional Privacy Measures

New Key Pair Per Transaction

"As an additional firewall, a new key pair should be used for each transaction to keep them from being linked to a common owner."

If you reuse the same address for multiple transactions, an observer can link all those transactions together, potentially revealing your spending patterns and total balance. Best practice: generate a new address for each transaction to maximize privacy. Modern wallets do this automatically.

Limitations of Privacy

"Some linking is still unavoidable with multi-input transactions, which necessarily reveal that their inputs were owned by the same owner. The risk is that if the owner of a key is revealed, linking could reveal other transactions that belonged to the same owner."

- **Multi-Input Linking**: When a transaction has multiple inputs, they must all be signed by the same private key, revealing they're controlled by the same owner
- **Chain Analysis**: If one address is linked to a real-world identity, blockchain analysis can potentially trace other transactions
- **Privacy Trade-off**: Full privacy requires careful address management and potentially additional techniques (like CoinJoin)

Privacy vs. Transparency Trade-off

The whitepaper acknowledges this trade-off: "The traditional banking model achieves a level of privacy by limiting access to information to the parties involved and the trusted third party. The necessity to announce all transactions publicly precludes this method." Blockchain's transparency enables verification but limits privacy compared to traditional banking.

4.15 Security Analysis: Attack Resistance

Attack Scenarios

The whitepaper analyzes the scenario of "an attacker trying to generate an alternate chain faster than the honest chain."

Understanding Attack Limitations

Even with majority hash power, an attacker's capabilities are limited. The whitepaper explains: "Even if this is accomplished, it does not throw the system open to arbitrary changes, such as creating value out of thin air or taking money that never belonged to the attacker."

Key Security Property: "Nodes are not going to accept an invalid transaction as payment, and honest nodes will never accept a block containing them. An attacker can only try to change one of his own transactions to take back money he recently spent."

What Attackers Cannot Do

- Create coins out of thin air (invalid transactions rejected)
- Steal coins they don't own (signatures required)
- Spend coins that don't exist (UTXO validation)
- Modify other people's transactions (cryptographic signatures prevent this)

What Attackers Can Do

- Try to reverse their own recent transactions
- Attempt double-spending attacks
- Create alternative chain history

The whitepaper's mathematical analysis shows that even these limited attacks become exponentially harder as confirmations increase.

Mathematical Analysis

Binomial Random Walk

"The race between the honest chain and an attacker chain can be characterized as a Binomial Random Walk. The success event is the honest chain being extended by one block, increasing its lead by +1, and the failure event is the attacker's chain being extended by one block, reducing the gap by -1."

The whitepaper's final security analysis uses probability to quantify how quickly an attacker's chances diminish as honest blocks accumulate. The intuition: catching up requires more sustained luck than the honest network needs to maintain its lead.

The probability of an attacker catching up is analogous to a gambler's ruin problem. The probability drops exponentially as the number of blocks increases.

Key Formula

For an attacker with probability q of finding the next block and honest nodes with probability p (where $p = 1 - q$), the probability of catching up from z blocks behind is:

- $q_z = 1$ if $p \leq q$
- $q_z = (q/p)^z$ if $p > q$

"Given our assumption that $p > q$, the probability drops exponentially as the number of blocks the attacker has to catch up with increases. With the odds against him, if he doesn't make a lucky lunge forward early on, his chances become vanishingly small as he falls further behind."

Confirmation Wait Times

The whitepaper calculates how long a recipient should wait before being certain a transaction cannot be reversed. The analysis considers:

- Attacker's potential progress (Poisson distribution)
- Probability of attacker catching up
- Number of confirmations needed for security

Security Thresholds

For $P < 0.1\%$ (probability of successful attack):

Table 4.1: Confirmation requirements by attacker hash power (P < 0.1%)

Attacker Hash Power	Confirmations
10%	5
15%	8
20%	11
25%	15
30%	24

This table shows "Solving for P less than 0.1%" — waiting for z confirmations reduces attack probability below 0.1%.

Real-World Application

- **Small Payments**: 1-2 confirmations may be sufficient (low risk)
- **Medium Payments**: 3-20 confirmations recommended (moderate risk)
- **Large Payments**: 6+ confirmations recommended (high risk)
- **Very Large Payments**: 10+ confirmations for maximum security

Exponential Security

As attacker's share of network power increases, exponentially more confirmations are needed for the same security level. The whitepaper demonstrates: "Given our assumption that $p > q$, the probability drops exponentially as the number of blocks the attacker has to catch up with increases."
Practical Example:

- If an attacker controls 10% of network power, waiting 5 blocks reduces attack probability to 0.09%
- If an attacker controls 30% of network power, you need 24 blocks for the same security level
- The relationship is exponential, not linear

This analysis provides mathematical proof that blockchain security increases with confirmations, giving users confidence in how long to wait before considering transactions final.

4.16 Conclusion: Trustless Electronic Transactions

Summary of Innovation

The Bitcoin whitepaper concludes by summarizing its contribution: "We have proposed a system for electronic transactions without relying on trust. We started with the usual framework of coins made from digital signatures, which provides strong control of ownership, but is incomplete without a way to prevent double-spending."

The Bitcoin protocol achieves trustless electronic transactions through a peer-to-peer network using proof-of-work to record a public history of transactions. The system becomes computationally impractical for an attacker to modify if honest nodes control a majority of CPU power, as stated: "To solve this, we proposed a peer-to-peer network using proof-of-work to record a public history of transactions that quickly becomes computationally impractical for an attacker to change if honest nodes control a majority of CPU power."

Architectural Properties

Robust Simplicity

"The network is robust in its unstructured simplicity. Nodes work all at once with little coordination." This property enables the system to operate without complex coordination protocols while maintaining security.

Anonymity and Pseudonymity

"They do not need to be identified, since messages are not routed to any particular place and only need to be delivered on a best effort basis." This property enables participation without identity disclosure.

Flexible Participation

"Nodes can leave and rejoin the network at will, accepting the longest proof-of-work chain as proof of what happened while they were gone." This property enables asynchronous participation and network resilience.

Consensus Mechanism

"They vote with their CPU power, expressing their acceptance of valid blocks by working on extending them and rejecting invalid blocks by refusing to work on them." This property establishes proof-of-work as the consensus mechanism.

Enforceability

"Any needed rules and incentives can be enforced with this consensus mechanism." This property demonstrates the extensibility of the consensus mechanism to enforce arbitrary protocol rules.

Impact and Historical Significance

The Bitcoin whitepaper introduced blockchain technology as a revolutionary approach to digital currency, solving the double-spending problem without requiring trusted third parties. As the whitepaper concludes: "We have proposed a system for electronic transactions without relying on trust."

Published in 2008, the whitepaper solved problems that had stumped cryptographers for decades:

- The double-spending problem (without central authority)
- The Byzantine Generals' Problem (distributed consensus)
- Trustless digital currency (cryptographic proof instead of trust)

Broader Impact

Its innovations have inspired thousands of blockchain projects and applications beyond cryptocurrency, including:

- **Smart Contracts**: Self-executing contracts on blockchain (Ethereum, etc.)
- **Decentralized Finance (DeFi)**: Financial services without intermediaries
- **Distributed Systems**: New approaches to distributed computing
- **Digital Identity**: Self-sovereign identity systems
- **Supply Chain**: Transparent and verifiable supply chains

Technical Legacy

The whitepaper's concepts continue to influence:

- Consensus mechanisms (Proof-of-Stake, Delegated Proof-of-Stake, etc.)
- Cryptocurrency design
- Distributed ledger technology
- Cryptographic protocols

The paper envisioned "a peer-to-peer network using proof-of-work to record a public history of transactions that quickly becomes computationally impractical for an attacker to change if honest nodes control a majority of CPU power." This vision has been realized and continues to evolve.

4.17 Key Takeaways

This chapter has covered the fundamental concepts from the Bitcoin whitepaper. Here are the essential takeaways:

1. **Double-Spending Solution**: Blockchain solves double-spending through public transaction announcement and consensus on transaction order. The fundamental insight is: "The only way to confirm the absence of a transaction is to be aware of all transactions."
2. **Proof-of-Work**: Computational work secures the network and creates immutable timestamps. "The proof-of-work involves scanning for a value that when hashed, such as with SHA-256, the hash begins with a number of zero bits."
3. **Distributed Consensus**: Longest chain rule ensures network-wide agreement. "Nodes always consider the longest chain to be the correct one."
4. **Economic Incentives**: Mining rewards align miner interests with network security. "The incentive may help encourage nodes to stay honest."
5. **Scalability**: Merkle trees enable efficient storage and verification. "Transactions are hashed in a Merkle Tree, with only the root included in the block's hash."
6. **Security**: Attack probability decreases exponentially with confirmations. "The probability drops exponentially as the number of blocks the attacker has to catch up with increases."

7. **Privacy**: Public keys can remain anonymous while transactions are public. "Privacy can still be maintained by breaking the flow of information in another place: by keeping public keys anonymous."
8. **Flexibility**: Multiple inputs/outputs enable flexible payment amounts. "To allow value to be split and combined, transactions contain multiple inputs and outputs."

4.18 What Comes Next

With the whitepaper's core ideas in place, the next challenge is the part where most implementations succeed or fail: turning concepts into **precise data structures and bytes**. The paper describes what the system must achieve; encoding is where those requirements become interoperable—where hashes, identifiers, scripts, and integers are represented so every node computes the same txids, Merkle roots, and block hashes.

The next chapter translates the whitepaper's "business objects" into **Rust types** and the **byte-level encoding rules** they imply. This is the bridge between theory and implementation, and precision matters.

Key Takeaways

- ✓ This chapter walked through all twelve sections of Satoshi Nakamoto's Bitcoin whitepaper, from the introduction of electronic cash to the probabilistic analysis of attacker success.
- ✓ Proof-of-work creates an immutable chain by making block production computationally expensive while verification remains cheap.
- ✓ The timestamp server, incentive mechanism, and simplified payment verification together enable a trustless peer-to-peer payment system.
- ✓ The mathematical foundations of blockchain security show that attack probability decreases exponentially with the number of confirmations.
- ✓ The economic model aligns miner incentives with network security, making attacks economically irrational despite their technical possibility.
- ✓ Chapter 5 translates these whitepaper concepts into concrete Rust data structures, bridging the gap between theory and implementation—where every byte representation must be agreed upon so that every node in the network computes the same hashes and reaches the same consensus.

5

Bitcoin Whitepaper in Rust

▷ **What you will learn in this chapter**

- Map each Bitcoin whitepaper concept to a concrete Rust data structure
- Explain the hashing and serialization rules that connect whitepaper theory to working code
- Trace how each whitepaper section corresponds to modules in the repository
- Understand the business objects that form the foundation of the implementation

THE whitepaper describes *what* Bitcoin does—how transactions become blocks, blocks form a chain, and nodes agree on which history is true—but the whitepaper says nothing about how to *encode* a transaction as bytes, which fields get hashed together, or what exact signatures prove authorization. These encoding decisions are where theory meets reality, and they must match across all nodes or the network fragments. In the sections that follow, we translate the whitepaper's abstract ideas into **concrete Rust modules and methods**, with complete code listings—calling out what we implement exactly, what we intentionally simplify, and where real-world Bitcoin Core adds rules the whitepaper left implicit.

> ▷ Note
>
> **Tip:** Read this chapter alongside Chapter 4 (The Bitcoin Whitepaper). Each section here maps directly to a whitepaper section, and understanding the theory first makes the Rust encoding decisions much clearer.

5.1 Rust Refresher (Optional)

If we want to brush up on Rust before working through the implementations, we read the Rust guide:

- **Chapter 33: Rust Language Guide** — start with **Rust Installation & Setup**, then continue to **Introduction**.

5.2 How to Read This Chapter (Node Lifecycle)

We structure this section around the core node pipeline, from parsing bytes to committing state. In Rust terms, the data path is:

bytes → structs → canonical bytes → hashes → validation → state update

- **We accept a transaction**: parse bytes into `Transaction` → serialize canonically → compute the `txid` (double-SHA256 of the canonical bytes) → validate (authorization + value rules) → check inputs are unspent in our UTXO view → add to mempool → relay.
- **We accept a block**: parse into `Block` → validate `BlockHeader` (prev link + PoW target) → validate tx set (including "not already spent") → apply UTXO transition atomically → maybe reorg → relay.

When we feel lost, we come back to this Rust checklist (whitepaper phrase → concrete implementation question):

- **Whitepaper says "hash"**: "What exact bytes are hashed, in what order, and with what endianness?" (consensus serialization)
- **Whitepaper says "sign"**: "What exact digest do we sign/verify per-input, and what prevout/script context is included?" (signature hashing / script context)
- **Whitepaper says "not already spent"**: "Does `TxIn.previous_output: OutPoint` exist in our UTXO view at the current best-chain tip?" (state + double-spend prevention)

5.3 Implementation Roadmap (With Rust Encoding)

Step 1 **Bytes (canonical encoding)**

Implement CompactSize/varints and deterministic serialization for the core objects. Outcome: "same object → same bytes" (always).

Step 2 **Identity (hashes as IDs)**

Implement `sha256d`, `txid`, Merkle root, and `block_hash`. Outcome: "same bytes → same IDs" across nodes.

Step 3 **Authorization (spends are permitted)**

Implement script/signature verification using the referenced output as the spend context. Outcome: "only the key-holder can spend" (no forged spends).

Step 4 **State (UTXO transitions)**

Implement UTXO updates as a pure state transition: spend inputs, create outputs. Outcome: "not already spent" is enforceable at the state layer.

Step 5 **Consensus (block acceptance + best chain)**

Implement block validation and chain selection (and reorg handling if needed). Outcome: nodes converge on the same history under the longest/most-work rule.

5.4 What the Whitepaper Specifies (and What It Doesn't)

In the summary chapter we focused on *what* the paper says. Here we focus on *how that becomes code* without losing the paper's intent and meaning.

The whitepaper specifies the *core relationships*:

- **Transactions** are transfers of ownership via digital signatures (Bitcoin Whitepaper Section 2).
- **Blocks** timestamp transactions by hashing them into a chain (Bitcoin Whitepaper Section 3).

- **Proof-of-work** makes rewriting history computationally impractical (Bitcoin Whitepaper Section 4).
- **Nodes** broadcast transactions and blocks and converge on the "longest" chain (Bitcoin Whitepaper Section 5).
- **Merkle trees** enable compact commitments and SPV proofs (Bitcoin Whitepaper Sections 7–8).

The deployed Bitcoin protocol adds important concrete details beyond the paper (still consistent with it), such as:

- **double-SHA256** ("hash twice") for txids and block hashes — applying SHA-256 twice guards against length-extension attacks on the underlying hash construction
- **CompactSize/varints** and strict little-endian **consensus serialization**
- **Script** (e.g., P2PKH/P2WPKH; see description in next section) and signature hashing ("sighash") rules
- a real P2P message protocol (inv/getdata, headers, etc.)

The whitepaper itself does **not** fully specify:

- exact wire encodings (byte-for-byte consensus serialization)
- Script details, signature hashing rules, and full validation edge cases
- production P2P protocol message formats

That's fine for learning: the whitepaper is the conceptual contract, and implementations supply the missing exactness. Our goal is to make the missing pieces explicit (especially byte encoding), because consensus is ultimately "agree on bytes".

5.5 Script: P2PKH vs P2WPKH

Before reaching the data structures themselves, we cover Script briefly: the next section's `TxOut` carries a `script_pubkey: Vec<u8>` field, and seeing what those bytes mean in the two most common standard forms makes the field's purpose concrete instead of opaque.

In Bitcoin, most outputs are "locked" by a **scriptPubKey** (a small stack program). Spending an output means providing data that makes that program succeed. Two common standard output types are:

▷ Deep Dive: P2PKH (Pay-to-PubKey-Hash)

P2PKH (Pay-to-PubKey-Hash): the output commits to a 20-byte `HASH160(pubkey)` (HASH160 is shorthand for RIPEMD-160 applied to SHA-256 — a 20-byte fingerprint shorter than raw SHA-256) and can be spent by providing a signature and the corresponding public key.

Locking form (scriptPubKey):

```
OP_DUP OP_HASH160 <20-byte pubKeyHash>
OP_EQUALVERIFY OP_CHECKSIG
```

Spending data (conceptually): `<sig> <pubkey>` (the node hashes `pubkey` to check it matches `pubKeyHash`, then verifies `sig` under the signature-hash rules).
Common address encoding: legacy Base58 addresses that start with `1...` on mainnet.

i

Why `HASH160(pubkey)` and not just `SHA256(pubkey)`?
In standard **Script/address constructions** (like P2PKH/P2WPKH), Bitcoin uses `HASH160 = RIPEMD160(SHA256(x))` for pubkey hashes largely because:

- It is **smaller** (20 bytes vs 32 bytes), which reduces output sizes and UTXO set footprint.
- It provides **defense in depth** by combining two hash functions (a practical break would need to affect both).
- It is a **historical standard** baked into early script/address conventions (changing it would be a broad compatibility and consensus break).

Note: this is separate from block/tx identifiers. **txids** (and **block hashes**) are computed with **double-SHA256** (i.e., `SHA256(SHA256(bytes))`) over consensus-serialized data (tx serialization for txids; block header serialization for block hashes).

▷ Deep Dive: P2WPKH (Pay-to-Witness-PubKey-Hash, SegWit v0)

P2WPKH (Pay-to-Witness-PubKey-Hash, SegWit v0): the same ownership model as P2PKH (pubkey hash), but signatures and pubkeys are carried in **witness** data (SegWit), not the legacy scriptSig path.

Locking form (witness program):

```
0 <20-byte pubKeyHash>
```

Spending data: witness stack provides `<sig>` `<pubkey>` (native P2WPKH has an empty `scriptSig`).
Why it matters: witness data is excluded from the legacy txid, which eliminates third-party malleability for signature data and makes blocks more space-efficient under weight rules.
Common address encoding: Bech32 addresses that start with `bc1q...` on mainnet. (For compatibility there is also P2SH-wrapped P2WPKH, often starting with `3...`.)

5.6 Core Data Structures (Whitepaper Sections 2–3)

The whitepaper describes Bitcoin's objects in prose: an electronic coin is "a chain of digital signatures," a block is a "timestamp" over transactions, and the ledger is a chain of such blocks anchored by proof-of-work. To implement this in Rust we need concrete *types*—structs whose fields name exactly what gets serialized, hashed, and stored. The seven types below are the minimum vocabulary; every later concept (txid, Merkle root, UTXO set, block hash) is a function of these fields.

The mental model to hold: **a transaction does not "move coins."** It *consumes* previously created outputs (`TxIn` pointing at an `OutPoint`) and *creates* new outputs (`TxOut`). The UTXO set is the derived index of which outputs remain spendable at a given chain tip. Everything else exists to make that rule globally auditable.

▷ **Deep Dive: The Seven Core Types**

`Block` — the unit we relay and validate as a whole; pairs the consensus header with the transaction list it commits to.

```
#[derive(Clone, Debug)]
pub struct Block {
    pub header: BlockHeader,
    pub txs: Vec<Transaction>,
}
```

BlockHeader — the fixed-size (80 bytes: $4 + 32 + 32 + 4 + 4 + 4$), consensus-critical commitment we hash for proof-of-work. `prev_hash` chains this header to the previous one; `merkle_root` commits to `txs`; `difficulty_bits` is the compact-encoded target; `nonce` is the value miners search.

```
#[derive(Clone, Debug)]
pub struct BlockHeader {
    pub version: i32,
    pub prev_hash: [u8; 32],
    pub merkle_root: [u8; 32],
    pub timestamp: u32,          // nTime
    pub difficulty_bits: u32,    // nBits
(compact target)
    pub nonce: u32,
}
```

Transaction — the atomic ledger transition: a list of `TxIn` (which prior outputs we spend) plus a list of `TxOut` (the new outputs we create). `lock_time` is the earliest block height (or Unix time, depending on its value) at which the transaction is allowed to be mined; if `lock_time` is less than 500,000,000, it is interpreted as a block height; otherwise, it is a Unix timestamp (seconds since January 1, 1970). This threshold-based convention allows both time-locking strategies without ambiguity. `0` means "valid immediately," which covers most transactions.

```
#[derive(Clone, Debug)]
pub struct Transaction {
    pub version: i32,
    pub inputs: Vec<TxIn>,
    pub outputs: Vec<TxOut>,
    pub lock_time: u32,
}
```

TxOut — spendable value (`value: u64` , in satoshis) plus a locking program (`script_pubkey: Vec<u8>`) defining *who* may spend it. The bytes are a serialized stack-based bytecode (Bitcoin Script); see §5.5 for example forms like P2PKH and P2WPKH.

```rust
#[derive(Clone, Debug)]
pub struct TxOut {
    pub value: u64,
    pub script_pubkey: Vec<u8>,
}
```

`OutPoint` — the canonical 36-byte identifier (`txid + vout`) for a specific output: a 32-byte transaction id plus a 4-byte output index inside that transaction. `TxIn` (next) consumes a UTXO by holding an `OutPoint` ; `UtxoSet` (below) uses `OutPoint` as its `HashMap` key, which is why it derives the hashmap-key trio `Hash + Eq + PartialEq` .

```rust
#[derive(Clone, Debug, Hash, Eq, PartialEq)]
pub struct OutPoint {
    pub txid: [u8; 32],
    pub vout: u32,
}
```

`TxIn` — a claim on an existing UTXO: a `previous_output: OutPoint` pointer to the output being spent, plus the `script_sig` unlocking data that must satisfy that output's lock. `sequence` is a per-input field originally intended as a signal for in-mempool replacement; today it mostly encodes relative timelocks (BIP68 is Bitcoin Improvement Proposal 68, which redefines the transaction `sequence` field as a relative timelock), and most transactions simply set it to `0xFFFFFFFF` (the maximum), disabling both features.

```rust
#[derive(Clone, Debug)]
pub struct TxIn {
    pub previous_output: OutPoint,
    pub script_sig: Vec<u8>,
    pub sequence: u32,
}
```

`UtxoSet` — the spendable-state index, derived from history. "Not already spent" is now a single hashmap lookup keyed by `OutPoint` .

```rust
use std::collections::HashMap;

pub type UtxoSet = HashMap<OutPoint, TxOut>;
```

i

Why the UTXO set is separate from the blockchain
The blockchain is the append-only history (blocks + transactions). The UTXO set is *derived state*: a fast index of "what remains spendable" after applying that history up to the chosen chain tip. We keep it separate because scanning the entire chain for every input would be unworkably slow. With a UTXO set, validating "is this output spendable?" is a direct `HashMap` lookup. On block connect we remove spent `OutPoint` s and insert new ones; on reorg we undo those changes for blocks we disconnect and reapply for the new branch.

5.7 Canonical Bytes: CompactSize and Transaction Serialization (Whitepaper Section 2)

With the structures defined, the next question is how to turn one of them into the byte string every node will hash. The whitepaper says "hash"; deployed Bitcoin says *exactly which bytes, in what order, with what endianness.* Two implementations agree on transaction identity (the `txid`) only if they produce *byte-identical* serialized transactions and apply double-SHA256 over those exact bytes. Consensus is ultimately "agree on bytes."

The two ingredients are `sha256d` (defined as `SHA256(SHA256(data))`) and `encode_compact_size` , Bitcoin's self-delimiting variable-length integer encoding used to length-prefix every variable-width field (input count, output count, script lengths).

▷ **Deep Dive: CompactSize, Legacy Tx Serialization, and**

The hashing primitive. `sha256d` is a thin wrapper around two SHA-256 invocations and is reused everywhere a consensus identifier (txid, block hash, Merkle parent) is computed.

```rust
use sha2::{Digest, Sha256};

/// Compute double-SHA256: SHA256(SHA256(data))
pub fn sha256d(data: &[u8]) -> [u8; 32] {
    let first = Sha256::digest(data);
    let second = Sha256::digest(&first);
    second.into()
}
```

CompactSize encoding. The first byte is either the value itself (for 0...252) or a marker (`0xFD`, `0xFE`, `0xFF`) telling the decoder to read 2, 4, or 8 more little-endian bytes. The thresholds are chosen so the marker bytes are never confused with small one-byte values: the value 253 in decimal is `0xFD` in hex, so the one-byte form must end at `0xFC` (decimal 252) to keep parsing unambiguous. Worked example: the value 300 encodes as the three bytes `FD 2C 01` —the `0xFD` marker followed by 300 = 0x012C written little-endian (low byte first).

```rust
pub fn encode_compact_size(n: u64, out: &mut Vec<u8>) {
    match n {
        // 0..=252: one byte, value is the byte itself
        0..=252 => out.push(n as u8),
        // marker 0xFD + 2-byte u16 LE
        253..=0xFFFF => {
            out.push(0xFD);
            out.extend_from_slice(&(n as u16).to_le_bytes());
        }
        // marker 0xFE + 4-byte u32 LE
        0x1_0000..=0xFFFF_FFFF => {
            out.push(0xFE);
            out.extend_from_slice(&(n as u32).to_le_bytes());
        }
        // marker 0xFF + 8-byte u64 LE
        _ => {
            out.push(0xFF);
            out.extend_from_slice(&n.to_le_bytes());
        }
    }
}
```

Legacy transaction serialization. Every variable-length field (input count, scriptSig, output count, scriptPubKey) is length-prefixed with CompactSize; every integer is little-endian. The result is the byte string we hash to get the `txid`.

```
pub fn serialize_tx_legacy(tx: &Transaction) ->
Vec<u8> {
    let mut out = Vec::new();
    out.extend_from_slice(&tx.version.to_le_bytes());
    encode_compact_size(tx.inputs.len() as u64,
&mut out);
    for input in &tx.inputs {
        out.extend_from_slice(&input.previous_output.txid);
        out.extend_from_slice(&input.previous_output.vout.to_le_bytes());

encode_compact_size(input.script_sig.len() as
u64, &mut out);

out.extend_from_slice(&input.script_sig);
        out.extend_from_slice(&input.sequence.to_le_bytes());
    }
    encode_compact_size(tx.outputs.len() as
u64, &mut out);
    for output in &tx.outputs {
        out.extend_from_slice(&output.value.to_le_bytes());

encode_compact_size(output.script_pubkey.len()
as u64, &mut out);

out.extend_from_slice(&output.script_pubkey);
    }
    out.extend_from_slice(&tx.lock_time.to_le_bytes());
    out
}

pub fn txid_legacy(tx: &Transaction) -> [u8;
32] {
    sha256d(&serialize_tx_legacy(tx))
}
```

The 32-byte hash is often shown reversed in block explorers and wallet user interfaces. Block explorers display hashes in little-endian byte order, a historical Bitcoin convention. Internally, we store hashes in their natural SHA-256 output order and reverse only at display boundaries.

▷ Note

SegWit note: Bitcoin's 2017 SegWit upgrade (BIP141, activated at block 481,824) moves the unlocking data (signatures and witness items) out of the legacy `script_sig` and into a separate witness structure. The legacy `txid` computed above remains stable for SegWit spends because witness bytes are excluded from it—this is what fixes signature malleability and enables Lightning-style payment channels. SegWit transactions also have a witness-including identifier called the `wtxid` —computed the same way as `txid` but over the serialization that does include the witness bytes, so changes to a signature change the `wtxid` but not the `txid` .

5.8 Proof-of-Work: Compact Targets and the Mining Loop (Whitepaper Section 4)

The whitepaper describes proof-of-work as "scanning for a value that when hashed begins with a number of zero bits" and notes that the work required is exponential in the number of zero bits. Deployed Bitcoin makes that intuition exact: the header carries a 4-byte `nBits` field that compactly encodes a 256-bit *target*, and a block is valid if and only if `block_hash <= target` . Mining is repeated hashing of the 80-byte header (varying `nonce`); verification is a single hash plus a single comparison. If SHA-256 outputs are uniform, then $P[\text{hash} \leq \text{target}] \approx \text{target}/2^{256}$, so halving the target roughly doubles the expected work.

▷ **Deep Dive: From to Target to a Mined Block**

Expanding `nBits` to a 256-bit target. The compact form stores the target as one exponent byte plus a 24-bit mantissa: `target = mantissa * 256^(exp - 3)` for `exp >= 3` , with a right-shift case for very small exponents (`exp <= 3`). The `-3` offset accounts for the mantissa being three bytes wide: at `exp == 3` the mantissa occupies the rightmost three positions (indexes 29–31) of the 32-byte buffer, and each increment of `exp` shifts it one byte leftward into a more significant position. Concretely, the function below writes the three mantissa bytes into the big-endian buffer so that the most significant mantissa byte lands at index `32 - exp`, meaning a larger `exp` produces a larger target. A larger target makes the inequality `block_hash <= target` easier to satisfy, which means *lower* difficulty (and faster expected mining time). Worked example: Bitcoin's genesis `nBits` is `0x1d00ffff`, so `exp = 0x1d = 29` and `mant = 0x00ffff`. The three mantissa bytes are written starting at index `32 - 29 = 3`, yielding the familiar difficulty-1 target `0x00000000FFFF0000...00`.

```rust
/// Expand nBits (4-byte compact) to target (32-byte big-endian).
pub fn bits_to_target(difficulty_bits: u32) -> [u8; 32] {
    let exp = (difficulty_bits >> 24) as u8;
    let mant = difficulty_bits & 0x00FF_FFFF;
    let mut target = [0u8; 32];

    if mant == 0 { return target; }

    if exp <= 3 {
        // Small-exponent branch: shrink mantissa by right-shifting.
        // Spec-completeness path; mainnet nBits values keep exp >= 3.
        let shift_bytes = (3 - exp) as u32;
        let m = (mant >> (8 * shift_bytes)) as u32;
        target[28..32].copy_from_slice(&m.to_be_bytes());
        return target;
    }

    // saturating_sub clamps to 0 if exp > 32 (corrupted nBits) instead of
    // underflowing usize; the bounds check below then prevents any write.
    let start = 32usize.saturating_sub(exp as usize);
    if start + 3 <= 32 {
        target[start]     = ((mant >> 16) & 0xFF) as u8;
        target[start + 1] = ((mant >>  8) & 0xFF) as u8;
        target[start + 2] = ( mant        & 0xFF) as u8;
    }
    target
}
```

Verification predicate. The target and the hash must be compared in the same byte order. `bits_to_target` writes a 32-byte big-endian buffer (most significant byte at index 0). SHA-256 produces its output in the opposite convention—Bitcoin historically treats a hash as a little-endian 256-bit integer, which is also why block explorers show txids and block hashes reversed—so `meets_target` reverses the hash bytes first. After that flip, a plain lexicographic `<=` on the two `[u8; 32]` arrays compares them as if they were MSB-first integers, which is exactly the check we want.

```
pub fn meets_target(hash: [u8; 32], target_be:
[u8; 32]) -> bool {
    // [u8; 32] is Copy, so this clones the
bytes; the caller's hash is intact.
    let mut h = hash;
    h.reverse();
    h <= target_be
}
```

The mining loop. Compute the target once; then iterate the `nonce` field, re-hash the 80-byte header, and stop when the hash falls below the target. Because finding a valid nonce is probabilistic and verification is one hash plus one compare, this captures exactly the whitepaper's "hard to find, easy to verify" property. We use a small `block_hash` helper that serializes the six header fields in the fixed 80-byte consensus order (little-endian integers, 32-byte hashes as-is) and applies `sha256d`—the same double-SHA256 primitive used for transaction ids. The rationale for double-hashing appears above: we hash twice (SHA-256 of SHA-256) to defend against length-extension attacks, a vulnerability in raw SHA-256 where knowing the hash of a message allows computing the hash of that message with appended data, without knowing the original message. Double hashing breaks this attack because the inner hash's output is a fixed-size input to the outer hash.

```
/// Serialize the 80-byte block header and
double-hash it.
pub fn block_hash(h: &BlockHeader) -> [u8; 32] {
    let mut buf = Vec::with_capacity(80);

buf.extend_from_slice(&h.version.to_le_bytes());
    buf.extend_from_slice(&h.prev_hash);
    buf.extend_from_slice(&h.merkle_root);
    buf.extend_from_slice(&h.timestamp.to_le_by
tes());
    buf.extend_from_slice(&h.difficulty_bits.to
_le_bytes());

buf.extend_from_slice(&h.nonce.to_le_bytes());
    sha256d(&buf)
}

pub fn mine(mut header: BlockHeader) ->
(BlockHeader, [u8; 32]) {
    let target =
bits_to_target(header.difficulty_bits);
    loop {
        let h = block_hash(&header);
        if meets_target(h, target) {
            return (header, h);
        }
        // wrapping_add (not +=) so the u32
silently rolls over at 2^32
        // instead of panicking in debug
builds; see the extranonce note below.
        // Rust's += operator panics on integer
overflow in debug builds (a safety feature that
catches bugs).
        // wrapping_add silently wraps around
to zero instead, matching the C-style semantics
that Bitcoin's mining loop expects.
        header.nonce =
header.nonce.wrapping_add(1);
    }
}
```

The 4-byte `nonce` field can be exhausted (2^{32} tries) before a valid hash is found at modern difficulty levels. Real miners then change something else that flows into the header—typically the *extranonce* bytes inside the **coinbase transaction**'s `script_sig`. The coinbase is the first transaction in every block, and it is special in two ways: it mints the block subsidy (the newly created BTC paid to the miner), and because it spends no prior UTXO, its `script_sig` is unconstrained and conventionally used to hold arbitrary miner data—which is exactly what makes it the natural home for the extranonce. Bumping the extranonce changes the coinbase, which changes its `txid`, which changes the Merkle root, which changes the header bytes being hashed. This implementation omits the rollover and would simply wrap the nonce; a production loop bumps an outer counter, rebuilds the coinbase, and recomputes `merkle_root` before resuming.

5.9 Merkle Trees and SPV (Whitepaper Sections 7–8)

The whitepaper introduces Merkle trees so that "only the root is included in the block hash" and uses them to build Simplified Payment Verification: a lightweight client that holds only the header chain can verify a payment is included in a particular block by checking a short *Merkle branch*. Two functions implement both halves: a full node *builds* a Merkle root from all the block's txids, and an SPV client *verifies* a leaf using the branch.

▷ **Deep Dive: Building a Merkle Root and Verifying a Branch**

Building the root. Pair leaves up, hash each pair with double-SHA256, and repeat until a single hash remains—that is the root. If a level has an odd number of nodes, Bitcoin duplicates the last one before pairing (a historical choice preserved for consensus compatibility; the duplication is also why two distinct leaf orderings can collide on the same root, the well-known CVE-2012-2459 that full nodes mitigate by independently checking transaction uniqueness). The empty-leaves branch is defensive: a real block always includes at least the coinbase transaction, so `leaves` is never empty in practice.

```
pub fn merkle_root(mut leaves: Vec<[u8; 32]>)
-> [u8; 32] {
    if leaves.is_empty() {
        // Real Bitcoin blocks always have >= 1
(coinbase).
        return [0u8; 32];
    }
    while leaves.len() > 1 {
        if leaves.len() % 2 == 1 {
            // Duplicate last node if odd count.

leaves.push(*leaves.last().unwrap());
        }
        let mut next =
Vec::with_capacity(leaves.len() / 2);
        for pair in leaves.chunks(2) {
            let mut b = Vec::with_capacity(64);
            b.extend_from_slice(&pair[0]);
            b.extend_from_slice(&pair[1]);
            // Merkle parent = sha256d(left ||
right)
            next.push(sha256d(&b));
        }
        leaves = next;
    }
    leaves[0]
}
```

Verifying a branch. An SPV proof gives the client a leaf (the `txid`), a list of sibling hashes from leaf to root, and the leaf's index (leftmost leaf is 0, next is 1, and so on). At each level the verifier inspects the low bit of `index`: 0 means the current hash is the left child (so concatenate `(self, sibling)`), 1 means it is the right child (so concatenate `(sibling, self)`). Shifting `index` right by one (`index /= 2`) discards the bit we just consumed and leaves the index of the parent node at the next level up. One way to picture this: the binary representation of the leaf's index spells out the path from root to leaf, where the top bit chooses left-or-right at the root and the bottom bit chooses left-or-right at the final step—so walking up the tree is the same as consuming those bits one at a time from the bottom. After consuming every sibling in the branch, the reconstructed hash should equal the Merkle root.

```
/// Reconstruct a Merkle root from a leaf and
its sibling branch.
/// Returns the reconstructed root; the caller
compares it to the
/// header's `merkle_root` to decide whether
the leaf is included.
pub fn verify_merkle_branch(
    leaf: [u8; 32],
    branch: &[[u8; 32]],
    mut index: usize,
) -> [u8; 32] {
    let mut h = leaf;
    for sibling in branch {
        let mut b = Vec::with_capacity(64);
        if index % 2 == 0 {
            // LEFT child: hash (h || sibling)
            b.extend_from_slice(&h);
            b.extend_from_slice(sibling);
        } else {
            // RIGHT child: hash (sibling || h)
            b.extend_from_slice(sibling);
            b.extend_from_slice(&h);
        }
        h = sha256d(&b);
        index /= 2;
    }
    h
}
```

If the reconstructed `h` equals the header's `merkle_root` , the leaf is committed by that block. Combined with a header chain (PoW + `prev_hash` links), this is a complete SPV inclusion proof—without ever validating the rest of the block's transactions.

i

What SPV proves and what it does not
SPV proves *inclusion in a proof-of-work-backed chain*: a transaction with this `txid` was committed by the Merkle root of a header that is on the most-work chain the client has seen. SPV does *not* verify Bitcoin's full consensus rules—it cannot independently enforce "not already spent" the way a full node does, because that requires the UTXO set and full transaction validation. Pruning and SPV use the same underlying idea (**commitment in the header, data in the body**) but make different storage and trust trade-offs: a pruned full node keeps the header chain plus the UTXO set; an SPV client keeps only the header chain.

5.10 Further Reading

- **Bitcoin Whitepaper** — Read alongside this chapter for the full context behind each Rust encoding. See https://bitcoin.org/bitcoin.pdf
- **serde Documentation** — The serialization framework used throughout the implementation. See https://serde.rs/
- **Bitcoin Developer Reference** — Technical specifications for Bitcoin data structures. See https://developer.bitcoin.org/reference/

Key Takeaways

✓ Every Bitcoin whitepaper concept maps to a concrete Rust data structure: the seven core types (`Block` , `BlockHeader` , `Transaction` , `TxIn` , `TxOut` , `OutPoint` , `UtxoSet`) are the minimum vocabulary for the whole system.

✓ Consensus is "agree on bytes." `encode_compact_size` and `serialize_tx_legacy` produce the byte-exact serialization that `txid_legacy` hashes to derive transaction identity.

✓ Proof-of-work compresses to a comparison: `bits_to_target` expands the 4-byte `nBits` field to a 256-bit threshold, `meets_target` tests `block_hash <= target` , and the `mine` loop scans the `nonce` until it succeeds.

✓ Merkle trees connect "a block contains transactions" to "the header commits to them." `merkle_root` builds the commitment;

`verify_merkle_branch` reconstructs the root from a leaf and its sibling hashes, giving SPV clients PoW-anchored inclusion proofs without full validation.

✓ In the next chapter, the Rust project's organization is examined — the crate workspace, dependency graph, and build configuration that make all of this compile and run.

6

Rust Blockchain Project

▷ **What you will learn in this chapter**

- Navigate the Cargo workspace and understand its crate organization
- Explain the dependency graph between crates and why it is structured this way
- Identify which crate owns each responsibility in the system
- Understand the build configuration and feature flags used across the project

CHAPTERS 4–5 used the Bitcoin whitepaper to build a minimal mental model and a "Bitcoin-shaped" implementation. This chapter switches from concepts to code, reading the Rust project as a working system and showing how the pieces connect in practice. A crate is Rust's term for a package or library—the fundamental unit of compilation and dependency management in Rust projects.

Chapter 5 closed with a five-step implementation roadmap: **Bytes** → **Identity** → **Authorization** → **State** → **Consensus**. The chapters ahead follow that same arc. Chapters 7–8 (Primitives and Utilities) cover *Bytes*—the canonical encodings every node must agree on. Chapter 9 (Cryptography) covers *Identity* (hashes as IDs) and *Authorization* (signatures that prove ownership). Chapters 10–18 (Blockchain Core) and 19 (Block Acceptance) cover *State* and *Consensus*—UTXO transitions, proof-of-work validation, and chain selection. From there, Chapters 20–23 build the surrounding infrastructure: storage, networking, node orchestration, and wallet. By

Chapter 24 (Web API), the full Bitcoin pipeline is implemented and exposed to the outside world.

6.1 Prerequisites: Clone the Repository

To follow along locally, clone the repository from GitHub (`https://github.com/bkunyiha/rust-blockchain`) and open it in your editor.

In the repository, the Rust implementation covered in this book lives under the `bitcoin/` crate.

6.2 How to Use This Chapter

While reading the codebase, keep two questions in mind:

- **What exact bytes are parsed, serialized, hashed, and verified here?**
- **What state is updated, and how would a node roll it back on a reorg?** A reorg (reorganization) occurs when a competing fork of the blockchain accumulates more proof-of-work than the node's current best chain. The node abandons its old tip and switches to the new one, undoing all state changes from discarded blocks.

The recommended reading order follows the same direction bytes flow through the system: primitives → crypto → PoW (proof-of-work)/validation → storage/chainstate (the in-memory UTXO set plus best-chain tip that every node maintains) → networking/node → wallet/client.

6.3 Rust Refresher

Chapter 33 (Rust Language Guide) appears at the end of the book, but it is designed to be read *before* the implementation chapters — not after. If ownership, traits, generics, or async/await feel rusty, read it now:

- **Chapter 33: Rust Language Guide** — start with **Rust Installation & Setup**, then continue to **Introduction**.

6.4 Guided Tour (Recommended Reading Order)

Each step below points to:

- the **book chapter** (documentation) that explains the subsystem
- the **code location** in the Rust project that implements it

> ▷ **Note**
>
> The crate names in this workspace (`bitcoin-blockchain`, `bitcoin-api`, etc.) are internal identifiers, not crates.io packages; all dependencies are local path dependencies within the workspace.

The order follows the path that bytes take through the system. First we define the structures and their binary encoding. Then we add the cryptographic machinery—hashing and signing—that makes those bytes tamper-evident. Next come the consensus rules that keep all nodes synchronized. Finally, we build the infrastructure layer (storage, networking) and user-facing tools (wallet, API, desktop) that make the system usable.

1. **Business objects and encoding (block, header, transaction)**
   - Chapter 7: Primitives
   - Code: `bitcoin/src/primitives/` (block, header, transaction)
2. **Utility helpers (bytes, plumbing, small reusable building blocks)**
   - Chapter 8: Utilities
   - Code: `bitcoin/src/util/`
3. **Crypto primitives (hashes, keys, signatures, address/script helpers)**
   - Chapter 9: Cryptography
   - Code: `bitcoin/src/crypto/`
4. **Proof-of-work and block acceptance**
   - Chapters 10–18: Blockchain — From Transaction to Block Acceptance
   - Code: `bitcoin/src/pow.rs` , `bitcoin/src/chain/`
5. **Storage and persistence**
   - Chapter 20: Storage Layer
   - Code: `bitcoin/src/store/` (persisting chain/wallet data)
6. **Chainstate / UTXO updates**
   - Chapter 11: Blockchain State Management
   - Code: `bitcoin/src/chain/chainstate.rs`, `bitcoin/src/chain/utxo_set.rs`
7. **Networking and message handling**
   - Chapter 21: Network Layer
   - Code: `bitcoin/src/net/` , `bitcoin/src/net/net_processing.rs`
8. **Node orchestration**
   - Chapter 22: Node Orchestration
   - Code: `bitcoin/src/node/` (peers, server, miner, mempool integration)
9. **Wallet/client**
   - Chapter 23: Wallet System
   - Code: `bitcoin/src/wallet/` (wallet implementation + service layer)

6.5 A Small Exercise

To turn reading into understanding, pick one end-to-end flow and trace it through code:

- **Receiving and confirming a transaction**: network receives a `tx` message → parse → validate → mempool → mine/include in block → connect block → wallet updates confirmation depth.

Being able to narrate that flow from memory and point to the relevant modules is a good sign of readiness for the deeper chapters that follow.

6.6 Further Reading

- **Cargo Workspaces**—The Rust Book's guide to multi-crate projects. See https://doc.rust-lang.org/book/ch14-03-cargo-workspaces.html
- **Cargo Reference: Features**—How conditional compilation and feature flags work in Cargo. See https://doc.rust-lang.org/cargo/reference/features.html

Key Takeaways

- ✓ This chapter navigated the Cargo workspace structure, identifying each crate and its responsibility within the blockchain system.
- ✓ The dependency graph between crates reflects a deliberate architecture that separates primitives, crypto, chain logic, and application layers.
- ✓ The build configuration, feature flags, and workspace-level settings coordinate compilation across the project.
- ✓ The next chapter covers the primitives crate—the Block, Transaction, and Blockchain structures that form the foundation everything else builds on.

7

Primitives

> ▷ **What you will learn in this chapter**
>
> - Define the Block, Transaction, and Blockchain data structures that form the system's foundation
> - Explain why transaction IDs use `Vec<u8>` rather than hex strings
> - Describe the role of each field in the block header and transaction structure
> - Understand how these pure data types are used by every other module in the codebase

WHEN a block arrives at your node over the network, it arrives as raw bytes. Before validation, before mining, before anything else happens, you must parse those bytes into a strongly typed `Block` struct. Every field must be in the right place, every field type must match exactly, or the whole system falls apart. The types you build in this chapter are the vocabulary that the entire codebase speaks—they define what a block *is*, not what you *do* with it. That job belongs to the chain, node, and validation modules.

By the end of this chapter, you will understand every field in a block and transaction, why we use `Vec<u8>` for hashes instead of strings, and how Serde derives turn raw bytes into type-safe Rust at parse time.

7.1 Overview

The types we define here flow through the rest of the system. Chapter 9 (Cryptography) hashes and signs them. Chapters 10–18 (Blockchain Core) validate them against consensus rules and manage UTXO state transitions. Chapter 20 (Storage Layer) persists them to disk via Sled. Chapter 21 (Network Layer) serializes them for peer-to-peer transmission. Understanding the shape of `Block`, `Transaction`, `TXInput`, and `TXOutput` is a prerequisite for every chapter that follows.

7.2 Block Structure

The `Block` structure represents a single block in the blockchain, containing both metadata (the header) and a list of transactions.

▷ Block Diagram

The diagram below shows the block structure with its header fields and transaction list:

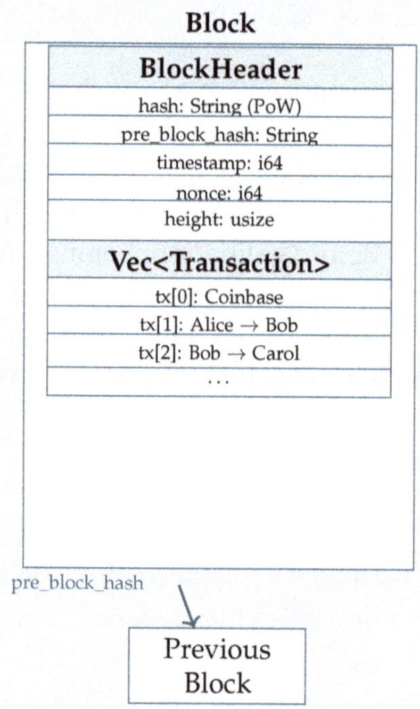

Figure 7.1: Block structure with header fields and transaction list

Clarification (this project vs Bitcoin Core): Bitcoin's block header includes fields like a Merkle root (a single hash summarizing every transaction in the block, so a tampered transaction instantly invalidates the header) and a compact difficulty target (the `nBits` field, which encodes the maximum hash value the block hash must fall below to qualify as valid proof-of-work). The block hash is then derived from these header bytes. In this book's implementation we keep the header minimal (and store hashes as `String`) so the first pass stays focused on chaining, proof-of-work, and transactions. As you read later chapters, treat this as an intentionally simplified—but functional—model of the core idea.

Block Header Components

The `BlockHeader` contains the metadata essential for blockchain operation:

- **Hash**: Cryptographic hash of the block (used as the identifier and as the "link" target for the next block)
- **Previous Hash** (`pre_block_hash`): Link to the parent block, creating the chain
- **Timestamp**: Unix timestamp of block creation
- **Nonce**: Proof-of-work value found by mining
- **Height**: Position of this block in the chain (zero-indexed)

Block Key Operations

- Block creation and validation
- Hash calculation
- Serialization/deserialization
- Transaction inclusion

7.3 Transaction Structure

Now that we have defined the container (a `Block`), we need to understand what those containers hold: transactions.

The `Transaction` structure represents a single transaction, which transfers value by consuming previous outputs and creating new ones. Those previous outputs that have not yet been spent are called *unspent transaction outputs*, or UTXOs — they are the atoms of balance in a Bitcoin-style system. A wallet's balance is the sum of UTXOs it can spend; sending coins means consuming some of those UTXOs as inputs and emitting fresh ones as outputs. Chapter 10 develops the UTXO model in detail; for now, treat UTXO as "a specific previous output that is still spendable."

Transaction Components

- **TXInput**: References to previous transaction outputs (UTXOs) being spent
- **TXOutput**: New outputs created by this transaction
- **Transaction ID**: SHA-256 hash of the transaction
- **Signatures**: Cryptographic signatures authorizing each spend

Transaction Types

- **Coinbase Transactions**: Mining rewards with no inputs
- **Regular Transactions**: Transfers between addresses
- **Wallet Transactions**: User-facing transaction representation

7.4 Blockchain Structure

The `Blockchain` structure represents the complete chain of blocks:

Blockchain Components

- **Blocks**: Collection of blocks in sequence
- **Tip Hash**: Hash of the latest block
- **Height**: Current chain height
- **Genesis Block**: First block in the chain

Key Operations

- Block addition
- Chain validation
- Block retrieval
- Chain traversal

7.5 Design Decisions

Why Pure Data Structures?

The primitives module deliberately contains no business logic – no validation, no persistence, no networking. This mirrors Bitcoin Core's `primitives/` directory and keeps the types reusable across every other module. A `Block` struct can be constructed, serialized, and passed around without pulling in database dependencies or consensus rules.

Why `Vec<u8>` for Hashes and IDs?

Transaction IDs and block hashes are stored as raw byte vectors rather than hex strings. This avoids repeated hex-encode/decode round-trips and keeps hashing deterministic (we hash bytes, not string representations). The following section explores this decision in depth, including comparisons with Bitcoin Core's approach.

> ▲ Warning
>
> Transaction IDs are stored as `Vec<u8>` (raw bytes) rather than hex strings throughout the codebase. This is a deliberate design choice: byte comparisons are faster, storage is more compact, and we avoid repeated hex encoding/decoding. You will see this pattern in every module that handles transaction IDs.

Serde for Serialization

Serde (short for *Serialize/Deserialize*) is Rust's standard framework for converting data structures to and from formats like JSON or binary. All primitives derive `Serialize` and `Deserialize`, enabling JSON serialization for the REST API (Chapter 24) and binary encoding via bincode for storage (Chapter 20). The `#[derive(Serialize, Deserialize)]` pattern appears on every struct in this module.

> ▲ Warning
>
> Changing any field in a block – even a single byte – invalidates the block hash and breaks the chain of hashes linking it to subsequent blocks. This is because SHA-256 is deterministic but *avalanche-sensitive*: the same input always produces the same hash, but flipping even one bit of the

> input produces a completely different 256-bit output. So any modification, no matter how small, yields a new hash that no longer matches the `pre_block_hash` stored in every subsequent block. This is what makes blockchain tamper-evident.

7.6 Transaction ID Format

Transaction identifiers may seem like a simple detail—an ID is just an identifier—but the representation choices made here have significant implications for memory efficiency, performance, and code clarity. A data representation decision can determine whether the system handles thousands of transactions per second or struggles with hundreds, and it affects everything from network protocol efficiency to database query performance.

This section examines why transaction IDs are stored as binary data rather than strings, how bytes and hex representations relate, and how Rust's ownership model enables zero-cost abstractions that keep the code both safe and fast.

Why `Vec<u8>` Instead of String?

The Fundamental Reason: Hash Output is Binary

In a blockchain, every transaction must be uniquely and deterministically identified — when one transaction spends an output from another, the reference uses the source transaction's ID.

The first design question for the transaction system is fundamental: how should transaction IDs be represented? The answer lies in understanding what transaction IDs actually are.

Transaction IDs are **SHA-256 hashes**, and hash functions produce **binary data**, not text. Here is what this means in practice:

```
// From src/primitives/transaction.rs
pub struct Transaction {
    txid: Vec<u8>,  // 32 bytes of binary data
    vin: Vec<TXInput>,
    vout: Vec<TXOutput>,
    // ...
}

// SHA-256 outputs raw bytes:
fn sha256(data: &[u8]) -> [u8; 32] {
    // Returns: [0x23, 0x2f, 0x3c, ..., 0xef]  (32 bytes)
    //     NOT: "9a2f3c...ef"  (64 character string)
}
```

Listing 1: Transaction ID storage in Rust

Memory Efficiency Comparison

Table 7.1: Memory usage: `Vec<u8>` vs hex string

Type	Size	Example
`Vec<u8>`	32 bytes	`[0x23, 0x2f, 0x3c, ...]`
`String` (hex)	64+ bytes	`"9a2f3c4d5e6f..."`
Savings	50%	Binary is half the size!

The Bitcoin Protocol Uses Binary

When we look at how Bitcoin actually works at the protocol level, we discover another important reason for using binary storage. The Bitcoin P2P protocol transmits **raw bytes**, not hex strings:

Bitcoin Wire Format (*inv* message)	
Count: 1	[varint]
Type: 0x01 (MSG_TX)	[4 bytes]
Hash: 0x9a2f3c... (raw bytes)	[32 bytes]

Figure 7.2: Bitcoin wire format for an *inv* message

Code Comparison Consider what this means in practice. If we stored transaction IDs as strings, we would need constant conversions:

```
// [X] BAD: String storage requires constant conversions
struct Transaction {
    id: String,  // Hex string "9a2f3c..."
}

// Send over network = decode hex every time
fn send_to_network(tx: &Transaction) {
    let bytes = hex::decode(&tx.id).unwrap();  // Expensive!
    network::send_inv(&bytes);
}
```

Listing 2: Inefficient string-based approach

But with binary storage, we get zero-cost network operations:

```rust
// [OK] GOOD: Binary storage, zero conversions
struct Transaction {
    id: Vec<u8>,   // Binary [0x23, 0x2f, ...]
}

// Send over network = direct
fn send_to_network(tx: &Transaction) {
    network::send_inv(&tx.id);  // Zero cost!
}
```

Listing 3: Efficient binary-based approach

From Our Codebase Here is how this works in the implementation:

```rust
// src/node/context.rs (line 99-110)
pub async fn process_transaction(
    &self,
    addr_from: &SocketAddr,
    tx: Transaction,
) -> Result<String> {
    // Add to memory pool
    add_to_memory_pool(tx, &self.blockchain).await;

    let my_node_addr = GLOBAL_CONFIG.get_node_addr();

    // Broadcast using BINARY format
    if my_node_addr.eq(&CENTRAL_NODE) {
        let nodes = self.get_nodes_excluding_sender(addr_from).await?;
        self.broadcast_transaction_to_nodes(&nodes, tx.get_id_bytes())
            .await;
        // ^^^^^^^^^^^^^^^^
        // Binary for network!
    }
    Ok(tx.get_tx_id_hex())  // Hex only for API response
}
```

Listing 4: Transaction processing with binary IDs

Performance Comparison

Binary format enables efficient operations:

```rust
// [OK] Binary: Direct byte comparison O(n)
fn compare_binary(a: &[u8], b: &[u8]) -> bool {
    a == b  // Fast: memcmp() at CPU level
}

// [X] Hex String: Character comparison O(2n)
fn compare_hex(a: &str, b: &str) -> bool {
    a == b  // Slower: must compare 64 chars instead of 32 bytes
}

// For Merkle tree operations, binary format is essential
// for hashing efficiency.
```

Listing 5: Binary vs hex comparison performance

Database Storage Efficiency

```rust
// [OK] Binary: Compact 32-byte keys
use sled::Db;

let db: Db = sled::open("blockchain.db")?;

// Store with binary key
db.insert(&tx.id, serialized_tx)?;  // 32-byte key

// Lookup with binary key
let tx = db.get(&tx.id)?;  // Fast lookup

// [X] String: Bloated 64-byte keys
let hex_key = hex::encode(&tx.id);
db.insert(hex_key.as_bytes(), serialized_tx)?;  // 64-byte key (2x space!)
```

Listing 6: Database key-value operations

```rust
// src/store/file_system_db_chain.rs
impl BlockchainFileSystem {
    pub async fn get_transaction(
        &self,
        id: &[u8],
    ) -> Result<Option<Transaction>> {
        // Binary for efficient DB lookup.
        let tx_tree = self.blockchain.db.open_tree(TRANSACTIONS_CF)?;

        match tx_tree.get(id)? {  // Direct binary key lookup
            Some(tx_bytes) => {
                let tx = bincode::deserialize(&tx_bytes)?;
                Ok(Some(tx))
            }
            None => Ok(None),
        }
    }
}
```

Listing 7: Database transaction lookup

Real-World Impact

For a blockchain processing 400,000 transactions per day (Bitcoin's approximate daily transaction volume):

```
Memory for 1 million transaction IDs:

Vec<u8> storage:
1,000,000 txids × 32 bytes = 32 MB

String storage:
1,000,000 txids × 64 bytes = 64 MB
Plus String overhead = ~88 MB total

SAVINGS: 56 MB (64% reduction!)
```

The same advantage applies to network bandwidth, where binary IDs reduce per-transaction overhead:

```
Network bandwidth (1000 tx/s sustained):

Vec<u8> transmission:
1000 tx/s × 32 bytes = 32 KB/s

String transmission:
1000 tx/s × 64 bytes = 64 KB/s

SAVINGS: 32 KB/s (50% bandwidth reduction!)
```

Bytes vs Hex: `get_id_bytes()` vs `get_tx_id_hex()`

As shown above, transaction IDs are fundamentally binary data—32 bytes produced by a SHA-256 hash function. However, different parts of the system need this data in different formats. Understanding when and why to use each format is crucial for writing efficient, maintainable code.

Both methods return the **same transaction ID**, just in different formats for different purposes. The key insight is recognizing that format conversion has costs, and we should minimize conversions by using the right format at the right time.

Method Definitions

```rust
// From src/primitives/transaction.rs
impl Transaction {
    /// Get transaction ID as raw bytes (for internal use)
    pub fn get_id_bytes(&self) -> Vec<u8> {
        self.txid.clone()
    }

    /// Get transaction ID as hex string (for display)
    pub fn get_tx_id_hex(&self) -> String {
        hex::encode(&self.txid)
    }

    /// Get transaction ID reference (most efficient)
    pub fn get_id(&self) -> &[u8] {
        &self.txid
    }
}
```

Listing 8: Transaction ID accessor methods

Use Cases Comparison

Table 7.2: When to use each transaction ID method

Method	Returns	Use Case
`get_id_bytes()`	`Vec<u8>`	Network protocol, storage, when ownership needed
`get_tx_id_hex()`	`String`	API responses, logging, UI display
`get_id()`	`&[u8]`	Comparisons, lookups, when borrowing is enough

Practical Examples from Our Codebase

Use case summary:

- Network Protocol: `Vec<u8>` (binary)
- API Response: `String` (hex)
- Logging: `String` (hex)
- Database: `Vec<u8>` (binary)

Conversion Cost Analysis

Understanding the cost of each operation helps us make informed decisions about when to use which method:

```
// Conversion costs for a 32-byte transaction ID:

// get_id() - FREE (just returns reference)
let id_ref: &[u8] = tx.get_id();
// Cost: 0 bytes allocated, 0 copies
//       Just returns a pointer (8 bytes) + length (8 bytes) = 16 bytes total
//       This is essentially free - no heap allocation, no data copying
//       CPU: ~1-2 nanoseconds (just pointer arithmetic)

// get_id_bytes() - CLONE COST
let id_vec: Vec<u8> = tx.get_id_bytes();
// Cost: 32 bytes copied + Vec overhead (24 bytes) = 56 bytes allocated
//       CPU: ~10-20 nanoseconds (memory copy operation)
//       This is necessary when you need ownership (e.g., storing in HashMap)

// get_tx_id_hex() - ENCODE + ALLOCATE
let id_hex: String = tx.get_tx_id_hex();
// Cost: 32 bytes read + 64 bytes allocated (hex string) + String overhead (24 bytes)
//       = 88 bytes allocated + encoding computation
//       CPU: ~50-100 nanoseconds (encoding each byte to 2 hex chars)
//       This conversion is necessary at API boundaries but should be avoided internally
```

Listing 9: Conversion costs for transaction IDs

Real-World Performance Impact

These costs might seem small, but they compound:

```
Scenario: Processing 1,000 transactions/second

Using get_id() (references) - 1,000 × 2ns = 2
microseconds/second
Using get_id_bytes() (cloning) - 1,000 × 15ns = 15
microseconds/second
Using get_tx_id_hex() (encoding) - 1,000 × 75ns = 75
microseconds/second

Over 1 day (86,400 seconds):
References: 172 milliseconds total
Cloning: 3 seconds total
Hex encoding: 6.5 seconds total

The difference becomes significant at scale!
```

Best Practices

```rust
// [OK] DO: Use get_id() for comparisons and lookups
if tx1.get_id() == tx2.get_id() {
    println!("Same transaction!");
}

// [OK] DO: Use get_id_bytes() when you need ownership
let txid_owned = tx.get_id_bytes();
store_in_database(txid_owned);

// [OK] DO: Use get_tx_id_hex() for user-facing output
println!("Transaction ID: {}", tx.get_tx_id_hex());
return Ok(json!({ "txid": tx.get_tx_id_hex() }));

// [X] DON'T: Convert unnecessarily
let hex = tx.get_tx_id_hex();
let bytes = hex::decode(&hex).unwrap(); // Wasteful!
// Just use: tx.get_id() or tx.get_id_bytes()

// [X] DON'T: Clone when borrowing is enough
let id = tx.get_id_bytes(); // Allocates!
compare(&id, &other);
// Better: compare(tx.get_id(), &other);
```

Listing 10: Best practices for transaction ID methods

References: `&tx.id` vs `tx.id.as_slice()`

As we have seen, using references (`&[u8]`) is crucial for performance. But Rust provides multiple ways to get a reference to the transaction ID bytes. Understanding the subtle differences between `&tx.id` and `tx.id.as_slice()` helps us write idiomatic Rust code and understand how the language's type system works.

These represent different ways to get a reference to the transaction ID bytes, and while they are often interchangeable, there are important distinctions that matter in certain contexts.

Type Difference

```
let tx = Transaction {
    txid: vec![0x23, 0x2f, 0x3c, /* ... */],
    // ...
};
// Different types:
let a: &Vec<u8> = &tx.id;             // Reference to Vec
let b: &[u8]    = tx.id.as_slice(); // Slice reference
```

Listing 11: Reference types for transaction IDs

Rust's Deref Coercion

Rust's `Deref` trait lets a function that accepts `&[u8]` (a byte slice) automatically accept `&Vec<u8>` as well — the compiler inserts the conversion, eliminating the need for explicit `.as_slice()` calls.

Rust's **deref coercion** is a powerful feature that automatically converts references to types that implement the `Deref` trait. `Vec<u8>` implements `Deref<Target = [u8]>`, which means Rust can automatically convert `&Vec<u8>` to `&[u8]` when needed. In **most cases**, they behave identically due to this automatic conversion:

```
fn takes_slice(data: &[u8]) {
    println!("Length: {}", data.len());
}
// Both work the same:
takes_slice(&tx.id);                // [OK] Auto-converts &Vec<u8> -> &[u8]
takes_slice(tx.id.as_slice());  // [OK] Explicit conversion
// For comparison:
if &tx.id == other_slice { }                    // [OK] Works
if tx.id.as_slice() == other_slice { }  // [OK] Same
```

Bitcoin Core Comparison

Our Rust implementation mirrors Bitcoin Core's approach to transaction identifiers but uses idiomatic Rust types instead of C++ primitives. Comparing the two side by side clarifies where the designs converge and where Rust's type system offers additional safety.

> ▷ Note
>
> The Bitcoin Core C++ excerpts in this section are reproduced under the MIT License. Copyright © 2009–present The Bitcoin Core developers. See https://github.com/bitcoin/bitcoin/blob/master/COPYING for the full license text.

Bitcoin Core Uses `uint256` (Binary)

```cpp
// Bitcoin Core: src/primitives/transaction.h
class CTransaction {
private:
    mutable uint256 hash;  // 256-bit binary hash
(like Vec<u8>)

public:
    // Get binary hash (like get_id_bytes())
    const uint256& GetHash() const {
        if (hash.IsNull())
            hash = SerializeHash(*this);
        return hash;  // Returns reference to binary
    }

    // Get hex string (like get_tx_id_hex())
    std::string GetHex() const {
        return hash.GetHex();  // Convert to hex
only when needed
    }
};
```

Listing 13: Bitcoin Core transaction ID storage (C++)

Bitcoin Core Pattern: Binary Internal, Hex External

```
// Bitcoin Core: src/rpc/rawtransaction.cpp
UniValue getrawtransaction(const JSONRPCRequest&
request) {
    uint256 hash = ParseHashV(request.params[0],
"txid");
    //                  ^^^^^^^^^^^
    //                  Parse hex from RPC -> binary
uint256

    CTransactionRef tx;
    if (!GetTransaction(hash, tx, ...)) {
        //                  ^^^^
        //                  Use binary for lookup
        throw
JSONRPCError(RPC_INVALID_ADDRESS_OR_KEY,
                            "No such transaction");
    }

    // Return hex to user
    return EncodeHexTx(*tx);
    //     ^^^^^^^^^^^
    //     Convert back to hex for RPC response
}
```

Listing 14: Bitcoin Core RPC transaction lookup

Our Implementation Mirrors Bitcoin Core

```rust
// Our implementation: src/primitives/transaction.rs
pub struct Transaction {
    txid: Vec<u8>,  // <- Like Bitcoin's uint256 (binary)
    // ...
}

impl Transaction {
    // Like Bitcoin's GetHash() - returns binary reference
    pub fn get_id(&self) -> &[u8] {
        &self.txid
    }

    // Like Bitcoin's GetHex() - converts to hex
    pub fn get_tx_id_hex(&self) -> String {
        hex::encode(&self.txid)
    }
}
```

Listing 15: Our transaction ID implementation

Protocol Messages (Binary Format)

Bitcoin Core (C++):

```cpp
// Bitcoin Core: src/net_processing.cpp
void SendInventory(CNode* node, const std::vector<CInv>& inventory) {
    for (const CInv& inv : inventory) {
        // inv.hash is uint256 (binary), sent as-is over network
        connman->PushMessage(node, NetMsgType::INV, inv);
    }
}
```

Listing 16: Bitcoin Core network message construction (C++)

Our Implementation (Rust):

```
// Our code: src/node/context.rs
async fn broadcast_transaction_to_nodes(&self,
nodes: &[Node], txid: Vec<u8>) {
    //
                ^^^^^^^^^^
    // Binary (like uint256)
    nodes.iter().for_each(|node| {
        tokio::spawn(async move {
            send_inv(&node_addr, OpType::Tx,
&[txid]).await;
            //                                          ^^^^
            //                                          Send
binary over network
        });
    });
}
```

Listing 17: Our network message construction

Database Storage (Binary Keys)

Bitcoin Core (C++):

```
// Bitcoin Core: src/txdb.cpp
bool CCoinsViewDB::GetCoin(const COutPoint
&outpoint, Coin &coin) const {
    // outpoint.hash is uint256 (binary) - used as
DB key
    return m_db->Read(DB_COIN, outpoint);  // Binary
key
}
```

Listing 18: Bitcoin Core database operations (C++)

Our Implementation (Rust):

```rust
// Our code: src/store/file_system_db_chain.rs
pub async fn get_transaction(&self, id: &[u8]) -> Result<Option<Transaction>> {
    //                                        ^^^^
    //                                        Binary key (like uint256)
    let tx_tree = self.blockchain.db.open_tree(TRANSACTIONS_CF)?;
    match tx_tree.get(id)? {  // Use binary key for lookup
        Some(tx_bytes) => Ok(Some(bincode::deserialize(&tx_bytes)?)),
        None => Ok(None),
    }
}
```

Listing 19: Our database operations

Best Practices for Transaction IDs

The rules below distill the patterns used throughout this project. Following them consistently prevents subtle bugs around format mismatches and unnecessary allocations.

1. Storage: Always Use `Vec<u8>`

```rust
// [OK] CORRECT: Store as binary
pub struct Transaction {
    txid: Vec<u8>,
    vin: Vec<TXInput>,
    vout: Vec<TXOutput>,
}

// [X] WRONG: Don't store as hex string
pub struct Transaction {
    txid: String,  // Wastes memory and requires conversions
    // ...
}
```

Listing 20: Storage best practices

2. Internal Operations: Use References (`&[u8]`)

```rust
// [OK] EFFICIENT: Pass by reference
fn verify_transaction(txid: &[u8], signature: &[u8])
-> bool {
    // Just reading, don't need ownership
    signature::verify(txid, signature)
}

// [X] WASTEFUL: Passing owned values
fn verify_transaction(txid: Vec<u8>, signature:
Vec<u8>) -> bool {
    // Forces cloning at call site
    signature::verify(&txid, &signature)
}
```

Listing 21: Internal operation best practices

3. Network Protocol: Use `Vec<u8>` or `&[u8]`

```rust
// [OK] Protocol messages use binary
async fn send_transaction_inv(peer: &SocketAddr,
txid: &[u8]) {
    let inv_msg = Message::Inv {
        inv_type: InvType::Tx,
        hash: txid.to_vec(),  // Binary
    };
    send_message(peer, inv_msg).await;
}
```

Listing 22: Network protocol best practices

4. API Responses: Convert to Hex

```rust
// [OK] Return hex in JSON/API responses
#[derive(Serialize)]
struct TransactionResponse {
    txid: String,  // Hex string for readability
    confirmations: u32,
}

impl From<Transaction> for TransactionResponse {
    fn from(tx: Transaction) -> Self {
        Self {
            txid: tx.get_tx_id_hex(),  // Convert to hex
            confirmations: 0,
        }
    }
}
```

Listing 23: API response best practices

5. Logging: Use Hex

```rust
// [OK] Log hex for human readability
use tracing::info;

info!("Processing transaction: {}", tx.get_tx_id_hex());
//                                  ^^^^^^^^^^^^^^^^^^
//                                  Hex is readable in logs

// [X] Don't log binary directly
info!("Processing transaction: {:?}", tx.get_id());
// Logs: [154, 47, 60, ...] - hard to read!
```

Listing 24: Logging best practices

6. Comparisons: Use References

```rust
// [OK] Compare without cloning
fn transaction_exists(tx: &Transaction, pool: &[Transaction]) -> bool {
    pool.iter().any(|t| t.get_id() == tx.get_id())
    //                  ^^^^^^^^^^     ^^^^^^^^^^
    //                  Returns &[u8] - no allocation
}

// [X] Don't convert to hex for comparison
fn transaction_exists(tx: &Transaction, pool: &[Transaction]) -> bool {
    let tx_hex = tx.get_tx_id_hex();  // Allocation!
    pool.iter().any(|t| t.get_tx_id_hex() == tx_hex)  // More allocations!
}
```

Listing 25: Comparison best practices

7. Database Keys: Use Binary

```rust
// [OK] Binary keys are compact
fn store_transaction(db: &Db, tx: &Transaction) -> Result<()> {
    db.insert(tx.get_id(), bincode::serialize(tx)?)?;
    //         ^^^^^^^^^^
    //         32-byte binary key
    Ok(())
}

// [X] Hex keys waste space
fn store_transaction(db: &Db, tx: &Transaction) -> Result<()> {
    let key = tx.get_tx_id_hex();  // 64 bytes!
    db.insert(key.as_bytes(), bincode::serialize(tx)?)?;
    Ok(())
}
```

Listing 26: Database key best practices

Performance Notes

The choice between `Vec<u8>` and `String` (hex) has runtime tradeoffs:

- **Memory**: Binary is 2-4x more efficient than hex string representation
- **CPU**: Hex conversion has minimal cost (~microseconds per transaction)
- **Database**: Binary keys are faster to compare and index

For a blockchain node processing 1000 tx/sec, the difference is negligible in absolute terms (microseconds), but storage savings can be significant: ~32GB for 1 billion transactions in binary vs ~128GB in hex.

Summary

Use `Vec<u8>` for internal storage and wire protocol.

Use `String` (hex) for external APIs and logging.

This matches Bitcoin Core's design and minimizes unnecessary conversions while keeping the API user-friendly.

7.7 Code Examples

Creating a Block

```rust
use blockchain::primitives::block::Block;
use blockchain::primitives::transaction::Transaction;

// Create block with transactions
let block = Block::new_block(
    previous_hash,
    &transactions,
    height
);
```

Listing 27: Creating a block with transactions

Creating a Transaction

```rust
use blockchain::primitives::transaction::{
    Transaction, TXInput, TXOutput
};

// Create coinbase transaction
let coinbase = Transaction::new_coinbase_tx(&mining_address)?;

// Create regular transaction
let tx = Transaction::new_utxo_transaction(
    &from_address,
    &to_address,
    amount,
    &utxo_set
)
.await?;
```

Listing 28: Creating transactions

Blockchain Operations

```
use blockchain::chain::BlockchainService;

// Initialize blockchain with genesis address
let blockchain_service =
BlockchainService::initialize(
    &genesis_address
).await?;

// Add block to the chain
blockchain_service.add_block(&block).await?;

// Get block by hash
let block =
blockchain_service.get_block_by_hash(&hash).await?;
```

Listing 29: Basic blockchain operations

7.8 Relationship to Bitcoin Core

This module aligns with Bitcoin Core's primitives directory:

- **Bitcoin Core's `primitives/block.h`** : Block data structure
- **Bitcoin Core's `primitives/transaction.h`** : Transaction data structure
- **Bitcoin Core's separation**: Pure data structures, no business logic

The separation of concerns maintained here—pure data types with no business logic—mirrors Bitcoin Core's architectural philosophy and ensures types remain reusable and dependency-free.

With these primitive types in place, the next chapter adds the utility functions — timestamps, functional helpers — that operate on them.

Key Takeaways

- ✓ Defined the Block, Transaction, and Blockchain structs that serve as atomic building blocks for every operation in the system
- ✓ Explained the Transaction ID format and the deliberate choice to store IDs as `Vec<u8>` rather than hex strings, optimizing for programmatic use
- ✓ Examined every field in the block header—hash, previous hash, timestamp, nonce, and height—and their roles in blockchain integrity
- ✓ Analyzed why binary storage reduces memory by 50%, saves network bandwidth, and enables efficient database operations
- ✓ Compared the Rust implementation with Bitcoin Core's approach to transaction IDs and consensus-critical data structures
- ✓ Demonstrated best practices for using `get_id()`, `get_id_bytes()`, and `get_tx_id_hex()` based on context (internal operations, network, API responses)
- ✓ How pure data types remain dependency-free, allowing every other module to build on them without circular references

In the next chapter, we build the utility functions that operate on these structures—timestamps, functional helpers, and cross-cutting concerns that every module in the system needs.

8

Utilities

▷ **What you will learn in this chapter**

- Use the timestamp generation utility for consistent time handling across the system
- Apply functional programming helpers that simplify operations throughout the codebase
- Understand cross-cutting concerns that serve multiple modules without belonging to any single domain

YOU're writing code in three different modules—the crypto layer, the network handler, and the miner—and all three need to format a timestamp the same way. All three need to filter collections with a consistent style. If each module implements its own helpers, you create circular dependencies or duplicate code. The `util` module solves this by collecting functions that are not blockchain domain concepts themselves, but that the entire codebase can depend on without creating tangles. This chapter shows you where to put the glue and how to design it so it stays invisible.

The code for this section lives in `bitcoin/src/util/` :

- `mod.rs` : module wiring + re-exports
- `utils.rs` : small, concrete helpers (currently: time)
- `functional_operations.rs` : optional functional-style helpers (map/filter/reduce patterns)

Because `bitcoin/src/lib.rs` re-exports the util module (`pub use util::*;`), utilities are typically called from within the crate as `crate::...` .

8.1 Why utilities matter in a Bitcoin implementation

The Bitcoin whitepaper frames the system in terms of a few big ideas—transactions, blocks, proof-of-work, and a shared notion of ordering over time. In practice, an implementation needs "small but everywhere" pieces:

- **Time**: We need a consistent way to place a timestamp into a block header when we create a new block.
- **Common transformations**: We frequently map/filter collections (transactions, outputs, UTXOs). Helpers can keep these pipelines explicit and readable.

The goal of `util` is not to be a dumping ground. The goal is to keep the core modules focused, while still making the rest of the code ergonomic.

8.2 Module wiring: `util/mod.rs`

Centralizing utilities in a dedicated module prevents circular dependencies — the situation where module A depends on module B and module B depends on module A, which prevents the project from compiling.

The `util` module exposes a small public surface area:

- `current_timestamp` is re-exported as a top-level util function.
- The `transaction` submodule in `functional_operations.rs` is re-exported as `functional_transaction` (an alias).

This is what lets us write code like `crate::current_timestamp()` instead of `crate::util::utils::current_timestamp()` .

8.3 Timestamp utility: `current_timestamp()`

The smallest utility in the codebase is also one of the most important: time.

In the whitepaper's language, the system uses proof-of-work to create a single history, and blocks include a timestamp as part of their header metadata. In our implementation, `current_timestamp()` produces a Unix timestamp in **milliseconds**:

```
use blockchain::current_timestamp;

let now_ms = current_timestamp();
```

Listing 30: Using the timestamp utility

Where the timestamp is used

Right now, the timestamp is set when a new block is constructed:

```
// bitcoin/src/primitives/block.rs
timestamp: crate::current_timestamp(),
```

Listing 31: Timestamp in block construction

Because `Block::new_block(...)` assigns the timestamp internally, callers do not pass a timestamp; they pass the previous block hash, the transactions to include, and
the height:

```
use blockchain::primitives::block::Block;

let block = Block::new_block(previous_hash,
&transactions, height);
```

Listing 32: Creating a block without explicit timestamp

A note on determinism

Time is a classic source of non-determinism. For consensus-critical code, we want deterministic behavior given the same inputs. In this project, the timestamp is part of block creation, so it is expected to vary across nodes and across runs; we keep the timestamp helper isolated in `util` so it does not "leak" unpredictability into unrelated code paths.

8.4 Functional helpers: `functional_operations.rs`

This file contains small, composable helpers that demonstrate a functional style: pass in a slice, pass in a function, get back transformed data. A closure is an anonymous function written inline — the `|x|` syntax names the parameter, and the expression after it is the logic. Closures are common in Rust for collection processing with methods like `filter` and `map`. In Rust, that "pass in a function" argument is typically a closure — an anonymous function literal written as `|x| expr` or `|x, y| { ... }` — that the helper stores or calls internally. The `|tx| tx.not_coinbase()` expression in Listing 33 is exactly this: a closure that takes one argument (`tx`) and returns a `bool`.

The transaction helpers are re-exported as `functional_transaction`:

```rust
use blockchain::functional_transaction;

// Keep only non-coinbase transactions (pure/synchronous predicate).
let non_coinbase = functional_transaction::process_transactions(
    &transactions,
    |tx| tx.not_coinbase(),
);
```

Listing 33: Using functional transaction helpers

Current status in the codebase

At the time of writing, these functional helpers are **not used by the production code** in `bitcoin/src/` — the mempool, validator, and chain modules currently use plain `for` loops and `Vec` mutation rather than calling `process_transactions` or `validate_transactions`. The helpers are exercised only by `#[cfg(test)]` unit tests, which compile into the test binary but not the release binary. We keep them in the book for two reasons:

- They provide a clean, "library-like" pattern that many Rust developers enjoy for collection-heavy code.
- They are a good refactoring target: readers can replace ad-hoc loops in mempool/chain logic with explicit `process_transactions` / `validate_transactions` pipelines.

These helpers illustrate a functional programming pattern you will encounter throughout the Rust ecosystem. If they serve your own code, use them; if they feel like scaffolding, the right choice is to remove them.

8.5 Related sections

- **Primitives**: The data structures we timestamp and transform
- **Blockchain State Management**: Where block headers and validation rules begin to matter
- **Transaction ID Format**: How transaction identifiers are derived and represented

8.6 Exercises

1. **Timestamp Consistency Check** — Call the timestamp utility in a loop 1,000 times. Verify that the returned values are monotonically non-decreasing. What guarantees does the implementation provide, and what edge cases could cause issues (e.g., system clock adjustments)?
2. **Functional Helper Exploration** — The functional helpers in this module are currently used in unit tests (not production code). Either (a) find three test cases that use them and explain the transformation, or (b) identify three places in mempool/chain logic where they *could* be refactored in for clarity.

8.7 Further Reading

- **Rust by Example: Functional Programming** — Closures, higher-order functions, and iterators in Rust.
- **chrono Crate Documentation** — Time handling in Rust, relevant to timestamp generation.

Key Takeaways

- ✓ Utility functions provide cross-cutting functionality used by every module in the blockchain system.
- ✓ Timestamp generation ensures consistent time handling across blocks and transactions.
- ✓ Functional programming helpers simplify common operations throughout the codebase.

In the next chapter, we add the cryptographic layer — hashing, signing, and key generation — that secures every transaction and block in the system.

9

Cryptography

▷ **What you will learn in this chapter**

- Implement SHA-256 hashing to create unique transaction and block identifiers
- Sign and verify transactions using Schnorr signatures on the secp256k1 curve
- Generate cryptographic key pairs and derive addresses via Base58Check encoding
- Understand why the crypto module exposes a minimal surface area: hash, sign, verify, and key generation
- Distinguish between hashing (which creates tamper-evident identifiers), signing (which proves authorization), and encoding (which makes bytes human-usable)

EVERY 32-byte hash is a fingerprint: a tamper-evident name for a block or transaction. Every signature proves ownership of a private key without ever revealing that key. Every address is a human-readable encoding of that ownership proof. In this chapter, you'll learn how these three mechanisms work together: cryptographic identities, tamper evidence, and authorization. You won't build cryptography from scratch (that's unsafe and belongs to libraries). Instead, you'll learn which library to use for which purpose, how to wire them into your blockchain, and why Rust's type system makes these operations safer than in most languages.

Satoshi's whitepaper relies on a few cryptographic building blocks. An **elliptic curve**, in this context, is a mathematical structure that makes it easy to combine two points into a third but practically impossible to reverse the operation—exactly the one-way property that cryptography needs. **secp256k1** is the specific curve that Bitcoin uses for key generation and digital signatures. It was chosen because it was less widely deployed than other standard curves at the time, reducing the risk that a pre-existing weakness might be known to a single curve's designers.

- **Hashing** creates tamper-evident fingerprints and powers proof-of-work.
- **Digital signatures** prove authorization without revealing the signing key.
- **Key generation** produces the identity material you sign with.
- **Address encoding** turns binary identifiers into strings humans can type.

In this project, the cryptography layer lives in `bitcoin/src/crypto/`. Cryptography is the part of a Bitcoin implementation that answers three practical questions:

- **How do we name things?** We use hashes as stable, tamper-evident identifiers (for transactions, blocks, and proof-of-work candidates).
- **How do we prove authorization?** We use digital signatures so only the key holder can authorize spends.
- **How do we represent these ideas as bytes?** We standardize key formats, signature formats, and address encodings so nodes can interoperate.

Some of this code is used by consensus-critical paths today (hashing and Schnorr verification). Some pieces exist as learning scaffolding or forward-looking building blocks (for example, alternative signature schemes), and we call that out explicitly where it matters.

9.1 Module Structure and Design

In Rust, a module is a namespace boundary. This approach keeps cryptographic concerns isolated and easy to audit: application code calls a small set of cryptographic functions, and the crypto module owns the details of which library implements what.

`bitcoin/src/crypto/mod.rs` is the entry point for this chapter's code. It defines four submodules, each representing a concrete cryptographic responsibility:

- **`hash`** : hashing bytes into fixed-size digests (identifiers and PoW work units)
- **`signature`** : producing and verifying signatures (authorization)
- **`keypair`** : generating private keys and deriving public keys (identity material)
- **`address`** : converting binary payloads to and from human-facing strings (encoding/decoding)

The crypto surface area is kept explicit and small by re-exporting only the functions the rest of the crate should call directly:

```rust
pub mod address;
pub mod hash;
pub mod keypair;
pub mod signature;

pub use address::{base58_decode, base58_encode};
pub use hash::{sha256_digest, taproot_hash};
pub use keypair::{get_schnorr_public_key,
new_key_pair, new_schnorr_key_pair};
pub use signature::{
    ecdsa_p256_sha256_sign_digest,
    ecdsa_p256_sha256_sign_verify,
    schnorr_sign_digest,
    schnorr_sign_verify,
};
```

Since `bitcoin/src/lib.rs` re-exports the crypto module (`pub use crypto::*;`), most call sites inside the crate simply use `crate::sha256_digest(...)` or `crate::schnorr_sign_verify(...)`. This is a deliberate ergonomics choice that keeps cryptographic call sites readable while centralizing cryptographic decisions inside `bitcoin/src/crypto/`.

9.2 Hash Functions: SHA-256 for Identifiers and Proof-of-Work

Hash functions are fundamental to blockchain operations. They create fixed-size fingerprints of arbitrary data, enabling efficient identification and verification. In this section, we explore how SHA-256 is used throughout our blockchain implementation for transaction IDs, block hashes, Merkle trees, and address generation.

The Role of Hashing in the Whitepaper

A **hash** (also called a *digest*) is the fixed-size output of a hash function. You can think of it as a compact "fingerprint" of some input bytes:

- **Determinism**: Same input $\rightarrow$ same hash
- **Avalanche effect**: Small change in input $\rightarrow$ very different hash
- **One-way**: Hash is easy to compute, but impossible to reverse (you cannot recover the original input from the hash)

In Bitcoin and in this project, hashes are used as *identifiers* ("this transaction / this block"), as *tamper-evidence* ("if the bytes change, the hash changes"), and as the work unit for proof-of-work ("find a hash below a target").

When we say "SHA-256," we are relying on specific properties:

- **Determinism**: Same bytes in, same bytes out. That is what allows every node to agree on identifiers.
- **Preimage resistance**: Given $h = \text{SHA256}(m)$, it is computationally infeasible to recover m. Breaking this property would let an attacker find a message that hashes to any chosen digest, enabling forgery attacks.
- **Second-preimage resistance**: Given m, it is infeasible to find $m' \neq m$ where $\text{SHA256}(m) = \text{SHA256}(m')$. Breaking this would let an attacker forge a different message with the same hash as an existing one, bypassing tamper detection.
- **Collision resistance**: It is infeasible to find any $m_1 \neq m_2$ with the same hash. Breaking this would let an attacker create two different inputs (e.g., two different transactions) that hash to the same value, colliding identifiers and breaking consensus.
- **Avalanche effect**: Flipping 1 bit of input tends to flip approximately 50% of output bits. This makes tampering obvious: any alteration to a block causes its hash to change completely, invalidating all subsequent blocks that link to it.

SHA-256 Digest: General-Purpose Hashing

The `sha256_digest` function provides general-purpose SHA-256 hashing using the `ring` crate for transaction IDs, block hashes, and Merkle tree calculations throughout the blockchain.

```
use ring::digest::{Context, SHA256};

pub fn sha256_digest(data: &[u8]) -> Vec<u8> {
    let mut context = Context::new(&SHA256);
    context.update(data);
    let digest = context.finish();
    digest.as_ref().to_vec()
}
```

Listing 34: SHA-256 hashing implementation (`hash.rs`)

Function signature:

- **Input**: `&[u8]` — Reference to byte slice (any length)
- **Output**: `Vec<u8>` — 32-byte SHA-256 hash

Process:

1. Create a new SHA-256 context
2. Update context with input data
3. Finalize and extract digest
4. Convert to vector of bytes

Why `ring` for SHA-256? The `ring` crate is a comprehensive cryptographic library based on BoringSSL. It provides security (well-audited, production-tested cryptographic primitives), performance (optimized C implementations), compatibility (used by other parts of our codebase), and reliability (battle-tested in production systems).

Transaction ID Generation

Every transaction gets a unique identifier by hashing its serialized contents. This ID is used throughout the blockchain to reference transactions.

> **i Why compute transaction hashes instead of trusting a supplied ID?**
>
> If we allowed an arbitrary `id` field to define identity, a sender could change the ID without changing the transaction's meaning—a critical security flaw. Instead, the ID is derived from the transaction's *content*. This content-addressed security model means nodes do not need to trust the sender's claimed ID; they recompute the hash locally and reject any transaction where the claimed ID does not match the bytes.

```rust
fn hash(&mut self) -> Result<Vec<u8>> {
    // IMPORTANT: we must NOT hash the transaction including its own id,
    // otherwise the definition becomes circular.
    let tx_copy = Transaction {
        // Exclude the id from the bytes we hash by setting it to empty.
        id: vec![],
        vin: self.vin.clone(),
        vout: self.vout.clone(),
    };
    // The transaction ID is the SHA-256 hash of the serialized transaction
    // (with id excluded).
    Ok(sha256_digest(tx_copy.serialize()?.as_slice()))
}
```

Listing 35: Computing transaction ID from content (`transaction.rs`)

Process:

1. Create a copy of the transaction without the ID field
2. Serialize the transaction to bytes
3. Hash the serialized bytes using SHA-256
4. Return the 32-byte hash as the transaction ID

▷ Important implementation note

In Bitcoin Core, many identifiers use **double SHA-256** — the function SHA256(SHA256(·)) that feeds one SHA-256 output straight into another SHA-256 as input. Satoshi adopted this pattern to harden against length-extension attacks that affected some uses of raw SHA-256. In this project, we currently use a **single** SHA-256 for simplicity. This is not a moral failing; it is a deliberate scope choice. But it is consensus-relevant: if you want byte-for-byte compatibility with Bitcoin's formats, you will need to align those hashing rules.

Block Hashing and Merkle-Ish Trees

Blocks are identified by their hash, calculated from header data. This hash serves as the block's immutable fingerprint.

```
pub fn hash_transactions(&self) -> Vec<u8> {
    let mut txhashs = vec![];
    for transaction in &self.transactions {
        txhashs.extend(transaction.get_id());
    }
    crate::sha256_digest(txhashs.as_slice())
}
```

Listing 36: Hashing block transactions (`block.rs`)

Process:

1. Collect all transaction IDs from the block
2. Concatenate them into a single byte vector
3. Hash the concatenated transaction IDs
4. Return the hash as the transactions hash

Why bother with a tree at all? A block header has room for only a single 32-byte hash, yet the block may contain thousands of transactions. The naive option — hashing every transaction ID together into one digest, as the code above does — commits to the set, but proving that any individual transaction is included forces a verifier to re-download and re-hash every other transaction. A Merkle tree solves this: with n leaves, an inclusion proof is just $\log_2 n$ sibling hashes, so a light client can verify membership in a 10,000-transaction block with roughly 14 hash comparisons instead of 10,000.

A **Merkle tree** is a binary hash tree: **leaves** are hashes of items (e.g., transaction IDs), and each **internal node** is the hash of its two child hashes. The **Merkle root** is the final hash at the top and serves as a compact *commitment* to the entire set and ordering of leaves. Changing any single transaction changes every hash on its path to the root, so the root transitively fingerprints the whole block body. This is what enables the efficient inclusion proofs sketched above.

> ▷ **Implementation note**
>
> In this project, `Block::hash_transactions()` currently computes a simplified "Merkle-ish" root by concatenating all transaction IDs and hashing once. That is useful for learning, but it is not the same as Bitcoin's full Merkle root construction, which uses pairwise hashing and handles odd-numbered levels by duplicating the last hash.

Proof-of-Work Mining

Proof-of-work mining uses hash functions to find valid block hashes. Miners repeatedly hash block data with different nonces until they find a hash below the target. The loop's upper bound, `MAX_NONCE`, is `i64::MAX` — a safety ceiling so the iteration variable never overflows. In practice, the loop exits almost immediately (after finding a valid hash) long before that ceiling is reached; if it ever were, a real miner would increment an *extranonce* in the coinbase transaction and restart the search.

```
pub fn run(&self) -> (i64, String) {
    let mut nonce = 0;
    let mut hash = Vec::new();

    while nonce < MAX_NONCE {
        let data = self.prepare_data(nonce);
        hash = crate::sha256_digest(data.as_slice());
        let hash_int = BigInt::from_bytes_be(Sign::Plus, hash.as_slice());

        if hash_int.lt(self.target.borrow()) {
            break; // Found valid hash!
        } else {
            nonce += 1; // Try next nonce
        }
        // A lower target means harder proof-of-work - fewer hash values qualify.
        // The network adjusts the target periodically so that, on average,
        // one valid block is found every ten minutes.
    }

    (nonce, HEXLOWER.encode(hash.as_slice()))
    //          ^^^^^^^^
    //          HEXLOWER is from the data-encoding crate and emits hex digits in lowercase --- Bitcoin convention for displaying hashes.
}
```

Listing 37: Proof-of-work mining loop (`pow.rs`)

Process:

1. Start with nonce = 0
2. Prepare block data with current nonce
3. Hash the block data
4. Convert hash to integer
5. Check if hash < target
6. If valid, return nonce and hash; if not, increment nonce and repeat

Taproot-Related Hashing for Address Generation

```
use sha2::{Digest as Sha2Digest, Sha256 as Sha2Hash};

pub fn taproot_hash(data: &[u8]) -> Vec<u8> {
    let mut hasher = Sha2Hash::new();
    hasher.update(data);
    hasher.finalize().to_vec()
}
```

Listing 38: Taproot-style SHA-256 hashing (`hash.rs`)

This function is also SHA-256, but implemented via the `sha2` library instead of `ring`. Conceptually, there is no new cryptographic primitive here; it is the same digest algorithm with a different implementation. In this project, `taproot_hash` is used by the wallet address pipeline (via `wallet_impl.rs` → `hash_pub_key`), where a 32-byte public-key hash is intentionally used as part of a Taproot-style address construction.

Why `sha2` for Taproot? The `sha2` crate is a focused hashing library that provides simplicity (lightweight, focused on hashing algorithms), Taproot compatibility (matches Bitcoin's Taproot upgrade requirements), modern standard (uses SHA-256 instead of RIPEMD160 for better security), and pure Rust implementation (no C dependencies, easier to audit).

9.3 Digital Signatures: Transaction Authorization

Digital signatures prove ownership and authorize transactions in the blockchain. Every transaction input must be signed with the private key corresponding to the public key that locks the output being spent.

Overview of Digital Signatures

A **digital signature** is a cryptographic primitive that binds a message to a keypair: the signer uses a private key to produce a signature over a message (or message digest), and anyone can use the corresponding public key to verify that (1) the signer knew the private key and (2) the message was not modified. Digital signatures provide authenticity and integrity, but not confidentiality.

Digital signatures serve three critical functions in blockchain systems:

1. **Authentication**: Prove that the signer owns the private key
2. **Authorization**: Authorize spending of transaction outputs
3. **Integrity**: Ensure transaction data has not been tampered with

Schnorr Signatures: Modern Bitcoin

Schnorr signatures are the modern signature scheme introduced with Bitcoin's Taproot upgrade. They provide better security properties, smaller signatures, and support for signature aggregation. This is the primary path used by transaction signing and verification in this project.

```rust
use secp256k1::{Keypair, Message, Secp256k1, SecretKey};

pub fn schnorr_sign_digest(
    private_key: &[u8],
    message: &[u8],
) -> Result<Vec<u8>> {
    let secp = Secp256k1::new();

    // Parse private key (32 bytes)
    let secret_key_array: [u8; 32] = private_key.try_into()
        .map_err(|_| BtcError::TransactionSignatureError(
            "Invalid private key length".to_string()
        ))?;
    let secret_key = SecretKey::from_byte_array(secret_key_array)?;
```

Listing 39: Schnorr signature creation: setup and key parsing (part 1 of 2)

With the private key successfully parsed into a `SecretKey`, the next step is to hash the message and prepare it for the cryptographic signing operation. This ensures the signing digest is correctly formatted for the secp256k1 elliptic curve operations:

```
    // Hash the message
    let message_hash = sha256_digest(message);
    let message_hash_array: [u8; 32] = message_hash.try_into()
        .map_err(|_| BtcError::TransactionSignatureError(
            "Invalid message hash length".to_string()
        ))?;

    // Create keypair and sign
    let keypair = Keypair::from_secret_key(&secp, &secret_key);
    let mut rng = rng();
    let signature = secp.sign_schnorr_with_rng(
        &message_hash,
        &keypair,
        &mut rng
    );

    Ok(signature.as_ref().to_vec())
}
```

Listing 40: Schnorr signature creation: hashing and signing (part 2 of 2)

Key Characteristics:

- **Key Format**: Raw 32-byte private keys (Bitcoin-native)
- **Curve**: secp256k1 (Bitcoin standard)
- **Library**: `secp256k1` crate (Bitcoin-optimized)
- **Signature Size**: Fixed 64 bytes (more efficient than ECDSA)
- **Message**: Transaction hash (32 bytes)

```rust
use secp256k1::{PublicKey, XOnlyPublicKey, schnorr};

pub fn schnorr_sign_verify(
    public_key: &[u8],
    signature: &[u8],
    message: &[u8]
) -> bool {
    let secp = Secp256k1::new();

    // Parse public key (33 bytes compressed)
    let public_key_array: [u8; 33] = match public_key.try_into() {
        Ok(arr) => arr,
        Err(_) => return false,
    };
    let public_key_obj = match
        PublicKey::from_byte_array_compressed(public_key_array)
    {
        Ok(pk) => pk,
        Err(_) => return false,
    };

    // Convert to XOnlyPublicKey for Schnorr
    let pk_bytes = public_key_obj.serialize();
```

Listing 41: Schnorr signature verification: public key parsing (part 1 of 3) (`signature.rs`)

After parsing and converting the public key, the function extracts the XOnly format. A compressed secp256k1 public key is 33 bytes: one parity byte (`0x02` or `0x03`) indicating the y-coordinate's parity, followed by 32 bytes of the x-coordinate. Schnorr signatures work with the x-coordinate alone, so we extract bytes 1 through 32. Specifically, `pk_bytes[1..33]` excludes the parity byte and retains the 32-byte x-coordinate:

```
    let xonly_array: [u8; 32] = match pk_bytes[1..33].try_into() {
        Ok(arr) => arr,
        Err(_) => return false,
    };
    let xonly_public_key = match XOnlyPublicKey::from_byte_array(xonly_array) {
        Ok(pk) => pk,
        Err(_) => return false,
    };

    // Hash the message
    let message_hash = sha256_digest(message);
    let message_hash_array: [u8; 32] = match message_hash.try_into() {
        Ok(arr) => arr,
        Err(_) => return false,
    };
```

Listing 42: Schnorr signature verification: XOnly extraction (part 2 of 3)

Then, the signature is parsed and verified against the message hash:

```
    // Parse signature (64 bytes)
    let signature_array: [u8; 64] = match signature.try_into() {
        Ok(arr) => arr,
        Err(_) => return false,
    };
    let signature_obj = schnorr::Signature::from_byte_array(signature_array);

    // Verify
    secp.verify_schnorr(&signature_obj, &message_hash, &xonly_public_key)
        .is_ok()
}
```

Listing 43: Schnorr signature verification: signature parsing and verification (part 3 of 3)

Verification Process:

1. Parse the compressed public key (33 bytes)
2. Convert to XOnlyPublicKey (32 bytes) for Schnorr verification
3. Hash the message using SHA-256
4. Parse the signature (64 bytes)
5. Verify the signature against the message hash

Why Schnorr? Schnorr signatures provide better security (improved security properties and linearity), smaller signatures (fixed 64 bytes vs. variable 70-72 bytes for ECDSA), signature aggregation (can combine multiple signatures efficiently), Bitcoin compatibility (native support for Taproot/P2TR addresses), and batch verification (can verify multiple signatures faster).

ECDSA Signatures: Legacy Support

ECDSA (Elliptic Curve Digital Signature Algorithm) is the traditional signature scheme used in older Bitcoin implementations. Our codebase provides ECDSA functions for legacy compatibility and alternative signature schemes.

```
use ring::signature::{ECDSA_P256_SHA256_FIXED_SIGNING, EcdsaKeyPair};

pub fn ecdsa_p256_sha256_sign_digest(
    pkcs8: &[u8],
    message: &[u8],
) -> Result<Vec<u8>> {
    let rng = ring::rand::SystemRandom::new();
    let key_pair = EcdsaKeyPair::from_pkcs8(
        &ECDSA_P256_SHA256_FIXED_SIGNING,
        pkcs8,
        &rng
    )?;
    let signature = key_pair.sign(&rng, message)?;
    Ok(signature.as_ref().to_vec())
}
```

Listing 44: ECDSA P-256 signature signing (`signature.rs`)

Key Characteristics:

- **Key Format**: PKCS#8 format (variable length, standardized)
- **Curve**: P-256 (secp256r1) — *different from Bitcoin's secp256k1*
- **Library**: `ring` crate (BoringSSL-based)
- **Signature Size**: Variable (typically 70-72 bytes)

> **⚠ Warning**
>
> ECDSA functions are available but not currently used in the primary transaction flow. The codebase primarily uses Schnorr signatures for modern Bitcoin operations. Bitcoin's historical ECDSA uses secp256k1; our ECDSA helpers use P-256 via `ring`, which is *not* Bitcoin-standard.

Transaction Signing Process

Transaction signing uses a *trimmed copy* strategy: strip the signature and public-key fields from the transaction, inject the locking script from the output being spent, then hash and sign the result. This ensures the signature commits to the transaction's substance without circular self-reference — the signature cannot be part of the data it signs, because it does not exist yet at signing time.

Transaction signing is a multi-step process that ensures only the private key owner can authorize spending.

```rust
async fn sign(
    &mut self,
    blockchain: &BlockchainService,
    private_key: &[u8],
) -> Result<()> {
    let mut tx_copy = self.trimmed_copy();

    for (idx, vin) in self.vin.iter_mut().enumerate() {
        // 1. Find the previous transaction
        let prev_tx_option = blockchain.find_transaction(vin.get_txid()).await?;
        let prev_tx = match prev_tx_option {
            Some(tx) => tx,
            None => {
                return Err(BtcError::TransactionNotFoundError(
                    "(sign) Previous transaction is not correct".to_string(),
                ));
            }
        };
```

Listing 45: Multi-input transaction signing: previous TX lookup (part 1 of 2)

After locating the previous transaction that created the output being spent, the signing process proceeds by injecting the previous output's locking data into the trimmed copy and computing the final signature:

```
            // 2. Prepare transaction copy for signing
            tx_copy.vin[idx].signature = vec![];
            tx_copy.vin[idx].pub_key =
prev_tx.vout[vin.vout].pub_key_hash.clone();
            tx_copy.id = tx_copy.hash()?;
            tx_copy.vin[idx].pub_key = vec![];

            // 3. Sign the transaction hash
            let signature =
schnorr_sign_digest(private_key, tx_copy.get_id())?;
            vin.signature = signature;
        }
        Ok(())
}
```

Listing 46: Multi-input transaction signing: trimmed copy and signature (part 2 of 2)

Detailed Process:

1. Create Trimmed Copy: Remove signatures and public keys from inputs
2. For Each Input:
    1. Find the previous transaction that created the output
    2. Set the public key hash in the trimmed copy
    3. Calculate the transaction hash
    4. Clear the public key from the trimmed copy
    5. Sign the transaction hash with the private key
    6. Attach the signature to the input

Transaction Verification Process

Transaction verification checks that signatures are valid and that the signer authorized the transaction.

```
pub async fn verify(&self, blockchain: &BlockchainService) -> Result<bool> {
    // Coinbase transactions don't need verification
    if self.is_coinbase() {
        return Ok(true);
    }

    let mut trimmed_self_copy = self.trimmed_copy();

    for (idx, vin) in self.vin.iter().enumerate() {
        // 1. Find the previous transaction
        let txid = vin.get_txid();
        let current_vin_tx_option = blockchain
            .find_transaction(txid)
            .await?;
        let current_vin_tx = match current_vin_tx_option {
            Some(tx) => tx,
            None => {
                return Err(BtcError::TransactionNotFoundError(
                    "(verify) Previous transaction is not correct".to_string(),
                ));
            }
        };
```

Listing 47: Multi-input transaction verification: setup (part 1 of 2)

With the previous transaction found, the verification process prepares the trimmed copy for each input and then validates the signature:

```
        // 2. Prepare transaction copy for verification
        trimmed_self_copy.vin[idx].signature = vec![];
        let pub_key_hash = current_vin_tx.vout[vin.vout]
            .pub_key_hash
            .clone();
        trimmed_self_copy.vin[idx].pub_key = pub_key_hash;
        trimmed_self_copy.id = trimmed_self_copy.hash()?;
        trimmed_self_copy.vin[idx].pub_key = vec![];

        // 3. Verify the signature
        if !schnorr_sign_verify(
            vin.get_pub_key(),
            vin.get_signature(),
            trimmed_self_copy.get_id()
        ) {
            return Ok(false); // Invalid signature
        }
    }

    Ok(true) // All signatures valid
}
```

Listing 48: Multi-input transaction verification: signature validation (part 2 of 2)

Detailed Process:

1. Check Coinbase: Coinbase transactions do not need verification
2. Create Trimmed Copy: Remove signatures and public keys
3. For Each Input:
    1. Find the previous transaction
    2. Set the public key hash in the trimmed copy
    3. Calculate the transaction hash
    4. Clear the public key from the trimmed copy
    5. Verify the signature against the public key and hash

   6. If invalid, return false
4. All Valid: Return true if all signatures are valid

Table 9.1: Signature schemes comparison

Aspect	ECDSA	Schnorr
Signature Size	Variable (70-72 bytes)	Fixed (64 bytes)
Security Properties	Well-established	Better (linearity, aggregation)
Bitcoin Compatibility	Traditional	Modern (Taproot)
Library	`ring` (BoringSSL)	`secp256k1` (Bitcoin-optimized)
Key Format	PKCS#8 (variable)	Raw 32-byte (Bitcoin-native)
Curve	P-256 (secp256r1)	secp256k1 (Bitcoin standard)
Current Usage	Legacy/Alternative	Primary (P2TR transactions)
Signature Aggregation	No	Yes
Batch Verification	Limited	Efficient

9.4 Key Pair Generation: Secure Key Management

Key pairs are the foundation of blockchain security. Every address is derived from a public key, and every transaction is signed with a private key. In this section, we focus on the exact key formats and libraries used by the code, and how those keys flow into wallets, addresses, and transaction signatures.

Overview of Key Pairs

Key pairs consist of two mathematically related keys:

1. **Private Key**: Secret key used for signing transactions (32 bytes — a 256-bit integer, because secp256k1 is defined over a 256-bit finite field and $256 \text{ bits} \div 8 = 32$ bytes)
2. **Public Key**: Public key used for verification (33 bytes compressed — a 1-byte parity prefix of `0x02` or `0x03` that identifies whether the y-coordinate is even or odd, followed by the 32-byte x-coordinate; the full y-coordinate is omitted since either parity and the curve equation are enough to recover it)

Key Pair Properties:

- **Mathematical Relationship**: Public key is derived from private key
- **One-Way Function**: Cannot derive private key from public key
- **Deterministic**: Same private key always produces same public key
- **Security**: Private key must be kept secret

Schnorr Key Pair Generation

Schnorr key pairs use the `secp256k1` crate and generate raw 32-byte private keys. This is the primary key pair type used for wallet creation in this project.

```rust
use secp256k1::{PublicKey, Secp256k1, SecretKey};

pub fn new_schnorr_key_pair() -> Result<Vec<u8>> {
    let mut secret_key_bytes = [0u8; 32];
    ring::rand::SystemRandom::new()
        .fill(&mut secret_key_bytes)
        .map_err(|e| BtcError::WalletKeyPairError(e.to_string()))?;

    let _secp = Secp256k1::new();
    let secret_key = SecretKey::from_byte_array(secret_key_bytes)
        .map_err(|e| BtcError::WalletKeyPairError(e.to_string()))?;
    Ok(secret_key.secret_bytes().to_vec())
}
```

Listing 49: Schnorr key pair generation (`keypair.rs`)

Process:

1. Generate Random Bytes: Fill 32-byte array with cryptographically secure random bytes
2. Create Secret Key: Convert bytes to `SecretKey` type
3. Validate: Ensure key is valid for secp256k1 curve
4. Return: Return private key as byte vector

Key Characteristics:

- **Format**: Raw 32-byte private key (Bitcoin-native)
- **Curve**: secp256k1 (Bitcoin standard)
- **Randomness**: Uses system random number generator
- **Library**: `secp256k1` crate

Public Key Derivation

Public keys are derived from private keys using elliptic curve multiplication. Elliptic curve multiplication is a one-way operation: multiplying a secret number by a fixed curve point produces another curve point (the public key). Computing this forward is fast, but reversing it — finding the secret from the public point — is computationally infeasible. This asymmetry is what makes private keys secret. In other words, you can derive the public key from the private key, but not vice versa.

```
pub fn get_schnorr_public_key(private_key: &[u8]) ->
Result<Vec<u8>> {
    let secp = Secp256k1::new();
    let secret_key_array: [u8; 32] =
private_key.try_into()
        .map_err(|_| BtcError::WalletKeyPairError(
            "Invalid private key length".to_string()
        ))?;
    let secret_key =
SecretKey::from_byte_array(secret_key_array)?;
    let public_key =
PublicKey::from_secret_key(&secp, &secret_key);
    Ok(public_key.serialize().to_vec())
}
```

Listing 50: Schnorr public key derivation (`keypair.rs`)

Process:

1. Parse Private Key: Convert byte slice to 32-byte array
2. Create Secret Key: Convert to `SecretKey` type
3. Derive Public Key: Use elliptic curve multiplication
4. Serialize: Convert to compressed format (33 bytes)
5. Return: Return public key as byte vector

Key Properties:

- **Deterministic**: Same private key always produces same public key
- **One-Way**: Cannot derive private key from public key
- **Compressed Format**: Public keys are 33 bytes (compressed)
- **Efficient**: Fast derivation operation

ECDSA Key Pair Generation (Legacy)

ECDSA key pairs use the `ring` crate and generate keys in PKCS#8 format. This path exists for legacy compatibility and is not used by the main wallet creation flow.

```
use ring::signature::{ECDSA_P256_SHA256_FIXED_SIGNING, EcdsaKeyPair};

pub fn new_key_pair() -> Result<Vec<u8>> {
    let rng = SystemRandom::new();
    let pkcs8 = EcdsaKeyPair::generate_pkcs8(
        &ECDSA_P256_SHA256_FIXED_SIGNING,
        &rng
    )?;
    Ok(pkcs8.as_ref().to_vec())
}
```

Listing 51: ECDSA P-256 key pair generation (`keypair.rs`)

Key Characteristics:

- **Format**: PKCS#8 (variable length, standardized)
- **Curve**: P-256 (secp256r1)
- **Randomness**: Uses system random number generator
- **Library**: `ring` crate

ECDSA key pairs are available but not currently used in the primary transaction flow. The codebase primarily uses Schnorr key pairs for modern Bitcoin operations, while ECDSA remains as a backward-compatible option.

9.5 Address Encoding: Base58Check for Human-Readable Addresses

We have generated keys and used them to sign transactions. Now we need a way to represent those keys as strings that humans can reliably copy, paste, and exchange — that representation is an address.

Address encoding is where raw key material becomes something a human can copy, paste, and exchange safely. In production Bitcoin, address formats vary (Base58Check for legacy scripts, Bech32/Bech32m for SegWit and Taproot). This project uses a **Base58Check-style** format for its wallet addresses: version byte || public key hash || checksum, then Base58-encode the bytes.

Overview of Address Encoding

An address is a compact, checksummed identifier derived from a public key. It is *not* the public key itself. In this project, we hash the public key, attach a version byte and checksum, then encode the result into a Base58 string.

Address Properties:

- **Human-Readable**: Easy to read and type
- **Compact**: More compact than hexadecimal
- **Error-Resistant**: Avoids ambiguous characters
- **Checksummed**: Includes checksum for error detection

> **i Address payload layout**
>
> In this project, we build an address by constructing a payload and then Base58-encoding it:
>
> `payload = version (1) || pub_key_hash (32) || checksum (4)`
>
> `version` : 0x01 (P2TR version tag) `pub_key_hash` : SHA-256(pubkey), 32 bytes `checksum` : first 4 bytes of SHA256(SHA256(version || hash))

Base58 Encoding Algorithm

Base58 encoding converts binary data into a human-readable string, excluding characters that could be confused (0, O, I, l).

```
pub fn base58_encode(data: &[u8]) -> Result<String> {
    Ok(bs58::encode(data).into_string())
}
```

Listing 52: Base58 encoding (`address.rs`)

Function Signature:

- **Input**: `&[u8]` — Reference to byte slice
- **Output**: `Result<String>` — Base58-encoded string

Why Base58?

- **Human Readability**: Easy to read and type
- **Error Prevention**: Avoids ambiguous characters (0/O, I/l)
- **Compactness**: More compact than hexadecimal
- **Bitcoin Standard**: Used by Bitcoin for addresses

Base58 Character Set:

`123456789ABCDEFGHJKLMNPQRSTUVWXYZabcdefghijkmnopqrstuvwxyz`

Excluded Characters:

- `0` (zero) — Can be confused with `O` (capital O)
- `O` (capital O) — Can be confused with `0` (zero)
- `I` (capital I) — Can be confused with `l` (lowercase L)
- `l` (lowercase L) — Can be confused with `I` (capital I)

Base58 Decoding Algorithm

Base58 decoding converts human-readable addresses back to binary data.

```
pub fn base58_decode(data: &str) -> Result<Vec<u8>> {
    bs58::decode(data)
        .into_vec()
        .map_err(|e|
BtcError::AddressDecodingError(e.to_string()))
}
```

Listing 53: Base58 decoding (`address.rs`)

Function Signature:

- **Input**: `&str` — Base58-encoded string
- **Output**: `Result<Vec<u8>>` — Decoded byte vector

Base58 decoding can fail if invalid characters are present, the string format is incorrect, or decoding fails. All errors are properly handled and returned as `BtcError::AddressDecodingError`.

P2TR Address Generation

P2TR (Pay-to-Taproot) addresses are generated from Schnorr public keys in this project, then encoded using the Base58Check-style format described above.

```rust
// 1. Generate key pair
let private_key = new_schnorr_key_pair()?;
let public_key = get_schnorr_public_key(&private_key)?;

// 2. Hash public key
let pub_key_hash = taproot_hash(&public_key);

// 3. Create address payload
let version_byte = 0x01; // P2TR version
let mut address_data = vec![version_byte];
address_data.extend_from_slice(&pub_key_hash);

// 4. Calculate checksum (double SHA-256, first 4 bytes)
let checksum = checksum(&address_data);
address_data.extend_from_slice(&checksum);

// 5. Encode to Base58
let address = base58_encode(&address_data)?;
```

Listing 54: P2TR address generation flow

Step-by-Step Process:

1. Hash Public Key: Use `taproot_hash` to hash public key
2. Add Version Byte: Prepend version byte (0x01 for P2TR)
3. Calculate Checksum: Double SHA-256 hash, take first 4 bytes
4. Append Checksum: Add checksum to address data
5. Base58 Encode: Convert to Base58 string

Address Validation

Address validation ensures addresses are correctly formatted and have valid checksums.

```rust
pub fn validate_address(address: &str) -> Result<bool> {
    // 1. Decode Base58
    let payload = base58_decode(address)?;

    // 2. Extract components
    let actual_checksum = payload[payload.len() - 4..].to_vec();
    let version = payload[0];
    let pub_key_hash = payload[1..payload.len() - 4].to_vec();

    // 3. Recompute checksum from version + hash
    let mut target_vec = vec![version];
    target_vec.extend(pub_key_hash);
    let target_checksum = checksum(target_vec.as_slice());

    // 4. Compare checksums
    Ok(actual_checksum.eq(target_checksum.as_slice()))
}
```

Listing 55: Address validation with checksum verification

Validation Steps:

1. Decode Base58: Convert address string to bytes
2. Extract Components: Split version, hash, and checksum
3. Recompute Checksum: Build `version || hash`, then double-SHA-256
4. Compare Checksums: Return true if the checksum matches

Why Validate?

- **Error Detection**: Catches transmission errors
- **Security**: Prevents invalid addresses
- **User Experience**: Provides clear error messages
- **Integrity**: Ensures address integrity

9.6 Security and Performance Considerations

Security is less about a single "best" library and more about disciplined and repeatable practices. The core idea is simple: protect private keys, validate every external input, and make the system behave predictably even under attack, even when the data is malformed or hostile.

Security Best Practices

▲ Threat model for the crypto layer

What to protect: private keys, authorization, tx/block ID integrity, address correctness
Who attacks: network attackers, local attackers, side-channel attackers, developers
How they attack: malformed inputs (DoS), memory scraping (logs, disk), timing observation, wrong implementation
Mitigations: validate all inputs and lengths, keep private keys out of logs, use well-audited crypto libraries, keep formats explicit

Secure Random Number Generation

Keys are only as strong as their randomness. This project uses the operating system's cryptographically secure RNG via `ring::rand::SystemRandom`:

```
let rng = ring::rand::SystemRandom::new();
```

Best Practices:

- Always use system random number generators
- Never use predictable random number generators
- Ensure sufficient entropy for key generation
- Test randomness quality in production

Constant-Time Operations

Cryptographic operations should be constant-time to reduce timing side channels. The libraries used in this project (`ring`, `secp256k1`) implement constant-time operations internally, so the safest path is to keep custom crypto logic minimal and delegate to those libraries.

Best Practices:
- Use libraries that implement constant-time operations
- Avoid timing-dependent code in cryptographic operations
- Test for timing vulnerabilities
- Use hardware acceleration when available

Input Validation

In a blockchain node, inputs are often attacker-controlled (network messages, transaction payloads, user-provided addresses). Validation is not a nice-to-have—it is an anti-DoS and correctness requirement.
Best Practices:
- Validate all inputs before cryptographic operations
- Check key lengths and formats
- Verify signature and message lengths
- Provide clear error messages

Error Handling

Error handling is part of the security model. Panics can become denial-of-service; ambiguous errors can hide bugs. This project returns `Result` for crypto operations to keep failure explicit.
Best Practices:
- Always return `Result` types for cryptographic operations
- Never panic on cryptographic errors
- Provide detailed error messages
- Handle errors gracefully

Private Key Protection

Private keys are the crown jewels. Treat them as toxic waste: never log them, never serialize them casually, and never keep them in memory longer than necessary.
Best Practices:
- Never log private keys
- Encrypt private keys at rest
- Use secure memory for private keys
- Limit access to private keys
- Implement secure key deletion

Performance Characteristics

Performance matters because every node replays the same cryptographic work: hashes for block/tx IDs, signature verification for every input, and address validation for every user-facing operation. The exact numbers are hardware-dependent, but the ordering and relative costs are stable across machines.

Table 9.2: Cryptographic operation performance (order-of-magnitude)

Operation	Speed	Latency	Notes
SHA-256 hash	200-300 MB/s	1-2 μs	Hardware-dependent
Schnorr sign	1000-2000 sigs/s	0.5-1 ms	Per signature
Schnorr verify	2000-4000 verifs/s	0.25-0.5 ms	Per verification
Key gen	100-200 pairs/s	5-24 ms	Bottleneck: RNG
Public key derivation	5000-10000/s	0.1-0.2 ms	Minimal overhead
Base58 encoding	10-20 MB/s	1-5 μs/address	User-facing

Optimization Strategies

Optimization comes after correctness. Start with clear, correct implementations, measure real bottlenecks, then apply targeted changes.

Common Optimization Patterns:

- **Batch Operations**: Process multiple signatures together to amortize fixed costs
- **Caching**: Cache frequently used results (like derived public keys)
- **Parallel Processing**: Verify multiple signatures in parallel when CPU cores are available
- **Hardware Acceleration**: Use hardware crypto when available to shift work to optimized CPU features

Library Choices and Trade-offs

Bitcoin implementations live and die by their dependency choices. You want well-audited code, deterministic behavior, and APIs that make mistakes hard. This project intentionally uses multiple libraries to mirror how real systems evolve:

- `ring` : ECDSA signatures, general SHA-256 hashing
- `secp256k1` : Schnorr signatures, secp256k1 curve operations
- `sha2` : Taproot-specific SHA-256 hashing
- `bs58` : Base58 encoding/decoding

Trade-offs:

Advantages:

- Best Tool for Each Job: Each library excels in its domain
- Bitcoin Compatibility: Native support for Bitcoin standards
- Flexibility: Can use different schemes as needed

Disadvantages:

- Dependency Count: More dependencies to manage
- Consistency: Different APIs and patterns
- Maintenance: More code to maintain and update

In a production system, we typically want a single SHA-256 implementation for consistency, reduced dependencies, and improved maintainability. However, both implementations are correct and produce identical results, so the current approach works well for a learning implementation.

Key Takeaways

- ✓ Cryptography in blockchain answers three practical questions: how do we name things (hashing), how do we prove authorization (signatures), and how do we represent bytes as humans can safely exchange them (encoding).
- ✓ SHA-256 hashing produces 32-byte digests used for transaction IDs, block hashes, and proof-of-work. It is deterministic, collision-resistant, and exhibits the avalanche effect.
- ✓ Schnorr signatures (secp256k1) are the primary authorization mechanism in this project. They provide better security properties and efficiency than legacy ECDSA schemes.
- ✓ Transaction signing requires computing a hash of the transaction, then signing that hash with the private key. Verification mirrors this: rebuild the same hash and verify the signature against the public key.
- ✓ Key pairs consist of a 32-byte private key and a 33-byte compressed public key. Public keys are derived deterministically from private keys via elliptic curve multiplication.
- ✓ Addresses are not keys. They are human-friendly Base58Check-encoded strings that combine a version byte, public key hash, and checksum. This format reduces transcription errors.
- ✓ The crypto module uses four specialized libraries: `ring` for ECDSA and SHA-256, `secp256k1` for Schnorr and secp256k1 curve operations, `sha2` for Taproot-specific hashing, and `bs58` for Base58 encoding.
- ✓ Security best practices include secure random generation, constant-time operations, input validation, explicit error handling, and private key protection. Never log private keys, and always encrypt them at rest.
- ✓ Performance is measured in hashes per second, signatures per second, and latency per operation. Signature verification is the most CPU-intensive operation in a typical node.
- ✓ Future improvements include hardware acceleration, better batch operation support, more sophisticated caching, and enhanced side-channel resistance.

Bibliography

[fips180] NIST. *FIPS 180-4: Secure Hash Standard (SHA-256).* https://csrc.nist.gov/publications/detail/fips/180/4/final

[fips186] NIST. *FIPS 186-5: Digital Signature Standard (DSS).* https://csrc.nist.gov/publications/detail/fips/186/5/final

[satoshi] Satoshi Nakamoto. *Bitcoin: A Peer-to-Peer Electronic Cash System.* https://bitcoin.org/bitcoin.pdf

[bip340] The Bitcoin Project. *BIP 340: Schnorr Signatures for secp256k1.* https://github.com/bitcoin/bips/blob/master/bip-0340.mediawiki

[bip341] The Bitcoin Project. *BIP 341: Taproot.* https://github.com/bitcoin/bips/blob/master/bip-0341.mediawiki

[bip342] The Bitcoin Project. *BIP 342: Validation of Taproot Scripts.* https://github.com/bitcoin/bips/blob/master/bip-0342.mediawiki

[sec2] Standards for Efficient Cryptography Group. *SEC 2: Recommended Elliptic Curve Domain Parameters.* https://www.secg.org/sec2-v2.pdf

[base58check] Bitcoin Wiki. *Base58Check encoding.* https://en.bitcoin.it/wiki/Base58Check_encoding

[ring] Bracing. *ring: Safe, fast, small crypto using Rust.* https://docs.rs/ring/latest/ring/

[secp256k1] Peter Westmacott. *secp256k1 Rust crate.* https://docs.rs/secp256k1/latest/secp256k1/

10

Chain: Domain Model

> ▷ **What you will learn in this chapter**
>
> - How blocks and block headers encode the whitepaper's chain of hashes
> - The UTXO model: why Bitcoin tracks *outputs*, not accounts
> - How `TXInput`, `TXOutput`, and `Transaction` encode spending
> - Where "unspent vs. spent" is tracked (the UTXO set, not the output itself)

When a block arrives over the network, the first thing your node does is parse the raw bytes into typed Rust structs. These domain types are the vocabulary the entire codebase speaks—if the types are wrong, the system cannot function. This section maps the whitepaper's abstract concepts to concrete Rust code, so you can confidently answer "what does this type *mean*?" and "where does it appear in the validation logic?"

The following files serve as the primary reference:

- `bitcoin/src/primitives/block.rs`
- `bitcoin/src/primitives/transaction.rs`
- `bitcoin/src/chain/utxo_set.rs` (for how outputs become "spendable")

10.1 Whitepaper Term → Rust Type Map

Table 10.1: Whitepaper concepts mapped to Rust types

Whitepaper Concept	Rust Type / Field
Block header	`BlockHeader`
Previous block hash	`BlockHeader.pre_block_hash`
Nonce	`BlockHeader.nonce`
Block hash	`BlockHeader.hash`
Transaction	`Transaction`
Transaction ID	`Transaction.id`
Input (spend)	`TXInput`
Output (new coin)	`TXOutput`
Locking condition	`TXOutput.pub_key_hash`
Signature	`TXInput.signature`

The following diagrams show how these types relate at runtime.

10.2 Domain Object Diagrams

The diagram below shows the *runtime relationship* between the main state buckets: the **blockchain** (append-only history), the **UTXO set** (derived "what is spendable right now" state), and **transactions** (which consume old outputs and create new ones).

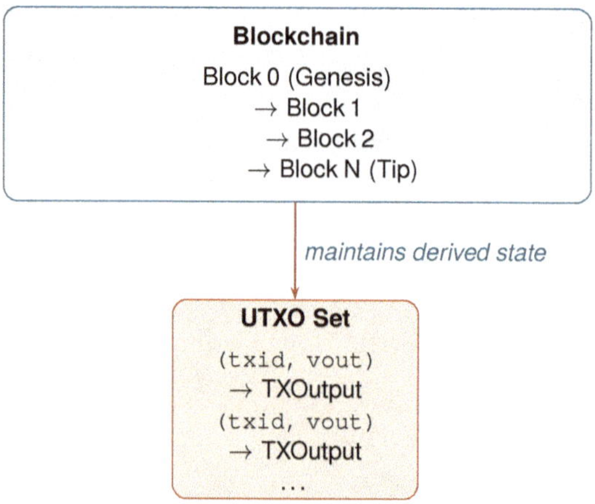

Figure 10.1: Blockchain and UTXO Set: Chain History and Derived State

Block

BlockHeader
– Previous Hash
– Timestamp
– Nonce
– Height
– (Merkle root / `hash_transactions()` simplification)

Transactions
→ Transaction 1
→ Transaction 2
→ Transaction N

Transaction

TXInputs (spends previous outputs)
→ Input 1: references `(prev_txid, vout)`
→ Input 2: references `(prev_txid, vout)`

TXOutputs (creates new outputs)
→ Output 1: becomes a future UTXO
→ Output 2: becomes a future UTXO

Figure 10.2: Block and Transaction Structure

10.3 Key Code Reading Checklist

As we follow the Rust code, we should be able to answer these questions from the structs alone:

- Where does the txid come from? (Search for `Transaction::hash()` .)
- Where does the signature live? (Look at `TXInput.signature` .)
- What does an output lock to? (`TXOutput.pub_key_hash` .)
- Where is "unspent vs. spent" tracked? (Not on the output—in `UTXOSet` .)

10.4 Step-by-Step Code Walkthrough

Goal: understand what the core structs *mean* and how the bytes flow between modules.

> i
>
> Source `bitcoin/src/primitives/block.rs` , `bitcoin/src/primitives/transaction.rs` , `bitcoin/src/chain/utxo_set.rs`

Step 1: Block and BlockHeader

In the Bitcoin whitepaper, a block is a **timestamped commitment** to two things: the previous block (so the history is tamper-evident by hash chaining) and a set of transactions (so the block anchors ownership transfers into the history).

The `BlockHeader` struct defines the smallest header needed to make those ideas concrete in code. In practice, the header matters because it defines the **proof-of-work input**—the fixed byte sequence that miners hash repeatedly while varying the `nonce` (a counter, free to change each iteration) until the resulting hash falls below the current **difficulty target**. That target is a 256-bit threshold the network agrees on: a "valid" block is one whose header hash, interpreted as a 256-bit number (in the protocol's standard byte order), is numerically smaller than the target. The smaller the target, the rarer a valid hash becomes, so lowering the target makes mining harder and raising it makes mining easier. The network adjusts this target periodically so that blocks arrive at a consistent ten-minute interval.

These bytes are assembled from the header fields in `ProofOfWork::prepare_data(...)`, which is why `BlockHeader` contains exactly the fields it does. Chapter 15 (Block Lifecycle and

Mining) covers the proof-of-work loop and the exact hashed byte layout.

```
pub struct BlockHeader {
    timestamp: i64,
    pre_block_hash: String,
    hash: String,
    nonce: i64,
    height: usize,
}

pub struct Block {
    header: BlockHeader,
    transactions: Vec<Transaction>,
}
```

Listing 56: Block and BlockHeader struct layout (`block.rs`)

What the fields mean:

- `pre_block_hash` : link to the previous block (whitepaper §3/§4).
- `nonce + hash` : PoW search result (whitepaper §4).
- `timestamp` : ordering signal; also part of the PoW header bytes.
- `height` : convenience for iteration/selection; not a Bitcoin header field.

▷ **Project-specific note**

This implementation does not use a **Merkle root** field. Instead, it concatenates transaction IDs and hashes once using `Block::hash_transactions()` . This approach keeps the code readable but does not support Merkle proofs or SPV.

To create a new block: `Block::new_block(..)` is the entry point that *defines* the header boundary. It takes the parent link and the transaction list as inputs, sets derived header fields such as `timestamp`, and then finalizes `nonce` and `hash` by running PoW.

```rust
pub fn new_block(
    pre_block_hash: String,
    transactions: &[Transaction],
    height: usize
) -> Block {
    let header = BlockHeader {
        timestamp: crate::current_timestamp(),
        pre_block_hash,
        hash: String::new(),
        nonce: 0,
        height,
    };
    let mut block = Block {
        header,
        transactions: transactions.to_vec(),
    };
    let pow = ProofOfWork::new_proof_of_work(block.clone());
    let (nonce, hash) = pow.run();
    block.header.nonce = nonce;
    block.header.hash = hash;
    block
}
```

Listing 57: `Block::new_block` — creating and mining a block

> **✓ Checkpoint**
>
> `pre_block_hash` is the chain link. `nonce` and `hash` are filled by PoW (`ProofOfWork::run()`), not supplied by the caller. `height` lives in the header as a convenience (not a Bitcoin header field).

Step 2: Transaction, Inputs, and Outputs

Each block contains a list of these transactions (the `transactions` field in `Block`). To understand what a transaction is, we now turn to how Bitcoin encodes the spending of previous coins.

Bitcoin is not an "account system." It is a system of **outputs**, and spending means consuming previous outputs as inputs.

> **i**
>
> Methods involved `Transaction::new_utxo_transaction()`, `Transaction::hash()`, `Transaction::sign()`

This step covers two topics: (1) defining what a transaction *is* by reading the struct fields, and (2) showing how a spending transaction is *constructed* in code.

```rust
#[derive(Clone, Default, Serialize, Deserialize)]
pub struct TXInput {
    txid: Vec<u8>,
    vout: usize,
    signature: Vec<u8>,
    pub_key: Vec<u8>,
}

#[derive(Clone, Serialize, Deserialize)]
pub struct TXOutput {
    value: i32,
    in_global_mem_pool: bool,
    pub_key_hash: Vec<u8>,
}

#[derive(Clone, Default, Serialize, Deserialize)]
pub struct Transaction {
    id: Vec<u8>,
    vin: Vec<TXInput>,
    vout: Vec<TXOutput>,
}
```

Listing 58: Transaction, TXInput, and TXOutput structs (`transaction.rs`)

They reveal the project's UTXO worldview: a transaction spends prior outputs by referencing an **outpoint** $(txid, vout)$ in `TXInput`, and it creates new spendable outputs in `TXOutput`. The outpoint is a two-part address: `txid` is the hash (ID) of the transaction that *created* the output, and `vout` is the zero-based index of that output in the creating transaction's `vout` array. Together they uniquely identify one coin in the entire ledger. The `Vec<u8>` fields— `txid`, `signature`, `pub_key`, `pub_key_hash` — are raw byte buffers (hashes, signatures, and keys); `String` would imply UTF-8 text, which these are not.

- A spend is identified by an outpoint $(txid, vout)$: `TXInput.{txid, vout}`. An *outpoint* is the lowest-level coordinate system of the ledger — "the n-th output of this specific earlier transaction."
- Authorization is per-input: `TXInput.signature + TXInput.pub_key`. `pub_key` carries the spender's full public key so any verifier can hash it and check that it matches the referenced UTXO's `pub_key_hash`, then verify `signature` against that public key. (During signing, `pub_key` is temporarily overwritten with the referenced output's locking `pub_key_hash` so the signature also commits to the UTXO being spent; see Chapter 14.)
- Outputs are locked by a pubkey-hash: `TXOutput.pub_key_hash` (no script engine). We store the hash rather than the public key itself so the full key is only revealed when the owner spends. This means that even if a future mathematical breakthrough makes it possible to derive private keys from public keys, coins that have not yet been spent remain safe—their public keys have never appeared on-chain. Locking by hash (rather than by the full key) historically added a margin of safety if a key's raw form were ever leaked. The `in_global_mem_pool` field is a local node hint — not a consensus rule — that marks whether this output is already referenced by a pending mempool transaction, helping the wallet avoid selecting the same coin twice in quick succession.

How a spending transaction is constructed:

1. **Select spendable outputs**: query the UTXO set for outpoints locked to the sender.
2. **Create inputs**: for each selected outpoint, create a `TXInput`.
3. **Create outputs**: payment to recipient, plus optional change back to sender.

4. **Compute the txid**: serialize a copy of the transaction with the `id` field set to the empty vector `[]` and hash those bytes. The `id` field is cleared first so the hash does not depend on itself (a non-circular definition).
5. **Sign**: produce per-input signatures and store into `TXInput.signature`.

The concrete entry point is `Transaction::new_utxo_transaction(...)` (full implementation in Chapter 14: Transaction Lifecycle).

You have now seen the blockchain structure (blocks containing transactions) and the transaction structure (inputs consuming outputs, outputs creating new coins). But where is the answer to "is this output spendable?" stored? Not on the output itself, but in a separate index called the UTXO set.

Step 3: History vs. Derived State (the UTXO Set)

UTXO (Unspent Transaction Output): a specific transaction output that is currently spendable—an output identified by an outpoint $(txid, vout)$ that has **not** been consumed by any later transaction input.

The **blockchain** is the append-only history (blocks and the transactions they contain). The **UTXO set** is derived state: a compact, query-friendly view of "what is spendable right now?" computed from that history.

The UTXO set is kept separate so the node can answer spendability questions efficiently without rescanning the entire chain every time it validates a transaction or connects a block.

```
const UTXO_TREE: &str = "chainstate";

pub struct UTXOSet {
    blockchain: BlockchainService,
}

impl UTXOSet {
    pub fn new(blockchain: BlockchainService) ->
UTXOSet {
        UTXOSet { blockchain }
    }
}
```

Listing 59: UTXOSet struct (`utxo_set.rs`)

▷ **Note**

Spendability is not a field on `TXOutput` ; it is tracked by membership in the UTXO database. This is the same design Bitcoin Core uses: the `chainstate` LevelDB stores only unspent outputs.

↪

See the full implementation The complete `find_spendable_outputs()` method, UTXO rebuild logic, and rollback handling are covered in Chapter 13 (UTXO Set).

11

Chain: Blockchain State Management

▷ **What you will learn in this chapter**

- How the `chain/` module serves as the public boundary between network events and state mutations
- The `BlockchainService` façade: read/write lock boundary for concurrent access
- Where reads take a shared lock and writes take an exclusive lock
- How persistence (storage layer) and derived state (UTXO set) are delegated from the boundary

MULTIPLE threads are running at once: the network handler receives blocks, the miner builds candidates, the wallet queries what it can spend, and the web server answers status requests. All of them need to read and write the same chain state simultaneously. One wrong move—a data race, an unserialized write, a forgotten lock—and your blockchain forks unexpectedly or loses consistency. The `chain/` module concentrates all of that shared state behind a single read/write lock façade. This section shows you the boundary: where readers take a shared lock, where writers get exclusive access, and how persistence and derived state are delegated.

This implementation concentrates "shared chain state" behind a single façade (`BlockchainService`) and controls mutation using an async read-

/write lock. The façade delegates persistence and fork-choice decisions to the storage layer (`BlockchainFileSystem`) and derived-state management to the UTXO set (`UTXOSet`).

11.1 Scope and Key Entry Points

This chapter covers the **API boundary level**: where reads vs. writes are controlled, and where the node delegates to persistence and derived state.

Key entry points in this chapter:

- **Read boundary**: `BlockchainService::read(...)` (the shared-read lock pattern)
- **Write boundary (peer blocks)**: `BlockchainService::add_block(...)` → `BlockchainFileSystem::add_block(...)`
- **Write boundary (local mining)**: `BlockchainService::mine_block(...)` → `BlockchainFileSystem::mine_block(...)`
- **Derived-state update/rollback**: `BlockchainService::update_utxo_set(...)` / `rollback_utxo_set(...)` → `UTXOSet::{update, rollback_block}(...)`

11.2 Architecture: Shared Chain API Used by Node and Web Layers

`BlockchainService` is a **high-level chain API** used in two ways:

- **Node runtime**: networking and mining code call `BlockchainService` directly (for example, to add a received block or mine a new one).
- **Web/API layer**: HTTP handlers call `NodeContext` (`bitcoin/src/node/context.rs`), which holds a `BlockchainService` internally. The web layer accesses the same chain façade **indirectly** through the node's coordination boundary.

Both the node runtime and the web handlers access the blockchain indirectly through `NodeContext`, the top-level coordination layer shown in the architecture diagram.

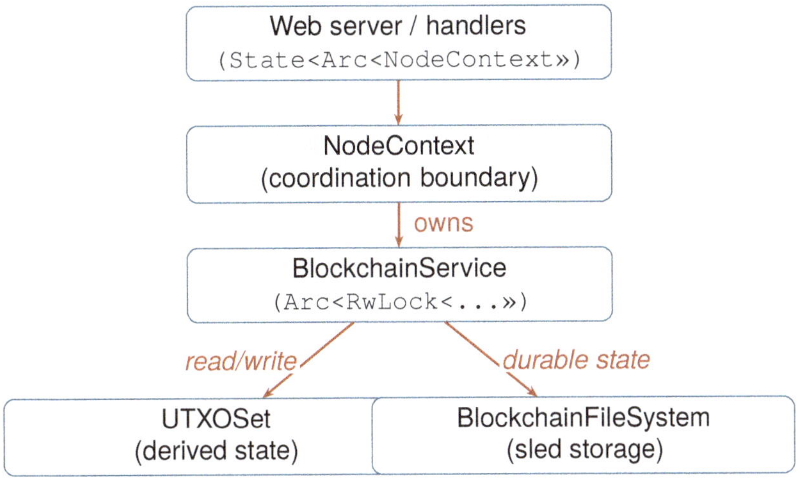

Figure 11.1: State Management Architecture: Web API Through Node Context to Blockchain Service

11.3 Step 1: The `chain/` Module Exports (Public API Boundary)

The types we import are re-exported here:

```rust
// Source: bitcoin/src/chain/mod.rs
pub mod chainstate;
pub mod utxo_set;

// Re-export main types for convenience
pub use chainstate::BlockchainService;
pub use utxo_set::UTXOSet;
```

Listing 60: Chain module exports (public boundary)

▷ Note

`chain/mod.rs` is intentionally small: it exposes the façade plus UTXO set without leaking internal layout. This boundary enforces that all chain access goes through the public API, never directly to the persistence engine.

11.4 Step 2: The Façade Type (`BlockchainService`)

```rust
// Source: bitcoin/src/chain/chainstate.rs
#[derive(Debug)]
pub struct BlockchainService(
    Arc<TokioRwLock<BlockchainFileSystem>>
);

impl BlockchainService {
    pub async fn initialize(
        genesis_address: &WalletAddress
    ) -> Result<BlockchainService> {
        let blockchain =
            BlockchainFileSystem::create_blockchain(
                genesis_address
            ).await?;
        Ok(BlockchainService(
            Arc::new(TokioRwLock::new(blockchain))
        ))
    }

    pub async fn default()
        -> Result<BlockchainService>
    {
        let blockchain =
            BlockchainFileSystem::open_blockchain()
                .await?;
        Ok(BlockchainService(
            Arc::new(TokioRwLock::new(blockchain))
        ))
    }
}
```

Listing 61: `BlockchainService` façade structure

i Key observations

`Arc<T>` (Atomically Reference Counted) gives us a thread-safe reference-counted handle to the same in-memory value; cloning an `Arc` bumps a reference count instead of duplicating the wrapped value, so the service is clonable and shareable across tasks without copying the underlying chainstate. `TokioRwLock<T>` is tokio's async-aware read/write lock: `RwLock` lets any number of readers share access but gives writers exclusive access, and it suspends awaiting tasks without blocking the thread (distinct from `std::sync::RwLock`, which blocks the OS thread). This is the standard Rust pattern for shared mutable state across async tasks.

11.5 Step 3: Read Helper (Shared Lock Pattern)

Understanding the locking model begins with the helper used for reads, which can then be compared to write paths.

```rust
// Source: bitcoin/src/chain/chainstate.rs
async fn read<F, Fut, T>(&self, f: F) -> Result<T>
where
    F: FnOnce(BlockchainFileSystem) -> Fut + Send,
    Fut: Future<Output = Result<T>> + Send,
    T: Send + 'static,
{
    // Acquire shared (read) lock...
    let blockchain_guard = self.0.read().await;
    // ...clone underlying chainstate handle,
    // run the operation.
    f(blockchain_guard.clone()).await
}
```

Listing 62: Read helper *read* lock + delegation

✓ Checkpoint

The public "read" methods (`get_tip_hash`, `get_block`, `find_transaction`, etc.) are thin wrappers around `read(...)`. We intentionally funnel reads through a single mechanism so it is easy to audit which operations require exclusive access. A read lock is sufficient here because we are only inspecting the current state, not modifying it.

> The exclusive write lock is acquired only when we are ready to persist the block.

11.6 Step 4: Write Lock Boundary (Adding a Block)

```
// Source: bitcoin/src/chain/chainstate.rs
pub async fn add_block(&self, block: &Block) ->
Result<()> {
    let mut blockchain_guard = self.0.write().await;
    blockchain_guard.add_block(block).await
}
```

Listing 63: Write-lock boundary example (`BlockchainService::add_block`)

> ▷ **Note**
>
> `add_block` is intentionally short: it takes the write lock and delegates to `BlockchainFileSystem::add_block(...)`. This delegation is important: **the storage layer is the acceptance boundary** where "validate → connect" belongs. By keeping the lock boundary thin, we avoid holding the exclusive lock longer than necessary, which would slow down concurrent readers.

11.7 Step 5: Mining Is Also a Write Path (With Double-Validation)

Mining is more complex than a simple `add_block`: it creates a new block from pending transactions, which introduces a race condition — another block may arrive between the time we validate candidates and the time we acquire the write lock.

Mining constructs a new block, persists it, advances the tip, and updates the UTXO set, so `mine_block` is also guarded by the write lock.

```
// Source: bitcoin/src/chain/chainstate.rs
pub async fn mine_block(
    &self,
    transactions: &[Transaction]
) -> Result<Block> {
    // Validate candidate transactions before we persist anything.
    for transaction in transactions {
        let is_valid = transaction.verify(self).await?;
        if !is_valid {
            return Err(BtcError::InvalidTransaction);
        }
    }
```

Listing 64: Mining boundary (`BlockchainService::mine_block` — part 1: pre-lock validation)

After validating all transactions with an open (read-lock) view of the blockchain, the function acquires an exclusive write lock and performs stale-mining protection by re-validating inputs once more under the lock. This double-check pattern prevents the node from creating blocks with already-spent transactions if a competing block was accepted between the pre-lock and lock-acquisition steps.

```rust
    // Acquire write lock
    let blockchain_guard = self.0.write().await;

    // Re-validate transaction inputs under the write lock.
    // Between pre-lock validation and here, a competing block may have
    // been accepted, spending the same inputs.
    let db = blockchain_guard.get_db();
    let utxo_tree = db.open_tree("chainstate")?;
    for tx in transactions {
        if tx.is_coinbase() { continue; }
        for input in tx.get_vin() {
            // Verify each input's UTXO still exists...
        }
    }

    // Mining + persistence happens inside the storage layer.
    blockchain_guard.mine_block(transactions).await
}
```

Listing 65: Mining boundary (`BlockchainService::mine_block` — part 2: write-lock and stale-mining protection)

▲ Stale Mining Protection

When multiple miners compete for the same transactions, there is a race condition:

1. **First validation** (read lock): checks each transaction's inputs are unspent (before write lock acquired).

2. Between steps 1 and 3, a **competing block** may arrive from the network and be processed via `add_block` (which takes the write lock), spending the same transaction inputs.
3. **Second validation** (write lock): re-checks inputs just before mining. If any inputs were spent by the competing block in step 2, mining is aborted with a "stale mining" error.

Without this re-validation, the node could produce a block whose inputs were already spent by the competing block — effectively creating coins from nothing, a consensus-critical failure. The `update_utxo_set` function silently skips missing inputs (those outpoints were already removed by the competing block) but still adds the coinbase output, so without the second check the node would effectively create money from nothing—a consensus-critical failure that stale-mining protection prevents.

11.8 Step 6: Derived-State Updates (UTXO Set)

```
// Source: bitcoin/src/chain/chainstate.rs
pub async fn update_utxo_set(
    &self,
    block: &Block
) -> Result<()> {
    let utxo_set = UTXOSet::new(self.clone());
    utxo_set.update(block).await
}

pub async fn rollback_utxo_set(
    &self,
    block: &Block
) -> Result<()> {
    let utxo_set = UTXOSet::new(self.clone());
    utxo_set.rollback_block(block).await
}
```

Listing 66: Derived-state delegation (UTXO update + rollback)

At this point, we have identified the most important "state boundaries" in code:

- read-only operations are funneled through `read(...)`,
- state mutations take the write lock and delegate to the storage layer,
- derived state is updated through the UTXO set.

Next, in Chapter 12, we trace the storage layer's write paths that make blocks durable on disk. Then, in Chapter 13, we study update and rollback rules in detail.

11.9 Summary

Key Takeaways

- ✓ **`BlockchainService` is the shared chain API**: one façade used across node runtime and indirectly by the web layer via `NodeContext`.
- ✓ **Read vs. write is explicit**: reads go through a shared lock; mutations take an exclusive lock before delegating to persistence.
- ✓ **Persistence and derived state are separate**: the storage layer persists blocks/tip; the UTXO set tracks spendability updates/rollbacks.
- ✓ **Double validation at mining boundary**: transaction verification happens before the write lock (pre-flight) and again inside the write lock (stale-mining protection).

12

Chain: Chain State and Storage

▷ **What you will learn in this chapter**

- How blocks are persisted to sled, the embedded key-value database
- The "tip pointer" pattern: where the current chain head lives in-memory and on-disk
- Entry points for reads (status queries) and writes (appending blocks)
- How the chain is initialized (genesis bootstrap) and reopened from disk
- Iterator pattern: walking the chain backward from tip to genesis

YOUR node is not a client of some central server. It is a sovereign copy of the entire blockchain—a complete, independent replica that synchronizes with other copies only by exchanging blocks over the network. Every node persists its own chain to its own local database. This decentralization is fundamental to blockchain's resilience: if one node goes offline, the others keep growing the chain. If one node gets attacked, the others can ignore it and follow the consensus rule. This section shows you how to store, retrieve, and update that sovereign copy using sled, Rust's embedded key-value store.

The following files are the primary references for this chapter:

- `bitcoin/src/chain/chainstate.rs` — the `BlockchainService` type that wraps storage behind a shared read/write lock
- `bitcoin/src/store/file_system_db_chain.rs` — the `BlockchainFileSystem` type that talks directly to sled

- `bitcoin/src/node/context.rs` — `NodeContext`, the top-level delegation layer that HTTP handlers call
- `bitcoin/src/web/handlers/blockchain.rs` — the status-read HTTP handler (entry point for chain queries)
- `bitcoin/src/web/handlers/mining.rs` — the mining HTTP handler (entry point for block creation)

i Key insight

When you see "chain state," think "this one node's view of history," not "the network's shared database." Each node runs the same storage and validation logic independently.

12.1 Status Read and Append-Block Write Entry Points

Entry point 1: Status read (GET blockchain info)

```rust
// Source: blockchain.rs --- router -> get_blockchain_info(handler)
pub async fn get_blockchain_info(
    State(node): State<Arc<NodeContext>>,
) -> Result<Json<ApiResponse<BlockchainInfoResponse>>, StatusCode> {
    let height = node
        .get_blockchain_height()
        .await
        .map_err(|_| StatusCode::INTERNAL_SERVER_ERROR)?;

    let last_block = node
        .blockchain()
        .get_last_block()
        .await?;
    let last_block_hash = last_block
        .map(|block| block.get_hash().to_string())
        .unwrap_or_else(|| "genesis".to_string());

    let mempool_size = node.get_mempool_size()?;
    // ... build response ...
    Ok(Json(ApiResponse::success(info)))
}
```

Listing 67: Status read handler: retrieve height and tip block

Entry point 2: Append-block write (POST mine to address)

```rust
// Source: mining.rs --- router -> generate_to_address(handler)
let mined_block = node
    .mine_block(&transactions)
    .await
    .map_err(|_| StatusCode::INTERNAL_SERVER_ERROR)?;
```

Listing 68: Mining write handler: mine and append a block

12.2 Height Read: The Shared-Lock Pattern Through Storage

The call chain for a height read goes:

> Axum router → `NodeContext::get_blockchain_height`
> → `BlockchainService::get_best_height` (shared lock)
> → `BlockchainFileSystem::get_best_height`

```rust
// Source: context.rs
pub async fn get_blockchain_height(&self) ->
Result<usize> {
    self.blockchain.get_best_height().await
}
```

Listing 69: `NodeContext::get_blockchain_height` delegates to service

```rust
// Source: chainstate.rs
pub async fn get_best_height(&self) -> Result<usize>
{
    self.read(|blockchain: BlockchainFileSystem|
async move {
        blockchain.get_best_height().await
    })
    .await
}
```

Listing 70: `BlockchainService::get_best_height` acquires shared lock

```rust
// Source: file_system_db_chain.rs
pub async fn get_best_height(&self) -> Result<usize>
{
    if self.is_empty() {
        Ok(0)
    } else {
        let block_tree = self.blockchain.db
            .open_tree(self.get_blocks_tree_path())?;
        let tip_block_bytes = block_tree
            .get(self.get_tip_hash().await?)?
            .ok_or(BtcError::BlockNotFound)?;
        let tip_block = Block::deserialize(
            tip_block_bytes.as_ref()
        )?;
        Ok(tip_block.get_height())
    }
}
```

Listing 71: `BlockchainFileSystem::get_best_height` hits sled

> ▷ **Note**
>
> `BlockchainService::get_best_height(...)` is a **shared-lock read**: it uses `read(...)` (shared lock) and delegates to `BlockchainFileSystem`. The persistence engine hits sled via `self.blockchain.db` and uses the current tip hash to load the tip block bytes.

Now that we have seen how reads retrieve cached data from the tip pointer and sled, we turn to writes — where atomicity is critical.

12.3 Tip-Block Read: Cache Then Lookup

```rust
// Source: file_system_db_chain.rs
pub async fn get_last_block(&self) -> Result<Option<Block>> {
    let tip_hash = self.get_tip_hash().await?;
    let block = self.get_block(tip_hash.as_bytes()).await?;
    Ok(block)
}

pub async fn get_tip_hash(&self) -> Result<String> {
    let tip_hash = self.blockchain.tip_hash.read().await;
    Ok(tip_hash.clone())
}
```

Listing 72: `BlockchainFileSystem::get_last_block` and cached tip pointer

✓ Checkpoint

This is a "tip pointer + lookup" pattern: the **tip pointer** is the hash of the current best block (the chain's head); reading a block requires two steps—fetch the cached tip hash from the in-memory lock, then use that hash as a sled key to load the block's serialized bytes, then deserialize. The pointer is cached because the tip changes only on writes; reads should not pay a disk hit to learn "where is the head?" on every query.

12.4 Where Chain State Lives: The Storage Container

```rust
// Source: file_system_db_chain.rs
#[derive(Clone, Debug)]
pub struct BlockchainFileSystem {
    blockchain: Blockchain<Db>,
    file_system_tree_dir: String,
}

// Source: blockchain.rs --- chain container
pub struct Blockchain<T> {
    pub tip_hash: Arc<TokioRwLock<String>>,
    pub db: T,                                  // sled Db handle
    pub is_empty: bool,
}
```

Listing 73: `BlockchainFileSystem` owns `Blockchain<Db>`

12.5 Create and Open: Bootstrap vs. Reopen

Constructors: initialize vs. default

```
// Source: chainstate.rs
impl BlockchainService {
    pub async fn initialize(
        genesis_address: &WalletAddress,
    ) -> Result<BlockchainService> {
        let blockchain =
            BlockchainFileSystem::create_blockchain(
                genesis_address
            ).await?;
        Ok(BlockchainService(Arc::new(
            TokioRwLock::new(blockchain)
        )))
    }

    pub async fn default() -> Result<BlockchainService> {
        let blockchain =
BlockchainFileSystem::open_blockchain().await?;
        Ok(BlockchainService(Arc::new(
            TokioRwLock::new(blockchain)
        )))
    }
}
```

Listing 74: `BlockchainService` constructor entry points

> ▷ **Note**
>
> `initialize(...)` delegates to `BlockchainFileSystem::create_blockchain(...)` (genesis bootstrapping lives there).
> `default()` delegates to `BlockchainFileSystem::open_blockchain(...)` (no genesis; fail if missing tip key).

Persisted Keys That Define "Chain Exists"

```
// Source: file_system_db_chain.rs
// persisted head pointer (sled key)
const DEFAULT_TIP_BLOCK_HASH_KEY: &str =
"tip_block_hash";
// sled tree: "<block_hash>" -> bytes(Block)
const DEFAULT_BLOCKS_TREE: &str = "blocks1";
// on-disk directory for the default sled DB
const DEFAULT_TREE_DIR: &str = "data1";
```

Listing 75: Storage constants for tip pointer and blocks

> ▷ **Note**
>
> The persisted head pointer is **one key** in the sled tree: the literal string `"tip_block_hash"` (defined as `DEFAULT_TIP_BLOCK_HASH_KEY`) maps to the hex-string hash of the current tip block. Every other entry in the same tree maps a block hash to that block's serialized bytes. The tip hash is stored as a hex string rather than raw binary, making it human-readable in debug logs and easier to work with via Rust's `String` type. The tip-pointer key is therefore the one well-known starting address that lets a freshly-restarted node find the rest of the chain.

Open path: load tip from sled

```
// Source: file_system_db_chain.rs
pub async fn open_blockchain()
    -> Result<BlockchainFileSystem>
{
    let db = sled::open(path)?;
    let blocks_tree = db
        .open_tree(file_system_tree_dir.clone())?;

    let tip_bytes = blocks_tree
        .get(DEFAULT_TIP_BLOCK_HASH_KEY)?
        .ok_or(BtcError::BlockchainNotFoundError(
            "No existing blockchain found.".to_string(),
        ))?;

    let tip_hash = String::from_utf8(tip_bytes.to_vec())?;

    Ok(BlockchainFileSystem {
        blockchain: Blockchain {
            tip_hash: Arc::new(TokioRwLock::new(tip_hash)),
            db,
            is_empty: false,
        },
        file_system_tree_dir,
    })
}
```

Listing 76: `BlockchainFileSystem::open_blockchain`

✓ Checkpoint

The **only "open" state we must recover** is the tip hash (`tip_block_hash` key). After this returns, reads like `get_tip_hash()` do **not** need to hit sled for the tip pointer (they read the in-memory lock).

Create path: bootstrap genesis if missing

```
// Source: file_system_db_chain.rs
pub async fn create_blockchain(
    genesis_address: &WalletAddress,
) -> Result<Self> {
    let db = sled::open(path)?;
    let blocks_tree =
        db.open_tree(file_system_tree_dir.clone())?;

    let data = blocks_tree.get(DEFAULT_TIP_BLOCK_HASH_KEY)?;

    let tip_hash = if let Some(data) = data {
        String::from_utf8(data.to_vec())?
    } else {
        let coinbase_tx = Transaction::new_coinbase_tx(
            genesis_address
        )?;
        let block = Block::generate_genesis_block(&coinbase_tx);
        Self::update_blocks_tree(&blocks_tree, &block).await?;
        String::from(block.get_hash())
    };

    Ok(BlockchainFileSystem {
        blockchain: Blockchain {
            tip_hash: Arc::new(TokioRwLock::new(tip_hash)),
            db,
            is_empty: false,
        },
        file_system_tree_dir,
    })
}
```

Listing 77: `BlockchainFileSystem::create_blockchain`

▷ **Note**

Genesis is created **exactly once** (when the tip key is absent). The persisted "chain exists" signal is: the `"tip_block_hash"` key is present.

12.6 Atomic Persistence Unit: Block Bytes + Tip Key

```
// Source: file_system_db_chain.rs
async fn update_blocks_tree(
    blocks_tree: &Tree,
    block: &Block
) -> Result<()> {
    let block_hash = block.get_hash();
    let block_ivec = IVec::try_from(block.clone())?;

    let transaction_result = blocks_tree.transaction(|tx_db| {
        tx_db.insert(block_hash, block_ivec.clone())?;
        tx_db.insert(DEFAULT_TIP_BLOCK_HASH_KEY, block_hash)?;
        Ok(())
    });

    transaction_result
        .map(|_| ())
        .map_err(|e| BtcError::BlockchainDBconnection(
            format!("{:?}", e)
        ))
}
```

Listing 78: Atomic persistence: write block and tip together

> Note

Atomic persistence here means either both the block file and the index entry are written, or neither is — we never persist one without the other, so a crash can never leave the database pointing at a block file that doesn't exist (or vice versa). In this context, **block bytes plus tip pointer** are updated together inside one sled transaction. This wraps the two inserts (block bytes and tip pointer) in a sled transaction. If the process crashes between inserts, sled's write-ahead log ensures either both writes complete or neither does — preventing the disk from reaching an inconsistent state where the tip points to a nonexistent block. Derived state (UTXO set) is **not** part of this transaction (it is updated as a later step).

12.7 Mining Boundary: Append Block via Local Mining

```
// Source: chainstate.rs
pub async fn mine_block(
    &self,
    transactions: &[Transaction]
) -> Result<Block> {
    for tx in transactions {
        if !tx.verify(self).await? {
            return Err(BtcError::InvalidTransaction);
        }
    }
    let blockchain_guard = self.0.write().await;
    blockchain_guard.mine_block(transactions).await
}
```

Listing 79: Mining: verify before acquiring write lock

```
// Source: file_system_db_chain.rs
pub async fn mine_block(
    &self,
    transactions: &[Transaction]
) -> Result<Block> {
    let best_height = self.get_best_height().await?;
    let block = Block::new_block(
        self.get_tip_hash().await?,
        transactions,
        best_height + 1,
    );
    let block_hash = block.get_hash();

    let blocks_tree = self.blockchain.db
        .open_tree(self.get_blocks_tree_path())?;
    Self::update_blocks_tree(&blocks_tree,
&block).await?;

    self.set_tip_hash(block_hash).await?;
    self.update_utxo_set(&block).await?;

    Ok(block)
}
```

Listing 80: Persistence engine: create, persist, cache, update UTXO

▷ Note

`BlockchainService::mine_block(...)` is the **exclusive lock boundary** for local chain extension. Persistence is split into:

- **Atomic persisted unit**: write `<block_hash> -> bytes(Block)` and `"tip_block_hash" -> <block_hash>`
- **Runtime cache update**: `set_tip_hash(...)` keeps the in-memory cached tip consistent with the persisted value
- **Derived state update**: UTXO updates happen after the block is persisted

12.8 Chain Iteration: Walking Backward from Tip to Genesis

```
// Source: chainstate.rs
pub async fn iterator(&self) ->
Result<BlockchainIterator> {
    self.read(|blockchain| async move {
        blockchain.iterator().await
    })
    .await
}
```

Listing 81: Iterator entry point (shared lock)

```
// Source: file_system_db_chain.rs
pub async fn iterator(&self) -> Result<BlockchainIterator> {
    let hash = self.get_tip_hash().await?;
    Ok(BlockchainIterator::new(
        hash,
        self.blockchain.db.clone(),
        self.get_blocks_tree_path(),
    ))
}

pub struct BlockchainIterator {
    db: Db,
    file_system_blocks_tree: String,
    current_hash: String,
}

impl BlockchainIterator {
    fn new(
        tip_hash: String,
        db: Db,
        file_system_blocks_tree: String,
    ) -> Self {
        BlockchainIterator {
            current_hash: tip_hash,
            file_system_blocks_tree,
            db,
        }
    }

}

impl Iterator for BlockchainIterator {
    type Item = Block;

    fn next(&mut self) -> Option<Self::Item> {
        let block_tree = self.db
.open_tree(self.file_system_blocks_tree.clone())
            .ok()?;

        let data = match block_tree.get(self.current_hash.clone()) {
            Ok(Some(d)) => d,
            Ok(None) => return None,
            Err(_) => return None,
        };

        let block = Block::deserialize(
            data.to_vec().as_slice()
        ).ok()?;
        self.current_hash =
```

```rust
// Source: chainstate.rs
pub async fn get_blocks_by_height(
    &self,
    initial_height: usize,
    height: usize,
) -> Result<Vec<Block>> {
    let mut blocks = Vec::new();
    let iterator = self.iterator().await?;
    for block in iterator {
        let h = block.get_height();
        if h > height || h < initial_height {
            break;
        }
        blocks.push(block);
    }
    Ok(blocks)
}
```

Listing 83: Higher-level API: blocks by height range

> ▷ Note
>
> The iterator is exposed at the **API boundary** (`BlockchainService::iterator`) and implemented in the persistence engine. Iteration starts at the current tip hash and repeatedly follows `pre_block_hash` "backward" through history.

12.9 Network Insertion: Add Block from Peer

```
// Source: chainstate.rs
pub async fn add_block(&self, block: &Block) ->
Result<()> {
    let mut blockchain_guard = self.0.write().await;
    blockchain_guard.add_block(block).await
}
```

Listing 84: Network block accepted into chain

```
// Source: file_system_db_chain.rs
pub async fn add_block(&mut self, new_block: &Block)
-> Result<()> {
    let block_tree = self.blockchain.db
        .open_tree(self.get_blocks_tree_path())?;

    if
block_tree.get(new_block.get_hash())?.is_some() {
        return Ok(());
    }

    let block_bytes = new_block.serialize()?;
    let tip_hash = self.get_tip_hash().await?;
```

Listing 85: Persistence layer: idempotence check and serialization (part 1)

After the idempotence check and serialization, the function wraps the database writes (block bytes and tip pointer update) in an atomic transaction. This ensures that the block and tip pointer are either both persisted or both rolled back in case of error, preventing inconsistent disk state.

```
    let transaction_result = block_tree.transaction(|tx| {
        tx.insert(new_block.get_hash(), block_bytes.clone())?;
        if new_block.get_height() > /* tip height */ {
            tx.insert(
                DEFAULT_TIP_BLOCK_HASH_KEY,
                new_block.get_hash()
            )?;
        }
        Ok(())
    });

    transaction_result
        .map_err(|e| BtcError::BlockchainDBconnection(
            format!("{:?}", e)
        ))?;

    Ok(())
}
```

Listing 86: Persistence layer: atomic transaction and error handling (part 2)

> ▷ **Note**
>
> The network-received block is persisted **before** the full "validate → connect" gate is enforced (that hard gate is still incomplete in this learning implementation). Tip updates use a simplified height-based fork-choice rule. This idempotent behavior handles the common case where the same block arrives from multiple peers — rather than returning an error, the node silently succeeds because the block is already persisted.

12.10 Summary

Key Takeaways

- ✓ **Two entry points**: status reads (shared lock), append-block writes (exclusive lock)
- ✓ **Tip pointer pattern**: in-memory cache of the canonical head hash, backed by the sled key `"tip_block_hash"`
- ✓ **Genesis bootstrapping**: created exactly once when the tip key is absent
- ✓ **Atomic persistence unit**: block bytes and tip pointer written together in one sled transaction
- ✓ **Chain iteration**: walk backward from tip by following `pre_block_hash` links
- ✓ **Network insertion**: accept candidate blocks, update tip if candidate wins by height

13

Chain: UTXO Set

▷ **What you will learn in this chapter**

- What a UTXO (Unspent Transaction Output) is and why Bitcoin tracks outputs, not accounts
- How the UTXO set is persisted in sled: one tree with `txid_bytes -> Vec<TXOutput>`
- Coin selection: how `find_spendable_outputs` chooses which coins to spend
- Block connection: updating the UTXO set when a block is accepted (remove spent, add created)
- Chain reorg support: rolling back the UTXO set when a block is disconnected
- Balance queries: deriving "account balance" from the collection of spendable UTXOs

In Bitcoin, a **UTXO** (Unspent Transaction Output) is a *specific coin* you can spend: an output created by some earlier transaction that has not yet been referenced as an input by any later transaction. Your "balance" is therefore not a single stored number; it is the sum of the values of all UTXOs you can unlock with your keys.

The **UTXO set** is the node's *current index of spendability*: the collection of all UTXOs that exist **right now** (keyed by $txid, vout$ and mapping to output details). It is updated when blocks are connected (remove spent outputs, add newly created outputs), and it is what wallets and validators consult to answer "is this input spendable?" efficiently.

This is different from the **blockchain**, which is an append-only history. The chain records *what happened*; the UTXO set represents the *resulting state* (what remains spendable after applying that history).

The following files are the primary references for this chapter:

- `bitcoin/src/chain/utxo_set.rs` — the `UTXOSet` type that manages the spendability index (find, update, rollback, balance queries)
- `bitcoin/src/primitives/transaction.rs` — the `Transaction`, `TXInput`, and `TXOutput` types that UTXOs reference

13.1 Storage Layout in sled

`sled` is an embedded key-value database written in Rust. There is no `UTXO` struct. The UTXO set is stored as a sled tree:

- Tree name: `chainstate` (constant `UTXO_TREE`)
- Key: `txid` (raw bytes—the 32-byte transaction hash)
- Value: `Vec<TXOutput>` serialized via `bincode`

```
// Source: utxo_set.rs
const UTXO_TREE: &str = "chainstate";

pub struct UTXOSet {
    // handle used to access the DB and chain data
    blockchain: BlockchainService,
}
```

Listing 87: UTXO tree structure and handle

> ▷ Note
>
> We persist **derived state** as: `txid_bytes -> bincode(Vec<TXOutput>)`. `bincode` is a compact binary serialization format for Rust types — significantly more efficient than JSON or XML for structured data. It converts a `Vec<TXOutput>` into a flat byte buffer for storage and back again on read. The *outpoint* $(txid, vout)$ is interpreted as "the output at index `vout` inside that stored `Vec<TXOutput>`"— `vout` is just a `usize` index into the array of outputs created by transaction `txid`.
>
> We use raw bytes as the database key (rather than hex strings) because they are more space-efficient (32 bytes vs. 64 characters) and faster to compare.

> When a transaction ID is displayed as hex in logs, that is the same value, just rendered for humans.

13.2 Core Data Types: TXInput and TXOutput

Understanding the UTXO set requires knowing what a transaction *points at* and what an output *contains*. A single transaction can create multiple outputs — for example, one paying the recipient and another returning change to the sender. The output index (`vout`) disambiguates which output within a transaction is being referenced.

```
// Source: transaction.rs
#[derive(Clone, Default, Serialize, Deserialize)]
pub struct TXInput {
    txid: Vec<u8>,                    // previous transaction hash
    vout: usize,                      // output index in that transaction
    signature: Vec<u8>,               // proof of authorization
    pub_key: Vec<u8>,                 // public key for verification
}

impl TXInput {
    pub fn new(txid: &[u8], vout: usize) -> TXInput {
        TXInput {
            txid: txid.to_vec(),
            vout,
            signature: vec![],
            pub_key: vec![],
        }
    }

    pub fn uses_key(&self, pub_key_hash: &[u8]) -> bool {
        let locking_hash = hash_pub_key(self.pub_key.as_slice());
        locking_hash.eq(pub_key_hash)
    }
}
```

Listing 88: `TXInput` : reference to a previous output and authorization

▷ **Note**

An **outpoint** is the pair $(txid, vout)$ that identifies which previous output an input is spending. It does not store "which address"; it stores the exact transaction and output index being consumed.

```rust
// Source: transaction.rs
#[derive(Clone, Serialize, Deserialize)]
pub struct TXOutput {
    value: i32,                          // amount locked by this output
    in_global_mem_pool: bool,            // local hint: reserved in mempool?
    pub_key_hash: Vec<u8>,               // ``lock'': who can spend this
}

impl TXOutput {
    pub fn new(
        value: i32,
        address: &WalletAddress
    ) -> Result<TXOutput> {
        let mut output = TXOutput {
            value,
            in_global_mem_pool: false,
            pub_key_hash: vec![],
        };
        output.lock(address)?;
        Ok(output)
    }

    fn lock(&mut self, address: &WalletAddress) -> Result<()> {
        self.pub_key_hash = get_pub_key_hash(address)?;
        Ok(())
    }

    pub fn set_in_global_mem_pool(&mut self, value: bool) {
        self.in_global_mem_pool = value;
    }
}
```

Listing 89: `TXOutput` : value and the "in mempool" flag

> Note

`pub_key_hash` is the "lock"—it is what `is_locked_with_key()` matches during coin selection. `in_global_mem_pool` is **not** a Bitcoin consensus concept; it is a local optimization: the node marks an output as reserved so that coin selection does not accidentally choose the same coin for two pending transactions. This flag is not enforced by consensus rules — other nodes never check it.

13.3 Coin Selection: Finding Spendable Outputs

Transaction creation requires the wallet to answer: "Which outpoints locked to me can cover *amount*, while avoiding outputs already used in the mempool?"

```
// Source: utxo_set.rs
pub async fn find_spendable_outputs(
    &self,
    from_pub_key_hash: &[u8],
    amount: i32,
) -> Result<(i32, HashMap<String, Vec<usize>>)> {
    let mut unspent_outputs_indexes = HashMap::new();
    let mut accumulated = 0;
    let db = self.blockchain.get_db().await?;
    let utxo_tree = db.open_tree(UTXO_TREE)?;
```

Listing 90: `UTXOSet::find_spendable_outputs` — setup and tree opening (part 1)

After setting up the accumulators and opening the UTXO tree, the function iterates over all stored outputs, deserializes each transaction's outputs, and selects outputs matching the owner's public key hash while staying unspent. The selected outpoints are collected in a map keyed by transaction ID.

```
    for item in utxo_tree.iter() {
        let (k, v) = item?;
        let txid_hex = HEXLOWER.encode(k.as_ref());
        let (tx_out, _) = bincode::serde::decode_from_slice(
            v.as_ref(),
            bincode::config::standard(),
        )?;

        for (vout_idx, out) in tx_out.iter().enumerate() {
            if out.not_in_global_mem_pool()
                && out.is_locked_with_key(from_pub_key_hash)
                && accumulated < amount
            {
                accumulated += out.get_value();
                unspent_outputs_indexes
                    .entry(txid_hex.clone())
                    .or_insert_with(Vec::new)
                    .push(vout_idx);
            }
        }
    }
    Ok((accumulated, unspent_outputs_indexes))
}
```

Listing 91: `UTXOSet::find_spendable_outputs` — output scanning and selection (part 2)

✓ Checkpoint

This method:

- Opens the `UTXO_TREE` and iterates the entire keyspace (this is $O(n)$ where n is the number of transactions with unspent outputs)
- Deserializes each `Vec<TXOutput>` and checks each output for ownership and reservation status
- Accumulates outputs until the sum covers the requested amount
- Returns a `HashMap<txid_hex -> [vout indexes]>` mapping transaction IDs to their selected output indices

Note that `find_spendable_outputs` iterates the entire UTXO tree ($O(n)$ where n is the number of transactions with unspent outputs). For small chains this is acceptable; production systems use secondary indexes for faster lookups.

13.4 Transaction Construction Using Selected Outputs

`Transaction::new_utxo_transaction` uses coin selection results to build the actual transaction:

```rust
// Source: transaction.rs
pub async fn new_utxo_transaction(
    from_wlt_addr: &WalletAddress,
    to_wlt_addr: &WalletAddress,
    tx_amount: i32,
    utxo_set: &UTXOSet,
) -> Result<Transaction> {
    let wallets = WalletService::new()?;
    let from_wallet =
wallets.get_wallet(from_wlt_addr)?;
    let from_pub_key_hash = hash_pub_key(
        from_wallet.get_public_key()
    );
    let (available_funds, valid_outputs) = utxo_set
        .find_spendable_outputs(&from_pub_key_hash,
tx_amount)
        .await?;

    if available_funds < tx_amount {
        return Err(BtcError::NotEnoughFunds);
    }

    let mut inputs = vec![];
    for (txid_hex, out_indexes) in valid_outputs {
        let txid =
HEXLOWER.decode(txid_hex.as_bytes())?;
        for vout_idx in out_indexes {
            inputs.push(TXInput::new(&txid,
vout_idx));
        }
    }
```

Listing 92: UTXO transaction construction: wallet and coin selection setup

With the inputs prepared from selected outputs, the transaction now constructs payment and change outputs, computes a transaction ID, and signs the result:

```
    let mut outputs = vec![TXOutput::new(tx_amount, to_wlt_addr)?];
    if available_funds > tx_amount {
        outputs.push(TXOutput::new(
            available_funds - tx_amount,
            from_wlt_addr,
        )?);
    }

    let mut tx = Transaction {
        id: vec![],
        vin: inputs,
        vout: outputs,
    };
    tx.id = tx.hash()?;
    tx.sign(utxo_set.get_blockchain(), from_wallet.get_pkcs8())
        .await?;
    Ok(tx)
}
```

Listing 93: UTXO transaction construction: output creation and signing

> ▷ **Note**
>
> The selected outpoints become `TXInput` s, value is re-expressed as payment and optional change `TXOutput` s, then we compute a txid and sign. This is the **mechanical implementation of the UTXO model**: spending consumes entire outputs, so leftover value must be recreated as a new change output.

13.5 Updating After a Block (Block Connect)

When a block is accepted, the UTXO set must be updated by removing spent outputs and adding newly created outputs.

```
// Source: utxo_set.rs
pub async fn update(&self, block: &Block) -> Result<()> {
    let db = self.blockchain.get_db().await?;
    let utxo_tree = db.open_tree(UTXO_TREE)?;

    // Step 1: Remove (spend) inputs referenced by this block
    for tx in block.get_transactions() {
        if !tx.is_coinbase() {
            for input in tx.get_vin() {
                let txid = input.get_txid();
                if let Ok(Some(mut outputs)) =
                    self.find_utxo(txid)
                {
                    if input.vout < outputs.len() {
                        outputs.remove(input.vout);
                        if outputs.is_empty() {
                            utxo_tree.remove(txid)?;
                        } else {
                            let data = bincode::serde::encode_to_vec(
                                &outputs,
                                bincode::config::standard(),
                            )?;
                            utxo_tree.insert(txid, data)?;
                        }
                    }
                }
            }
        }
    }
```

Listing 94: Update the UTXO set when a block is connected: spending inputs

After removing spent outputs, the block's newly created outputs are inserted into the UTXO set, making them available for future spending:

```rust
    // Step 2: Add (create) outputs produced by this block
    for tx in block.get_transactions() {
        let txid = tx.get_id();
        let outputs = tx.get_vout();
        let data = bincode::serde::encode_to_vec(
            &outputs,
            bincode::config::standard(),
        )?;
        utxo_tree.insert(txid, data)?;
    }

    Ok(())
}
```

Listing 95: Update the UTXO set when a block is connected: creating outputs

> ▷ **Note**
>
> Block connection is a two-step atomic transformation:
>
> 1. **Spend phase**: for each input in each transaction, locate the previous transaction's outputs and remove the one at index `input.vout`. If that empties the `Vec<TXOutput>`, delete the txid key entirely so the tree does not accumulate empty entries; otherwise re-serialize the trimmed vector and write it back.
> 2. **Create phase**: for each transaction in the block, insert all its outputs into the UTXO set (keyed by the transaction's ID).

13.6 Rollback: Disconnecting a Block (Reorg Support)

If a block must be disconnected (e.g., during a chain reorg), its UTXO effects are undone by removing created outputs and restoring spent outputs.

```
// Source: utxo_set.rs
pub async fn rollback_block(&self, block: &Block) -> Result<()> {
    let db = self.blockchain.get_db().await?;
    let utxo_tree = db.open_tree(UTXO_TREE)?;

    // Step 1: Remove outputs created by this block
    for tx in block.get_transactions() {
        utxo_tree.remove(tx.get_id())?;
    }

    // Step 2: Restore outputs spent by this block
    for tx in block.get_transactions() {
        if !tx.is_coinbase() {
            for input in tx.get_vin() {
                let prev_txid = input.get_txid();
                if let Ok(Some(prev_tx)) =
                    self.blockchain.find_transaction(prev_txid)
                {
                    let data = bincode::serde::encode_to_vec(
                        prev_tx.get_vout(),
                        bincode::config::standard(),
                    )?;
                    utxo_tree.insert(prev_txid, data)?;
                }
            }
        }
    }

    Ok(())
}
```

Listing 96: Rollback the UTXO set when a block is disconnected

▷ Note

Rollback is the inverse of block connect:

1. **Remove phase**: delete all transactions created by this block from the UTXO set
2. **Restore phase**: for each input spent by this block, look up the original transaction and restore its full output set to the UTXO tree

This allows the node to support chain reorganizations: if a better chain is discovered, blocks can be disconnected from the old chain and reconnected to the new one, with UTXO state updated correctly each step.

13.7 Balance and UTXO Queries

Beyond the core update/rollback loop, higher-level query methods provide functionality for wallets and debugging.

```
// Source: utxo_set.rs
pub async fn find_utxo(
    &self,
    pub_key_hash: &[u8],
) -> Result<Vec<TXOutput>> {
    let mut result = Vec::new();
    let db = self.blockchain.get_db().await?;
    let utxo_tree = db.open_tree(UTXO_TREE)?;

    for item in utxo_tree.iter() {
        let (_, v) = item?;
        let (tx_out, _) =
bincode::serde::decode_from_slice(
            v.as_ref(),
            bincode::config::standard(),
        )?;
        for output in tx_out {
            if
output.is_locked_with_key(pub_key_hash) {
                result.push(output);
            }
        }
    }
    Ok(result)
}
```

Listing 97: Find UTXOs and compute balance: UTXO discovery

With UTXOs discovered by ownership, higher-level queries derive wallet balance and count:

```
pub async fn get_balance(
    &self,
    address: &WalletAddress,
) -> Result<i32> {
    let pub_key_hash = get_pub_key_hash(address)?;
    let utxos = self.find_utxo(&pub_key_hash).await?;
    Ok(utxos.iter().map(|o| o.get_value()).sum())
}

pub async fn utxo_count(
    &self,
    address: &WalletAddress,
) -> Result<usize> {
    let pub_key_hash = get_pub_key_hash(address)?;
    let utxos = self.find_utxo(&pub_key_hash).await?;
    Ok(utxos.len())
}
```

Listing 98: Find UTXOs and compute balance: balance and count queries

> ▷ Note
>
> These query methods iterate the UTXO tree and filter by ownership (`pub_key_hash`). They answer:
>
> - "What UTXOs do I own?" (`find_utxo`)
> - "What is my total balance?" (`get_balance`)
> - "How many unspent coins do I have?" (`utxo_count`)

13.8 Summary

Key Takeaways

- ✓ **UTXO set** is the derived state that answers "what is spendable right now?"
- ✓ **Storage**: sled tree `chainstate` with `txid_bytes -> Vec<TXOutput>`
- ✓ **Coin selection**: `find_spendable_outputs` scans the UTXO tree, filtering by ownership and reservation status
- ✓ **Block connect**: two-phase update (spend inputs, create outputs)
- ✓ **Block disconnect**: two-phase rollback (remove created, restore spent) for reorg support
- ✓ **Balance queries**: derive wallet balance by summing owned UTXOs
- ✓ **Local mempool flag**: `in_global_mem_pool` is a hint to avoid local double-selection, not a consensus rule

14

Chain: Transaction Lifecycle

▷ **What you will learn in this chapter**

- How a transaction flows from wallet creation through network propagation to mining boundary
- Transaction construction: selecting inputs from UTXO set and creating outputs
- Signing: the "trimmed copy" pattern that authorizes spending without circular signatures
- Verification: checking signatures at the mining boundary
- Mempool admission: accepting pending transactions and avoiding local conflicts
- Mining trigger: when and how the system decides to start mining

When you want to send coins to someone, what actually happens behind the scenes? This section traces a transaction through its complete lifecycle—from the moment you decide to send coins, through construction and signing, verification and mempool admission, to network propagation and eventual inclusion in a block.

The following files are the primary references for this chapter:

- `bitcoin/src/primitives/transaction.rs` — `Transaction`, `TXInput`, and `TXOutput` construction, the "trimmed copy" signing pattern, and coinbase creation
- `bitcoin/src/node/context.rs` — `NodeContext` entry points for transaction creation and processing

- `bitcoin/src/node/txmempool.rs` — the global mempool: pending transaction admission, duplicate detection, and retrieval
- `bitcoin/src/chain/chainstate.rs` — mining-boundary verification (signature re-check under the write lock)

14.1 Overview: The Complete Transaction Journey

A transaction goes through several distinct stages, each handled by different parts of the system:

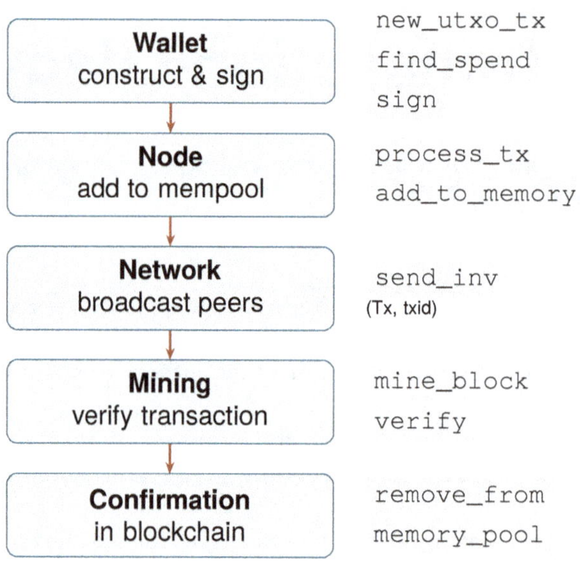

Figure 14.1: Transaction Lifecycle: From Wallet to Blockchain Confirmation

The complete flow: **construct** → **sign** → **submit** → **mempool** → **(async) broadcast/mining** → **verify at mining boundary** → **confirmation**.

14.2 Step 1: Entry Point — Top-Level Send Payment

This is the highest-level orchestration method: it creates a transaction and hands it to the node for mempool/network processing.

```rust
// Source: context.rs
pub async fn btc_transaction(
    &self,
    wlt_frm_addr: &WalletAddress,
    wlt_to_addr: &WalletAddress,
    amount: i32,
) -> Result<String> {
    // Create a UTXOSet handle (derived-state accessor).
    // Why: transaction construction needs coin selection;
    // signing needs previous-tx lookups via chainstate.
    let utxo_set = UTXOSet::new(self.blockchain.clone());

    // Build + sign the transaction (wallet-side responsibility).
    // Why: the node should not ``invent'' spends;
    // it only accepts/relays what the wallet constructed.
    let utxo = Transaction::new_utxo_transaction(
        wlt_frm_addr, wlt_to_addr, amount, &utxo_set,
    ).await?;

    // Submit to the node's mempool/network pipeline.
    // Why: once constructed, a tx must enter the node's
    // pending set before it can be mined/relayed.
    let addr_from = crate::GLOBAL_CONFIG.get_node_addr();
    self.process_transaction(&addr_from, utxo).await
}
```

Listing 99: `NodeContext::btc_transaction` — send payment entry point

> ▷ **Note**
>
> This method separates responsibilities: wallet-side work (construction + signing) is followed by node-side work (mempool/network processing). The return value is the transaction ID for the caller to track.

14.3 Step 2: Construct a Spending Transaction

Now we see how the transaction is actually built. This is where the wallet selects which coins to spend, creates the payment and change outputs, computes the transaction ID, and signs everything.

```rust
// Source: transaction.rs
pub async fn new_utxo_transaction(
    from_wlt_addr: &WalletAddress,
    to_wlt_addr: &WalletAddress,
    tx_amount: i32,
    utxo_set: &UTXOSet,
) -> Result<Transaction> {
    let wallets = WalletService::new()?;
    let from_wallet = wallets.get_wallet(from_wlt_addr)?;
    let from_pub_key_hash = hash_pub_key(
        from_wallet.get_public_key()
    );
    let (available_funds, valid_outputs) = utxo_set
        .find_spendable_outputs(&from_pub_key_hash, tx_amount)
        .await?;

    if available_funds < tx_amount {
        return Err(BtcError::NotEnoughFunds);
    }
```

Listing 100: `Transaction::new_utxo_transaction` — wallet setup and fund validation (part 1 of 2)

After validating that sufficient funds are available, the function assembles inputs and creates payment and change outputs:

```
    let mut inputs = vec![];
    for (txid_hex, out_indexes) in valid_outputs {
        let txid = HEXLOWER.decode(txid_hex.as_bytes())?;
        for vout_idx in out_indexes {
            inputs.push(TXInput::new(&txid, vout_idx));
        }
    }

    let mut outputs = vec![TXOutput::new(tx_amount, to_wlt_addr)?];
    if available_funds > tx_amount {
        let change = available_funds - tx_amount;
        outputs.push(TXOutput::new(change, from_wlt_addr)?);
    }

    let mut tx = Transaction {
        id: vec![],
        vin: inputs,
        vout: outputs,
    };
    tx.id = tx.hash()?;
    tx.sign(utxo_set.get_blockchain(), from_wallet.get_pkcs8())
        .await?;
    Ok(tx)
}
```

Listing 101: `Transaction::new_utxo_transaction` — input/output assembly and signing (part 2 of 2)

✓ Checkpoint

This method:

1. Loads the sender's keys and derives the sender's `pub_key_hash`
2. Performs coin selection via `find_spendable_outputs`
3. Turns selected outpoints into `TXInput` s (empty signatures for now)
4. Builds `TXOutput` s: payment plus optional change
5. Finalizes by computing txid (`tx.hash()`) and signing (`tx.sign(...)`)

In a UTXO-based system, each output must be consumed entirely — there is no concept of a partial spend. If a 100-coin output is used to pay 60 coins, the remaining 40 must be explicitly created as a new output (change) locked to the sender's own address. Change is a *new output*, not "leftover in an account", because UTXO-based systems must explicitly create all spendable coins.

14.4 Step 3: Sign and Verify (Trimmed Copy Pattern)

Once the transaction is constructed, it must be authorized. Signatures prove that the sender owns the coins being spent.

```rust
// Source: transaction.rs
fn trimmed_copy(&self) -> Transaction {
    let inputs = self.vin.iter()
        .map(|i| TXInput::new(i.get_txid(),
i.get_vout()))
        .collect();
    Transaction {
        id: self.id.clone(),
        vin: inputs,
        vout: self.vout.clone()
    }
}
```

Listing 102: Trimmed copy helper — clearing signatures (part 1)

Why the "copy with signatures stripped" dance? The signature cannot be part of the data being hashed, because the signature does not exist yet at the time of hashing. Both signer and verifier agree to hash a canonical form with signatures removed — the "trimmed copy" — so that both sides compute the same digest.

The trimmed copy is exactly that canonical form: a signature has to cover the transaction's contents, but it cannot cover itself — once the signature is written into the input, the bytes the signer hashed no longer exist anywhere. Signers and verifiers therefore agree on a canonical pre-signature form: take the transaction, clear every input's `signature` and `pub_key` fields, and hash *that*. Both sides reproduce the same bytes and therefore the same digest, and the signature is verified against a canonical view neither side can quietly alter.

The signing function iterates over each input, temporarily injects the referenced output's locking condition (`pub_key_hash`) so that the signature commits to the exact UTXO being spent. This prevents the signature from being replayed against a different output. It hashes that copy, and computes a Schnorr signature over that digest. The signature is then stored in the original input.

```
async fn sign(
    &mut self,
    blockchain: &BlockchainService,
    private_key: &[u8],
) -> Result<()> {
    let mut tx_copy = self.trimmed_copy();
    for (idx, vin) in self.vin.iter_mut().enumerate() {
        let prev_tx = blockchain
            .find_transaction(vin.get_txid())
            .await??;

        // Temporarily inject the referenced output's lock
        tx_copy.vin[idx].pub_key =
            prev_tx.vout[vin.vout].pub_key_hash.clone();
        tx_copy.id = tx_copy.hash()?;
        let signature = schnorr_sign_digest(
            private_key,
            tx_copy.get_id()
        )?;
        vin.signature = signature;
        tx_copy.vin[idx].pub_key = vec![];
    }
    Ok(())
}
```

Listing 103: Digital signature — signing each input (part 2)

Verification mirrors the signing process: it reconstructs the same digest for each input and validates that the stored signature authenticates the digest. If any signature is invalid, the verification fails immediately.

```
pub async fn verify(
    &self,
    blockchain: &BlockchainService
) -> Result<bool> {
    if self.is_coinbase() { return Ok(true); }
    let mut trimmed_copy = self.trimmed_copy();
    for (idx, vin) in self.vin.iter().enumerate() {
        let prev_tx = blockchain
            .find_transaction(vin.get_txid())
            .await??;
```

Listing 104: Digital signature verification: setup (part 3a)

After retrieving the previous transaction, the code verifies each signature:

```
        let pkh = prev_tx.vout[vin.vout]
            .pub_key_hash.clone();
        trimmed_copy.vin[idx].pub_key = pkh;
        trimmed_copy.id = trimmed_copy.hash()?;
        let is_valid = schnorr_sign_verify(
            vin.get_pub_key(),
            vin.get_signature(),
            trimmed_copy.get_id(),
        );
        if !is_valid {
            return Ok(false);
        }
        // Reset before the next input: each iteration injects only the
        // current input's pub_key_hash, so we must clear it before moving
        // on or the next input's digest would include leftover data.
        trimmed_copy.vin[idx].pub_key = vec![];
    }
    Ok(true)
}
```

Listing 105: Digital signature verification: signature validation (part 3b)

▷ **Note**

The trimmed copy pattern avoids circular signing (the signature cannot sign itself):

1. Create a copy with signatures cleared (`vec![]` on each `TXInput`) and other signing-related fields blank. The copy keeps the `vin` / `vout` structure but removes anything that would make the digest depend on itself.
2. For each input: inject the referenced output's `pub_key_hash` to bind the signature to the exact outpoint being spent
3. Hash that temporary copy (the `.id` field on `tx_copy` is overwritten with the hash of the trimmed bytes; the original transaction's `.id` is untouched)
4. Sign the hash (which represents the transaction *shape* and referenced outputs)
5. Verification recomputes that same digest and verifies the signature

> This ensures signatures commit to the exact outpoint and locking data, preventing signature reuse across different spends.

14.5 Step 4: Accept into Mempool and Spawn Background Work

This is the node's acceptance boundary: reject duplicates, add to the mempool, then spawn propagation/mining trigger in the background.

```
// Source: context.rs
pub async fn process_transaction(
    &self,
    addr_from: &std::net::SocketAddr,
    utxo: Transaction,
) -> Result<String> {
    if transaction_exists_in_pool(&utxo) {
        let txid = utxo.get_tx_id_hex();
        return Err(

BtcError::TransactionAlreadyExistsInMemoryPool(
                txid
            )
        );
    }
    add_to_memory_pool(utxo.clone(),
&self.blockchain)
        .await?;
```

Listing 106: `NodeContext::process_transaction` — duplicate check and mempool add (part 1 of 2)

After adding to the mempool, the transaction is propagated in a background task:

```
    let context = self.clone();
    let addr_copy = *addr_from;
    let tx = utxo.clone();
    tokio::spawn(async move {
        let _ = context
.submit_transaction_for_mining(&addr_copy, tx)
            .await;
    });
    Ok(utxo.get_tx_id_hex())
}
```

Listing 107: `NodeContext::process_transaction` — async propagation (part 2 of 2)

> ▷ **Note**
>
> This method:
>
> - **Synchronously** checks for duplicate (by `txid`)
> - **Synchronously** adds to mempool via `add_to_memory_pool`
> - **Asynchronously** (spawns background task) propagates and triggers mining
> - Returns the `txid` immediately to the caller
>
> Important: this method does **not** call `Transaction::verify` before storing. Signature verification is enforced at the **mining boundary** (`BlockchainService::mine_block`). This is a learning simplification; production systems validate at mempool admission too.

14.6 Step 5: Mempool Internals

How does the mempool store, track, and manage pending transactions?

```
1  // Source: txmempool.rs
2  pub async fn add_to_memory_pool(
3      tx: Transaction,
4      blockchain: &BlockchainService,
5  ) -> Result<()> {
6      let tx_id = tx.get_tx_id_hex();
7      if GLOBAL_MEMORY_POOL.lock().await.contains_key(&tx_id) {
8          return Err(BtcError::TransactionAlreadyExistsInMemoryPool(
9              tx_id
10         ));
11     }
12     GLOBAL_MEMORY_POOL
13         .lock()
14         .await
15         .insert(tx_id, tx.clone());
```

Listing 108: Mempool — duplicate check and insertion (part 1 of 2)

Notice that the mutex lock is acquired twice: once for the `contains_key` check (line 7) and once for the `insert` (line 12). Between those two calls, the lock is released and re-acquired. This is a deliberate simplification — in a production mempool, you would hold a single lock across both operations to prevent a race where two concurrent tasks both pass the duplicate check and insert the same transaction. In our single-node implementation, the trade-off is acceptable because it keeps each critical section short.

After adding to the mempool, the function marks all referenced inputs as reserved to prevent double-spending. The mempool is stored as a global variable (protected by a mutex) so that multiple async tasks — networking, mining, and the web server — can access and update it without requiring an explicit handle to be passed through every call chain.

```
    // Mark referenced inputs as reserved
    let utxo_set = UTXOSet::new(blockchain.clone());
    for input in tx.get_vin() {
        if let Ok(Some(mut outputs)) =
utxo_set.find_utxo_by_txid(input.get_txid()).await
        {
            if input.vout < outputs.len() {
                outputs[input.vout]
                    .set_in_global_mem_pool(true);
            }
        }
    }
    Ok(())
}
```

Listing 109: Mempool — marking inputs as reserved (part 2 of 2)

A quick existence check avoids duplicate processing when the same transaction arrives from multiple peers:

```
pub fn transaction_exists_in_pool(tx: &Transaction) -> bool {
    let tx_id = tx.get_tx_id_hex();
    GLOBAL_MEMORY_POOL.blocking_lock().contains_key(&tx_id)
}
```

Listing 110: Mempool — existence check

The `remove_from_memory_pool` function mirrors the add operation: it removes the transaction and clears the "in-pool" flag from all inputs that reference UTXOs in the blockchain. This reservation flag is checked by coin selection: `find_spendable_outputs` skips any output with `in_global_mem_pool` set to `true`, preventing the same coin from being selected in two concurrent pending transactions.

```
pub async fn remove_from_memory_pool(
    tx: &Transaction,
    blockchain: &BlockchainService,
) -> Result<()> {
    let tx_id = tx.get_tx_id_hex();
    GLOBAL_MEMORY_POOL.lock().await.remove(&tx_id);

    // Unmark referenced inputs
    let utxo_set = UTXOSet::new(blockchain.clone());
    for input in tx.get_vin() {
        if let Ok(Some(mut outputs)) =

utxo_set.find_utxo_by_txid(input.get_txid()).await
        {
            if input.vout < outputs.len() {
                outputs[input.vout]
                    .set_in_global_mem_pool(false);
            }
        }
    }
    Ok(())
}
```

Listing 111: Mempool operations — remove

▷ Note

The mempool is a process-wide in-memory map of `txid -> Transaction` held in a global `Mutex` (`GLOBAL_MEMORY_POOL`). `vin` is the array of inputs (each input pointing at one previous output the transaction wants to spend); `vout` is the array of new outputs the transaction creates. When a transaction is added:

- It is stored in `GLOBAL_MEMORY_POOL`
- Its referenced inputs are marked with `in_global_mem_pool = true` to reserve them locally

When removed (after confirmation):

- It is deleted from the mempool

- Its referenced inputs are unmarked

This reservation mechanism reduces (but does not eliminate) the chance that the node builds conflicting pending spends.

14.7 Step 6: Propagation and Mining Trigger

After mempool admission, a background task propagates the transaction to peers and may trigger mining.

```rust
// Source: context.rs (simplified)
async fn submit_transaction_for_mining(
    &self,
    addr_from: &std::net::SocketAddr,
    tx: Transaction,
) -> Result<()> {
    // Broadcast transaction to peers by sending INV message
    self.send_inv_for_transaction(&tx).await?;

    // If this is a mining node and mempool
    // is large enough, trigger mining
    let mempool_size = self.get_mempool_size()?;
    if self.is_mining_enabled()
        && mempool_size >= TRANSACTION_THRESHOLD
    {
        self.trigger_mining_with_candidate_txs().await?;
    }

    Ok(())
}
```

Listing 112: Background task: submit for mining and relay

▷ **Note**

The background task handles two concerns:

1. **Propagation**: announces the transaction to peers via INV (inventory) message
2. **Mining trigger**: if mining is enabled and mempool exceeds a threshold, initiates mining with the pending transactions. `TRANSACTION_THRESHOLD` is set to 3—a deliberately low value chosen so that mining triggers quickly during development and testing. A production node would raise this to batch more transactions per block, balancing latency against throughput.

> This decoupling (background task) allows the initial mempool submission to return immediately without waiting for network I/O or mining computation.

14.8 Step 7: Mining Boundary — Defensive Verification

Before a transaction can be included in a block, it is verified again at the mining boundary. This second verification is essential: between the time a transaction entered the mempool and the time mining begins, the UTXO set may have changed — a competing block may have been accepted that spends the same outputs. Without re-verification here, the miner could produce a block containing a now-invalid transaction, which every other node would reject.

```
// Source: chainstate.rs
pub async fn mine_block(
    &self,
    transactions: &[Transaction],
) -> Result<Block> {
    // Gate: validate before mutating state.
    for transaction in transactions {
        let is_valid =
transaction.verify(self).await?;
        if !is_valid {
            return Err(BtcError::InvalidTransaction);
        }
    }
```

Listing 113: Mining boundary: pre-lock signature verification (part 1)

After verifying all transaction signatures with a read lock, the function acquires an exclusive write lock to perform stale-mining protection. This re-validates each input under the lock to catch any that were spent by a competing block that arrived between the pre-lock verification and lock acquisition.

```
    // Acquire write lock
    let blockchain_guard = self.0.write().await;

    // Re-validate transaction inputs under the write lock
    // (stale mining protection)
    let db = blockchain_guard.get_db();
    let utxo_tree = db.open_tree("chainstate")?;
    for tx in transactions {
        if tx.is_coinbase() { continue; }
        for input in tx.get_vin() {
            // Verify each input's UTXO still exists...
        }
    }

    // Mining + persistence happens inside the storage layer.
    blockchain_guard.mine_block(transactions).await
}
```

Listing 114: Mining boundary: write-lock and stale-mining protection (part 2)

> ▷ **Note**
>
> **The mining boundary** is the final defensive gate before blocks are created:
> 1. **Pre-lock verification**: each transaction signature is checked before acquiring the exclusive write lock
> 2. **Lock acquisition**: the write lock is taken to ensure atomic block creation
> 3. **Stale-mining protection**: transaction inputs are re-checked under the lock to catch any inputs that were spent by a competing block between pre-lock and lock acquisition
> 4. **Persistence**: only after all checks pass is the block actually persisted and UTXO state updated
>
> If we only verified before taking the write lock, a competing block could arrive between the pre-check and lock acquisition, spending the same in-

> puts. Without the second check, the node would produce a block with already-spent inputs — an invalid block the network would reject. This double-check pattern prevents the node from creating blocks with invalid or already-spent transactions.

14.9 Step 8: Mining Trigger Entry Points

The system decides to start mining in response to two events:

```
// Trigger 1: Mempool size reaches threshold
if is_mining_enabled()
    && get_mempool_size()
        >= TRANSACTION_THRESHOLD
{
    prepare_candidate_txs_and_mine().await?;
}
```

Listing 115: Mining trigger 1: mempool threshold

```
// Trigger 2: Manual/on-demand mining
// (e.g., via API: POST
/api/v1/mining/generatetoaddress)
pub async fn generate_to_address(
    State(node): State<Arc<NodeContext>>,
    Json(req): Json<GenerateToAddressRequest>,
) -> Result<Json<Block>> {
    let block = node
        .mine_block_to_address(&req.address)
        .await?;
    Ok(Json(block))
}
```

Listing 116: Mining trigger 2: on-demand mining (manual trigger)

▷ Note

Mining is triggered in two ways:

1. **Automatic**: when the mempool reaches a size threshold (e.g., during transaction flooding)
2. **On-demand**: via API request or other explicit signals (e.g., "mine now to address X")

Once mining is triggered, the system prepares candidate transactions from the mempool, verifies them, and calls `BlockchainService::mine_block`, which performs the final verification and persistent storage.

14.10 Summary

Key Takeaways

- ✓ **Entry point**: `NodeContext::btc_transaction` orchestrates wallet-side (construction + signing) and node-side (mempool/network) work
- ✓ **Construction**: `Transaction::new_utxo_transaction` selects inputs from UTXO set and creates outputs (payment + optional change)
- ✓ **Signing**: the **trimmed copy pattern** computes signatures without circular self-reference by temporarily injecting locking data, hashing, and signing
- ✓ **Mempool admission**: `process_transaction` checks for duplicates, stores the transaction, and spawns background propagation/mining trigger
- ✓ **Reservation**: the `in_global_mem_pool` flag is set on referenced outputs to reduce local double-selection
- ✓ **Propagation**: asynchronous task sends INV messages to peers to announce the transaction
- ✓ **Mining trigger**: automatic (mempool threshold) or on-demand (API request) initiation of block mining
- ✓ **Mining boundary**: `BlockchainService::mine_block` performs defensive verification before creating and persisting the block
- ✓ **Stale-mining protection**: transaction inputs are re-verified under the write lock to catch competing blocks
- ✓ **Confirmation**: once a block is accepted, its transactions are removed from the mempool

15

Chain: Block Lifecycle and Mining

▷ **What you will learn in this chapter**

- How pending transactions transition to a mined block
- The three critical boundaries: mining verification, persistence, and peer acceptance
- How proof-of-work is performed and why nonce search is necessary
- Where the UTXO set advances after a block connects
- Block relay mechanics: INV, GETDATA, and BLOCK messages

In the previous chapter (Chapter 14, **Transaction Lifecycle**), we followed a transaction from construction and signing, through mempool admission and propagation. That brings us to the natural next question: **what happens to those pending transactions next?** In the previous chapter we followed transactions from creation through mempool admission. Now we answer the next question: what happens when those pending transactions are assembled into a block?

This section traces the rest of the path: how the node assembles a candidate block from the mempool, performs proof-of-work, persists the new tip, advances the UTXO set, and relays the new block to peers. The code is walked through with key methods printed and each listing followed by a succinct explanation of what the code does and why.

The following files are the primary references for this chapter:

- `bitcoin/src/node/miner.rs` — candidate assembly: mempool snapshot, coinbase creation, and the mining trigger
- `bitcoin/src/pow.rs` — the `ProofOfWork` engine: nonce search, target comparison, and difficulty encoding
- `bitcoin/src/primitives/block.rs` — `Block` and `BlockHeader` construction
- `bitcoin/src/chain/chainstate.rs` — block persistence and UTXO set advancement after a block connects
- `bitcoin/src/store/file_system_db_chain.rs` — atomic block-plus-tip write to sled
- `bitcoin/src/net/net_processing.rs` — block relay: INV, GETDATA, and BLOCK message handling

15.1 Scope

This chapter covers **Steps 5–7** of the blockchain pipeline (from transaction to block acceptance): candidate assembly, proof-of-work, persistence, and the UTXO state transition after a block is connected.

15.2 Reader Promise

After reading this section, you should be able to explain—using concrete method names—how the code moves from **pending transactions** to a **mined, persisted, and relayed block**, including where the implementation:

- Builds the candidate transaction list (mempool snapshot + coinbase).
- Constructs a block header and commits to transaction data.
- Performs proof-of-work (the nonce search and the bytes being hashed).
- Persists the new tip and applies the UTXO state transition.
- Announces blocks to peers and handles block download (INV → GETDATA → BLOCK).

Quick Terminology

- **mempool**: an in-memory pool of **accepted transactions** that are **waiting to be included in a block** (implemented here as `GLOBAL_MEMORY_POOL`)
- **coinbase transaction**: by convention, the **first transaction in a block** is a coinbase transaction. It has no real inputs (there are no earlier coins to spend), and it **creates new coins owned by the miner** as the block reward—this is the Bitcoin whitepaper's incentive mechanism (§6: "the first transaction in a block is a special transaction that starts a new coin owned by the creator of the block"). In this implementation it is created with `Transaction::new_coinbase_tx(...)`.
- **tip**: the current best block hash this node considers canonical (the "head" of the chain)
- **blocks tree**: the on-disk key/value store of blocks (hash → serialized block)
- **UTXO set / chainstate**: derived state answering "what outputs are spendable right now?" (stored under the `"chainstate"` tree)
- **INV / GETDATA / BLOCK**: announce an object by id → request bytes → transmit full bytes

The Three Boundaries to Watch For

This section is easiest to follow if you keep three "boundaries" in mind:

- **mining boundary**: the "last step" before doing proof-of-work—every candidate transaction must be verified before we are willing to mine it (`BlockchainService::mine_block`)
- **persistence + state-transition boundary**: the moment a mined block becomes part of our local chain—write the block as the new tip, then update the UTXO set so spendability matches the new tip (`BlockchainFileSystem::mine_block` → `update_utxo_set`)
- **peer acceptance boundary**: the moment we receive a full block from the network and attempt to add it to our chain (`process_stream` handling `Package::Block` → `node_context.add_block`)

Primary Files

i Code locations

- `bitcoin/src/node/miner.rs`
- `bitcoin/src/chain/chainstate.rs`
- `bitcoin/src/store/file_system_db_chain.rs`
- `bitcoin/src/primitives/block.rs`
- `bitcoin/src/pow.rs`
- `bitcoin/src/net/net_processing.rs`

15.3 Block Lifecycle at a Glance (Two Zoom Levels)

High-Level Stages

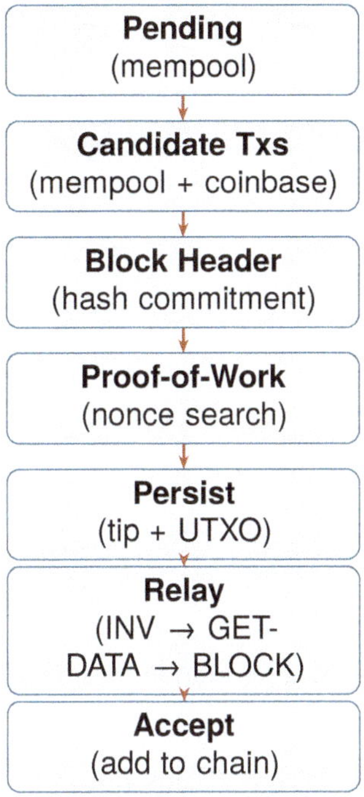

Figure 15.1: Block Lifecycle: From Pending Transactions to Blockchain Acceptance

In this diagram, "selected from the mempool for this block" means a fixed list of transactions the miner will try to include in the next block; those transactions are still unconfirmed until the block is mined and accepted.

Code-Level Call Sequence

Figure 15.2: Mining call sequence and network message flow

15.4 Whitepaper Connections

Timestamp Chaining (Whitepaper §3)

The "timestamp server" concept creates an immutable, chronological chain by linking each block to its predecessor through cryptographic hashing. The key insight is that changing any block would require redoing all subsequent proof-of-work, making the history tamper-resistant.

In this implementation, the proof-of-work hash input includes five components that together create this chain:

```
prev_hash + tx_commitment + timestamp + difficulty +
nonce
```

The `prev_hash` links this block to the previous block's hash, creating the chain structure. Changing any historical block would change its hash, breaking the link and requiring all subsequent blocks to be re-mined. The `tx_commitment` is a hash (simplified Merkle root via `hash_transactions()`) that commits to the exact set of transactions in this block. Changing any transaction would change this commitment, invalidating the block's proof-of-work.

The `timestamp` records when the block was created, providing chronological ordering. It prevents miners from manipulating block ordering by using timestamps from the future, and ensures the chain reflects real-world time progression. The `difficulty` field encodes the target threshold (as `TARGET_BITS`) that determines how hard the proof-of-work must be. This is included in the hash so that changing the difficulty would require re-mining, maintaining consensus on the difficulty adjustment rules.

Finally, the `nonce` is the variable that miners increment during proof-of-work search. It's the only field that changes between hash attempts, allowing miners to search for a hash below the target without changing the block's content.

The first four components are fixed for a given candidate block, while the `nonce` is varied during mining. This means the block header commits to its position in the chain (`prev_hash`), its contents (`tx_commitment`), its creation time (`timestamp`), and the consensus rules (`difficulty`). The resulting block hash serves as both the proof-of-work result and the link that the next block will reference, creating an unbreakable chain.

Proof-of-Work (Whitepaper §4)

Proof-of-work is the mechanism that secures the blockchain by making block creation computationally expensive. The miner's task is to find a nonce value that, when combined with the block header data and hashed, produces a hash value numerically below a predetermined target threshold.

The algorithm works through brute-force search: the miner repeatedly hashes the block header with different nonce values until finding one that satisfies the difficulty requirement. Since hash functions are unpredictable, there's no shortcut—the miner must try many nonce values, making the process computationally intensive.

Here's how the proof-of-work algorithm operates:

```
function mine_block(block_header):
    target = calculate_target(TARGET_BITS)
    nonce = 0

    while nonce < MAX_NONCE:
        data = concatenate(
            block_header.prev_hash,
            block_header.tx_commitment,
            block_header.timestamp,
```

```
            block_header.difficulty_bits,
            nonce
        )
        hash = SHA256(data)
        hash_as_integer = convert_to_integer(hash)

        if hash_as_integer < target:
            return (nonce, hash)
        else:
            nonce = nonce + 1

    return error
```

The key insight is that the first four components of the data (`prev_hash` , `tx_commitment` , `timestamp` , `difficulty_bits`) are fixed for a given candidate block, while the `nonce` is the only variable that changes between attempts. The other header fields — previous hash, transaction commitment, timestamp, difficulty — are fixed for this candidate block. The nonce is the only field the miner varies, so incrementing it is the sole mechanism for producing a different hash output. This allows miners to search through nonce values without altering the block's content or position in the chain. The difficulty target determines how rare a valid hash is—lower targets mean fewer valid hashes exist, requiring more computational work on average.

The difficulty adjusts over time to maintain a consistent block production rate. As more miners join the network and computational power increases, blocks would be mined too quickly if difficulty remained constant. To compensate, the network periodically adjusts the `TARGET_BITS` value (which encodes the difficulty threshold) to make mining harder. When difficulty increases, the target value decreases, meaning miners must find rarer hashes—those with more leading zeros when interpreted as a number. This adjustment typically occurs every few blocks, ensuring that blocks continue to be produced at roughly the intended interval despite changes in total network hash rate.

Incentives (Whitepaper §6)

Mining is rewarded by a coinbase transaction (`Transaction::new_coinbase_tx(...)`). This implementation appends coinbase to the candidate list during `prepare_mining_utxo(...)`.

Merkle Roots vs. Our Simplification (Whitepaper §8)

Bitcoin commits to transactions via a Merkle root in the block header. This implementation uses a simplified `hash_transactions()` commitment (a hash over concatenated transaction ids). That keeps the learning focus on the byte layout and the PoW loop, but it is not a substitute for Merkle proofs.

15.5 Step-by-Step Code Walkthrough

Goal: understand block production and propagation in code: mempool → coinbase → PoW → persist tip → broadcast → peer acceptance path.

Roadmap

- **Step 1**: mining trigger (`should_trigger_mining`) → Listing 117
- **Step 2**: candidate tx list (`prepare_mining_utxo`) → Listing 118
- **Step 3**: mine + announce (`process_mine_block`) → Listing 119
- **Step 3a**: mining boundary verification (`BlockchainService::mine_block`) → Listing 120
- **Step 3b**: block construction + tx commitment (`Block::new_block` , `hash_transactions`) → Listing 121
- **Step 3c**: proof-of-work engine (`ProofOfWork`) → Listing 122
- **Step 3d**: persist new tip + update derived state (`BlockchainFileSystem::mine_block`) → Listing 123
- **Step 3e**: UTXO state transition (`update_utxo_set`) → Listing 124
- **Step 4**: block relay handshake (INV → GETDATA → BLOCK) → Listings 125–127

Whitepaper anchors:

- Section 3 (Timestamp server intuition: linking via previous hash)
- Section 4 (Proof-of-Work)
- Section 5 (Network operation loop: broadcast txs/blocks; accept; build on accepted tip)
- Section 6 (Incentive mechanism: coinbase/subsidy)

Step 1 — Decide Whether to Mine

Mining is only attempted when the node is configured as a miner and the mempool has reached a minimum size.

```
pub fn should_trigger_mining() -> bool {
    // Read mempool size (how many pending transactions we currently have).
    let pool_size = GLOBAL_MEMORY_POOL.len()
        .expect("Memory pool length error");
    // Configuration flag: only nodes explicitly configured as miners should mine.
    let is_miner = GLOBAL_CONFIG.is_miner();
    // Teaching policy: mine only when there is "enough" work and we are a miner.
    // (Production miners build templates continuously and do not wait for a
    // fixed threshold.)
    pool_size >= TRANSACTION_THRESHOLD && is_miner
}
```

Listing 117: Mining trigger (`should_trigger_mining`)

What to notice:

- It checks two conditions—mempool size and "am I a miner?"—and returns a boolean.
- It makes miner scheduling explicit and easy to reason about: the node mines only when there is enough pending work to justify it.

Step 2 — Build Candidate Transaction List

This step constructs the exact list of transactions to be included in the next block.

In this project: The miner takes a snapshot of the entire mempool using `GLOBAL_MEMORY_POOL.get_all()` (the same process-wide map introduced in Chapter 14), which returns all pending transactions without filtering or ordering. There is no fee-based selection or size optimization—this is a simplified learning implementation that prioritizes clarity over production efficiency. Mining is triggered when the mempool contains at least 3 transactions (`TRANSACTION_THRESHOLD = 3` , an arbitrary small number chosen so the system mines often during local testing without firing on every single transaction), and when mining occurs, all transactions in the mempool are included in the candidate block.

In Bitcoin whitepaper: Production miners use sophisticated transaction selection algorithms to maximize revenue. Transactions are selected based on their fee rate (satoshis per byte), with higher fee-rate transactions prioritized. Bitcoin applies the same concept (select from mempool, prepend a coinbase) but adds an optimization: transactions are ranked by fee rate (satoshis per byte) and the highest-fee transactions are included first to maximize miner revenue. This does not change the learning structure. Miners aim to fill blocks up to the size limit (originally 1MB, now approximately 4MB with SegWit) with the most profitable transactions first. The Bitcoin whitepaper doesn't specify a particular selection algorithm, but the economic incentive is clear: "If the output value of a transaction is less than its input value, the difference is a transaction fee that is added to the incentive value of the block containing the transaction" (Whitepaper §6). This creates a fee market where users compete by offering higher fees for faster confirmation.

After selecting transactions, the miner appends a coinbase transaction, creating the candidate transaction list that will be packaged into the new block.

Diagram — candidate assembly (mempool snapshot + coinbase)

```
candidate_txs =
  GLOBAL_MEMORY_POOL.get_all()
  + [Transaction::new_coinbase_tx(mining_address)]
```

```rust
pub async fn prepare_mining_utxo(
    mining_address: &WalletAddress,
    blockchain: &BlockchainService,
) -> Result<Vec<Transaction>> {
    let txs = GLOBAL_MEMORY_POOL.get_all()?;

    // Validate each transaction's inputs are still unspent
    let db = blockchain.get_db().await?;
    let utxo_tree = db.open_tree("chainstate")?;

    let mut valid_txs = Vec::new();
    for tx in txs {
        if tx.is_coinbase() { continue; }
        let mut inputs_valid = true;
        for input in tx.get_vin() {
            match utxo_tree.get(input.get_txid()) {
                Ok(Some(outs_bytes)) => {
                    let outputs: Vec<TXOutput> =
                        decode(outs_bytes)?;
                    if input.get_vout() >= outputs.len() {
                        inputs_valid = false;
                        break;
                    }
                }
                _ => { inputs_valid = false; break; }
            }
        }
        if inputs_valid {
            valid_txs.push(tx);
        } else {
            remove_from_memory_pool(tx, blockchain).await;
        }
    }

    if valid_txs.is_empty() {
        return Err(BtcError::InvalidValueForMiner(
            "No valid transactions to mine".to_string(),
        ));
    }

    let coinbase_tx =
        create_mining_coinbase_transaction(mining_address)?;
    let mut final_txs = valid_txs;
    final_txs.push(coinbase_tx);
    Ok(final_txs)
}
```

What to notice:

- It snapshots the current mempool and validates each transaction's inputs against the UTXO set. This prevents mining blocks with already-spent inputs when a competing block has been accepted during the race between miners.
- Transactions with spent inputs are removed from the mempool (they were already confirmed in a competing block).
- If no valid transactions remain (all were stale), mining is aborted.
- It appends a coinbase transaction, which is the mechanism by which new coins (subsidy) are created for the miner.
- The function is now `async` and accepts a `BlockchainService` parameter for UTXO validation.

> ▷ **Note**
>
> Why does validation happen in `prepare` AND again in `mine_block`? `prepare_mining_utxo` validates with a *read lock*—other operations can proceed concurrently. Between this validation and the actual `mine_block` call (which requires the *write lock*), a competing block may arrive from the network and be processed via `add_block`. That competing block spends the same transaction inputs. If we didn't re-validate under the write lock, we'd mine a block with already-spent inputs—creating a duplicate coinbase subsidy (money from nothing). The second validation in `BlockchainService::mine_block` catches this race condition.

Step 3 — Mine, Persist, and Clean Up Mempool

```
pub async fn process_mine_block(
    txs: Vec<Transaction>,
    blockchain: &BlockchainService,
) -> Result<Block> {
    // Prevent concurrent mining --- only one mining task at a time
    if MINING_IN_PROGRESS
        .compare_exchange(false, true, Ordering::SeqCst,
                                   Ordering::SeqCst)
        .is_err()
    {
        let msg = "Mining already in progress";
        return Err(BtcError::InvalidValueForMiner(
            msg.to_string()));
    }

    // Reset cancellation flag before starting
    reset_mining_cancellation();

    let result = async {
        // Check for cancellation before mining
        // (a competing block may have arrived)
        if is_mining_cancelled() {
            let msg = "Mining cancelled";
            return Err(BtcError::InvalidValueForMiner(
                msg.to_string()));
        }
        // ... (continue to mine_block call)
    }.await;

    MINING_IN_PROGRESS.store(false, Ordering::SeqCst);
    result
}
```

Listing 119: Mine → mempool cleanup → announce (`process_mine_block`)

Step 3a — Mining Boundary Verification

Before a mined block is constructed, every transaction is verified to ensure it is not already spent.

```
pub async fn mine_block(
    &self,
    transactions: &[Transaction]
) -> Result<Block> {
    for tx in transactions {
        let is_valid = tx.verify(self).await?;
        if !is_valid {
            return Err(BtcError::InvalidTransaction);
        }
    }
    // ... (locking mechanism)
    
self.0.write().await.mine_block(transactions).await
}
```

Listing 120: Mining boundary verification (`BlockchainService::mine_block`)

Step 3b — Block Construction and Transaction Commitment

```rust
pub fn new_block(
    pre_block_hash: String,
    transactions: &[Transaction],
    height: usize,
) -> Block {
    let header = BlockHeader {
        timestamp: crate::current_timestamp(),
        pre_block_hash,
        hash: String::new(),
        nonce: 0,
        height,
    };
    let mut block = Block {
        header,
        transactions: transactions.to_vec(),
    };
    // Run PoW to find nonce such that
    // hash < target difficulty
    let pow = ProofOfWork::new_proof_of_work(
        block.clone()
    );
    let (nonce, hash) = pow.run();
    block.header.nonce = nonce;
    block.header.hash = hash;
    block
}
```

Listing 121: Block construction + proof-of-work (`Block::new_block`)

Step 3c — Proof-of-Work Loop

The hash is converted to a big-endian integer and compared numerically against the target threshold. A valid block is one whose header hash, interpreted this way, falls below the target.

```
pub fn run(&self) -> (i64, String) {
    let mut nonce = 0;
    let mut hash = Vec::new();
    while nonce < MAX_NONCE {
        let data = self.prepare_data(nonce);
        hash = crate::sha256_digest(
            data.as_slice());
        let hash_int = BigInt::from_bytes_be(
            Sign::Plus, hash.as_slice());
        if hash_int.lt(self.target.borrow()) {
            // Found valid hash < target difficulty
            break;
        } else {
            nonce += 1;
        }
    }
    (nonce, HEXLOWER.encode(hash.as_slice()))
}
```

Listing 122: Proof-of-work search (`ProofOfWork::run`)

What to notice:

- The nonce starts at 0 and increments by 1 each iteration—a brute-force search over the integer keyspace.
- Each iteration hashes the block header (plus the current nonce) and reads the 256-bit result as a big integer (`BigInt::from_bytes_be`, "big-endian unsigned").
- `hash_int.lt(self.target.borrow())` returns `true` when the hash interpreted as an integer is strictly less than the difficulty target. `.borrow()` hands the comparator a shared reference to the target without moving or cloning the underlying `BigInt` .
- Once a hash below the target is found, the loop breaks and returns the nonce and the hex-encoded hash.

Step 3d — Persist New Tip + Update Derived State

```
pub async fn mine_block(
    &self,
    transactions: &[Transaction]
) -> Result<Block> {
    let best_height = self.get_best_height().await?;
    let block = Block::new_block(
        self.get_tip_hash().await?,
        transactions,
        best_height + 1
    );
    let block_hash = block.get_hash();
    // ... (persist to sled, update tip hash)
    self.update_utxo_set(&block).await?;
    Ok(block)
}
```

Listing 123: Persist block and update state (`BlockchainFileSystem::mine_block`)

Step 3e — UTXO State Transition

```
pub async fn update_utxo_set(
    &self,
    block: &Block
) -> Result<()> {
    // For each transaction in the block:
    for tx in block.get_transactions() {
        // Remove spent outputs (coinbase has no inputs)
        if !tx.is_coinbase() {
            for input in tx.get_vin() {
                self.spend_output(
                    input.get_txid(),
                    input.get_vout()
                ).await?;
            }
        }
        // Add newly created outputs
        for (idx, output) in
            tx.get_vout().iter().enumerate()
        {
            self.add_unspent_output(
                tx.get_id_bytes(),
                idx,
                output
            ).await?;
        }
    }
    Ok(())
}
```

Listing 124: UTXO set update after block (`update_utxo_set`)

Step 4 — Block Relay Handshake

Blocks propagate over the P2P network using a three-message pattern: INV (announce), GETDATA (request), and BLOCK (deliver).

```
pub async fn broadcast_new_block(
    block: &Block
) -> Result<()> {
    // Get all connected peers
    let peers = GLOBAL_NODES.get_nodes()?;
    for peer in peers {
        // Spawn a task to send INV to each peer
        let block_hash = block.get_hash();
        tokio::spawn(async move {
            send_inv(
                &peer.get_addr(),
                OpType::Block,
                &[block_hash.into_bytes()]
            ).await;
        });
    }
    Ok(())
}
```

Listing 125: Announce new block (`broadcast_new_block`)

```
pub async fn send_inv(
    addr_to: &SocketAddr,
    op_type: OpType,
    items: &[Vec<u8>],
) {
    send_data(addr_to, Package::Inv {
        addr_from: GLOBAL_CONFIG.get_node_addr(),
        op_type,
        items: items.to_vec(),
    }).await;
}

pub async fn send_get_data(
    addr_to: &SocketAddr,
    op_type: OpType,
    id: &[u8],
) {
    send_data(addr_to, Package::GetData {
        addr_from: GLOBAL_CONFIG.get_node_addr(),
        op_type,
        id: id.to_vec(),
    }).await;
}

pub async fn send_block(
    addr_to: &SocketAddr,
    block: &Block,
) {
    send_data(addr_to, Package::Block {
        addr_from: GLOBAL_CONFIG.get_node_addr(),
        block: block.serialize()
            .expect("Serialization error"),
    }).await;
}
```

Listing 126: P2P broadcast primitives (`send_inv`, `send_get_data`, `send_block`)

```
// Source: bitcoin/src/net/net_processing.rs
match pkg {
    // Peer says: "I have block_hash"
    Package::Inv {
        addr_from,
        op_type: OpType::Block,
        items
    } => {
        let block_hash = items.first()
            .expect("INV items empty");
        // Request the full block bytes
        send_get_data(
            &addr_from,
            OpType::Block,
            block_hash
        ).await;
    }

    // Peer sends: full block bytes
    Package::Block {
        addr_from,
        block
    } => {
        let block = Block::deserialize(
            block.as_slice())
            .expect("Block deserialization error");
        // Validate and add to blockchain
        node_context.add_block(&block).await
            .expect("Blockchain write error");
    }

    _ => {}
}
```

Listing 127: P2P receive: block from peer (`process_stream` , block arms)

15.6 Summary

Key Takeaways

- ✓ Pending transactions in the mempool are selected and combined with a coinbase transaction to form a candidate block.
- ✓ The mining boundary enforces that all transactions are valid before any proof-of-work is attempted.
- ✓ Proof-of-work is a nonce search where miners increment a counter until the block header hashes to a value below the target threshold.
- ✓ The persistence boundary updates the blockchain tip and advances the UTXO set only after mining succeeds.
- ✓ Block relay uses a three-message INV/GETDATA/BLOCK pattern to efficiently propagate blocks across the network without requiring all peers to simultaneously download each block.

16

Chain: Consensus and Validation

▷ **What you will learn in this chapter**

- How consensus is implemented: validation (local correctness) vs. fork choice (global rules)
- The critical "accept only if valid and not already spent" gate (Step 5 from the whitepaper)
- Transaction signature verification and proof-of-work validation
- Fork choice hierarchy: height, cumulative work, and deterministic tie-breaks
- How reorganizations roll back and re-apply UTXO state
- Double-spend protection through the UTXO set membership test

A block arrives over the network. Your node has milliseconds to decide: is it valid, or is it an attack? If it's valid and doesn't conflict with what you've already accepted, you add it to your chain. If it's invalid, you discard it and disconnect from the peer who sent it. If it conflicts with your current chain but has more cumulative proof-of-work, you reorganize your chain to follow it instead. This decision boundary is the heart of consensus. This chapter covers two complementary concepts: *validation* (is this block internally correct?) and *fork choice* (when multiple competing chains exist, which one is canonical?). Together they form the consensus mechanism that all nodes use to converge on a single authoritative history. This section shows you the two halves: **validation** (local correctness checks) and **fork choice** (which competing history to follow when ambiguity arises).

Three primary code locations are used:

- `bitcoin/src/primitives/transaction.rs` (transaction construction, signing, verification)
- `bitcoin/src/pow.rs` + `bitcoin/src/primitives/block.rs` (proof-of-work and block construction)
- `bitcoin/src/store/file_system_db_chain.rs` (block insertion, fork choice, reorg, UTXO maintenance)

16.1 Scope

This chapter covers the rules behind **Steps 3 and 8** of the blockchain pipeline (from transaction to block acceptance): transaction validity checks and the block acceptance boundary (validate → connect).

16.2 Conceptual Model: What "Consensus" Means

The following distinction is used throughout the chapter:

- **Validation (local correctness checks)**: "Is this object internally consistent and authorized?" Examples: transaction signatures verify; a block contains exactly one coinbase transaction; a block hash satisfies proof-of-work.
- **Consensus / fork choice (global convergence rule)**: "Given multiple competing histories, which one is canonical?" In Bitcoin, the rule is "the chain with the most cumulative proof-of-work wins." In this learning implementation, fork choice is modeled as a deterministic hierarchy: **height → cumulative work → hash tie-break**.

The most important engineering rule is the Step 5 gate from the whitepaper (§5): **do not mutate durable chain state (tip + UTXO set) unless the block is valid and its spends are not already spent**. When this boundary is violated, you can "mint" money or accept double-spends even if proof-of-work is present elsewhere.

16.3 Acceptance Boundary Diagram

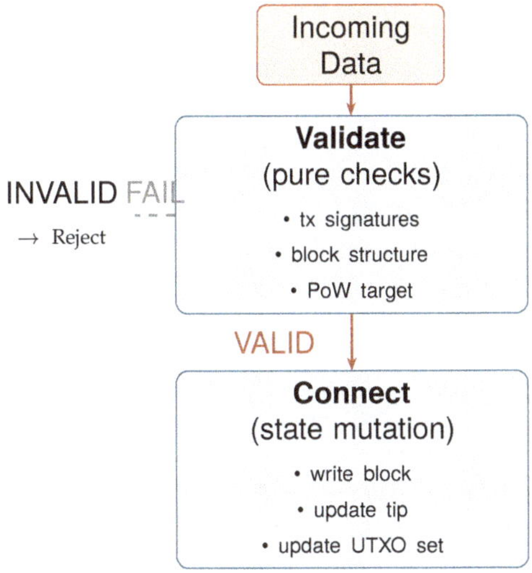

Figure 16.1: Consensus Acceptance Boundary: Validate Then Connect

In the current codebase, transaction signature verification is implemented and used during mining. The full Step 5 block acceptance gate is explicitly noted as a FIXME in `BlockchainFileSystem::add_block` and is explored further in the dedicated Step 5 chapter.

> ▲ **Warning**
>
> The current implementation does **not** consistently enforce the Bitcoin whitepaper's Step 5 contract ("**valid AND not already spent**") as a hard **Validate → Connect** gate for inbound blocks before mutating durable state (tip + UTXO set). For the concrete "what's missing + how to implement it" deep dive, read **Chapter 19 (Whitepaper Step 5: Block Acceptance)**.

16.4 Transaction Validation (Signature Verification)

Validation is performed in `Transaction::verify(...)`. Conceptually, this method answers:

> "Does each input prove authorization to spend the referenced previous output?"

It reconstructs the signed digest for each input and then verifies the Schnorr signature against the input's public key.

```
pub async fn verify(
    &self,
    blockchain: &BlockchainService
) -> Result<bool> {
    if self.is_coinbase() {
        return Ok(true);
    }
    let mut trimmed_self_copy = self.trimmed_copy();
    for (idx, vin) in self.vin.iter().enumerate() {
        let current_vin_tx = blockchain
            .find_transaction(vin.get_txid())
            .await??;
        // ... (set up trimmed copy with
        // previous output's pub_key_hash)
        trimmed_self_copy.id =
            trimmed_self_copy.hash()?;
        // Verify Schnorr signature against
        // reconstructed digest
        let verify = schnorr_sign_verify(
            vin.get_pub_key(),
            vin.get_signature(),
            trimmed_self_copy.get_id(),
        );
        if !verify {
            return Ok(false);
        }
    }
    Ok(true)
}
```

Listing 128: Transaction validity (signature verification) (`Transaction::verify`)

What to notice:

- For each input, the code looks up the referenced previous transaction to pull the locking data.
- The digest being verified is a "trimmed copy" digest (signatures don't sign themselves).
- Coinbase transactions short-circuit verification.

Whitepaper mapping:

- §2: signatures enforce the chain of ownership for spent outputs.

16.5 Proof-of-Work and Block Construction

Mining is implemented at two layers:

- `BlockchainService::mine_block(...)` performs a simple "do not mine invalid txs" gate.
- `BlockchainFileSystem::mine_block(...)` constructs the block on the current tip and updates the UTXO set.

In addition, block construction itself (`Block::new_block`) runs proof-of-work using `ProofOfWork::run` .

Mining-time validation gate code: `bitcoin/src/chain/chainstate.rs`

Before a mined block is constructed, `BlockchainService::mine_block` verifies each transaction:

```
pub async fn mine_block(
    &self,
    transactions: &[Transaction]
) -> Result<Block> {
    for tx in transactions {
        let is_valid = tx.verify(self).await?;
        if !is_valid {
            return Err(BtcError::InvalidTransaction);
        }
    }
    // ... (locking mechanism)
    self.0.write().await.mine_block(transactions).await
}
```

Listing 129: Mining-time validation gate (`BlockchainService::mine_block`)

```
1  pub async fn mine_block(
2      &self,
3      transactions: &[Transaction]
4  ) -> Result<Block> {
5      let best_height = self.get_best_height().await?;
6      let block = Block::new_block(
7          self.get_tip_hash().await?,
8          transactions,
9          best_height + 1
10     );
11     let block_hash = block.get_hash();
12     // ... (persist to sled, update tip hash, UTXO set)
13     Ok(block)
14 }
```

Listing 130: Block mining (construct + update state) (`BlockchainFileSystem::mine_block`)

The `// ...` comment on line 10 hides three operations that must succeed atomically: (1) persist the raw block bytes to sled, (2) update the tip-hash pointer so subsequent queries see the new chain head, and (3) apply the block's transactions to the UTXO set, consuming spent outputs and creating new ones. If the process crashes between any two of these steps, the chain is left in an inconsistent state — which is why the storage layer wraps them in a sled transaction (see Chapter 12, Listing 70).

```rust
pub fn new_block(
    pre_block_hash: String,
    transactions: &[Transaction],
    height: usize,
) -> Block {
    let header = BlockHeader {
        timestamp: crate::current_timestamp(),
        pre_block_hash,
        hash: String::new(),
        nonce: 0,
        height,
    };
    let mut block = Block {
        header,
        transactions: transactions.to_vec(),
    };
    // Run PoW to find nonce such that
    // hash < target difficulty
    let pow = ProofOfWork::new_proof_of_work(
        block.clone()
    );
    let (nonce, hash) = pow.run();
    block.header.nonce = nonce;
    block.header.hash = hash;
    block
}
```

Listing 131: Block construction + proof-of-work (`Block::new_block`)

The inner loop converts the SHA-256 output to a big integer using `BigInt::from_bytes_be` (*big-endian*, i.e., most-significant byte first) before comparing it to the target. SHA-256 emits its 32 output bytes in the order $h_0, h_1, \ldots, h_{31}$ where h_0 is the high-order byte; reading that buffer big-endian produces the same numeric value Bitcoin's protocol convention treats as "the hash." The comparison `hash_int < target` is a single 256-bit integer comparison—no per-byte logic required.

```
pub fn run(&self) -> (i64, String) {
    let mut nonce = 0;
    let mut hash = Vec::new();
    while nonce < MAX_NONCE {
        let data = self.prepare_data(nonce);
        hash = crate::sha256_digest(
            data.as_slice());
        let hash_int = BigInt::from_bytes_be(
            Sign::Plus, hash.as_slice());
        if hash_int.lt(self.target.borrow()) {
            // Found valid hash < target difficulty
            break;
        } else {
            nonce += 1;
        }
    }
    (nonce, HEXLOWER.encode(hash.as_slice()))
}
```

Listing 132: Proof-of-work loop (`ProofOfWork::run`)

What to notice:

- Mining path is defensive: it refuses to mine invalid transactions.
- This is not a substitute for Step 5 acceptance on inbound blocks (network blocks still need a hard gate).

Whitepaper mapping:

- §5 steps 2–4: nodes collect transactions and work on PoW; mining should build on valid transactions.

16.6 Block Acceptance and Fork Choice

Fork-choice and block acceptance code: `bitcoin/src/store/file_system_db_chain.rs`

The acceptance point for inbound blocks is the storage layer's `add_block(...)` function. This is where:

- the block is inserted into sled,
- the tip may or may not update,
- consensus/tie-breaking and reorg logic runs.

Because this chapter is intended to stand alone, we print the method in full. While reading it, pay special attention to two boundaries:

- **DB insertion vs. consensus decision**: the sled transaction closure is synchronous, while the fork-choice logic is async and runs afterwards. All received blocks are stored in the database as candidates, even if they are not yet accepted as the canonical tip. This is intentional: retaining non-canonical blocks allows future reorganizations to walk both branches of a fork.
- **Validation gate (FIXME)**: the method currently contains a whitepaper Step 5 FIXME ("accept only if all txs valid and not already spent") that must be enforced before state mutation in a production node.

```rust
pub async fn add_block(
    &mut self,
    new_block: &Block
) -> Result<()> {
    let block_tree = self.blockchain.db
        .open_tree(self.get_blocks_tree_path())?;

    // 1) Empty chain: first block always becomes tip
    if self.is_empty() { /* ... accept and update UTXO ... */ }

    // 2) Dedup: skip if already present
    if block_tree.get(new_block.get_hash())?
        .is_some()
    { return Ok(()); }

    // 3) Persist inside sled transaction (block is now in DB
    // regardless of fork choice)
    block_tree.transaction(|tx| {
        tx.insert(
            new_block.get_hash(),
            new_block.serialize()?
        )
    })?;

    // 4) Fork-choice: three-level consensus hierarchy
    let current_tip = self.get_tip_hash().await?;
    let current_height = self.get_best_height().await?;

    match new_block.get_height()
        .cmp(&current_height)
    {
        Ordering::Greater => {
            if new_block.get_pre_block_hash()
                == current_tip
            {
                // Normal case: extends our current chain
                self.set_tip_hash(
                    new_block.get_hash()).await?;
                self.update_utxo_set(new_block).await?;
            } else {
                // FORK: reorganize to rollback old
                // branch's UTXO
                self.reorganize_chain(
                    new_block.get_hash()).await?;
            }
        }
```

Key design decisions in `add_block`:

> **i Key design decisions**
>
> - **The fork-choice dispatch uses `Ordering`.** `height.cmp(&other)` returns one of three variants— `Greater`, `Equal`, or `Less` —which the `match` arms handle explicitly. This is Rust's idiomatic way to compare two values without if/else chains: each arm names exactly which case it handles, so the compiler refuses to compile a comparison that forgets one branch. `reorganize_chain(...)` is the routine that handles the harder case when the new block's parent is *not* the current tip: it walks back to the common ancestor of the two branches, rolls back UTXO state along the old branch, then re-applies blocks along the new branch.
> - **Step 3 inserts the block BEFORE fork-choice runs.** This means ALL received blocks end up in the database, even if they're rejected by consensus. This is intentional— `find_common_ancestor()` needs to walk both branches during future reorganizations, and it can only do so if the blocks are in the DB.
> - **`Ordering::Greater` checks for forks.** A higher-height block might be on a DIFFERENT branch (its `pre_block_hash` —the hash of its parent—does not match our current tip). This can happen when block relay delivers blocks out of order. Without the fork check, the old branch's UTXO (including coinbase subsidies) would never be rolled back—creating money from nothing.
> - **`Ordering::Less` blocks are retained, not deleted.** During `rollback_to_block()`, blocks are also NOT deleted from the database. This ensures `find_common_ancestor()` always works, matching Bitcoin Core's behavior where all blocks are kept in `blk*.dat` files regardless of whether they are on the active chain.

What to notice:

- This is the canonical "fork-choice" boundary in this codebase: it may update tip and may reorganize.
- UTXO updates happen when the code decides the new block/branch is canonical.
- **`Ordering::Greater` now detects forks**: If a higher-height block's parent does NOT match our current tip, it is on a different branch. The code calls `reorganize_chain()` instead of directly updating the tip. Without this, the old branch's UTXO (including coinbase subsidies) would remain, creating money from nothing.

- **`Ordering::Less` blocks are retained**: Blocks at lower heights are stored in the DB (by the Sled transaction) but not accepted as the tip. They remain available for `find_common_ancestor()` during future reorganizations. Rolled-back blocks are also never deleted from the database.
- **Block relay**: When the `Package::Block` handler in `net_processing.rs` processes a new block, it relays the block's `Inv` to all peers (except the sender). This ensures blocks propagate across multi-hop network topologies, not just to the miner's direct neighbors.

Whitepaper mapping:

- §5 (Step 6): nodes express acceptance by working on the next block (i.e., building on the chosen tip).
- §11: the whole explains why "more work" makes history harder to rewrite (fork-choice must be deterministic).

Cumulative Work and Deterministic Tie-Break

Fork choice needs a notion of "how strong is this branch?" In Bitcoin this is "cumulative proof-of-work". In this codebase, that is computed by walking parent links back to genesis and summing each block's `get_work()` value. Each block's work value is derived from its difficulty target — blocks with lower targets (harder to mine) have higher work values. The sum of all blocks' work along a chain quantifies the total computational investment in that chain.

```
pub async fn get_chain_work(
    &self,
    block_hash: &str
) -> Result<u64> {
    let mut work = 0u64;
    let mut current_hash = block_hash.to_string();
    // Walk backwards through parent links,
    // summing each block's work value
    while let Some(block) = self
        .get_block(current_hash.as_bytes()).await?
    {
        work += block.get_work();
        current_hash = block.get_pre_block_hash();
        // ... (break at genesis)
    }
    Ok(work)
}
```

Listing 134: Cumulative chain work (`BlockchainFileSystem::get_chain_work`)

When two blocks have the same height but are *not* direct parent/child, the code treats them as a fork and compares chains.

```
Ordering::Equal => {
    if new_block.get_pre_block_hash()
        == current_tip
    {
        return Ok(());
    }
    let current_work = self
        .get_chain_work(&current_tip).await?;
    // ... (ensure block in DB for traversal)
    let new_work = self
        .get_chain_work(
            new_block.get_hash()).await?;
    match new_work.cmp(&current_work) {
        Ordering::Greater => {
            self.reorganize_chain(
                new_block.get_hash()).await?;
        }
        Ordering::Equal if self
            .accept_new_block_tie_break(
                new_block,
                &current_tip
            ).await? => {
            self.reorganize_chain(
                new_block.get_hash()).await?;
        }
        _ => { /* reject or clean up */ }
    }
}
```

Listing 135: Equal-height competitors (compute work, then reorganize or reject)

What to notice:

- Height alone is not enough when forks happen at the same depth; the code explicitly computes "cumulative work".
- The project temporarily inserts blocks so `get_chain_work(...)` can traverse a chain that exists in the DB (this is a pragmatic learning-implementation trick, not a production approach).

Deterministic Tie-Break

When work is equal, the project resolves the fork deterministically by comparing hashes:

```
async fn accept_new_block_tie_break(
    &self,
    new_block: &Block,
    current_tip: &str,
) -> Result<bool> {
    let current_block = self
        .get_block(current_tip.as_bytes())
        .await??;
    // Deterministic tie-break: lexicographic hash
    // ordering
    Ok(new_block.get_hash_string()
        > current_block.get_hash_string())
}
```

Listing 136: Deterministic tie-break (lexicographic hash ordering)

What to notice:

- This is not "Bitcoin's exact rule"; it is a deterministic rule chosen so all nodes converge the same way in this teaching implementation.

Reorganization: Rollback to Common Ancestor

If a stronger branch wins (higher work or tie-break), the project reorganizes:

```
pub async fn reorganize_chain(
    &mut self,
    new_tip_hash: &str
) -> Result<()> {
    let current_tip = self.get_tip_hash().await?;
    let ancestor = self
        .find_common_ancestor(
            &current_tip,
            new_tip_hash
        ).await??;
    // Rollback UTXO effects from old tip back
    // to ancestor
    self.rollback_to_block(&ancestor).await?;
    self.apply_chain_from_ancestor(
        &ancestor,
        new_tip_hash
    ).await?;
    Ok(())
}
```

Listing 137: Reorganization contract (rollback to common ancestor, then apply new branch)

Because this chapter is intended to be repo-independent, we also include the two stateful helpers that make reorgs correct:

- `rollback_to_block(...)` (remove blocks from the old tip back to the ancestor and rollback UTXO effects)
- `update_utxo_set(...)` (incrementally apply UTXO changes for blocks on the winning branch)

In production systems these functions must be carefully audited: any mismatch between "block history" and "UTXO state" is a consensus failure. Reorganization is a three-step process: (1) find the block both chains have in common (the common ancestor), (2) reverse the UTXO changes from the old chain back to the ancestor, and (3) apply the UTXO changes from the ancestor forward on the new chain. The actual block data is never deleted — blocks remain in the database regardless of canonical status.

What to notice:

- "Fork-choice" is not just "pick a tip hash"; it requires derived state (UTXO set) to be rolled back and re-applied to remain consistent.
- This is the concrete embodiment of the whitepaper's claim that nodes follow the strongest chain (and that later blocks can cause reorganization).

16.7 Double-Spending: The Core Protection

The double-spend problem is simple to state and easy to accidentally reintroduce in code:

- An attacker creates two different transactions that spend the **same outpoint** $(txid, vout)$.
- If different peers accept different spends (even temporarily), your node's notion of "balance" and "ownership" becomes inconsistent.

In our implementation, the core protection is: **only mutate the canonical chain tip + UTXO set after we are sure the block is valid.**

Diagram: Conflicting Spends of the Same Outpoint

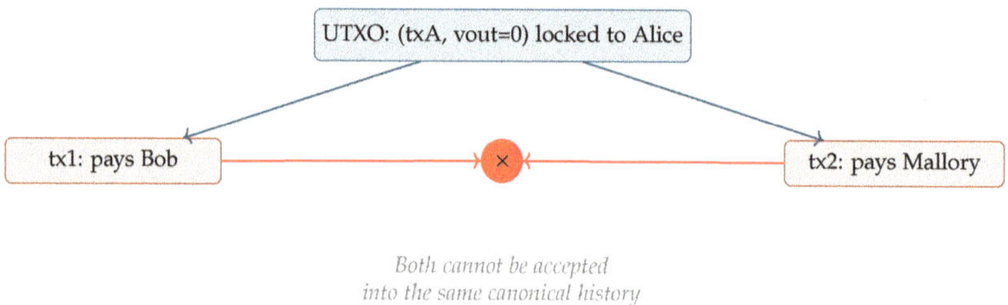

Figure 16.2: Double-spending conflict: UTXO can only be spent once

Where the Protection Lives in Code

- **Transaction-level check:** `Transaction::verify(...)` proves authorization (signatures).
- **State-level check:** the UTXO set determines whether an outpoint is **already spent.**
- **Block-level gate:** `BlockchainFileSystem::add_block(...)` is where "accept only if..." must hold before updating tip/UTXO.

For the whitepaper-aligned "Validate → Connect" explanation (Step 5), continue to:

- **Block Acceptance (Whitepaper §5, Step 5)**

16.8 Simplifications and Missing Features

These whitepaper or Bitcoin Core features are intentionally simplified:

- Difficulty retargeting (`TARGET_BITS` is constant).
- Full Merkle tree verification.
- Full mempool policy and conflict tracking.
- Robust fork reorg logic in normal operation.

16.9 Reorganizations and Chain Rewriting

In Bitcoin, nodes sometimes learn about a competing branch that becomes "better" (more cumulative work). When that happens, the node must **reorganize**:

1. Find the common ancestor of the old tip and the new tip.
2. Undo state changes from blocks that are no longer on the best chain.
3. Apply blocks on the winning branch in order.

In practical terms, a correct reorg requires the ability to **roll back and re-apply UTXO updates** deterministically. Our codebase contains a reorg path (`reorganize_chain` plus UTXO rollback/apply helpers).

Critical rule: rolled-back blocks are **never deleted** from the database. They remain as non-canonical entries so that `find_common_ancestor()` can always walk both branches during future reorganizations. This matches Bitcoin Core's behavior where all blocks are kept in `blk*.dat` files.

Critical implementation details for correct reorgs:

- **UTXO rollback for fully-spent transactions**: When `rollback_block()` restores a spent output, the original transaction's UTXO entry may have been completely removed from the database (because all its outputs were spent). The code handles this by creating a fresh vector when the entry is missing, rather than silently losing the output. Without this, coins would be permanently lost during reorganization.
- **Reverse transaction order**: During rollback, transactions are processed newest-first (reverse order). This correctly handles intra-block dependencies where a later transaction spends an earlier transaction's output within the same block.
- **Blocks are never deleted during rollback**: The `rollback_to_block()` method only rolls back the UTXO set and moves the tip pointer — it does NOT delete blocks from the database. Rolled-back blocks must remain available for `find_common_ancestor()` to work during future reorganizations. This matches Bitcoin Core's behavior where all blocks stay in `blk*.dat` files.

16.10 Multi-Node Consensus

When multiple miners compete in a multi-node network, several additional mechanisms ensure correct consensus:

Block Relay

When a node receives a block and it is **new** (not already in the database), the node relays the block's `Inv` to all its peers (except the sender). This ensures blocks propagate across the full network, not just one hop from the miner. Without relay, in a linear topology ($1 \to 2 \to 3 \to 4 \to 5 \to 6 \to 7$), a block mined by Node 4 would only reach Nodes 3 and 5 — the rest of the network would never see it.

The `block_is_new` check prevents infinite relay loops where nodes keep forwarding the same block back and forth.

Mining Concurrency and Cancellation

When transactions arrive at a node, mining is triggered in a background task. Two guards prevent problems:

1. **`MINING_IN_PROGRESS` flag**: Prevents concurrent mining tasks from running simultaneously on the same node.
2. **`MINING_CANCELLED` flag**: Set by the `Package::Block` handler when a competing block arrives. Checked before mining starts — if a competing block was already accepted, mining is aborted.

Critical rule: Cancellation is NEVER checked after `mine_block()` completes. Once the block is created and added to the local chain, it MUST be broadcast. Skipping the broadcast would leave an unbroadcast block in the node's chain, creating a permanent fork where this node has a block nobody else knows about.

Stale Mining Protection

Between `prepare_mining_utxo()` (which validates transaction inputs with a read lock) and the actual `mine_block()` call (which requires the write lock), a competing block may be accepted — spending the same transaction inputs. The `chainstate.rs` wrapper re-validates all inputs under the write lock just before mining. If any inputs are already spent, mining is aborted with a "stale mining" error. Without this check, the node would create a block with already-spent inputs, and `update_utxo_set` would silently add the coinbase transaction — creating money from nothing.

16.11 Whitepaper Connections

Network Operation Steps (Whitepaper §5)

The whitepaper's Section 5 lists the "network operation" loop. In this codebase, the closest mapping is:

1. **New transactions are broadcast**: Entry point: `NodeContext::process_transaction(...)`. Propagation primitive: `send_inv(...)` in `bitcoin/src/net/net_processing.rs`
2. **Nodes collect new transactions into a block**: `miner::prepare_mining_utxo(...)` pulls from `GLOBAL_MEMORY_POOL`
3. **Nodes work on proof-of-work**: `ProofOfWork::run()` in `bitcoin/src/pow.rs`
4. **When a node finds PoW, it broadcasts the block**: `send_inv(...)` announces the new block hash
5. **Nodes accept the block only if all transactions are valid and not already spent**: This is the Step 5 acceptance gate. In this book, it's covered explicitly in **Block Acceptance (Whitepaper §5, Step 5)**
6. **Nodes express acceptance by working on the next block**: Mining continues on the best tip selected by `add_block(...)` logic.

Security Analysis (Whitepaper §11)

The whitepaper's Section 11 quantifies the "attacker catching up" probability. You don't need the exact math to understand the implementation impact:

- **More confirmed blocks → harder to rewrite history** because rewriting requires redoing PoW from the fork point forward.
- **Chain selection must be deterministic** across nodes (height/work/tie-break) or the network will diverge.
- **Step 5 correctness is non-negotiable**: if we accept invalid spends or double-spends, PoW cannot "save" the system.

16.12 Summary

Key Takeaways

- ✓ Consensus requires both *validation* (local correctness checks) and *fork choice* (global history selection).
- ✓ Transaction validity is checked via signature verification; the node confirms that each input is authorized to spend the referenced output.
- ✓ Block acceptance uses a three-level fork-choice rule: height $\times$ cumulative work $\times$ deterministic tie-break.
- ✓ Reorganizations require rolling back the UTXO set to the common ancestor, then re-applying state changes on the new branch.
- ✓ Double-spend protection depends on the UTXO set membership test: an outpoint is spendable only if it exists in the UTXO set.
- ✓ The critical Step 5 gate ("valid and not already spent") is currently incomplete and is the subject of Chapter 19.

17

Chain: Node Orchestration

▷ What you will learn in this chapter

- What a blockchain node is and how it maintains its own copy of the blockchain
- Node orchestration: the coordination layer that wires subsystems together
- Global singletons: `GLOBAL_MEMORY_POOL`, `GLOBAL_NODES`, `GLOBAL_BLOCKS_IN_TRANSIT`
- How `NodeContext` serves as the central coordination API
- Runtime event flow: web/network messages route to the right handlers
- How background tasks (broadcast, mining) run concurrently with API responses

In the Transaction Lifecycle (Chapter 14), Block Lifecycle (Chapter 15), and Consensus (Chapter 16) chapters, we studied individual subsystems in isolation. This chapter answers the integration question: how do these pieces coordinate at runtime? Previous chapters explored how transactions are constructed and signed (Chapter 14), how blocks are mined and persisted (Chapter 15), and how the UTXO set tracks spendable outputs (Chapter 13). But how does all of this come together at runtime? How does a node coordinate between incoming network messages, the mempool, mining operations, and blockchain state updates?

17.1 What Is a Node?

A blockchain node is a running instance of the blockchain software that maintains its own local copy of the blockchain, validates transactions and blocks, participates in the peer-to-peer network, and (optionally) mines new blocks.

A crucial distributed systems concept: **each node stores its own complete copy of the blockchain** (as seen in Chapter 20, where `BlockchainFileSystem` persists blocks to a local sled database). Nodes synchronize by exchanging blocks and transactions over the network, but each node's storage is independent—there's no central database that all nodes share. This decentralization makes blockchains resilient: even if some nodes go offline, others continue operating with their own copies.

In this implementation, a node is the complete runtime system that coordinates blockchain state (stored locally in `BlockchainFileSystem`), transaction mempool, network communication, and mining operations.

17.2 Node Orchestration

Node orchestration is the coordination layer that wires these subsystems together—it routes network messages to the right handlers, manages shared state (like the mempool and peer list), coordinates between mining and network propagation, and ensures all components work together as a cohesive system. Think of it as the "conductor" that directs when and how different parts of the node interact.

This section walks through the **node orchestration layer**—the code that wires everything together and makes the blockchain node function as a cohesive system, tracing how external events (network messages, API requests) flow through the system, how global state is managed, and how different subsystems coordinate their work.

What you'll learn: How the node runtime coordinates blockchain operations, how global singletons manage shared state, how `NodeContext` serves as the central coordination point, and how network messages route into the appropriate subsystems. After reading, you'll understand the complete runtime architecture and be able to trace any operation from entry point to completion.

i Primary code files

- `bitcoin/src/node/server.rs` — global singletons and TCP server loop
- `bitcoin/src/node/context.rs` — central coordination API (`NodeContext`)
- `bitcoin/src/net/net_processing.rs` — network message routing and handling
- `bitcoin/src/node/txmempool.rs` — mempool management
- `bitcoin/src/node/miner.rs` — mining coordination

17.3 Scope

This chapter covers the **orchestration layer** that coordinates **Steps 4–8** of the blockchain pipeline (from transaction to block acceptance): how web/network events route into mempool admission, mining triggers, propagation, and block acceptance. While previous chapters focused on *what* happens (transaction lifecycle, block mining), this chapter focuses on *how* it all connects at runtime.

17.4 Runtime Event Flow Diagram

This diagram shows how external events flow through the orchestration layer and get routed to the appropriate subsystems:

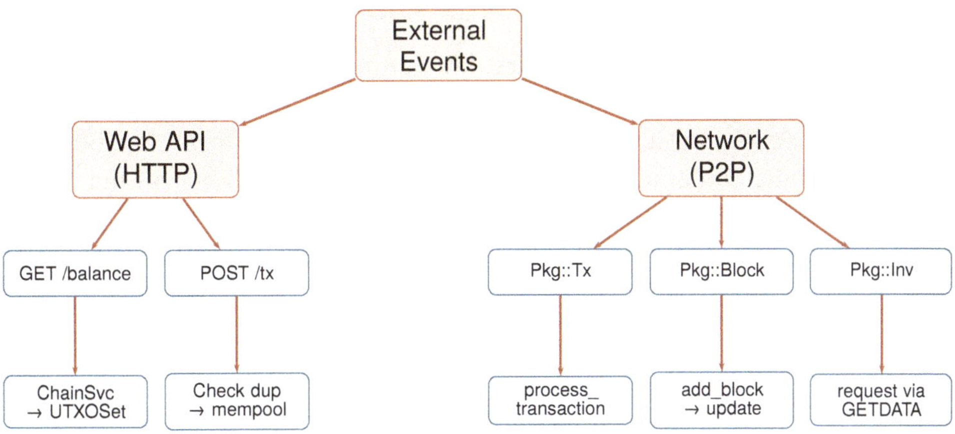

Figure 17.1: Node Orchestration: Event Routing Through Web API and Network Layers

What this diagram shows: The orchestration layer (`NodeContext` and `process_stream`) acts as a **message router and coordinator** that:

- **Receives events from multiple sources**: Web API requests (HTTP handlers) and network messages (P2P peers) arrive concurrently and need routing to the right handlers.
- **Routes events to appropriate subsystems**:
  - Transaction events → mempool admission (`add_to_memory_pool`) → background broadcast/mining
  - Block events → blockchain validation (`add_block`) → mempool cleanup → chain state update
  - Query events → blockchain reads (`get_balance`, `get_blockchain_height`) → UTXO set queries
- **Coordinates background work asynchronously**: Long-running operations (network broadcast, mining) are spawned as separate tasks using `tokio::spawn` , allowing the node to respond immediately to API requests while background work continues.
- **Manages shared state**: Global singletons (`GLOBAL_MEMORY_POOL`, `GLOBAL_NODES`, `GLOBAL_BLOCKS_IN_TRANSIT`) are accessed by multiple subsystems concurrently, and the orchestration layer ensures consistent access patterns.
- **Handles concurrency**: Multiple peers can send messages simultaneously, multiple API requests can arrive concurrently, and mining/broadcast tasks run in parallel—the orchestration layer coordinates all of this safely.

17.5 Node Architecture at a Glance

Before diving into the code, we first lay out the big picture. A blockchain node is fundamentally a **coordinator** that manages multiple subsystems: blockchain state, transaction mempool, network communication, and mining operations. Understanding how these pieces fit together will make our detailed code walkthrough much easier to follow.

High-Level Architecture Diagram

This diagram shows the overall architecture: external interfaces communicate with `NodeContext` , which coordinates between subsystems, and all persistent state ultimately lives in the storage layer.

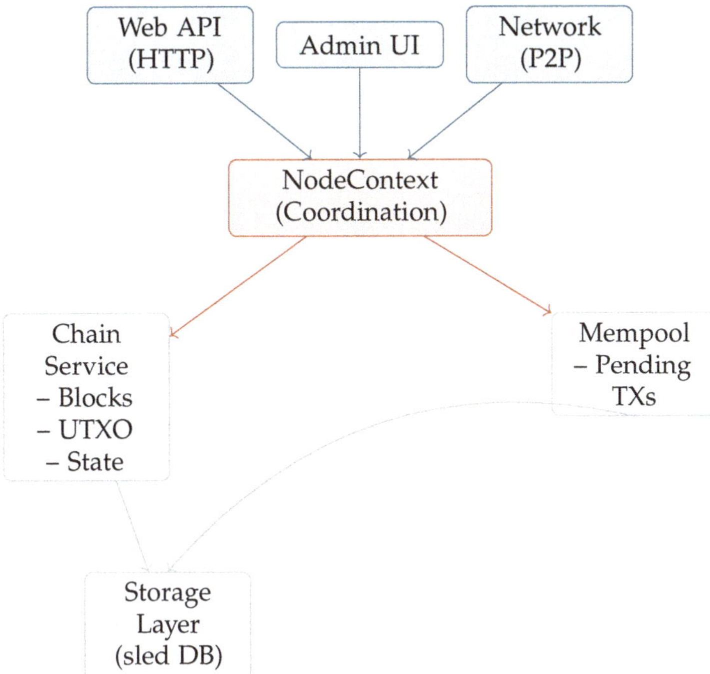

Figure 17.2: External interfaces architecture: coordination through NodeContext

What this diagram shows: The separation of concerns in our implementation. External interfaces (web API, network peers) all communicate through `NodeContext`, which acts as a central coordinator. `NodeContext` delegates to specialized subsystems (chain state, mempool), and all persistent data ultimately lives in the storage layer.

Call Hierarchy and Shared State

This diagram shows the call relationships: how external code calls `NodeContext`, how `NodeContext` delegates to subsystems, and where global state is accessed.

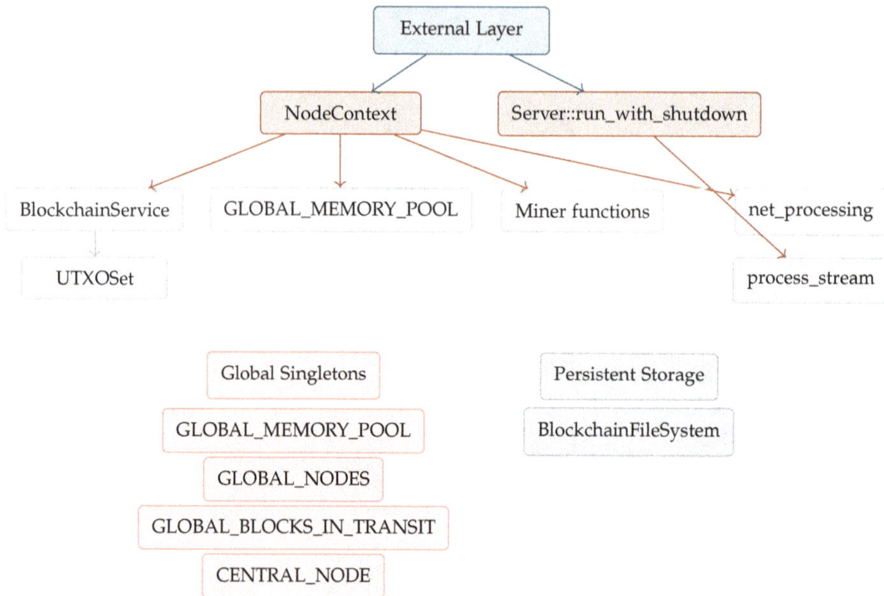

Figure 17.3: Call hierarchy and shared state architecture

What this diagram shows: The call hierarchy and shared state. `NodeContext` is the primary entry point, but subsystems also access global singletons directly (e.g., `GLOBAL_MEMORY_POOL`). The server loop spawns per-connection tasks that handle network messages.

17.6 Concrete Example Flows

Example 1: Get Balance Query

This diagram traces how a balance query flows from the web API through the system.

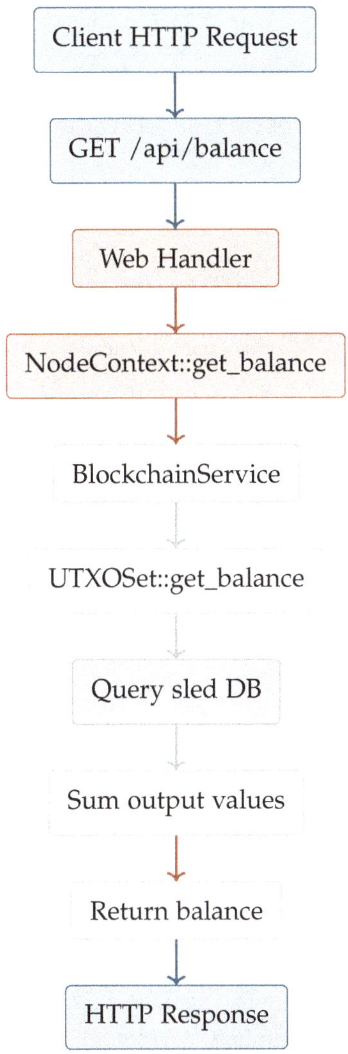

Figure 17.4: HTTP balance query flow through system layers

What this shows: A simple read operation that doesn't modify state. The query flows through `NodeContext` to the blockchain service, which queries the UTXO set, and the result flows back up the same path.

Example 2: Send Bitcoin Transaction

This diagram traces a concrete write operation: create a signed transaction spending UTXOs from A to B, accept it into the mempool, then propagate it to peers.

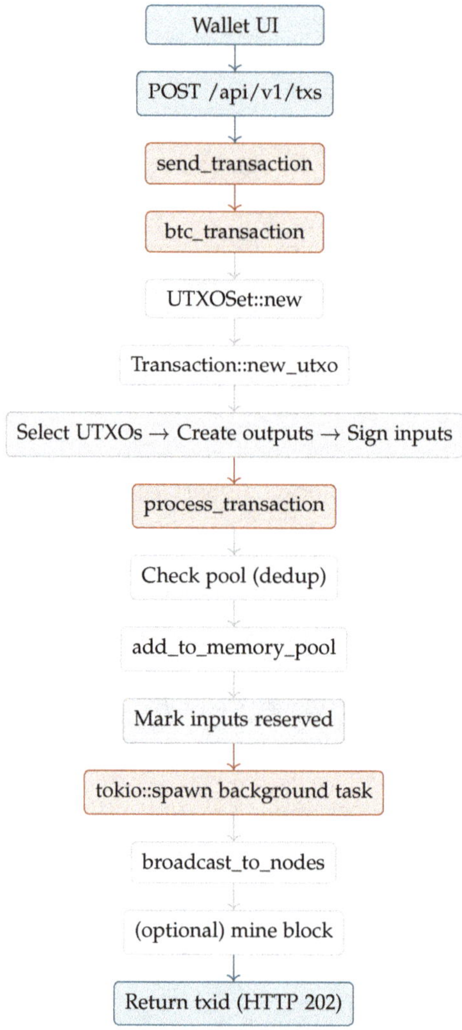

Figure 17.5: Send transaction flow: validation, mempool, and propagation

What this shows: A state-changing write path. The API handler delegates to `NodeContext::btc_transaction`, which builds a signed UTXO transaction, accepts it into the global mempool, and then uses a background task to broadcast an INV to peers and optionally trigger mining.

17.7 Step-by-Step Code Walkthrough

Now that we understand the architecture, we walk through the code that implements it. We'll start with global state management, then examine the coordination API, and finally trace the runtime paths for transactions, blocks, and mining.

Our goal: Understand the runtime wiring—where global state lives, which entry points receive network messages, and how those messages route into chainstate/mempool/mining.

Roadmap

Here's the path we'll follow through the code. Each step leads naturally to the next:

- **Step 1**: Global singletons (`GLOBAL_MEMORY_POOL` , `GLOBAL_NODES` , etc.) → Listing 138
- **Step 2**: `NodeContext` initialization and structure → Listing 140
- **Step 3**: Transaction processing path (`process_transaction`) → Listing 142
- **Step 4**: Block processing path (`add_block`) → Listing 144
- **Step 5**: Network message routing (`process_stream`) → Listing 145
- **Step 6**: Server runtime loop (`run_with_shutdown`) → Listing 148

Step 1 — Global Singletons

Node runtime globals code: `bitcoin/src/node/server.rs`

The node uses several process-wide singletons that are shared across all subsystems. These globals provide a single source of truth for shared state like the mempool, peer list, and blocks in transit.

```rust
use once_cell::sync::Lazy;
use parking_lot::RwLock;

// The global memory pool: all pending transactions
// accepted by this node but not yet confirmed
pub static GLOBAL_MEMORY_POOL: Lazy<
    Arc<Mutex<MemoryPool>>
> = Lazy::new(|| {
    Arc::new(Mutex::new(MemoryPool::new()))
});

// The global node peer list: addresses of all
// connected peers in the network
pub static GLOBAL_NODES: Lazy<
    Arc<RwLock<Vec<Node>>>
> = Lazy::new(|| {
    Arc::new(RwLock::new(Vec::new()))
});
```

Listing 138: Global state: memory pool singleton (part 1 of 2) (`server.rs`)

The remaining global singletons track blocks in transit and the bootstrap node address:

```
// Blocks in transit: tracking which blocks we've
// asked for but haven't received yet
pub static GLOBAL_BLOCKS_IN_TRANSIT: Lazy<
    Arc<Mutex<Vec<Vec<u8>>>>
> = Lazy::new(|| {
    Arc::new(Mutex::new(Vec::new()))
});

// The bootstrap/central node address
pub static CENTRAL_NODE: SocketAddr =
    SocketAddr::from(([127, 0, 0, 1], 3000));
```

Listing 139: Global state: blocks and bootstrap node (part 2 of 2)

What to notice:

- These are `static` variables that are lazily initialized on first access using `once_cell::sync::Lazy`—the closure passed to `Lazy::new(...)` runs exactly once, the first time the static is dereferenced, and the value is reused forever after. `once_cell::sync::Lazy` ensures the static variable is initialized exactly once, on first access. Rust statics must be compile-time constants; `Lazy` defers initialization to runtime while guaranteeing thread-safe, one-time execution. This avoids the chicken-and-egg problem that ordinary Rust statics cannot call non- `const` constructors.
- Each is wrapped in an `Arc` for shared ownership across async tasks and threads (cloning bumps a refcount; it does not duplicate the wrapped collection).
- `Mutex` (exclusive access) and `RwLock` (many readers OR one writer) protect concurrent access. The mempool uses `Mutex` because every operation either reads-and-modifies or atomically re-checks before inserting; the peer list uses `RwLock` because reads ("who are my peers?") vastly outnumber writes ("a new peer joined").
- These globals are accessed from multiple parts of the codebase without passing through function parameters—a deliberate simplification for this learning implementation; production code typically threads a context handle through call sites instead.

Step 2 — NodeContext

Central coordination API code: `bitcoin/src/node/context.rs`

`NodeContext` is the primary coordination point. It holds references to the blockchain service and provides methods that route requests to appropriate subsystems.

```
#[derive(Clone)]
pub struct NodeContext {
    // Reference to the shared blockchain service
    pub blockchain: BlockchainService,
}

impl NodeContext {
    pub fn new(blockchain: BlockchainService)
        -> Self
    {
        NodeContext { blockchain }
    }

    // Coordinate transaction creation and submission
    pub async fn btc_transaction(
        &self,
        from_addr: &WalletAddress,
        to_addr: &WalletAddress,
        amount: i32,
    ) -> Result<String> {
        // ... (builds + submits transaction)
    }
```

Listing 140: NodeContext structure and constructor (part 1 of 2) (`context.rs`)

The NodeContext provides entry points for transactions, blocks, and queries. All major operations delegate to specialized subsystems:

```
    // Entry point for all transaction admission
    pub async fn process_transaction(
        &self,
        addr_from: &SocketAddr,
        tx: Transaction,
    ) -> Result<String> {
        // ... (mempool acceptance)
    }

    // Entry point for all block admission
    pub async fn add_block(&self, block: &Block)
        -> Result<()>
    {
        // ... (blockchain validation + persistence)
    }

    // Query methods
    pub async fn get_balance(
        &self,
        address: &WalletAddress
    ) -> Result<i32> {
        // ... (UTXO query)
    }
}
```

Listing 141: NodeContext transaction/block/query methods (part 2 of 2)

What to notice:

- NodeContext is Clone, allowing cheap sharing via Arc<NodeContext> across tasks.
- BlockchainService is an async-safe wrapper (Arc<TokioRwLock<BlockchainFileSyst that provides thread-safe read-write access to the underlying storage. The Arc enables sharing across tasks; the TokioRwLock allows concurrent readers or one exclusive writer.
- All major operations (btc_transaction, process_transaction, add_block) are async.
- Methods delegate to subsystems (blockchain service, mempool, miner) without implementing the logic directly.

Step 3 — Transaction Processing

Transaction submission code: `bitcoin/src/node/context.rs`

```
pub async fn process_transaction(
    &self,
    addr_from: &std::net::SocketAddr,
    utxo: Transaction,
) -> Result<String> {
    // 1) Reject duplicates early (important to
    // prevent loops and redundant work)
    if transaction_exists_in_pool(&utxo) {
        return Err(
BtcError::TransactionAlreadyExistsInMemoryPool(
                utxo.get_tx_id_hex()
            )
        );
    }

    // 2) Add to the global mempool and mark outputs
    // as "reserved" by mempool policy
    add_to_memory_pool(utxo.clone(),
        &self.blockchain).await?;

    Ok(utxo.get_tx_id_hex())
}
```

Listing 142: Mempool acceptance entry point (part 1) (`NodeContext::process_transaction`)

After rejecting duplicates and admitting the transaction to the mempool, the function spawns a background task to handle propagation and mining triggers without blocking the caller's response.

```
    // 3) Background work: propagation and
    // (if this node is a miner) mining trigger
    // Spawned so caller (HTTP handler or P2P handler)
    // returns quickly
    let context = self.clone();
    let addr_copy = *addr_from;
    let tx = utxo.clone();
    tokio::spawn(async move {
        let _ = context
            .submit_transaction_for_mining(
                &addr_copy, tx).await;
    });

    // 4) Return txid immediately (accept-to-mempool)
    Ok(utxo.get_tx_id_hex())
}
```

Listing 143: Mempool acceptance entry point (part 2) — background mining trigger

What to notice:

- Duplicate detection happens early to prevent redundant work.
- The mempool admit operation is `await` ed (synchronous from the caller's perspective).
- Background broadcast/mining is spawned with `tokio::spawn` , allowing the function to return immediately.
- The caller gets a txid right away, even before broadcast completes.

Step 4 — Block Processing

Block submission code: `bitcoin/src/node/context.rs`

```rust
pub async fn add_block(&self, block: &Block)
    -> Result<()>
{
    // Delegate to blockchain service for validation
    // and persistence
    self.blockchain.add_block(block).await?;

    // Remove confirmed txs from the mempool
    for tx in block.get_transactions() {
        if !tx.is_coinbase() {
            remove_from_memory_pool(tx, &self.blockchain)
                .await;
        }
    }

    Ok(())
}
```

Listing 144: Block acceptance entry point (`NodeContext::add_block`)

What to notice:

- Block validation is delegated to the blockchain service (which checks signatures, PoW, fork choice).
- After a block is accepted, its transactions are removed from the mempool (they are now confirmed).
- This ensures the mempool contains only unconfirmed transactions.

Step 5 — Network Message Routing

P2P message dispatch code: `bitcoin/src/net/net_processing.rs`

Each TCP connection to a peer is handled by a task that calls `process_stream`. This function deserializes messages and routes them based on type.

```
pub async fn process_stream(
    node_context: Arc<NodeContext>,
    mut stream: std::net::TcpStream,
) -> Result<()> {
    loop {
        // Deserialize a message from the peer
        let pkg: Package = deserialize(&stream)?;

        match pkg {
            // Peer announces a transaction
            Package::Inv {
                addr_from,
                op_type: OpType::Tx,
                items
            } => {
                let txid = items.first()
                    .expect("INV items empty");
                if !GLOBAL_MEMORY_POOL
                    .contains(txid_hex.as_str())?
                {
                    send_get_data(&addr_from,
                        OpType::Tx, txid).await;
                }
            }
```

Listing 145: P2P message dispatcher (part 1) — message loop setup and transaction inventory

Transaction bodies are then passed to the node context for mempool acceptance:

```
// Peer sends a transaction
Package::Tx {
    addr_from,
    transaction
} => {
    let tx = Transaction
        ::deserialize(
            transaction.as_slice())?;
    let _ = node_context
        .process_transaction(
            &addr_from, tx).await;
}

// Peer announces a block
Package::Inv {
    addr_from,
    op_type: OpType::Block,
    items
} => {
    let block_hash = items.first()
        .expect("INV items empty");
    send_get_data(&addr_from,
        OpType::Block, block_hash).await;
}
```

Listing 146: P2P message dispatcher (part 2) — transaction data and block handling

Block bodies complete the dispatch routing:

```
                // Peer sends a block
                Package::Block {
                    addr_from,
                    block
                } => {
                    let block = Block
                        ::deserialize(
                            block.as_slice())?;
                    node_context.add_block(&block)
                        .await?;
                }

                _ => {}
            }
        }
    }
```

Listing 147: P2P message dispatcher (part 3) — block data and loop termination

What to notice:

- This is the central message dispatcher for incoming P2P messages.
- Transaction INVs trigger GETDATA requests; transaction bodies trigger `process_transaction`.
- Block INVs trigger GETDATA requests; block bodies trigger `add_block`.
- All routes eventually call methods on `node_context`, which coordinates the actual work.

Step 6 — Server Runtime Loop

TCP server code: `bitcoin/src/node/server.rs`

```rust
pub async fn run_with_shutdown(
    &self,
    addrs: &SocketAddr,
    connect_nodes: HashSet<ConnectNode>,
    mut shutdown: tokio::sync::broadcast
        ::Receiver<()>,
) {
    // Bind the TCP listener
    let listener = TcpListener::bind(addrs)
        .await
        .expect("TcpListener bind error");

    // Bootstrap: if not central node, send version
    if !addrs.eq(&CENTRAL_NODE) {
        let best_height = self.node_context
            .get_blockchain_height().await
            .expect("Blockchain read error");
        send_version(&CENTRAL_NODE, best_height)
            .await;
    }
```

Listing 148: P2P accept loop: TCP listener setup and bootstrap

After listening begins and bootstrap is complete, the server enters the main event loop that multiplexes incoming peer connections with shutdown signals:

```
        loop {
            tokio::select! {
                _ = shutdown.recv() => break,
                accept_res = listener.accept() => {
                    if let Ok((stream, _)) = accept_res {
                        let blockchain = self
                            .node_context.clone();
                        tokio::spawn(async move {
                            if let Ok(std_stream) =
                                stream.into_std()
                            {
                                let _ =
                                    net_processing
                                    ::process_stream(
                                        blockchain,
                                        std_stream
                                    ).await;
                            }
                        });
                    }
                }
            }
        }
    }
```

Listing 149: P2P accept loop: connection handling and shutdown

What to notice:

- The server binds to a TCP socket and accepts incoming connections in a loop.
- Each accepted connection is handled by a separate task spawned with `tokio::spawn`.
- `tokio::select!` waits for either a shutdown signal or a new connection.
- This allows the server to accept multiple concurrent peer connections.

17.8 Rust Concepts We'll Encounter

This section uses several Rust-specific patterns that are essential for async network programming:

- **`async` / `await`**: Functions marked `async` return `Future` s. The `await` keyword suspends execution until the future completes, allowing other tasks to run. This enables efficient concurrent I/O without blocking threads.
- **`tokio::spawn`**: Spawns a new async task that runs concurrently. Tasks are lightweight (unlike OS threads) and can number in the thousands.
- **`tokio::select!`**: A macro that waits for multiple futures and executes the branch for the first one that completes. Used for handling multiple concurrent events (e.g., shutdown signal vs incoming connection).
- **`Lazy`** (from `once_cell`): Thread-safe lazy initialization of static variables. Initializes on first access and ensures single initialization.
- **`Clone`**: Allows copying types. In async Rust, we often clone values to move them into closures/tasks. `NodeContext` implements `Clone` to allow sharing across tasks.
- **`Send + Sync`**: Marker traits for thread safety. `Send` means a type can be moved between threads. `Sync` means a type can be shared between threads via `&T`.
- **Pattern matching (`match`)**: Exhaustively handles enum variants. Used extensively for routing network messages based on their type.
- **`Result<T, E>`**: Rust's error handling type. `Ok(T)` for success, `Err(E)` for errors. The `?` operator propagates errors.
- **Iterator chains**: Rust's iterator API (`iter()`, `filter()`, `map()`, `collect()`) provides a functional programming style for data transformations.

17.9 Summary

Key Takeaways

- ✓ A blockchain node is a complete runtime system that maintains its own copy of the blockchain and participates in the peer-to-peer network.
- ✓ Node orchestration wires together multiple subsystems: blockchain state, mempool, network I/O, and optional mining.
- ✓ Global singletons (`GLOBAL_MEMORY_POOL`, `GLOBAL_NODES`, etc.) provide shared state that is accessed by multiple subsystems concurrently.
- ✓ `NodeContext` is the central coordination API that routes external events (web API requests, P2P messages) to the appropriate subsystems.
- ✓ External events flow through `NodeContext` and `process_stream`, which dispatch them to blockchain/mempool/miner handlers.
- ✓ Background tasks (broadcast, mining) run concurrently with API responses, enabled by `tokio::spawn`.
- ✓ The P2P server loop uses `tokio::select!` to multiplex between accepting new connections and handling shutdown signals.

18

Chain: Transaction to Block

▷ **What you will learn in this chapter**

- Follow the complete path from user input to mined block
- Understand how two-node architecture separates web server (API) from miner
- Runtime wiring: entry points, message flow, and coordination
- The HTTP API entry point and method dispatch
- How transactions propagate over P2P and reach miners
- Mining triggers, block construction, and broadcast
- The complete end-to-end path from `main()` to block creation

This is the capstone walkthrough for the chain chapter series. We trace the complete runtime flow from `main()` all the way to block creation, building on the Transaction Lifecycle, Block Lifecycle, Consensus, and Node Orchestration chapters. This section is the **final code walkthrough** for the `chain/` chapter series. The goal is explicit:

> Follow the first instruction executed in `main`, and trace the call chain all the way to a block being created.

Unlike earlier sections (which focus on individual subsystems), this chapter covers **wiring and flow**: the runtime entry points, the message boundaries, and the concrete method-to-method path that transforms "a user wants to send bitcoin" into "a miner produces a new block".

18.1 A Practical Constraint: Web and Miner Are Separate Roles

In `bitcoin/src/main.rs` , `startnode` enforces that **a node cannot run the web server and be a miner simultaneously**. In this implementation, the web server and miner are configured as exclusive roles (controlled by command-line flags). This is a simplification for clarity — in production Bitcoin, a single node can run both simultaneously. Mining only runs on nodes started with `is_miner=yes` , while HTTP transaction creation requires `is_web_server=yes` .

The end-to-end story naturally involves two processes:

- **Node A (Web/API node)**: accepts an HTTP request and creates a transaction, then propagates it over P2P.
- **Node B (Miner node)**: receives the transaction over P2P, places it in the mempool, and mines a block once mining is triggered.

This is not a limitation of Bitcoin as a protocol—it is simply how this learning implementation is configured in `main` .

18.2 Diagram: The Full Pipeline

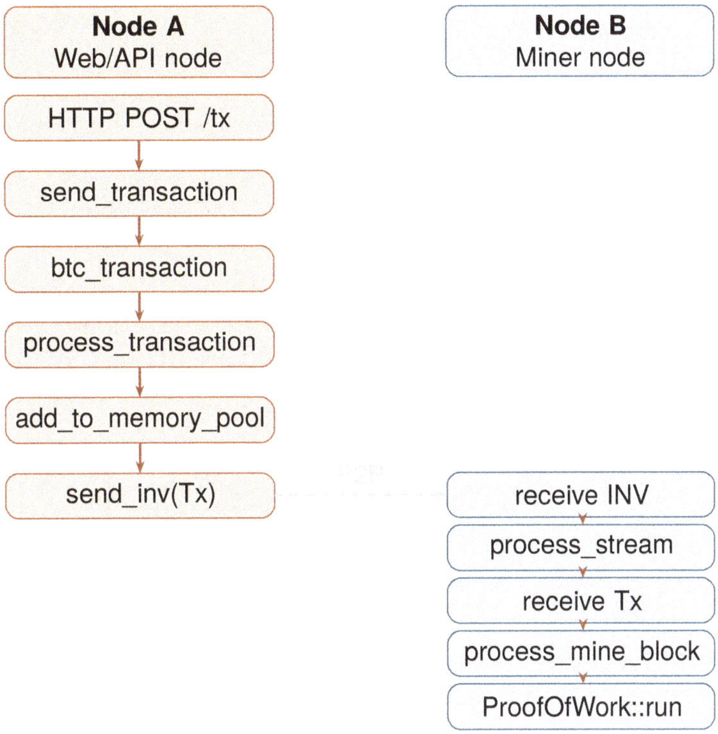

Figure 18.1: End-to-End Flow: Transaction from Web API Node to Miner Block Creation

18.3 Method Index

We will walk these methods, in the order you reach them at runtime:

- `bitcoin/src/main.rs`
  - `main`
  - `process_command`
  - `start_node`
- `bitcoin/src/node/server.rs`
  - `Server::run_with_shutdown`
- `bitcoin/src/net/net_processing.rs`
  - `process_stream` (only the message arms relevant to tx/block flow)
  - `send_inv`, `send_get_data`, `send_tx`, `send_block`
- `bitcoin/src/web/server.rs` + `bitcoin/src/web/routes/api.rs` + `bitcoin/src/web/handlers/transaction.rs`
  - `WebServer::start_with_shutdown`
  - `create_api_routes` (the POST `/transactions` route)
  - `send_transaction` (HTTP handler)
- `bitcoin/src/node/context.rs`
  - `NodeContext::btc_transaction`
  - `NodeContext::process_transaction`
  - `NodeContext::submit_transaction_for_mining`
  - `NodeContext::broadcast_transaction_to_nodes`
- `bitcoin/src/node/txmempool.rs`
  - `add_to_memory_pool`
- `bitcoin/src/node/miner.rs`
  - `should_trigger_mining`
  - `prepare_mining_utxo`
  - `process_mine_block`

Only the methods that form the end-to-end chain are shown, with unrelated class and struct definitions omitted.

18.4 Step 1 — The Process Starts

The first executed instructions in the node runtime are in `main`, where the CLI is parsed and control routes to `start_node(...)`.

```
#[tokio::main]
#[deny(unused_must_use)]
async fn main() {
    // 1) Initialize the global tracing subscriber
    // so later components can log.
    initialize_logging();

    // 2) Parse CLI args (subcommands like
    // startnode/createwallet/etc.).
    let opt = Opt::parse();

    // 3) Dispatch the selected command.
    // For end-to-end node runtime, we care about
    // Command::StartNode.
    if let Err(e) =
process_command(opt.command).await
    {
        eprintln!("Error: {}", e);
        std::process::exit(1);
    }
}
```

Listing 150: Process entrypoint (`main`)

```
async fn process_command(command: Command)
    -> Result<()>
{
    match command {
        // ... other commands omitted
        Command::StartNode {
            is_miner,
            is_web_server,
            connect_nodes,
            wlt_mining_addr,
        } => {
            // Validate and normalize mining address
            let validated_addr =
                WalletAddress::validate(
                    wlt_mining_addr)?;

            // Enter the runtime wiring path
            start_node(
                is_miner,
                is_web_server,
                connect_nodes,
                validated_addr
            ).await
        }
        _ => Ok(()),
    }
}
```

Listing 151: CLI dispatch (`process_command`)

```
async fn start_node(
    is_miner: IsMiner,
    is_web_server: IsWebServer,
    connect_nodes: Vec<ConnectNode>,
    wlt_mining_addr: WalletAddress,
) -> Result<()> {
    // Configure the process-level GLOBAL_CONFIG
    validate_miner_config(
        &wlt_mining_addr,
        &is_miner,
        &is_web_server
    )?;

    // Open or create blockchain
    let blockchain = open_or_create_blockchain(
        &wlt_mining_addr,
        &connect_nodes
    ).await?;

    let node_context = NodeContext::new(blockchain);
    let socket_addr = GLOBAL_CONFIG.get_node_addr();

    // Convert CLI nodes into a set for bootstrapping
    let connect_nodes_set: HashSet<ConnectNode> =
        connect_nodes.into_iter().collect();

    // Create shutdown signal channel
    let (shutdown_tx, _) =
        tokio::sync::broadcast::channel::<()>(1);

    // Start the P2P network server
    let network_server = Server::new(
        node_context.clone());
    let net_shutdown_rx = shutdown_tx.subscribe();
    let network_handle = tokio::spawn(async move {
        network_server
            .run_with_shutdown(
                &socket_addr,
                connect_nodes_set,
                net_shutdown_rx
            )
            .await;
    });

    // ... (continue with optional web server)
}
```

Listing 152: Wiring the node runtime (`start_node`)

Once the network server is initialized, the function checks whether to launch an optional HTTP web server (for wallet nodes) or handle miner-only mode. Both paths wait for a shutdown signal:

```
    match (is_web_server, is_miner) {
        (IsWebServer::Yes, IsMiner::No) => {
            let web_server =
                create_web_server(node_context);
            let web_handle = tokio::spawn(async move
{
                let _ = web_server
                    .start_with_shutdown().await;
            });
            // ... (wait for Ctrl+C or task
completion)
            Ok(())
        }
        (IsWebServer::Yes, _) => {
            Err(BtcError::InvalidConfiguration(
                "Web server and miner cannot \
                 be enabled at the same time"
                    .to_string(),
            ))
        }
        _ => {
            // ... (wait for Ctrl+C or task
completion)
            Ok(())
        }
    }
}
```

18.5 Step 2 — The P2P Runtime Loop

Once `start_node` runs, the P2P server is spawned and begins accepting TCP connections. Each accepted stream is handed to the P2P message dispatcher `net_processing::process_stream`.

```rust
pub async fn run_with_shutdown(
    &self,
    addrs: &SocketAddr,
    connect_nodes: HashSet<ConnectNode>,
    mut shutdown: tokio::sync::broadcast
        ::Receiver<()>,
) {
    // Bind the TCP listener
    let listener = TcpListener::bind(addrs)
        .await
        .expect("TcpListener bind error");

    // Bootstrap: if not central node,
    // send version handshake
    if !addrs.eq(&CENTRAL_NODE) {
        let best_height = self.node_context
            .get_blockchain_height().await
            .expect("Blockchain read error");
        send_version(&CENTRAL_NODE, best_height)
            .await;
    }
    // ... (collect and share known nodes)

    loop {
```

Listing 153: P2P accept loop — setup and bootstrap (`Server::run_with_shutdown`)

Once the listener is bound and the node announces itself to the network, the server enters a loop awaiting either a shutdown signal or an incoming TCP connection.

```
            tokio::select! {
                _ = shutdown.recv() => break,
                accept_res = listener.accept() => {
                    if let Ok((stream, _)) = accept_res {
                        let blockchain = self
                            .node_context.clone();
                        tokio::spawn(async move {
                            if let Ok(std_stream) =
                                stream.into_std()
                            {
                                let _ =
                                    net_processing
                                    ::process_stream(
                                        blockchain,
                                        std_stream
                                    ).await;
                            }
                        });
                    }
                }
            }
        }
}
```

Listing 154: P2P accept loop — connection handling

18.6 Step 3 — The HTTP Entrypoint (Node A)

The web server is only enabled for non-miner nodes. Its purpose is to provide a client-friendly HTTP API for creating wallets, querying balances, and creating transactions.

```
pub async fn start_with_shutdown(
    &self,
) -> Result<(), Box<dyn std::error::Error
                            + Send + Sync>>
{
    let app = self.create_app()?;
    let addr = SocketAddr::from((
        [0, 0, 0, 0],
        self.config.port
    ));
    let listener = tokio::net::TcpListener
        ::bind(addr).await?;
    let shutdown_signal = async {
        tokio::signal::ctrl_c().await?
    };
    axum::serve(
        listener,
        app.into_make_service_with_connect_info::<
            SocketAddr
        >()
    )
        .with_graceful_shutdown(shutdown_signal)
        .await?;
    Ok(())
}
```

Listing 155: Web server startup (`WebServer::start_with_shutdown`)

```
pub fn create_api_routes()
    -> Router<Arc<NodeContext>>
{
    Router::new()
        // ... other routes omitted ...
        .route(
            "/transactions",
            post(transaction::send_transaction)
        )
        // ... other routes omitted ...
}
```

Listing 156: Route mapping: POST `/api/v1/transactions`

```
pub async fn send_transaction(
    State(node): State<Arc<NodeContext>>,
    Json(request): Json<SendTransactionRequest>,
) -> Result<
    Json<ApiResponse<SendBitCoinResponse>>,
    StatusCode
> {
    let txid = node
        .btc_transaction(
            &request.from_address,
            &request.to_address,
            request.amount
        )
        .await
        .map_err(|_| StatusCode::BAD_REQUEST)?;
    let response = SendBitCoinResponse {
        txid,
        timestamp: chrono::Utc::now(),
    };
    Ok(Json(ApiResponse::success(response)))
}
```

Listing 157: HTTP handler: `send_transaction`

18.7 Step 4 — From Send to Mempool Accept

Now we enter the core node orchestration API.

```
pub async fn btc_transaction(
    &self,
    wlt_frm_addr: &WalletAddress,
    wlt_to_addr: &WalletAddress,
    amount: i32,
) -> Result<String> {
    // 1) Build a UTXO view over the current
    // chain state. This is used to select
    // spendable outputs owned by the sender.
    let utxo_set = UTXOSet::new(
        self.blockchain.clone());

    // 2) Construct and sign the transaction.
    // Transaction::new_utxo_transaction selects
    // inputs, creates outputs (including change),
    // and signs the inputs using sender's key.
    let tx = Transaction::new_utxo_transaction(
        wlt_frm_addr,
        wlt_to_addr,
        amount,
        &utxo_set
    ).await?;

    // 3) Submit to mempool + propagation via
    // shared processing entrypoint.
    let addr_from = crate::GLOBAL_CONFIG
        .get_node_addr();
    self.process_transaction(&addr_from, tx).await
}
```

Listing 158: Create and submit signed UTXO transaction (`NodeContext::btc_transaction`)

```
pub async fn process_transaction(
    &self,
    addr_from: &std::net::SocketAddr,
    utxo: Transaction,
) -> Result<String> {
    // 1) Reject duplicates early
    if transaction_exists_in_pool(&utxo) {
        return Err(
            BtcError
            ::TransactionAlreadyExistsInMemoryPool(
                utxo.get_tx_id_hex()
            )
        );
    }

    // 2) Add to the global mempool and mark
    // outputs as ``reserved'' by mempool policy
    add_to_memory_pool(utxo.clone(),
        &self.blockchain).await?;

    // 3) Background work: propagation and
    // (if miner) mining trigger
    let context = self.clone();
    let addr_copy = *addr_from;
    let tx = utxo.clone();
    tokio::spawn(async move {
        let _ = context
            .submit_transaction_for_mining(
                &addr_copy, tx).await;
    });

    // 4) Return txid immediately (accept-to-mempool)
    Ok(utxo.get_tx_id_hex())
}
```

Listing 159: Mempool acceptance entrypoint (`NodeContext::process_transaction`)

```
pub async fn add_to_memory_pool(
    tx: Transaction,
    blockchain_service: &BlockchainService,
) -> Result<()> {
    // 1) Store the transaction in the global
    // in-memory pool.
    GLOBAL_MEMORY_POOL.add(tx.clone())
        .expect("Memory pool add error");

    // 2) Mark referenced outputs as ``in mempool''
    // inside the UTXO view. This is a local
    // double-spend protection mechanism: it prevents
    // two mempool txs from spending the same output
    // concurrently.
    let utxo_set = UTXOSet::new(
        blockchain_service.clone());
    utxo_set.set_global_mem_pool_flag(
        &tx.clone(), true).await?;

    Ok(())
}
```

Listing 160: Mempool insert (`txmempool::add_to_memory_pool`)

18.8 Step 5 — P2P Propagation: INV → GETDATA → TX

Transactions propagate over the P2P layer, not the HTTP layer. The web layer exists only for local clients (UIs/admin tooling).

```
async fn submit_transaction_for_mining(
    &self,
    addr_from: &std::net::SocketAddr,
    utxo: Transaction,
) -> Result<()> {
    // Propagate tx to peers if this is central node
    if GLOBAL_CONFIG.get_node_addr()
        .eq(&CENTRAL_NODE)
    {
        let nodes = self
            .get_nodes_excluding_sender(addr_from)
            .await?;
        self.broadcast_transaction_to_nodes(
            &nodes,
            utxo.get_id_bytes()
        ).await;
    }
    // Trigger mining if threshold met
    if should_trigger_mining() {
        if let Some(mining_address) =
            GLOBAL_CONFIG.get_mining_addr()
        {
            if let Ok(txs) =
                prepare_mining_utxo(&mining_address)
            {
                if !txs.is_empty() {
                    process_mine_block(txs,
                        &self.blockchain).await?;
                }
            }
        }
    }
    Ok(())
}
```

Listing 161: Background "after accept" hook (`submit_transaction_for_mining`)

```rust
async fn broadcast_transaction_to_nodes(
    &self,
    nodes: &[Node],
    txid: Vec<u8>
) {
    // For each peer, spawn a task that sends
    // an INV message. INV ("inventory") is a
    // lightweight announcement: "I have txid"
    // -- the peer can request the full bytes
    // later via GETDATA if it wants them.
    // OpType::Tx tells the peer this inventory
    // entry is a transaction (vs OpType::Block).
    // tokio::spawn fans the sends out concurrently
    // so a slow peer cannot block the rest.
    let txid_clone = txid.clone();
    nodes.iter().for_each(|node| {
        let node_addr = node.get_addr();
        let txid = txid_clone.clone();
        tokio::spawn(async move {
            send_inv(&node_addr, OpType::Tx,
                &[txid]).await;
        });
    });
}
```

Listing 162: Broadcast tx inventory to peers (`broadcast_transaction_to_nodes`)

```rust
pub async fn send_get_data(
    addr_to: &SocketAddr,
    op_type: OpType,
    id: &[u8]
) {
    send_data(addr_to, Package::GetData {
        addr_from: GLOBAL_CONFIG.get_node_addr(),
        op_type,
        id: id.to_vec(),
    }).await;
}

pub async fn send_inv(
    addr_to: &SocketAddr,
    op_type: OpType,
    blocks: &[Vec<u8>],
) {
    send_data(addr_to, Package::Inv {
        addr_from: GLOBAL_CONFIG.get_node_addr(),
        op_type,
        items: blocks.to_vec(),
    }).await;
}

pub async fn send_tx(
    addr_to: &SocketAddr,
    tx: &Transaction
) {
    send_data(addr_to, Package::Tx {
        addr_from: GLOBAL_CONFIG.get_node_addr(),
        transaction: tx.serialize()
            .expect("Serialization error"),
    }).await;
}

pub async fn send_block(
    addr_to: &SocketAddr,
    block: &Block
) {
    send_data(addr_to, Package::Block {
        addr_from: GLOBAL_CONFIG.get_node_addr(),
        block: block.serialize()
            .expect("Serialization error"),
    }).await;
}
```

Listing 163: P2P send primitives (`send_inv`, `send_get_data`, `send_tx`, `send_block`)

```rust
// Source: bitcoin/src/net/net_processing.rs
match pkg {
    // Peer says: "I have txid"
    Package::Inv {
        addr_from,
        op_type: OpType::Tx,
        items
    } => {
        let txid = items.first()
            .expect("INV items empty");
        let txid_hex = HEXLOWER.encode(txid);

        // If not already in mempool, request
        // the full tx bytes
        if !GLOBAL_MEMORY_POOL
            .contains(txid_hex.as_str())
            .expect("mempool contains error")
        {
            send_get_data(&addr_from, OpType::Tx,
                txid).await;
        }
    }

    // Peer sends: full tx bytes
    Package::Tx { addr_from, transaction } => {
        let tx = Transaction::deserialize(
            transaction.as_slice())
            .expect("Transaction deserialization");

        // Admit to mempool; may also trigger mining
        let _ = node_context
            .process_transaction(&addr_from, tx)
            .await;
    }

    // Peer sends: full block bytes
    Package::Block { addr_from, block } => {
        let block = Block::deserialize(
            block.as_slice())
            .expect("Block deserialization");
        node_context.add_block(&block).await
            .expect("Blockchain write error");
    }

    _ => {}
}
```

Listing 164: P2P receive: miner gets full tx (`process_stream`, tx-related arms)

18.9 Step 6 — Mining: Mempool to Block

The mining module is the last step in the pipeline. It is only active when the process is started as a miner (`GLOBAL_CONFIG.is_miner()`).

```rust
pub fn should_trigger_mining() -> bool {
    let pool_size = GLOBAL_MEMORY_POOL.len()
        .expect("Memory pool length error");
    let is_miner = GLOBAL_CONFIG.is_miner();
    pool_size >= TRANSACTION_THRESHOLD && is_miner
}

// Mining is triggered only when the mempool reaches a
// threshold size (three transactions in this implementation).
// Below that threshold, transactions accumulate so that blocks
// are more efficiently filled. In production, miners build
// candidate blocks continuously without waiting for a fixed size.

pub fn prepare_mining_utxo(
    mining_address: &WalletAddress,
) -> Result<Vec<Transaction>> {
    // Pull all mempool txs and append a
    // coinbase tx for the miner reward
    let txs = GLOBAL_MEMORY_POOL.get_all()?;
    let coinbase_tx =
        Transaction::new_coinbase_tx(mining_address)?;
    let mut final_txs = txs;
    final_txs.push(coinbase_tx);
    Ok(final_txs)
}
```

Listing 165: Mining trigger and block assembly (part 1) — mining decision and transaction preparation

Once the miner has collected candidate transactions and created a coinbase transaction, it runs the proof-of-work algorithm to construct the new block and updates the global mempool to remove mined transactions.

```
pub async fn process_mine_block(
    txs: Vec<Transaction>,
    blockchain: &BlockchainService,
) -> Result<Block> {
    // Construct+mine a new block on the
    // current tip
    let new_block = blockchain.mine_block(&txs)
        .await?;

    // Remove txs from mempool once mined
    for tx in &txs {
        remove_from_memory_pool(
            tx.clone(), blockchain).await;
    }

    // Announce new block hash to peers (INV)
    broadcast_new_block(&new_block).await?;
    Ok(new_block)
}
```

Listing 166: Mining trigger and block assembly (part 2) — block construction and propagation

Where the Block Is Actually Created

The exact method call edge where a "block comes into existence" is:

```
miner::process_mine_block
  +-> BlockchainService::mine_block
        +-> BlockchainFileSystem::mine_block
              +-> Block::new_block
                    +-> ProofOfWork::run
```

You have already studied these methods in detail in **Chapter 16 (Consensus and Validation)**; this chapter's purpose is to show **how we reach them at runtime** from `main`.

18.10 Summary

Key Takeaways

- ✓ The end-to-end flow from user input to block creation spans two separate nodes: a web/API node and a miner node.
- ✓ `main()` parses CLI arguments and dispatches to `start_node`, which initializes the blockchain and spawns P2P and optional web servers.
- ✓ The HTTP API receives a POST request, constructs a signed UTXO transaction, and submits it to the mempool via `NodeContext::process_transaction`.
- ✓ Transactions propagate over P2P using INV/GETDATA/TX messages, reaching other nodes including miners.
- ✓ When the mempool reaches a threshold size and the node is a miner, `should_trigger_mining` initiates mining.
- ✓ `prepare_mining_utxo` snapshots the mempool and appends a coinbase transaction for the block.
- ✓ `Block::new_block` constructs the header and runs proof-of-work via `ProofOfWork::run`.
- ✓ Once mining completes, the mined block is broadcast via INV/GETDATA/BLOCK messages to peers.
- ✓ Understanding this end-to-end path clarifies how individual subsystems (transaction construction, signing, mining, consensus) integrate into a complete node runtime.

19

Block Acceptance

▷ **What you will learn in this chapter**

- Explain the whitepaper's Step 5 gate: "Nodes accept the block only if all transactions in it are valid and not already spent"
- Map this safety rule to concrete code boundaries in the implementation
- Identify the exact point where ownership and scarcity are enforced
- Understand the validate-first, connect-only-if-valid pattern that prevents double spending

BITCOIN's whitepaper compresses the most important safety rule in the entire system into one sentence:

> "Nodes accept the block only if all transactions in it are valid and not already spent." — *Bitcoin Whitepaper, Section 5*

This is the moment where your node decides whether incoming data becomes **durable state**. Getting this wrong allows the chain to "look like a blockchain" while quietly violating the two rules that make Bitcoin Bitcoin:

- **Ownership**: only the holder of the right key can spend an output.
- **Scarcity**: each output can be spent **at most once** (no double-spends).

Previous chain chapters covered the pieces: This chapter builds on the transaction validation logic (Chapter 14), block construction (Chapter 15), and consensus rules (Chapter 16). It isolates the acceptance boundary — the gate that every block must pass before its state changes take effect.

- **Validity** lives in code like `Transaction::verify(...)` (signatures, structure).

- **Spendability** lives in the UTXO set (what is unspent right now).
- **Fork choice** decides which branch we build on.

This capstone is about the *boundary* where those pieces must be composed correctly:

> **i Validate First, Connect Only If Valid**
>
> This chapter isolates the missing piece and shows the exact boundary where it must be implemented in the code.

19.1 Scope: Where Step 5 Appears in Our Codebase

In this repository, the "block became canonical" boundary is in:

- `bitcoin/src/store/file_system_db_chain.rs` → `BlockchainFileSystem::add_block(...)`

That's the method that must enforce the Step 5 gate **before** mutating the canonical tip and the UTXO set.

19.2 The Runtime Story: "A Block Just Arrived"

Imagine your node receives a `Package::Block` from a peer. At that moment, there is a choice:

1. Treat it as *data you can store* (fine: you can persist blocks as candidates).
2. Treat it as *state you will build on* (dangerous: this is where Step 5 applies).

The whitepaper's Step 5 concerns the second choice:

> "Accept the block" means "allow this block to change the node's authoritative view of money."

This includes:

- Moving the canonical tip pointer.
- Updating derived state (UTXO set) so "what is spendable" matches the new tip.
- Potentially reorganizing (disconnect old tip blocks, connect new branch blocks).

Step 5 is not a "nice-to-have validation"—it is the contract that prevents your node from turning invalid history into real balances.

19.3 A Rust Mental Model: The Acceptance Boundary Is an API Boundary

For a Rust developer, thinking about Step 5 cleanly means:

- **Validation** is a *pure function*: it can read chain state and UTXO state, but must not mutate durable state.
- **Connection** is a *state transition*: it mutates tip + UTXO (and maybe indexes), and must be atomic or rollback-safe.

That gives you a two-phase acceptance interface:

```
validate(block, view) -> Ok(()) or Err(...)
connect(block, state) -> Ok(()) or Err(...)
```

This pattern prevents partial state transitions from leaving the node inconsistent.

19.4 Block Validation Pipeline

Here is the diagram you should keep in your head while reading code:

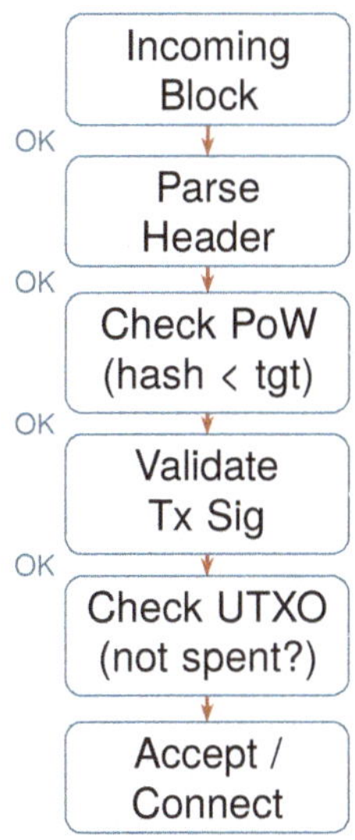

Figure 19.1: Block Validation Pipeline: Parse, PoW, Signatures, and UTXO Checks

If your code discovers invalidity "mid-update", you have already violated the contract: you let invalid data partially become state.

19.5 Step 5, Expanded: What "Valid" and "Not Already Spent" Mean

The whitepaper is minimal, so we'll be explicit. In a learning implementation like this repo, the smallest useful Step 5 set is:

Block-Level Sanity (Structural)

At minimum:

- **Coinbase rules**: a block should contain **exactly one coinbase** transaction (simplified rule used throughout the book).
- **Parent linkage**: if we are connecting the block, its parent must be known (or we keep it as an orphan/candidate).
- **Proof-of-work**: if your chain is PoW-secured, the header hash must satisfy the target (some paths in this repo intentionally simplify/todo this).

Transaction-Level Validity (Authorization)

> ▲ Critical Gate
>
> The UTXO check in block validation is the single gate that prevents double spending. Without it, an attacker could include two transactions in the same block that both spend the same output, effectively creating money from nothing.

> ▷ Note
>
> The in-memory UTXO set maintained during validation is a cache/index derived from applied blocks, not the source of truth — the on-disk block files are the canonical history. The UTXO set is rebuilt on startup by replaying blocks from the genesis block forward.

For each non-coinbase transaction, "valid" includes:

- **Signature verification** against the reconstructed digest — that is, the hash the verifier recomputes from scratch over the same trimmed-copy representation the signer committed to. If the two don't match, the signature is not valid for this transaction. A valid signature proves that the key holder authorized a particular spend, but it does *not* answer "is the output I am trying to spend still available?" That is a state-level question answered by the UTXO set. A transaction can be validly signed and yet attempt to spend an output that was already consumed in a prior block.

In this repo, that primitive already exists:

- `bitcoin/src/primitives/transaction.rs` → `Transaction::verify(&BlockchainService)`

State-Level Validity ("Not Already Spent")

The key phrase is **"not already spent"**, which is *not* a signature property. It is a statement about the current UTXO view.

This is outpoint-level logic:

- **Outpoint**: $(txid, vout)$
- **Rule**: every input must reference an outpoint that is currently unspent in the UTXO view.

Two pitfalls that Step 5 must guard against:

- **Inter-block double spend**: spending an outpoint that was already spent in the current canonical chain.
- **Intra-block double spend**: the same outpoint appears twice as an input across the block's transactions.

The intra-block case is easy to miss and easy to fix:

- Build a `HashSet<(txid, vout)>` while scanning the block. A `HashSet` gives $O(1)$ membership lookups: `seen.insert(outpoint)` returns `false` if the outpoint was already in the set, immediately detecting a duplicate spend. A `Vec` would require $O(n)$ linear scans, which matters for full blocks with hundreds or thousands of transactions. This matters because we check every input of every transaction in the block — an $O(n^2)$ scan would be noticeable on full blocks.
- If you see the same `(txid, vout)` pair twice across any of the block's inputs — meaning two different transactions in this same block both try to spend the same prior output — reject the block immediately.

19.6 Mapping Step 5 to Our Repo

The core acceptance entry point is already labeled in the code with a FIXME.

The Acceptance Boundary in Code

`bitcoin/src/store/file_system_db_chain.rs` → `BlockchainFileSystem::add_block(...)`

Inside this method, you'll find a comment like:

```
// FIXME: From bitcoin whitepaper, only add block if:
// A) "All transactions in it are valid"
// B) "Not already spent"
```

That is the right instinct, and it points to the right place: **Step 5 belongs in `add_block`**.

The important subtlety is what "add" means here:

- It's fine to *store the block* as "data we've heard about."
- It is not fine to *connect the block* (tip + UTXO mutation) without Step 5 validation.

19.7 A Concrete Design: Implement "Validate → Connect"

This section is intentionally practical. It's not "Bitcoin Core"; it's a clear shape you can implement in Rust in this codebase.

Phase 1: Validate (Read-Only)

Inputs:

- The block being considered.
- A read-only chain API (`BlockchainService`) to locate referenced previous transactions (needed for signature verification).
- A UTXO view to answer "is this outpoint unspent?"

Outputs:

- `Ok(())` if Step 5 holds.
- A domain error that explains which rule was violated.

Rust shape (documentation-level pseudocode):

```rust
use std::collections::HashSet;

#[derive(Clone, Debug, PartialEq, Eq, Hash)]
pub struct OutPoint {
    pub txid: Vec<u8>,   // id of the transaction that produced the output
    pub vout: usize,     // index into that transaction's vout array
}

// An outpoint uniquely identifies an unspent transaction output
// as a pair: the transaction ID and the zero-based index of that
// output within the transaction.

pub async fn validate_step5(
    block: &Block,
    chain: &BlockchainService,
    utxo: &UTXOSet,
) -> Result<()> {
    // 1) Exactly one coinbase (simplified)
    let txs = block.get_transactions().await?;
    let coinbase_count = txs.iter()
        .filter(|tx| tx.is_coinbase()).count();
    if coinbase_count != 1 {
        return Err(BtcError::InvalidTransaction);
    }

    // 2) No outpoint spent twice in the same block
    let mut seen: HashSet<OutPoint> = HashSet::new();
```

Listing 167: Step 5 validation pseudocode (part 1 of 3) — setup and coinbase check

For each non-coinbase transaction, the validator verifies the signature and checks UTXO spendability:

```
    for tx in &txs {
        if tx.is_coinbase() {
            continue;
        }

        // 3) Authorization (signatures)
        if !tx.verify(chain).await? {
            return Err(BtcError::InvalidSignature);
        }
```

Listing 168: Step 5 validation pseudocode (part 2 of 3) — signature verification

After signature verification, each input is checked against the UTXO set to ensure no intra-block double spends:

```
        // 4) Spendability (UTXO view)
        for vin in tx.get_vin() {
            let op = OutPoint {
                txid: vin.get_txid().to_vec(),
                vout: vin.get_vout(),
            };

            if !seen.insert(op.clone()) {
                // Intra-block double spend
                return Err(
                    BtcError::InvalidTransactionInput
                );
            }

            // Your UTXO API wants to answer:
            // is (txid, vout) currently unspent?
            utxo.assert_unspent(&op).await?;
        }
    }

    Ok(())
}
```

Listing 169: Step 5 validation pseudocode (part 3 of 3) — UTXO and double-spend checks

> ▷ **Key Insight**
>
> Step 5 needs an outpoint-level query (`assert_unspent`), not just "find UTXOs by owner".

Phase 2: Connect (Mutating)

Once validation passes, connecting the block is "just" the state transition:

- Spend the referenced outpoints.
- Insert the new outputs.
- Advance tip (or apply reorg logic).

But there is one critical systems requirement:

> ▲ **Atomicity Requirement**
>
> Connecting must be atomic or rollback-safe.

If your UTXO update is multiple DB writes and you can fail mid-way, your node can end up in a state that doesn't correspond to any valid chain. For instance, if the UTXO update removes output X in transaction 1 but crashes before inserting output Y in transaction 2, the database now reflects a state that never existed on the actual chain. Wrapping all updates in a database transaction ensures either all succeed atomically or all are rolled back.

In this repo, the connector is implemented as UTXO update logic (e.g. `UTXOSet::update(...)`), and the persistence layer is sled. The design goal is:

- compute the delta
- apply the delta in one sled transaction (or a clearly defined "write then commit tip" transaction)

19.8 Reorgs: Step 5 Is Not Optional on the "Apply Blocks" Path

A common misunderstanding is: "we validated blocks when we first saw them, so reorg apply is safe."

In a real node, and in this repo's learning node, reorg application still needs the same gate:

- When you **disconnect** blocks: rollback derived state safely.
- When you **connect** blocks on the winning branch: each connected block must satisfy Step 5 against the evolving UTXO view.

So any method that effectively does "connect a sequence of blocks" must call the same validator you use for normal extension.

In the current codebase, look for reorg helpers like:

- `reorganize_chain(...)`

- `apply_chain_from_ancestor(...)`

and treat them as "batch connect": Step 5 validation should be enforced per block.

19.9 A Practical Note About UTXO Representation

Step 5 is an outpoint-level rule. Your UTXO layer must preserve stable outpoint identity:

- In Bitcoin, $(txid, vout)$ is stable forever.
- If your UTXO storage is `txid -> Vec<TXOutput>` and you *remove elements* from the `Vec`, you can accidentally shift indices and break the meaning of `vout`.

That's why many implementations model UTXO state as something like:

- `outpoint -> TXOutput`

or keep a stable vector plus a spent marker rather than physically removing entries.

You don't have to implement a perfect data model for this book, but you do need one property:

> ▷ **Note**
>
> `vout` must keep its meaning, so "is $(txid, vout)$ unspent?" is deterministic.

19.10 Conclusion

The whitepaper's Step 5 is not a comment, and not "an error we hope happens during update".

It is a hard gate:

- **Validate all transactions** (authorization).
- **Reject double spends** (state-level spendability).
- **Only then** mutate the canonical tip and the UTXO set.

That's the moment where consensus becomes state.

19.11 Exercises

1. **Construct a Double-Spend Block** — Create a block containing two transactions that both attempt to spend the same UTXO. Predict at which validation step the block will be rejected. Trace through the code to verify your prediction.
2. **Validation Order Analysis** — The validate-first pattern checks transactions before connecting the block to the chain. Describe what could go wrong if the order were reversed (connect first, validate second). What specific attack would this enable?

Key Takeaways

- ✓ The whitepaper's Step 5 gate — "Nodes accept the block only if all transactions in it are valid and not already spent" — maps directly to concrete code boundaries.
- ✓ The validate-first, connect-only-if-valid pattern emerges as the key mechanism that prevents double spending at the consensus layer.
- ✓ The exact boundary where ownership and scarcity are enforced lies at the UTXO check, ensuring every input references an unspent output.
- ✓ This capstone validation rule connects backward to the transaction lifecycle, consensus rules, and chain state management covered in previous chapters.

In the next chapter, we move from validation to persistence — how all of this data is stored on disk using the Sled embedded database.

20

Storage Layer

▷ **What you will learn in this chapter**

- Use the Sled embedded database for persistent block and chain state storage
- Understand how the `BlockchainFileSystem` abstracts low-level storage operations
- Implement efficient persistence and retrieval of blocks, chain state, and UTXO data
- Explain the trade-offs in the storage design and why Sled was chosen

WITHOUT durable storage, a node would lose all blockchain history every time it restarts — it would have to re-download and re-validate the entire chain from peers. The storage layer also enforces a critical invariant: the tip hash and the blocks tree must always be consistent. If the node crashes halfway through writing a new block, the database must either contain both the block and the updated tip, or neither. This is why atomicity is the central design concern of this chapter.

The primary reference for this chapter is:

- `bitcoin/src/store/file_system_db_chain.rs` — the `BlockchainFileSystem` type that wraps sled and provides every read, write, and fork-choice operation for on-disk block storage

20.1 What "Storage" Means in Our Rust Bitcoin Implementation

In this codebase, "storage" is not a separate service; it is an embedded key-value database (**sled**) with a small set of conventions.

What Is Sled?

Sled is a pure-Rust embedded database — think of it as a persistent `BTreeMap<Vec<u8>, Vec<u8>»` backed by a log-structured merge tree on disk. It requires no external process, no TCP connection, and no configuration file: you open a directory path and get a `sled::Db` handle. This implementation uses Sled because it provides atomic batch writes (critical for "insert block + move tip" in one operation) and compiles on every platform Rust targets. If you have used RocksDB or LevelDB before, sled fills the same niche with a Rust-native API.

Conventions on top of sled:

- a **blocks tree** that maps `block_hash -> serialized Block bytes`
- a stable **tip key** (`"tip_block_hash"`) that points at the canonical tip hash
- atomic updates for "insert block + move tip" (sled transactions)

Think of sled as a persistent in-memory data structure (like a `BTreeMap`) that writes changes to disk atomically. If the process crashes, the database either contains both the block and the updated tip, or neither — it never gets stuck in an inconsistent state.

> ▷ **Debugging Tip**
>
> When debugging storage issues, Sled's `Db::export()` and `Db::import()` methods can dump the entire database contents for inspection. This is invaluable during development.

The key methods are `BlockchainFileSystem::create_blockchain` and `open_blockchain` (lifecycle), `get_tip_hash` and `get_last_block` (reads), and `update_blocks_tree` (the internal atomic write that inserts a block and advances the tip in a single sled transaction).

20.2 Sled Layout: The Minimum Schema

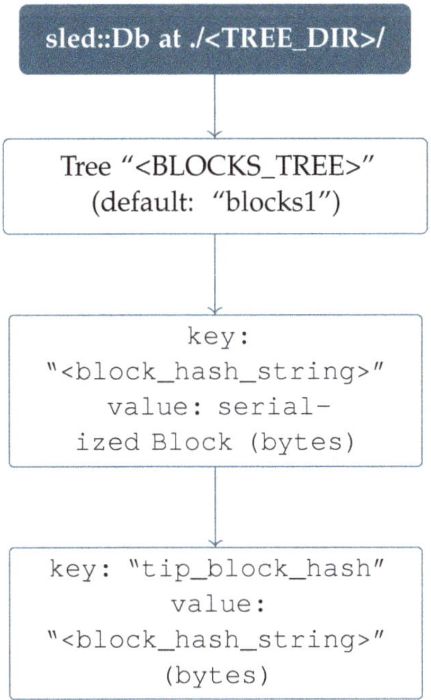

This chapter is about making those two invariants true:

- if a block exists, it can be fetched by hash
- tip always points at a block that exists (or a known "empty" sentinel)

20.3 Initialization: Creating or Opening the DB

The storage location is chosen by environment variables:

- `TREE_DIR` (directory on disk; default `"data1"`)
- `BLOCKS_TREE` (sled tree name; default `"blocks1"`)

Diagram: Config → Path → DB + Tree

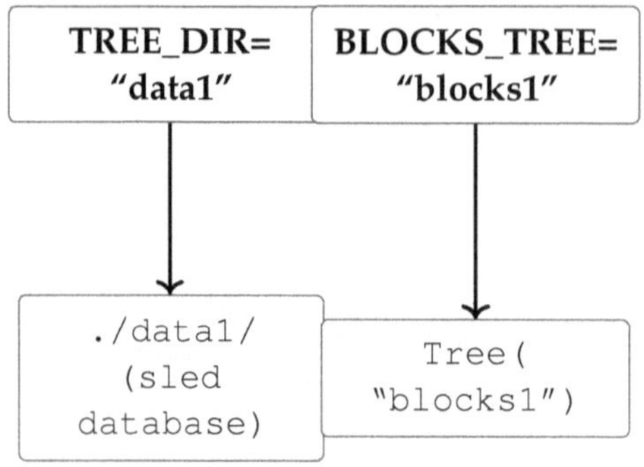

Type Definition and Blockchain Creation

```rust
use crate::error::{BtcError, Result};
use crate::primitives::block::Block;
use crate::primitives::blockchain::Blockchain;
use crate::primitives::transaction::Transaction;
use crate::wallet::WalletAddress;
use sled::{Db, Tree};
use std::env;
use std::sync::Arc;
use tokio::sync::RwLock as TokioRwLock;

const DEFAULT_TIP_BLOCK_HASH_KEY: &str = "tip_block_hash";
// Sentinel string written under DEFAULT_TIP_BLOCK_HASH_KEY before the
// genesis block has been mined. A real block hash is 32 raw bytes, so the
// ASCII string "empty" can never collide with any valid hash and unambiguously
// signals "this database is fresh; no chain has been built yet."
const DEFAULT_EMPTY_TIP_BLOCK_HASH_VALUE: &str = "empty";
const DEFAULT_BLOCKS_TREE: &str = "blocks1";
const DEFAULT_TREE_DIR: &str = "data1";

#[derive(Clone, Debug)]
pub struct BlockchainFileSystem {
    blockchain: Blockchain<Db>,
    file_system_tree_dir: String,
}
```

Listing 170: Type definition and blockchain creation — imports and type def

The `create_blockchain` method initializes a new blockchain by resolving tree paths from environment variables, opening the sled database, and creating a genesis block if the chain does not yet exist.

```rust
impl BlockchainFileSystem {
    pub async fn create_blockchain(
        genesis_address: &WalletAddress,
    ) -> Result<Self> {
        let blocks_tree_name = env::var("BLOCKS_TREE")
            .unwrap_or_else(|_| DEFAULT_BLOCKS_TREE.to_string());
        let dir = env::var("TREE_DIR")
            .unwrap_or_else(|_| DEFAULT_TREE_DIR.to_string());
        let path = std::env::current_dir()?
            .join(dir.clone());

        let db = sled::open(path)?;
        let blocks_tree = db.open_tree(blocks_tree_name.clone())?;
```

Listing 171: Type definition and blockchain creation (part 1) — DB setup

After resolving the database path, the code checks whether a chain already exists or must initialize a genesis block.

```rust
        // Check if chain exists, else create genesis
        let tip_hash =
            if let Some(data) =
                blocks_tree.get(DEFAULT_TIP_BLOCK_HASH_KEY)? {
                String::from_utf8(data.to_vec())?
            } else {
                // Initialize: create genesis block,
                // persist + set tip atomically
                let coinbase_tx =
                    Transaction::new_coinbase_tx(genesis_address)?;
                let block =
                    Block::generate_genesis_block(&coinbase_tx);
                Self::update_blocks_tree(&blocks_tree, &block)
                    .await?;
                String::from(block.get_hash())
            };
```

Listing 172: Type definition and blockchain creation (part 2) — tip hash lookup

Two separate conditions drive that branch. If `blocks_tree.get(DEFAULT_TIP_BLOCK_HASH_KEY)` returns `None`, the key is missing — no one has ever initialized this database, so we create a genesis block and write it along with the tip. If the key returns `Some(data)`, the chain is already initialized and we load whatever tip was last persisted. The sentinel `"empty"` described earlier is a distinct third state — the key exists but its value is the sentinel, signaling "this database has been primed but a genesis block has not yet been mined." In this codebase only the first two states are exercised by `create_blockchain`; the sentinel is used by the database-level reset path (emptying the chain while keeping the file open).

With the tip hash established, the method constructs and returns the initialized blockchain state.

```
        Ok(BlockchainFileSystem {
            blockchain: Blockchain {
                tip_hash: Arc::new(TokioRwLock::new(tip_hash)),
                db,
                is_empty: false,
            },
            file_system_tree_dir: blocks_tree_name,
        })
    }
}
```

Listing 173: Type definition and blockchain creation (part 3) — blockchain state construction

20.4 Open Existing or Empty Blockchain

```
impl BlockchainFileSystem {
    pub async fn open_blockchain() -> Result<Self> {
        let blocks_tree_name = env::var("BLOCKS_TREE")
            .unwrap_or_else(|_| DEFAULT_BLOCKS_TREE.to_string());
        let dir = env::var("TREE_DIR")
            .unwrap_or_else(|_| DEFAULT_TREE_DIR.to_string());
        let path = std::env::current_dir()?.join(dir);

        let db = sled::open(path)?;
        let blocks_tree = db.open_tree(blocks_tree_name.clone())?;
```

Listing 174: Open existing or empty blockchain (part 1) — existing chain initialization

Once the database and blocks tree are open, the method fetches the tip pointer from persistent storage.

```
        let tip_bytes = blocks_tree
            .get(DEFAULT_TIP_BLOCK_HASH_KEY)?
            .ok_or(BtcError::BlockchainNotFoundError(
                "No blockchain found".into(),
            ))?;
        let tip_hash = String::from_utf8(tip_bytes.to_vec())?;

        Ok(BlockchainFileSystem {
            blockchain: Blockchain {
                tip_hash: Arc::new(TokioRwLock::new(tip_hash)),
                db,
                is_empty: false,
            },
            file_system_tree_dir: blocks_tree_name,
        })
    }
```

Listing 175: Open existing or empty blockchain (part 2) — retrieving the tip hash

The `open_blockchain_empty` variant creates an empty blockchain state without reading from disk, used for testing or fresh setup when no prior chain exists.

```
    pub async fn open_blockchain_empty() -> Result<Self> {
        let blocks_tree_name = env::var("BLOCKS_TREE")
            .unwrap_or_else(|_| DEFAULT_BLOCKS_TREE.to_string());
        let dir = env::var("TREE_DIR")
            .unwrap_or_else(|_| DEFAULT_TREE_DIR.to_string());
        let path = std::env::current_dir()?.join(dir);

        let db = sled::open(path)?;
        Ok(BlockchainFileSystem {
            blockchain: Blockchain {
                tip_hash: Arc::new(
                    TokioRwLock::new("empty".to_string())),
                db,
                is_empty: true,
            },
            file_system_tree_dir: blocks_tree_name,
        })
    }
}
```

Listing 176: Open existing or empty blockchain — empty chain

20.5 Atomic Storage Primitive: `update_blocks_tree`

When creating genesis or mining locally, "block insert" and "tip pointer update" must happen as a single atomic unit.

```rust
async fn update_blocks_tree(
    blocks_tree: &Tree,
    block: &Block
) -> Result<()> {
    // Hash is the key; serialized block is the value.
    // IVec is sled's owned byte buffer (similar to Vec<u8> but
    // reference-counted so reads are cheap). The TryFrom impl
    // calls Block::serialize() under the hood, so this line both
    // serializes the block and wraps the bytes in sled's container.
    let block_hash = block.get_hash();
    let block_ivec = IVec::try_from(block.clone())?;
    // IVec::try_from consumes ownership of the block, which is why we clone() it here.
    // The resulting IVec is reference-counted internally, so subsequent reads are cheap.

    // sled transactions give us atomicity across
    // multiple inserts into the same Tree.
    let transaction_result: TransactionResult<(), ()> =
        blocks_tree.transaction(|tx_db| {
        // 1) Persist the block bytes under its hash.
        let _ = tx_db.insert(
            block_hash,
            block_ivec.clone()
        )?;
```

Listing 177: Atomic insert + tip update (part 1) — block serialization

After inserting the block bytes, the transaction atomically updates the tip pointer to the same hash, ensuring both changes succeed or both fail.

```
        // 2) Move the "tip pointer" to the same hash.
        // If the process crashes after this transaction
        // commits, both updates are present.
        let _ = tx_db.insert(
            DEFAULT_TIP_BLOCK_HASH_KEY,
            block_hash
        )?;
        Ok(())
    });
    transaction_result
        .map(|_| ())
        .map_err(|e|
            BtcError::BlockchainDBconnection(
                format!("{:?}", e)))
}
```

Listing 178: Atomic insert + tip update (part 2) — tip pointer update

20.6 Tip Pointer API

The tip is also cached in memory (an async `RwLock<String>`) for fast access during runtime. The choice of `RwLock` (rather than `Mutex`) reflects the access pattern: many concurrent reads of the tip — by relay tasks, query handlers, and mining loops — but rare writes (only when a new best block is connected). `tokio::sync::RwLock` permits unlimited concurrent read holders and exactly one writer, and crucially is async-aware: a contended `.read().await` or `.write().await` suspends the calling task instead of blocking the whole runtime thread. Wrapping it in an `Arc` (atomically reference-counted shared pointer) is what lets the same lock travel into every task spawned with `tokio::spawn` .

```rust
pub async fn get_tip_hash(&self) -> Result<String> {
    // Read-lock: multiple readers can read
    // the cached tip concurrently.
    let tip_hash =
self.blockchain.tip_hash.read().await;
    Ok(tip_hash.clone())
}

async fn set_tip_hash(&self, new_tip_hash: &str)
    -> Result<()> {
    // Write-lock: tip updates are exclusive.
    let mut tip_hash =
        self.blockchain.tip_hash.write().await;
    // Update the in-memory cached tip
    // (DB tip key updates happen elsewhere).
    *tip_hash = String::from(new_tip_hash);
    Ok(())
}
```

Listing 179: Tip pointer helpers

20.7 Read Path: Height, Get-by-Hash, and Inventory

The network layer and UI need:

- current height (`get_best_height`)
- fetch-by-hash (`get_block`)
- list hashes (`get_block_hashes`) for sync inventory

```
pub async fn get_best_height(&self) -> Result<usize> {
    if self.is_empty() {
        // An "empty handle" reports height 0
        // (genesis is height 1 in this codebase).
        info!("Blockchain is empty, returning height 0");
        Ok(0)
    } else {
        // Open the blocks tree so we can fetch
        // the tip block bytes.
        let block_tree = self
            .blockchain.db
            .open_tree(self.get_blocks_tree_path())
            .map_err(|e|
                BtcError::OpenBlockchainTreeError(
                    e.to_string()))?;
        // Use the cached tip hash to look up the
        // corresponding block record.
        let tip_block_bytes = block_tree
            .get(self.get_tip_hash().await?)
            .map_err(|e|
                BtcError::GetBlockchainError(
                    e.to_string()))?
            .ok_or(BtcError::GetBlockchainError(
                "tip is invalid".to_string()))?;
```

Listing 180: Read path operations (part 1) — empty blockchain check

For non-empty blockchains, we retrieve the block bytes and deserialize to extract its height.

```
            // Deserialize bytes back into a Block
            // so we can read its height.
            let tip_block =

Block::deserialize(tip_block_bytes.as_ref())?;
            Ok(tip_block.get_height())
        }
}
```

Listing 181: Read path operations (part 1b) — height extraction from tip block

The complementary method fetches a block by its hash, useful for responding to peer requests or validating block references during chain validation.

```
pub async fn get_block(
    &self,
    block_hash: &[u8]
) -> Result<Option<Block>> {
    // Read-by-hash is a straight key-value lookup.
    let block_tree = self
        .blockchain.db
        .open_tree(self.get_blocks_tree_path())
        .map_err(|e|
            BtcError::OpenBlockchainTreeError(
                e.to_string()))?;
    let block_bytes = block_tree
        .get(block_hash)
        .map_err(|e|

BtcError::GetBlockchainError(e.to_string()))?;
```

Listing 182: Read path operations (part 2a) — block tree setup and lookup

If the block is found, we deserialize the bytes; otherwise, we return None.

```
    if let Some(block_bytes) = block_bytes {
        // Found a record: decode it back into a Block.
        let block =
Block::deserialize(block_bytes.as_ref())?;
        Ok(Some(block))
    } else {
        // Missing key: caller gets None (not an error).
        Ok(None)
    }
}
```

Listing 183: Read path operations (part 2b) — deserialization and result

The storage layer also provides inventory and iteration support for chain synchronization. The final read-path method walks the canonical chain and collects block hashes for peer synchronization.

```
pub async fn get_block_hashes(&self)
    -> Result<Vec<Vec<u8>>> {
    // "Inventory" for sync: walk the chain
    // backward and collect hashes.
    let mut iterator = self.iterator().await?;
    let mut blocks = vec![];
    loop {
        match iterator.next() {
            None => break,
            Some(block) => {
                blocks.push(block.get_hash_bytes());
            }
        }
    }
    Ok(blocks)
}
```

Listing 184: Read path operations (part 3) — block hash inventory

20.8 Mining Write Path: `mine_block`

Now that we have traced the read path — height lookups, tip-block retrieval, and block iteration — we turn to the write path, where atomicity becomes critical. Local mining creates a new `Block`, writes it into sled, updates the in-memory tip, then updates derived state. This is the "fast path" for locally-mined blocks: we skip the full consensus validation (fork choice, tie-breaking, reorganization) because we built the block ourselves at exactly `best_height + 1`, so we know it is valid and canonical. In contrast, inbound blocks from peers (next section) must run full validation.

```
pub async fn mine_block(
    &self,
    transactions: &[Transaction]
) -> Result<Block> {
    let best_height = self.get_best_height().await?;
    let block = Block::new_block(
        self.get_tip_hash().await?,
        transactions,
        best_height + 1,
    );
    let block_hash = block.get_hash();

    let blocks_tree = self
        .blockchain.db
        .open_tree(self.get_blocks_tree_path())
        .map_err(|e|
            BtcError::BlockchainDBconnection(
                e.to_string()))?;
    Self::update_blocks_tree(&blocks_tree, &block)
        .await?;
    self.set_tip_hash(block_hash).await?;
    self.update_utxo_set(&block).await?;

    Ok(block)
}
```

Listing 185: Mining write path

> ▷ **Stale Mining Protection**
>
> The `BlockchainService::mine_block()` wrapper re-validates transaction inputs under the write lock before calling this method. Between `prepare_mining_utxo` (which validates with a read lock) and the actual mining (which requires the write lock), a competing block may have been accepted, spending the same inputs. The wrapper catches this race

> condition and aborts mining with a "stale mining" error rather than creating a block with already-spent inputs. This prevents duplicate mining subsidies when multiple miners compete for the same transactions.

20.9 Inbound Write Path: `add_block`

Inbound blocks are first persisted, then the node runs consensus decisions to determine whether the tip should move or whether a reorganization is required.

```
pub async fn add_block(&mut self, new_block: &Block)
    -> Result<()> {
    // Inbound: persist first -> then consensus
    // decision -> maybe reorg.
    let block_tree = self.blockchain.db
        .open_tree(self.get_blocks_tree_path())?;

    if self.is_empty() {
        // First block always becomes tip
        self.set_not_empty();
        Self::update_blocks_tree(&block_tree,
new_block)
            .await?;

self.set_tip_hash(new_block.get_hash()).await?;
        self.update_utxo_set(new_block).await?;
        return Ok(());
    }

    // Dedup: skip if already present
    if block_tree.get(new_block.get_hash())?
        .is_some() {
        return Ok(());
    }
```

Listing 186: Inbound block persistence and dedup (part 1a) — empty blockchain and dedup checks

After checking for duplicates, we persist the new block and conditionally update the tip pointer.

```
    // Atomic insert within transaction
    let block_bytes = new_block.serialize()?;
    let tip_hash = self.get_tip_hash().await?;
    block_tree.transaction(|txn| {
        txn.insert(
            new_block.get_hash(),
            block_bytes.clone()
        )?;
        // Eagerly move tip if block is strictly higher
        if new_block.get_height() >
            Block::deserialize(
                txn.get(tip_hash.clone())?
                    .ok_or(...)?)?
            ).get_height() {
            txn.insert(
                DEFAULT_TIP_BLOCK_HASH_KEY,
                new_block.get_hash()
            )?;
        }
        Ok(())
    })?;
```

Listing 187: Inbound block persistence and dedup (part 1b) — atomic block insert and tip update

After persisting the block, we run consensus rules to decide whether to update the tip or *reorganize*. A chain **reorganization** ("reorg") is the repair operation that fires when a longer chain arrives on a fork: the node walks back from the current tip to the common ancestor, unwinds every block on the losing branch (rolling its UTXO changes back out of the set), then walks forward along the winning branch, re-applying each block's UTXO changes. The node ends up on the new canonical tip with a UTXO set consistent with the chain that has the most work. First, we handle blocks that are strictly higher than the current tip:

```
    // Fork choice: compare height, work, then tie-break
    let current_tip = self.get_tip_hash().await?;
    let current_height = self.get_best_height().await?;

    match new_block.get_height().cmp(&current_height) {
        Ordering::Greater => {
            // Check if block extends our chain
            // or is on a different branch
            if new_block.get_pre_block_hash()
                == current_tip {
                // Normal case: extends our current chain
                self.set_tip_hash(
                    new_block.get_hash()
                ).await?;
                self.update_utxo_set(new_block).await?;
            } else {
                // FORK: block is on a different branch
                // at a higher height.
                // Must reorganize to properly rollback
                // old branch's UTXO.
                self.reorganize_chain(
                    new_block.get_hash()
                ).await?;
            }
        }
```

Listing 188: Fork choice and reorg decision (part 2a) — higher blocks and fork detection

When a block arrives at the same height as the current tip, we must compare cumulative work and apply tie-breaking rules to decide on chain reorg:

```
        Ordering::Equal => {
            if new_block.get_pre_block_hash()
                == current_tip {
                return Ok(());
            }
            // Competing tips: compare cumulative work
            let current_work =
                self.get_chain_work(&current_tip).await?;
            let new_work = self.get_chain_work(
                new_block.get_hash()
            ).await?;
            match new_work.cmp(&current_work) {
                Ordering::Greater => {
                    self.reorganize_chain(
                        new_block.get_hash()
                    ).await?
                }
```

Listing 189: Fork choice and reorg decision (part 2b) — work comparison and reorganization

When work is equal, we apply tie-breaking rules; when work is lower, we reject the block.

```
                Ordering::Equal => {
                    if self.accept_new_block_tie_break(
                        new_block,
                        &current_tip
                    ).await? {
                        self.reorganize_chain(
                            new_block.get_hash()
                        ).await?;
                    }
                }
                Ordering::Less => {}
            }
        }
        Ordering::Less => {
            // Block stored in DB but not accepted as tip.
            // Available for future reorganizations when
            // higher blocks on this branch arrive.
        }
    }
    Ok(())
}
```

Listing 190: Fork choice and reorg decision (part 2c) — tie-breaking and lower work

> ▷ **Important Fork Detection Notes**
>
> 1. **`Ordering::Greater` fork detection:** The original code assumed higher-height blocks always extended the current chain. With block relay across multi-hop networks, a higher-height block on a *different branch* can arrive. Without checking `get_pre_block_hash() == current_tip`, the old branch's UTXO (including coinbase subsidies) would never be rolled back, creating money from nothing. The fix calls `reorganize_chain()` to properly rollback and apply.

2. **`Ordering::Less` block retention**: Blocks at lower heights are now kept in the database. They are NOT deleted. This is critical because `find_common_ancestor()` needs to walk both chain branches during reorganization. If rolled-back blocks were deleted, future reorganizations would fail with "No common ancestor found." This matches Bitcoin Core's behavior where all received blocks are kept in `blk*.dat` files.
3. **`rollback_to_block` no longer deletes blocks**: During chain reorganization, only the UTXO set is rolled back and the tip pointer is moved. Blocks remain in the database as non-canonical entries. This ensures `find_common_ancestor()` and `apply_chain_from_ancestor()` can always find the necessary blocks.

20.10 Exercises

1. **Storage Round-Trip Test** — Write a test that creates a block, stores it using `BlockchainFileSystem`, retrieves it, and verifies all fields match the original. Pay attention to serialization: does every field survive the round trip?
2. **UTXO Retrieval Performance** — Examine how UTXO lookups work in the Sled storage layer. If the blockchain has 10,000 transactions with an average of 2 outputs each, how many entries are in the UTXO set? What data structure does Sled use internally that makes lookups efficient?

20.11 Common Errors

▷ Troubleshooting: Storage Layer

"sled lock file already exists" — Another process (or a crashed previous run) still holds the database lock. Delete the `db/__sled__/lock` file manually, or ensure the previous node process has fully exited.
Deserialization panic after code changes — If you modify the `Block` struct and restart without clearing the database, sled will try to deserialize old bytes into the new struct layout. Delete the `db/` directory to start fresh, or implement a migration path.
"tree not found" on a fresh database — Ensure `create_blockchain` is called before `open_blockchain`. The blocks tree must be explicitly created on first run.

Key Takeaways

- ✓ This chapter explained how the `BlockchainFileSystem` uses the Sled embedded database to persist blocks, chain state, and UTXO data to disk.
- ✓ The storage operations enable efficient insertion and retrieval of blockchain data.
- ✓ The storage abstraction decouples chain logic from persistence details, making it possible to swap storage backends.
- ✓ Atomic transactions are critical for ensuring consistency across crashes and failures.

In the next chapter, we build the networking layer that enables nodes to communicate, propagate blocks, and maintain consensus across a distributed network.

21

Network Layer

▷ **What you will learn in this chapter**

- Process peer-to-peer messages for blockchain synchronization
- Manage peer connections and handle discovery of new nodes
- Coordinate blockchain synchronization across a distributed network
- Understand the network protocol that enables decentralized consensus

A blockchain that cannot communicate with peers is just a local database. The network layer is what turns isolated nodes into a consensus system: it propagates new transactions so miners can include them in blocks, relays newly mined blocks so all nodes converge on the same chain, and synchronizes new nodes that need to catch up with the canonical history. Every guarantee Bitcoin makes — immutability, double-spend prevention, censorship resistance — depends on this protocol layer working correctly.

▷ **Scope**

This chapter implements a simplified P2P protocol for blockchain synchronization. We do not cover NAT traversal, relay nodes, the full Bitcoin protocol message set, or Tor/I2P privacy layers.

21.1 Chapter Map: What "Network" Means in This Repo

This repository's P2P layer is deliberately small:

- **Transport**: TCP streams
- **Encoding**: JSON via `serde_json`
- **Message model**: `Package` enum + `OpType` enum
- **Dispatcher**: `process_stream(...)` (routes each inbound package to the right action)
- **Send primitives**: `send_data(...)` and typed wrappers (`send_inv`, `send_get_data`, `send_block`, `send_tx`, `send_version`,...)
- **Peer bootstrap**: central-node concept + "known nodes" exchange

A fresh node needs at least one peer to talk to before it can learn about any others — the classic chicken-and-egg problem of peer discovery. This implementation solves it with a *central node*: a well-known address (injected via the `CENTRAL_NODE` environment variable) that every new node contacts on startup to exchange its known-nodes list. Real Bitcoin clients hard-code a list of DNS seeds that resolve to volunteer-run bootstrap nodes; the mechanism is different, but the purpose is the same. Once bootstrap is complete, all nodes are peers — the central node has no special privileges in consensus.

The core implementation lives in:

- `bitcoin/src/net/net_processing.rs`
- `bitcoin/src/node/server.rs` (TCP accept loop + bootstrap wiring)

> ▲ Implementation Note
>
> This implementation uses a simplified P2P protocol suitable for learning. It does not implement NAT traversal, relay nodes, or the full Bitcoin protocol message set. Production networking would require significantly more robust connection handling.

21.2 The Minimal Protocol Loop

Bitcoin uses a **gossip and fetch** strategy to minimize bandwidth: peers announce what they have by sharing only the hash (the gossip phase), peers request the full object by hash (the fetch phase), and peers deliver the full object.

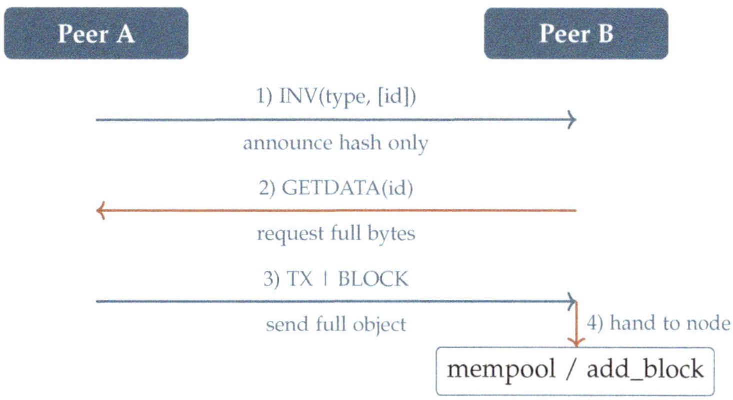

This three-message pattern—announce, request, deliver—is the heartbeat of blockchain peer-to-peer communication.

21.3 Message Model: The Wire-Level Vocabulary

Before reading any runtime flow, we need to understand what messages exist and what fields they carry.

```
// Bumped whenever a wire-incompatible change is made to a
// message variant (a new field, a new opcode, or a renamed
// type). Peers exchange this in the version handshake and
// refuse to talk to anyone whose number they don't recognize.
pub const NODE_VERSION: usize = 1;

// Discriminator: tells the receiver of an Inv or GetData
// message whether the 32-byte hash payload should be looked
// up in the mempool (Tx) or in the block store (Block).
#[derive(Debug, Serialize, Deserialize)]
pub enum OpType { Tx, Block }

#[derive(Debug, Serialize, Deserialize)]
pub enum MessageType {
    Error, Success, Info, Warning, Ack
}

// Admin operations (not part of P2P protocol)
#[derive(Debug, Serialize, Deserialize)]
pub enum AdminNodeQueryType {
    GetBalance { wlt_address: String },
    GetAllTransactions,
    GetBlockHeight,
    MineEmptyBlock,
    ReindexUtxo,
}
```

Listing 191: Network globals and message type enums — version and type discriminators

The `Package` enum encapsulates all wire-level messages exchanged between peers, including block/transaction broadcast, inventory announcements, version handshakes, and admin queries.

```rust
// Wire envelope: every JSON message is one Package
#[derive(Debug, Serialize, Deserialize)]
pub enum Package {
    Block { addr_from: SocketAddr, block: Vec<u8> },
    GetBlocks { addr_from: SocketAddr },
    GetData {
        addr_from: SocketAddr,
        op_type: OpType,
        id: Vec<u8>
    },
    Inv {
        addr_from: SocketAddr,
        op_type: OpType,
        items: Vec<Vec<u8>>
    },
    Tx { addr_from: SocketAddr, transaction: Vec<u8> },
    SendBitCoin {
        addr_from: SocketAddr,
        wlt_frm_addr: String,
        wlt_to_addr: String,
        amount: i32,
    },
    // NOTE: SendBitCoin is a high-level wallet operation (from address, to address, amount)
    // typically triggered by the user interface. Tx is the serialized on-chain transaction
    // that peers exchange over the network. A SendBitCoin request is converted into a Tx
    // before broadcast.
```

Listing 192: Network globals and message type enums (part 1) — block and transaction messages

The remaining variants handle peer discovery, version negotiation, and admin operations.

```
    KnownNodes { addr_from: SocketAddr, nodes: Vec<SocketAddr> },
    Version {
        addr_from: SocketAddr,
        version: usize,
        best_height: usize
    },
    Message {
        addr_from: SocketAddr,
        message_type: MessageType,
        message: String,
    },
    AdminNodeQuery {
        addr_from: SocketAddr,
        query_type: AdminNodeQueryType
    },
}
```

Listing 193: Network globals and message type enums (part 2) — peer discovery and admin messages

21.4 TCP Server Loop: How Nodes Accept Connections

This is the runtime entry point for inbound peer connections. It binds a TCP listener, does initial bootstrap, and then spawns one task per accepted connection.

```
#[derive(Debug, Clone)]
pub struct Server {
    node_context: NodeContext,
}

impl Server {
    pub fn new(blockchain: NodeContext) -> Server {
        Server { node_context: blockchain }
    }

    pub async fn run_with_shutdown(
        &self,
        addrs: &SocketAddr,
        connect_nodes: HashSet<ConnectNode>,
        mut shutdown:
            tokio::sync::broadcast::Receiver<()>,
    ) {
        let listener = TcpListener::bind(addrs)
            .await
            .expect("TcpListener bind error");
        info!("Server listening on {:?}",
            listener.local_addr());
```

Listing 194: TCP server setup and bootstrap (part 1a) — struct definition and TCP binding

After binding, the server either announces itself to the central node (if it's a regular peer) or collects peer addresses (if it's the central node).

```
if !addrs.eq(&CENTRAL_NODE) {
    let best_height = self
        .node_context
        .get_blockchain_height()
        .await
        .expect("Blockchain read error");
    send_version(&CENTRAL_NODE, best_height)
        .await;
} else {
    let remote_nodes: HashSet<SocketAddr> =
        connect_nodes
            .iter()
            .filter(|node| node.is_remote())
            .map(|node| node.get_addr())
            .collect();

    GLOBAL_NODES
        .add_nodes(remote_nodes.clone())
        .expect("Global nodes add error");
}
```

Listing 195: TCP server setup and bootstrap (part 1b) — peer registration and bootstrap

With bootstrap complete, the server enters its main event loop using `tokio::select!` to multiplex shutdown signals and incoming connections. The `tokio::select!` macro polls multiple async expressions concurrently and runs the branch belonging to whichever one finishes first — here, either "a shutdown signal arrived" or "a TCP client connected." Whichever wins, all the other branches are cancelled cleanly. This is how a single thread can wait on many independent events without writing a manual state machine.

```
// Serve incoming connections with
// graceful shutdown.
loop {
    tokio::select! {
        _ = shutdown.recv() => {
            info!(
                "Network server shutdown signal
received"
            );
            break;
        }
```

Listing 196: TCP server setup and bootstrap (part 1c) — main event loop setup

The server spawns each accepted connection as a background task that calls the message dispatcher. The connection acceptance and task spawning logic is extracted into separate listings:

```
accept_res = listener.accept() => {
    match accept_res {
        Ok((stream, _peer)) => {
            let blockchain =
                self.node_context.clone();
            tokio::spawn(async move {
                match stream.into_std() {
                    Ok(std_stream) => {
                        let _ = std_stream
                            .set_nonblocking(false);
                        if let Err(e) =
                            net_processing
                            ::process_stream(
                                blockchain,
                                std_stream,
                            ).await {
                            error!(
                                "Serve error: {}",
                                e
                            );
                        }
                    }
```

Listing 197: Network server bootstrap and connection loop (part 2a) — accept result handling

Error handling for stream conversions and accept failures completes the event loop logic.

```
                                    Err(e) => {
                                        error!(
                                            "Stream conversion error: {}",
                                            e
                                        );
                                    }
                                }
                            });
                        }
                        Err(e) => {
                            error!("Accept error: {}", e);
                        }
                    }
                }
            }
        }
    }
}
```

Listing 198: Network server bootstrap and connection loop (part 2b) — error handling

21.5 Message Dispatcher: Routing Inbound Messages

The dispatcher routes inbound messages to the node context, which decides how to respond. The dispatcher is the heart of message routing. It reads JSON from the TCP stream, deserializes into a `Package`, and routes based on the variant.

```
pub async fn process_stream(
    node_context: NodeContext,
    stream: std::net::TcpStream,
) -> Result<()> {
    let reader = std::io::BufReader::new(
        stream.try_clone()?);

    // JSON message stream
    let mut deserializer =

serde_json::Deserializer::from_reader(reader);

    // For each JSON message from the stream...
    loop {
        match serde_json::Value::deserialize(
            &mut deserializer) {
            Ok(value) => {
                // Parse the wire envelope
                match
serde_json::from_value::<Package>(
                    value) {
                    Ok(pkg) => {
                        // Dispatch by variant
                        if let Err(e) =
                            match pkg {
```

Listing 199: Message dispatcher: stream reading and deserialization (simplified)

Once the JSON is deserialized into a `Package` envelope, the dispatcher examines the variant and routes to the appropriate handler. Transaction and block messages are deserialized from their binary format and passed to the chainstate. Inventory and peer discovery messages trigger their respective handlers.

```
Package::Tx { addr_from, transaction } => {
    let tx = Transaction
        ::deserialize(&transaction)?;
    node_context
        .process_transaction(
            &addr_from,
            tx
        ).await
        .map(|_| ())
}
Package::Block {
    addr_from, block
} => {
    let blk = Block
        ::deserialize(&block)?;
    node_context
        .add_block(&blk)
        .await
}
```

Listing 200: Message dispatcher: routing by message type (part 1) — block and transaction handlers

After transaction and block processing, inventory and data requests are handled, followed by peer version information and error management.

```
Package::Inv {
    addr_from,
    op_type,
    items
} => {
    handle_inv(
        &node_context,
        &addr_from,
        op_type,
        items
    ).await
}
Package::GetData {
    addr_from,
    op_type,
    id
} => {
    handle_get_data(
        &node_context,
        &addr_from,
        op_type,
        id
    ).await
}
```

Listing 201: Message dispatcher: routing by message type (part 2a) — inventory and data requests

The remaining arms handle version negotiation, catch-all fallback, and the outer error-handling layers that close the connection on failure.

```
                            Package::Version {
                                addr_from,
                                version,
                                best_height
                            } => {
                                // Record peer info
                                GLOBAL_NODES
                                    .add_node(addr_from)
                                    .map(|_| ())
                            }
                            _ => Ok(()),
                        } {
                            error!("Handler error: {}", e);
                        }
                    }
                    Err(e) => {
                        error!("Deserialization error: {}", e);
                        // Malformed JSON terminates the connection.
                        // This is a deliberate design choice: malformed data suggests
                        // a buggy or malicious peer rather than a transient error, so
                        // dropping the connection is the safest response.
                        break;
                    }
                }
            }
            Err(e) if e.is_eof() => {
                // Peer disconnected
                break;
            }
            Err(e) => {
                error!("JSON read error: {}", e);
                break;
            }
        }
    }
    Ok(())
}
```

Listing 202: Message dispatcher: routing by message type (part 2b) — version, errors, and connection teardown

21.6 Send Primitives: Broadcasting to Peers

The dispatcher routes inbound messages to the node context, which decides how to respond. The send primitives below handle the outbound direction — relaying data back to peers. The send primitives are typed wrappers around a base `send_data(...)` function that opens a fresh TCP connection and sends one JSON message.

```rust
pub async fn send_inv(
    addr: &SocketAddr,
    op_type: OpType,
    items: &[Vec<u8>],
) {
    let pkg = Package::Inv {
        addr_from: GLOBAL_CONFIG.get_node_addr(),
        op_type,
        items: items.to_vec(),
    };
    let _ = send_data(addr, pkg).await;
}

pub async fn send_get_data(
    addr: &SocketAddr,
    op_type: OpType,
    id: Vec<u8>,
) {
    let pkg = Package::GetData {
        addr_from: GLOBAL_CONFIG.get_node_addr(),
        op_type,
        id,
    };
    let _ = send_data(addr, pkg).await;
}

pub async fn send_version(
    addr: &SocketAddr,
    best_height: usize,
) {
    let pkg = Package::Version {
        addr_from: GLOBAL_CONFIG.get_node_addr(),
        version: NODE_VERSION,
        best_height,
    };
    let _ = send_data(addr, pkg).await;
}
```

Listing 203: Send primitives (part 1) — inventory and version announcements

The remaining send primitives handle full block and transaction bodies by serializing the objects and propagating errors for retry logic.

```
pub async fn send_block(
    addr: &SocketAddr,
    block: &Block,
) -> Result<()> {
    let pkg = Package::Block {
        addr_from: GLOBAL_CONFIG.get_node_addr(),
        block: block.serialize()?,
    };
    send_data(addr, pkg).await
}

pub async fn send_tx(
    addr: &SocketAddr,
    tx: &Transaction,
) -> Result<()> {
    let pkg = Package::Tx {
        addr_from: GLOBAL_CONFIG.get_node_addr(),
        transaction: tx.serialize()?,
    };
    send_data(addr, pkg).await
}
```

Listing 204: Send primitives (part 2a) — block and transaction relay

The base `send_data` function handles the actual TCP connection and JSON serialization used by all send primitives.

```
// Base send primitive: open connection, send message.
// For simplicity, this implementation opens a new TCP connection for each
// outbound message. A production node would maintain persistent connections
// to peers and multiplex messages over them.
// NOTE: std::net::TcpStream::connect blocks the current
// runtime thread until the TCP handshake completes.
// In an `async fn` this can stall every other task
// scheduled on that thread. A production node would use
// tokio::net::TcpStream::connect(addr).await; this code
// keeps std::net for parity with the per-message
// open-and-close model described above.
async fn send_data(
    addr: &SocketAddr,
    pkg: Package,
) -> Result<()> {
    let mut stream = std::net::TcpStream::connect(addr)?;
    let _ = serde_json::to_writer(&mut stream, &pkg);
    let _ = stream.flush();
    Ok(())
}
```

Listing 205: Send primitives (part 2b) — base send implementation

21.7 Peer Discovery: Bootstrap and Known Nodes

The network layer maintains a peer set and exchanges known nodes to bootstrap new peers. The central node concept provides an initial meeting point.

> ▷ **Bootstrap Strategy**
>
> Nodes start with a hardcoded central node address. They announce their presence by sending a `Version` message. The central node collects these addresses and redistributes them via `KnownNodes`. This provides the initial peer discovery mechanism without requiring a separate DHT or seed server.

21.8 Trade-offs: Transport Layer Architecture

The network layer currently uses `std::net::TcpStream` for compatibility with existing JSON deserialization code. This choice trades scaling for simplicity:

- **Advantage**: Direct compatibility with `serde_json::Deserializer::from_reader(`
- **Disadvantage**: Potential to block Tokio worker threads under high peer load.

A future migration to `tokio::net::TcpStream` would require:

1. Moving from `serde_json::from_reader(...)` to async frame parsing
2. Implementing message framing (length-delimited or newline-delimited)
3. Updating connection handling to use async I/O primitives

This would enable better scalability for production networks with many peers.

21.9 Exercises

1. **Message Flow Trace** — Run two nodes locally and submit a transaction to one node. Trace the P2P messages exchanged as the transaction propagates to the second node. Document the message sequence: which message types are sent, in what order, and what each contains.
2. **Partition Recovery Scenario** — Imagine a network partition splits your nodes into two groups. Each group mines blocks independently for 5 minutes. When the partition heals, describe the chain synchronization process. Which chain wins, and what happens to transactions in the losing chain?

21.10 Common Errors

▷ Troubleshooting: Network Layer

"Connection refused" when connecting to a peer — The peer node is not running, or it is listening on a different port/interface than expected. Verify the peer's bind address (check for `0.0.0.0` vs `127.0.0.1`) and that no firewall rules are blocking the port.

Timeout during block synchronization — If a new node is catching up with a long chain, the default read timeout may be too short. Increase the TCP timeout or implement chunked block transfer. Also check that the sending peer is not blocked on a lock while the receiver waits.

"Address already in use" on startup — The previous node process did not release the TCP port. Wait a few seconds for the OS to reclaim it, or use `SO_REUSEADDR` in the socket options.

Peers connect but no blocks propagate — Check that the message dispatcher is routing `NewBlock` messages to the chainstate handler. A common mistake is registering the handler for `NewTransaction` but forgetting `NewBlock`.

Key Takeaways

- ✓ This chapter presented the peer-to-peer networking layer that enables blockchain nodes to communicate and synchronize.
- ✓ Message processing handles block and transaction propagation across the network.
- ✓ Peer connection management enables discovery, handshake, and ongoing communication.
- ✓ The network synchronization protocol keeps all nodes' chain state consistent.
- ✓ Trade-offs exist between simplicity (blocking TCP) and scalability (async I/O).

In the next chapter, we bring all these subsystems together under a unified `NodeContext` API that coordinates blockchain state, mempool, network, and mining.

22

Node Orchestration

> ▷ **What you will learn in this chapter**
>
> - Coordinate blockchain state, mempool, network, mining, and validation through the `NodeContext` API
> - Understand how the node module provides a unified interface over multiple subsystems
> - Trace how an incoming request flows through the node context to the appropriate handler
> - Explain why centralized orchestration simplifies the interaction between blockchain components

A peer sends your node a block. Who decides what happens next? Is it validation? Relay? Tip advancement? The answer is the node orchestrator. Every incoming message—a network packet from a peer, a transaction broadcast, a local mining trigger—flows through `NodeContext` to the right subsystem: chainstate gets the block, mempool gets unconfirmed transactions, mining gets a signal to build a new block. This chapter explains the `bitcoin/src/node` module—the coordination router that sits at the heart of your blockchain node.

The following files are the primary references for this chapter:

- `bitcoin/src/node/context.rs` — `NodeContext` : the central coordination struct that routes every request to the right subsystem
- `bitcoin/src/node/miner.rs` — mining trigger and block construction logic

- `bitcoin/src/node/txmempool.rs` — the global mempool: pending transaction storage, admission, and retrieval
- `bitcoin/src/node/peers.rs` — peer set management: add, evict, query, and iteration
- `bitcoin/src/node/server.rs` — TCP listener and inbound connection handling

22.1 What "Node Orchestration" Means

The runtime flow is:

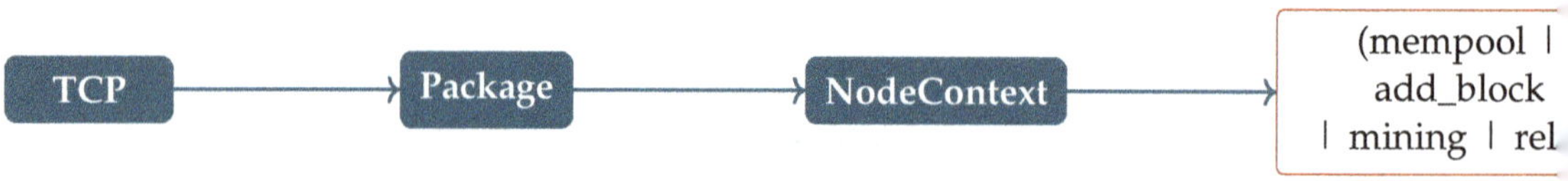

The key entry points are:

- `NodeContext::process_transaction` (mempool admission)
- `NodeContext::add_block` (chain extension from a peer)
- `NodeContext::mine_empty_block` (local mining trigger)

These delegate to:

- `txmempool::{add_to_memory_pool, remove_from_memory_pool}` for mempool state
- `miner::{should_trigger_mining, process_mine_block, broadcast_new_blo` for the mining pipeline

> **▲ Critical Role**
>
> `NodeContext` is the single entry point for all blockchain operations. Every user-facing interface — the web API, the desktop admin UIs, and the wallet applications — communicates with the blockchain exclusively through `NodeContext`. Understanding this module is essential for understanding how the system's components fit together.

22.2 The Façade: `NodeContext` is the Coordinator

`NodeContext` is the central façade used by other layers (network server, web/API) to interact with the node. It owns a `BlockchainService` handle and reaches out to:

- the global mempool (`GLOBAL_MEMORY_POOL`) via `txmempool`
- the peer set (`GLOBAL_NODES`) via `peers`
- the network send primitives (`send_inv`) to announce inventory
- the mining pipeline (`miner`) to build blocks and broadcast new tips

Transaction Ingestion: Accept → Relay → Maybe Mine

This is the path you will trace most often when debugging "why didn't my transaction propagate / get mined?"

The orchestration call graph for transactions:

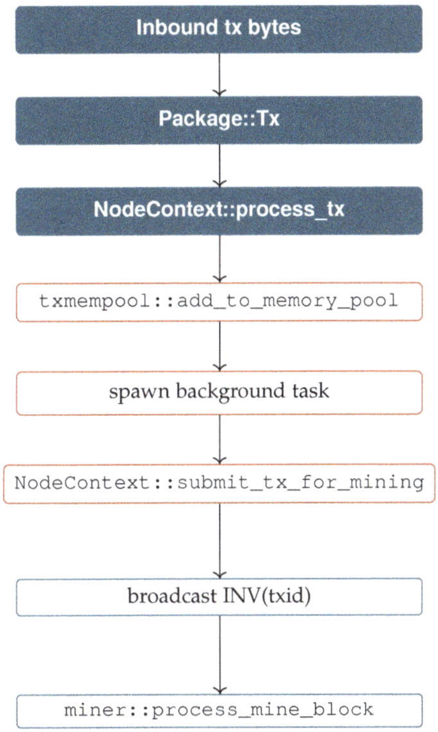

```
use crate::chain::{BlockchainService, UTXOSet};
use crate::error::{BtcError, Result};
use crate::node::miner::*;
use crate::node::txmempool::*;
use crate::node::GLOBAL_NODES;
use crate::{Block, Transaction, WalletAddress};
use std::net::SocketAddr;

#[derive(Clone, Debug)]
pub struct NodeContext {
    blockchain: BlockchainService,   // Only owned dependency
}

impl NodeContext {
    pub fn new(blockchain: BlockchainService) -> Self {
        Self { blockchain }
    }
```

Listing 206: NodeContext struct and dependencies (part 1)

The `NodeContext` constructor wraps a single owned dependency: the `BlockchainService`. This simplicity is intentional—all stateful operations delegate to the blockchain and its subsystems rather than maintaining complex internal state. The `btc_transaction` method shows how a caller constructs a transaction from a wallet and routes it through the node's admission and mining pipeline.

```
    pub async fn btc_transaction(
        &self,
        wlt_frm_addr: &WalletAddress,
        wlt_to_addr: &WalletAddress,
        amount: i32,
    ) -> Result<String> {
        let utxo_set = UTXOSet::new(
            self.blockchain.clone());
        // UTXOSet (introduced in Chapter~\ref{ch:utxo-set}) provides access to the
        // unspent-output index, allowing the node to check which coins are available
        // for spending.
        let utxo = Transaction::new_utxo_transaction(
            wlt_frm_addr,
            wlt_to_addr,
            amount,
            &utxo_set
        ).await?;
        let addr_from =
            crate::GLOBAL_CONFIG.get_node_addr();
        self.process_transaction(&addr_from, utxo)
            .await
    }
```

Listing 207: Transaction creation via NodeContext (part 2)

After creating a transaction, the node must accept it into the mempool. The `process_transaction` method enforces a duplicate check and then adds the transaction to the mempool, marking its outputs as "in mempool" to prevent double-spending.

```
    pub async fn process_transaction(
        &self,
        addr_from: &SocketAddr,
        utxo: Transaction,
    ) -> Result<String> {
        // 1) Dedupe check
        if transaction_exists_in_pool(&utxo) {
            return Err(BtcError
                ::TransactionAlreadyExistsInMemoryPool(
                    utxo.get_tx_id_hex(),
                ));
        }

        // 2) Accept into mempool
        // (flags outputs as "in mempool")
        add_to_memory_pool(utxo.clone(), &self.blockchain)
            .await?;

        // 3) Fire-and-forget: broadcast + mining
        // in background task. After mempool admission, the node spawns a background
        // task for relay and mining. This fire-and-forget design means the main path
        // returns immediately --- if the background task fails (for example, a peer is
        // unreachable), the transaction remains in the mempool and can be retried later.
        let context = self.clone();
        let addr_copy = *addr_from;
        let tx = utxo.clone();
        tokio::spawn(async move {
            let _ = context
                .submit_transaction_for_mining(
                    &addr_copy,
                    tx
                ).await;
        });

        Ok(utxo.get_tx_id_hex())
    }
}
```

Listing 208: Transaction admission with duplicate detection (part 3)

After accepting a transaction into the mempool, the node spawns background tasks for relay and mining decisions. The background submission begins by checking if this node is the central relay point, and if so, propagates the transaction hash to peers via INV messages.

```
impl NodeContext {
    async fn submit_transaction_for_mining(
        &self,
        addr_from: &SocketAddr,
        utxo: Transaction,
    ) -> Result<()> {
        // Background: relay to peers (if central node)
        // and maybe trigger mining. For teaching simplicity, this codebase uses a
        // single well-known node (CENTRAL_NODE) as the relay hub. Real Bitcoin nodes
        // relay transactions peer-to-peer; this centralized topology makes the message
        // flow easier to follow in a learning context. CENTRAL_NODE is a hardcoded
        // bootstrap address (typically 127.0.0.1:3000) that this teaching codebase
        // designates as the sole transaction relayer.
        let my_node_addr =
            GLOBAL_CONFIG.get_node_addr();
        if my_node_addr == crate::node::CENTRAL_NODE {
            let nodes = self

                .get_nodes_excluding_sender(addr_from)
                .await?;
            for node in &nodes {
                send_inv(
                    &node.get_addr(),
                    OpType::Tx,
                    &[utxo.get_id_bytes()],
                )
                .await;
            }
        }
```

Listing 209: Background transaction relay to peers (part 4a) — peer relay

After relaying the transaction hash to peers, the method checks whether the mempool has reached the mining threshold and, if so, triggers block construction.

```
        // Mining: trigger if mempool reaches threshold
        if should_trigger_mining() {
            if let Some(addr) =
                GLOBAL_CONFIG.get_mining_addr() {
                if let Ok(txs) =
                    prepare_mining_utxo(&addr) {
                    if !txs.is_empty() {
                        process_mine_block(
                            txs,
                            &self.blockchain
                        ).await?;
                    }
                }
            }
        }
        Ok(())
    }
```

Listing 210: Background transaction relay to peers (part 4b) — mining trigger

The `get_nodes_excluding_sender` helper performs peer set filtering to avoid relaying back to the sender or to ourselves. This method demonstrates a common pattern: acquiring a read lock on the global peer set, filtering the peer vector, and collecting it into a result.

```
    async fn get_nodes_excluding_sender(
        &self,
        addr_from: &SocketAddr,
    ) -> Result<Vec<Node>> {
        let nodes = GLOBAL_NODES
            .get_nodes()?
            .into_iter()
            .filter(|node| {
                let node_addr = node.get_addr();
                node_addr != *addr_from
                    && node_addr !=
                    GLOBAL_CONFIG.get_node_addr()
            })
            .collect();
        Ok(nodes)
    }
}
```

Listing 211: Helper: filter peer set excluding sender (part 5)

Block Ingestion and Chain/Peer Queries

This is the subset of `NodeContext` that the network layer and UI/API use for:

- pushing blocks into chainstate (`add_block`)
- answering sync queries (height, hashes, block lookup)
- basic peer introspection (who are we connected to?)

```
impl NodeContext {
    pub fn get_blockchain(&self)
        -> &BlockchainService {
        &self.blockchain
    }

    pub async fn add_block(
        &self,
        block: &Block
    ) -> Result<()> {
        self.blockchain.add_block(block).await
    }

    pub async fn get_blockchain_height(
        &self
    ) -> Result<usize> {
        self.blockchain.get_best_height().await
    }

    pub async fn get_block_hashes(
        &self
    ) -> Result<Vec<Vec<u8>>> {
        self.blockchain.get_block_hashes().await
    }
```

Listing 212: NodeContext block and chain queries (part 1: read operations)

The remaining methods handle individual block retrieval, mining delegation, and peer introspection. Each delegates to the appropriate subsystem while keeping the façade layer thin.

```
    pub async fn get_block(
        &self,
        block_hash: &[u8]
    ) -> Result<Option<Block>> {
        self.blockchain.get_block(block_hash).await
    }

    pub async fn mine_empty_block(
        &self,
        wallet_address: &WalletAddress,
    ) -> Result<Block> {
        miner::mine_empty_block(
            &self.blockchain,
            wallet_address
        ).await
    }
```

Listing 213: NodeContext block and chain queries (part 2: block retrieval and mining)

Finally, the peer introspection methods expose the node's view of the network. Both delegate to `GLOBAL_NODES`, a thread-safe global that tracks active connections.

```
    pub fn get_peer_count(&self) -> Result<usize> {
        use crate::node::GLOBAL_NODES;
        let nodes = GLOBAL_NODES.get_nodes()?;
        Ok(nodes.len())
    }

    pub fn get_peers(&self)
        -> Result<Vec<SocketAddr>> {
        use crate::node::GLOBAL_NODES;
        let nodes = GLOBAL_NODES.get_nodes()?;
        Ok(nodes.into_iter()
            .map(|n| n.get_addr())
            .collect())
    }
}
```

Listing 214: NodeContext block and chain queries (part 3: peer introspection)

22.3 The Mempool Primitives

The mempool module is deliberately small: it is a thin wrapper around `GLOBAL_MEMORY_POOL` plus a UTXO-side flag update so outputs can be marked "in mempool". The `add_to_memory_pool` function stores the transaction in the global pool and then marks all of its outputs in the UTXO set with a "in mempool" flag to prevent double-spending.

```
use crate::error::Result;
use crate::node::GLOBAL_MEMORY_POOL;
use crate::{BlockchainService, Transaction, UTXOSet};

pub async fn add_to_memory_pool(
    tx: Transaction,
    blockchain_service: &BlockchainService,
) -> Result<()> {
    // Store in pool + mark outputs
    // "in mempool" to prevent double-spend
    GLOBAL_MEMORY_POOL.add(tx.clone())?;

    let utxo_set = UTXOSet::new(
        blockchain_service.clone());
    utxo_set.set_global_mem_pool_flag(&tx, true)
        .await?;
    // When the wallet later runs coin selection, find_spendable_outputs skips any output
    // with this flag set to true, preventing the mempool from accepting a second
    // transaction that spends the same coin.

    Ok(())
}
```

Listing 215: Mempool admission and flag management (part 1)

When transactions are confirmed in a block, or when the mempool reaches capacity, `remove_from_memory_pool` clears both the global pool entry and the UTXO flags. The `transaction_exists_in_pool` helper provides a quick membership check used during ingestion deduplication.

```
pub async fn remove_from_memory_pool(
    tx: Transaction,
    blockchain: &BlockchainService,
) {
    // Remove from pool + clear "in mempool" flags
    let _ = GLOBAL_MEMORY_POOL.remove(tx.clone());
    let utxo_set = UTXOSet::new(
        blockchain.clone());
    let _ = utxo_set
        .set_global_mem_pool_flag(&tx, false)
        .await;
}

pub fn transaction_exists_in_pool(
    tx: &Transaction
) -> bool {
    GLOBAL_MEMORY_POOL.contains_transaction(tx)
        .unwrap_or(false)
}
```

Listing 216: Mempool removal and queries (part 2)

22.4 Mining Pipeline

Mining is triggered by **policy** (`should_trigger_mining`) and executed by `process_mine_block` . The output of mining is a new block which is then announced to peers using `INV(block_hash)` .

The mining trigger → mining → relay flow:

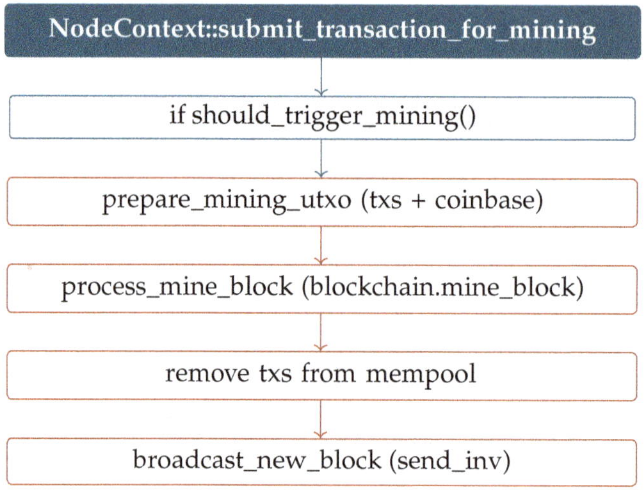

```rust
// Policy knob: mine once the mempool holds this many
// txs. 3 is a deliberate teaching value --- small enough
// that a hand-driven demo produces blocks promptly, large
// enough that blocks are not empty. Production miners
// tune this much higher (50-100+) to amortize the fixed
// per-block overhead across more fee revenue.
const TRANSACTION_THRESHOLD: usize = 3;

pub fn should_trigger_mining() -> bool {
    // Policy: mine if miner configured AND
    // mempool size exceeds threshold
    GLOBAL_MEMORY_POOL.len().unwrap_or(0)
        >= TRANSACTION_THRESHOLD
        && GLOBAL_CONFIG.is_miner()
}

pub async fn prepare_mining_utxo(
    mining_address: &WalletAddress,
) -> Result<Vec<Transaction>> {
    // Snapshot mempool and validate each tx's inputs
    // are still unspent. This prevents mining blocks
    // with already-spent inputs when a competing block
    // has been accepted during the race between miners.
    let txs = GLOBAL_MEMORY_POOL.get_all()?;
    let mut valid_txs = Vec::new();
    for tx in txs {
        if tx.is_coinbase() { continue; }
        // ... (validate each input exists in UTXO tree)
        // Stale transactions are removed from mempool
    }
    valid_txs.push(
        Transaction::new_coinbase_tx(mining_address)?);
    Ok(valid_txs)
}
```

Listing 217: Mining trigger and block construction

Once we have a validated transaction set, `process_mine_block` performs the actual proof-of-work and clears the mempool. It uses an atomic compare-and-exchange to prevent concurrent mining, then runs the proof-of-work computation inside an inner async block so the lock can be released before broadcasting.

```rust
pub async fn process_mine_block(
    txs: Vec<Transaction>,
    blockchain: &BlockchainService,
) -> Result<Block> {
    // Prevent concurrent mining: atomically swap the flag from false to true.
    // Two concurrent background tasks could both reach this point simultaneously.
    // The atomic compare_exchange ensures only one proceeds to mine; the other
    // returns early. The two Ordering::SeqCst arguments give the strongest memory
    // ordering on both the success and failure paths --- relaxed would be enough for
    // a simple flag, but SeqCst keeps the teaching example unambiguous.
    if MINING_IN_PROGRESS.compare_exchange(
        false,
        true,
        Ordering::SeqCst,
        Ordering::SeqCst
    ).is_err() {
        return Err("Mining already in progress".into());
    }
    reset_mining_cancellation();

    let result = async {
        // 1) Mine: PoW + chainstate integration
        // (with stale-mining protection)
        let new_block =
            blockchain.mine_block(&txs).await?;

        // CRITICAL: Do NOT cancel after block creation
        // the block is in our chain and MUST be
        // broadcast, or we create a permanent
        // minority fork.

        // 2) Remove confirmed txs from mempool
        for tx in &txs {
            remove_from_memory_pool(
                tx.clone(),
                blockchain
            ).await;
        }

        // 3) Announce block hash to peers (INV-first)
        broadcast_new_block(&new_block).await?;
        Ok(new_block)
    }.await;
```

After mining completes, the `broadcast_new_block` helper announces the new block's hash to all peers via INV messages. This is done asynchronously per peer to avoid blocking the mining thread on network I/O.

```
pub async fn broadcast_new_block(
    block: &Block
) -> Result<()> {
    let my_addr = GLOBAL_CONFIG.get_node_addr();
    let nodes = GLOBAL_NODES.get_nodes()?;
    for node in nodes {
        if node.get_addr() != my_addr {
            let addr = node.get_addr();
            let hash = block.get_hash_bytes();
            tokio::spawn(async move {
                send_inv(&addr, OpType::Block, &[hash])
                    .await;
            });
        }
    }
    Ok(())
}
```

Listing 219: Block announcement to peer network (part 2)

22.5 Peer Set

The peer set is a thread-safe wrapper around a `HashSet<Node>` guarded by an `RwLock`.

```rust
use crate::error::Result;
use std::collections::HashSet;
use std::net::SocketAddr;
use std::sync::RwLock;

#[derive(Clone, Debug, Eq, PartialEq, Hash)]
pub struct Node { addr: SocketAddr }

impl Node {
    fn new(addr: SocketAddr) -> Self {
        Node { addr }
    }
    pub fn get_addr(&self) -> SocketAddr {
        self.addr
    }
}

// Thread-safe peer set: many reads, occasional
writes
pub struct Nodes {
    inner: RwLock<HashSet<Node>>
}

impl Nodes {
    pub fn new() -> Self {
        Nodes {
            inner: RwLock::new(HashSet::new())
        }
    }
```

Listing 220: Peer data structures and initialization

The `Nodes` structure wraps a thread-safe `RwLock` around a hash set of peer addresses. The mutating methods `add_node`, `add_nodes`, and `evict_node` all acquire write locks, and their implementations demonstrate the pattern of protecting stateful modifications.

```
    pub fn add_node(&self, addr: SocketAddr)
        -> Result<()> {
        self.inner.write()?
            .insert(Node::new(addr));
        Ok(())
    }

    pub fn add_nodes(
        &self,
        nodes: HashSet<SocketAddr>
    ) -> Result<()> {
        let mut inner = self.inner.write()?;
        for node in nodes {
            inner.insert(Node::new(node));
        }
        Ok(())
    }

    pub fn evict_node(&self, addr: &SocketAddr)
        -> Result<bool> {
        Ok(self.inner.write()?
            .remove(&Node::new(*addr)))
    }
```

Listing 221: Peer set mutations: add and evict

The second half of the peer set API provides read operations for querying membership and retrieving the full peer list. These methods acquire read locks rather than write locks, enabling concurrent read access when no mutations are in flight.

```
    pub fn get_nodes(&self)
        -> Result<Vec<Node>> {
        Ok(self.inner.read()?
            .iter()
            .cloned()
            .collect())
    }

    pub fn node_is_known(&self, addr: &SocketAddr)
        -> Result<bool> {
        Ok(self.inner.read()?
            .iter()
            .any(|x| x.get_addr() == *addr))
    }
}

impl Default for Nodes {
    fn default() -> Self { Self::new() }
}
```

Listing 222: Peer set query and iteration methods

22.6 Integration Point: Network Routing Uses NodeContext

The network router is responsible for **decoding** and **dispatching**, and then calling into `NodeContext` for stateful operations.

At the key boundary:

- `Package::Tx` → `NodeContext::process_transaction(...)`
- `Package::Block` → `NodeContext::add_block(...)`

This is the "runtime wiring" that makes the node feel like a single system rather than a set of disconnected modules.

22.7 Exercises

1. **Request Flow Tracing** — Pick any REST API endpoint (e.g., submit transaction) and trace the request from the HTTP handler through `NodeContext` to the final blockchain state change. Identify every module boundary the request crosses.
2. **Subsystem Interaction Map** — Draw a diagram showing how `NodeContext` interacts with each subsystem: chain state, mempool, network, mining, and validation. For each interaction, label the function called and the data exchanged.

22.8 Summary: What to Remember

- `NodeContext` is a façade: it routes high-level requests into mempool, mining, relay, and chainstate.
- `process_transaction` is intentionally **fast**: it accepts to mempool and then spawns relay/mining in the background.
- Mining is policy-driven (`should_trigger_mining`) and ends by relaying an `INV` for the new block.
- The peer set is a simple RwLock<HashSet<Node» and is used by both relay and mining.
- Network messages are dispatched to `NodeContext` methods, which coordinate subsystems without owning them.

Key Takeaways

✓ This chapter presented the `NodeContext` , the central coordination point for all blockchain node operations.

✓ Interactions between blockchain state, transaction mempool, network operations, mining, and validation are unified behind a single API.

✓ The node module abstracts the complexity of coordinating multiple subsystems into clean, testable interfaces.

✓ Transaction and block ingestion paths flow from network packets to persistent blockchain state.

✓ Mining policy, peer relay, and consensus validation integrate into a coherent runtime system.

In the next chapter, we build the wallet system — key generation, address derivation, and transaction signing — that gives users the ability to hold and spend cryptocurrency.

23

Wallet System

▷ **What you will learn in this chapter**

- Generate cryptographic key pairs and create wallet addresses
- Sign transactions to authorize spending from a wallet
- Persist wallet data securely across application restarts
- Understand the key management lifecycle from creation through usage to storage

YOUR wallet doesn't hold coins—it holds **keys**. Your "balance" is just the sum of all unspent outputs your keys can unlock. This chapter explains how the wallet system (`bitcoin/src/wallet`) derives addresses from those keys, validates them, and persists them safely on disk. We walk through the code in two files:

- `bitcoin/src/wallet/wallet_impl.rs` (key generation and address derivation)
- `bitcoin/src/wallet/wallet_service.rs` (local persistence across application restarts)

i Prerequisites

This chapter depends on the cryptographic primitives from Chapter 9 (key generation, hashing, signing) and the UTXO model from Chapter 13. You do not need to have read the network or node chapters—the wallet module is a standalone library that the node and UI layers consume.

23.1 Overview and Scope

The wallet system implements three concrete responsibilities:

1. **Keypair creation**: `Wallet::new()` generates a Schnorr keypair (Taproot-style).
2. **Address derivation + validation**: `Wallet::get_address()` derives addresses; `WalletAddress::validate(..)` verifies them. Both use a Base58 payload format with a version byte + hash + checksum.
3. **Local persistence**: `WalletService` loads/saves a map of wallets to a single file (default `wallets.dat`) using `bincode` .

> ▲ What we do not implement
>
> **Transaction signing** is handled elsewhere (crypto and transaction logic). This wallet module focuses on keys, addresses, and persistence of wallet material. We also do not cover BIP-32 hierarchical deterministic (HD) wallets, multi-signature schemes, hardware wallet integration, or Lightning Network payment channels.

> ▲ Key reuse risk
>
> Never reuse a private key across wallets. If a key is compromised in one wallet, all funds associated with that key are at risk regardless of which wallet holds them.

23.2 Mental Model: Three Layers, One Responsibility Each

The wallet module is easier to understand if you separate it into three responsibilities:

1. **Key material**: create and hold a Schnorr keypair (`Wallet`)
2. **Address format**: derive and validate a Base58-encoded payload (`WalletAddress` , `convert_address` , `get_pub_key_hash`)
3. **Local persistence**: store multiple wallets in a file (`WalletService` , default `wallets.dat`)

The diagram below shows the runtime relationship between key creation, address derivation, and file persistence:

```
WalletService::create_wallet
    |
    |-- Wallet::new()                   // generates
keypair
    |-- Wallet::get_address()           // derives
Base58 address from public key
    |-- insert into HashMap             // address ->
wallet
    |-- save_to_file()                  // bincode ->
wallets.dat
```

23.3 Address Format and Validation

The address format used by our Rust Bitcoin implementation is based on three fields:

- **version byte** (1 byte)
- **pub_key_hash** (the "data" bytes)
- **checksum** (4 bytes), derived from a double-SHA-256 digest

Address Payload Structure

This wallet implementation uses a payload that matches the "classic" Base58Check idea (version + data + checksum), but note the version byte and hashing choices are specific to our implementation. This is intentional for teaching purposes; Bitcoin's actual address format is slightly different.

```
payload bytes:
  [ version: 1 byte ] [ pub_key_hash: N bytes ] [
  checksum: 4 bytes ]

encoded as:
  Base58(payload)
```

The address pipeline flows through `Wallet::get_address` (constructs the payload), `get_pub_key_hash` (hashes the public key), and `WalletAddress::validate` (verifies checksum and version on decode). `convert_address` extracts the public key hash from a Base58 address string.

Step 1: WalletAddress Validation and Checksum

i Methods involved

`WalletAddress::validate(...)`, `WalletAddress::validate_address(...)` (internal), `convert_address(...)`, `get_pub_key_hash(...)`, `checksum(...)` (internal)

```rust
use crate::error::{BtcError, Result};
use serde::{Deserialize, Serialize};
use utoipa::ToSchema;

// Address-format version byte. The first byte of every address
// payload is reserved so that future address schemes (different
// hash functions, longer keys, witness programs) can coexist on
// the same wire by changing only this byte. 0x01 identifies
// addresses produced by this implementation. Versioning allows future
// address schemes --- different hash functions, longer keys, witness
// programs --- to coexist on the same network by changing only this byte.
const VERSION: u8 = 0x01;
// Length of the Base58Check-style checksum appended to every
// address. Four bytes is enough to make accidental typos detectable
// with overwhelming probability (1 in 2^32 ~ 4 billion of slipping
// through) while keeping the address short.
pub const ADDRESS_CHECK_SUM_LEN: usize = 4;

#[derive(Clone, Serialize, Deserialize, PartialEq, Eq, Hash, Debug, ToSchema)]
pub struct WalletAddress(String);

impl WalletAddress {
    pub fn validate(address: String) -> Result<Self> {
        if Self::validate_address(&address)? {
            Ok(Self(address))
        } else {
            Err(BtcError::InvalidAddress(address))
        }
    }
}
```

Listing 223: `WalletAddress` validation and checksum (part 1: struct and public validate method) (`wallet_impl.rs`)

The core validation logic checks the address by decoding the Base58 payload and verifying its embedded checksum against the version and public key hash. This internal validation method is shown next.

```
    fn validate_address(address: &str) -> Result<bool> {
        let payload = crate::base58_decode(address)?;
        let actual_checksum =
            payload[payload.len() - ADDRESS_CHECK_SUM_LEN..]
                .to_vec();
        let version = payload[0];
        let pub_key_hash =
            payload[1..payload.len() - ADDRESS_CHECK_SUM_LEN]
                .to_vec();

        let mut target_vec = vec![];
        target_vec.push(version);
        target_vec.extend(pub_key_hash);
        let target_checksum = checksum(target_vec.as_slice());
        Ok(actual_checksum.eq(target_checksum.as_slice()))
    }
}

// Bitcoin's standard Base58Check checksum: SHA-256 applied
// twice. The double application defeats length-extension attacks
// against SHA-256 (a class of attack where knowing H(x) allows computing
// H(x || y) without knowing x; double hashing eliminates this vulnerability).
// The first 4 bytes of the second hash are then used as the trailing checksum.
fn checksum(payload: &[u8]) -> Vec<u8> {
    let first_sha = crate::sha256_digest(payload);
    let second_sha = crate::sha256_digest(first_sha.as_slice());
    second_sha[0..ADDRESS_CHECK_SUM_LEN].to_vec()
}
```

Listing 224: `WalletAddress` validation and checksum (part 2: internal validation) (`wallet_impl.rs`)

The struct also exports convenience methods for accessing and cloning the inner address string, which are useful for downstream code that needs to pass the address to APIs or persist it.

```
impl WalletAddress {
    pub fn as_str(&self) -> &str {
        &self.0
    }

    pub fn as_string(&self) -> String {
        self.0.clone()
    }
}
```

Listing 225: `WalletAddress` validation and checksum (part 3: accessor methods) (`wallet_impl.rs`)

✓ Checkpoint

The validation flow is: (1) Base58-decode the address string, (2) split into version, pub_key_hash, and checksum fields, (3) recompute the checksum from version + pub_key_hash, (4) verify the recomputed checksum matches the embedded one.

Address Creation and Extraction Helpers

Address creation and extraction helper functions construct Base58-encoded addresses with checksums and decode them back to retrieve the public key hash:

```
pub fn convert_address(pub_hash_key: &[u8]) -> Result<WalletAddress> {
    let mut payload: Vec<u8> = vec![];
    payload.push(VERSION);
    payload.extend(pub_hash_key);
    let checksum = checksum(payload.as_slice());
    payload.extend(checksum.as_slice());
    let address_str = crate::base58_encode(payload.as_slice())?;
    WalletAddress::validate(address_str)
}

pub fn get_pub_key_hash(address: &WalletAddress) -> Result<Vec<u8>> {
    let payload = crate::base58_decode(address.as_str())?;
    let pub_key_hash =
        payload[1..payload.len() - ADDRESS_CHECK_SUM_LEN].to_vec();
    Ok(pub_key_hash)
}
```

Listing 226: Address creation and extraction (`wallet_impl.rs`)

23.4 Wallet: Keypair Creation and Address Derivation

In this codebase, a `Wallet` is just two byte vectors:

- `private_key: Vec<u8>`
- `public_key: Vec<u8>`

Keypairs are created using Schnorr helpers from the crypto layer.

Key Generation Flow

The keypair derivation pipeline flows through five stages:

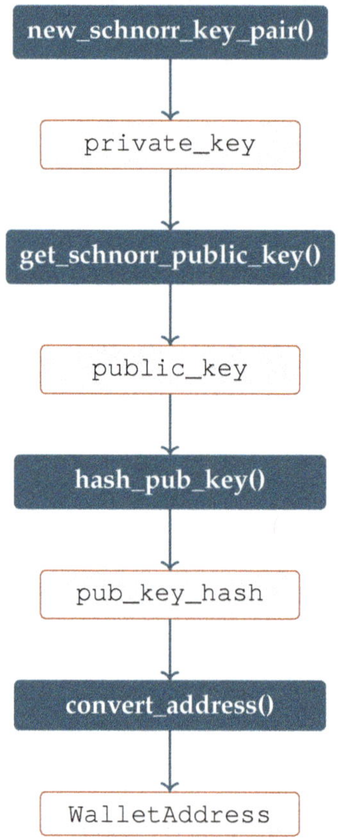

Step 2: Wallet Implementation

i Methods involved

`Wallet::new()`, `Wallet::get_address()`, `Wallet::{get_public_key, get_public_key_hash, get_private_key, get_pkcs8}`, `hash_pub_key(...)`, `convert_address(...)`

The `Wallet` struct holds the private and public key material. Keys are created and persisted as raw bytes, which are then used directly as cryptographic signing material elsewhere in the codebase.

```
#[derive(Clone, Serialize, Deserialize)]
pub struct Wallet {
    // Stored as raw bytes; callers use these bytes as signing material
    // elsewhere in the codebase.
    private_key: Vec<u8>,
    // Stored as raw bytes; used for deriving addresses and for signature
    // verification contexts.
    public_key: Vec<u8>,
}

impl Wallet {
    pub fn new() -> Result<Wallet> {
        // 1) Create a new Schnorr secret key.
        let private_key = new_schnorr_key_pair()?;
        // 2) Derive the corresponding Schnorr public key.
        let public_key = get_schnorr_public_key(&private_key)?;
        Ok(Wallet {
            private_key,
            public_key,
        })
    }
}
```

Listing 227: `Wallet` implementation (part 1: struct and constructor) (`wallet_impl.rs`)

Note: The `new()` method uses the `new_schnorr_key_pair()` and `get_schnorr_public_key()` helpers from the crypto layer (Chapter 9). The cryptography layer (Chapter 9) separates key generation from public-key derivation as distinct operations, reflecting the mathematical relationship: the public key is deterministically computed from the private key.

The `get_address()` method is the primary public API for deriving an address from the wallet's public key. It delegates to the address helpers from the address module.

```
impl Wallet {
    pub fn get_address(&self) -> Result<super::WalletAddress> {
        // 1) Hash the public key into the payload "data" bytes.
        let pub_key_hash = super::hash_pub_key(self.public_key.as_slice());

        // 2) Construct and validate the final Base58 string.
        super::convert_address(pub_key_hash.as_slice())
    }
}
```

Listing 228: `Wallet` implementation (part 1b: address derivation) (`wallet_impl.rs`)

The remaining accessor methods provide callers with access to the private and public key material, as well as a legacy PKCS8-style interface for compatibility with existing signing code.

```rust
impl Wallet {
    pub fn get_public_key(&self) -> &[u8] {
        self.public_key.as_slice()
    }

    pub fn get_public_key_hash(&self) -> Vec<u8> {
        super::hash_pub_key(self.get_public_key())
    }

    pub fn get_private_key(&self) -> &[u8] {
        self.private_key.as_slice()
    }

    pub fn get_pkcs8(&self) -> &[u8] {
        // Kept for compatibility with older signing code that expects
        // "pkcs8-like" bytes.
        self.private_key.as_slice()
    }
}

pub fn hash_pub_key(pub_key: &[u8]) -> Vec<u8> {
    // Taproot-oriented hashing (single SHA256-like digest).
    // The concrete implementation is delegated to `crate::taproot_hash`.
    crate::taproot_hash(pub_key)
}
```

Listing 229: `Wallet` implementation (part 2: key accessors) (`wallet_impl.rs`)

> **✓ Checkpoint**
>
> `Wallet::new()` creates both the private and public keys using Schnorr primitives. `get_address()` hashes the public key and constructs a Base58-encoded payload. The private key is stored as raw bytes and is used as signing material elsewhere in the codebase.

23.5 WalletService: Multiple Wallets and File Persistence

WalletService is a small manager around:

- an in-memory HashMap<WalletAddress, Wallet>
- load/save to a file (default wallets.dat)

Persistence Flow

The diagram below shows the load-mutate-save flow:

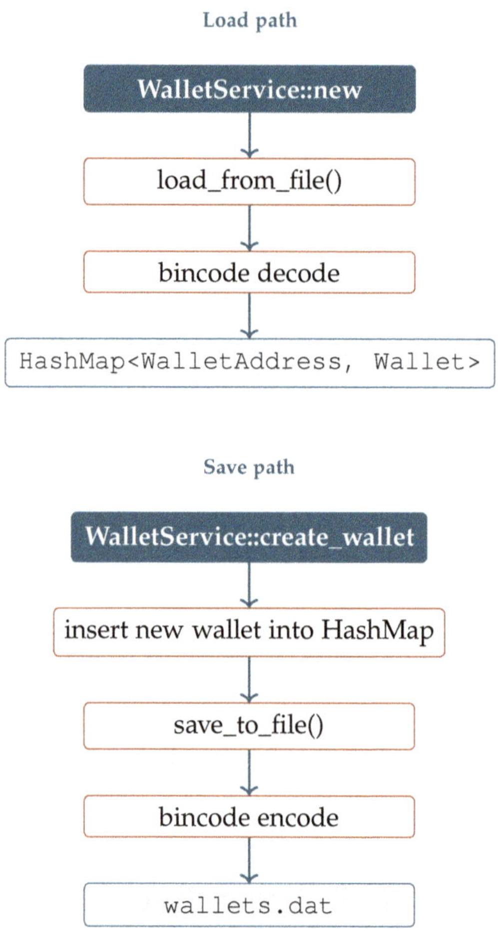

Step 3: WalletService Implementation

> **i Methods involved**
>
> `WalletService::{new, create_wallet, get_addresses, get_wallet}`, `WalletService::{load_from_file, get_wallet_file_path}`, `WalletService::save_to_file(...)` (internal)

```
use crate::error::{BtcError, Result};
use crate::wallet::{Wallet, WalletAddress};
use std::collections::HashMap;
use std::env;
use std::env::current_dir;
use std::fs::{File, OpenOptions};
use std::io::{BufWriter, Read, Write};

pub const DEFAULT_WALLETS_FILE: &str = "wallets.dat";

pub struct WalletService {
    wallets: HashMap<WalletAddress, Wallet>,
}

impl WalletService {
    pub fn new() -> Result<WalletService> {
        let mut wallets = WalletService {
            wallets: HashMap::new(),
        };
        wallets.load_from_file()?;
        Ok(wallets)
    }
}
```

Listing 230: `WalletService` implementation (part 1: imports and struct setup) (`wallet_service.rs`)

The `new()` constructor loads existing wallets from disk. The `create_wallet()` method instantiates a new wallet, inserts it into the in-memory map, and immediately persists the collection via `save_to_file()`.

```
impl WalletService {
    pub fn create_wallet(&mut self) -> Result<WalletAddress> {
        let wallet = Wallet::new()?;
        let address = wallet.get_address()?;
        self.wallets.insert(address.clone(), wallet);
        self.save_to_file()?;
        Ok(address)
    }
}
```

Listing 231: `WalletService` implementation (part 1b: wallet creation) (`wallet_service.rs`)

The remaining methods provide read-only access to the wallet store.

```
    pub fn get_addresses(&self) -> Vec<WalletAddress> {
        self.wallets.keys().cloned().collect()
    }

    pub fn get_wallet(&self, address: &WalletAddress) -> Option<&Wallet> {
        self.wallets.get(address)
    }
}
```

Listing 232: `WalletService` implementation (part 2: query methods) (`wallet_service.rs`)

File I/O: Loading Wallets

The file I/O methods handle persistence by reading and writing a bincode-encoded map to disk:

```
pub fn load_from_file(&mut self) -> Result<()> {
    let path = current_dir()
        .map_err(|e| BtcError::WalletsFilePathError(e.to_string()))?
        .join(self.get_wallet_file_path());

    if !path.exists() {
        return Ok(());
    }

    let mut file = File::open(path).map_err(|e| {
        BtcError::WalletsFileOpenError(e.to_string())
    })?;
    let metadata = file
        .metadata()
        .map_err(|e| BtcError::WalletsFileMetadataError(e.to_string()))?;
    let mut buf = vec![0; metadata.len() as usize];
    let _ = file
        .read(&mut buf)
        .map_err(|e| BtcError::WalletsFileReadError(e.to_string()))?;
```

Listing 233: Loading wallets from disk (part 1: file operations) (`wallet_service.rs`)

After constructing the path and checking for file existence, the method opens the file, reads its metadata to allocate a correctly-sized buffer, and reads the entire file contents. The deserialization step then follows.

```
        // decode_from_slice returns Ok((decoded_value, bytes_read)).
        // The .0 picks the decoded value; the bytes_read count would
        // matter only if we expected trailing data after the wallets
        // record in the same buffer, which we don't.
        let wallets = bincode::serde::decode_from_slice(
            &buf[..],
            bincode::config::standard(),
        )
        .map_err(|e| {
            BtcError::WalletsDeserializationError(e.to_string())
        })?
        .0;
        self.wallets = wallets;
        Ok(())
    }

    pub fn get_wallet_file_path(&self) -> String {
        env::var("WALLET_FILE").unwrap_or(DEFAULT_WALLETS_FILE.to_string())
    }
```

Listing 234: Loading wallets from disk (part 2: deserialization) (`wallet_service.rs`)

✓ Checkpoint

If the wallet file does not exist, `load_from_file()` returns `Ok(())` with an empty HashMap. This allows new wallets to be created from scratch. The file path is determined by the `WALLET_FILE` environment variable or defaults to `wallets.dat`.

File I/O: Saving Wallets

The save operation mirrors the load, but opens the file for writing and flushes the encoded bytes:

```
fn save_to_file(&self) -> Result<()> {
    let path = current_dir()
        .map_err(|e| BtcError::WalletsFilePathError(e.to_string()))?
        .join(self.get_wallet_file_path());

    let file = OpenOptions::new()
        .create(true)
        .truncate(true)
        .write(true)
        .open(&path)
        .map_err(|e| BtcError::SavingWalletsError(e.to_string()))?;
    let mut writer = BufWriter::new(file);
```

Listing 235: Saving wallets to disk (part 1: file setup) (`wallet_service.rs`)

Once the file is opened (with truncation enabled to clear the old wallet data), a `BufWriter` wraps it for efficient buffered writing. The next part serializes the wallet map and writes it to the file.

```
    let wallets_bytes = bincode::serde::encode_to_vec(
        &self.wallets,
        bincode::config::standard(),
    )
    .map_err(|e| {
        BtcError::WalletsSerializationError(e.to_string())
    })?;

    writer
        .write_all(wallets_bytes.as_slice())
        .map_err(|e| BtcError::SavingWalletsError(e.to_string()))?;
    writer
        .flush()
        .map_err(|e| BtcError::SavingWalletsError(e.to_string()))?;
    Ok(())
}
```

Listing 236: Saving wallets to disk (part 2: serialization and flush) (`wallet_service.rs`)

▷ Atomicity note

`OpenOptions::truncate(true)` truncates the file before writing, which provides a simple form of atomicity: the old file is cleared before new data is written. If the write or flush fails, the wallet file is left in an inconsistent state. For production systems, consider writing to a temporary file and then renaming it atomically.

23.6 Key Reading Checklist

As we follow the Rust code, you should be able to answer these questions from the structs and method signatures alone:

- Where does a wallet get its address? (Search for `Wallet::get_address()`.)
- How is the public key hashed? (Look at `hash_pub_key(...)`.)
- How does checksum validation work? (`WalletAddress::validate_address(...)`.)
- Where are multiple wallets stored? (In-memory `HashMap`; persisted via `wallets.dat`.)
- What format are wallets serialized as? (`bincode` standard configuration.)

23.7 Exercises

1. **Multi-Wallet Transfer** — Generate two wallets, fund the first with a coinbase transaction, then send coins from the first wallet to the second. Verify the UTXO set reflects the transfer. Attempt to spend more than the first wallet's balance and confirm the transaction is rejected.
2. **Key Persistence Verification** — Create a wallet, generate an address, and save the wallet. Restart the application, reload the wallet, and verify the same key pair and address are available. This confirms the persistence layer correctly serializes and deserializes cryptographic keys.

23.8 Further Reading

- **BIP-32 (HD Wallets)** — Defines hierarchical deterministic key derivation, allowing an entire tree of key pairs to be generated from a single seed. The `bitcoin` crate in the Rust ecosystem implements this.
- **BIP-39 (Mnemonic Seed Phrases)** — Specifies how a random seed is encoded as a human-readable list of 12 or 24 words. The `bip39` crate provides a Rust implementation.
- **BIP-44 (Multi-Account Hierarchy)** — Builds on BIP-32 to define a standard derivation path (`m/44'/0'/0'/...`) for organizing keys by coin type and account.
- **rust-bitcoin wallet module** — The community's production-grade Bitcoin library for Rust. Studying its wallet implementation reveals the gap between our teaching implementation and production requirements.

Key Takeaways

- ✓ This chapter covered the wallet system that generates key pairs, creates addresses, and persists keys securely.
- ✓ A Base58Check address format with version byte, pub-key-hash, and checksum verification was implemented.
- ✓ The key management lifecycle flows from Schnorr keypair generation through address derivation and wallet persistence.
- ✓ `WalletService` manages multiple wallets in an in-memory `HashMap`, serialized to disk using `bincode`.

24

Web API Architecture

> ▷ **What you will learn in this chapter**
>
> - How to structure a REST API using Axum and Tokio
> - Request handlers, extractors, and middleware patterns
> - Authentication, CORS, logging, and error handling
> - Automatic OpenAPI documentation with Utoipa
> - Rate limiting, security, and production best practices

EVERY desktop app, web UI, and CLI tool talks to your blockchain node through one boundary: the REST API (Representational State Transfer API — an HTTP-based convention where each URL identifies a resource and the HTTP verb says what to do with it: `GET` to read, `POST` to create, and so on). One endpoint mines a block. Another broadcasts a transaction. A third checks your balance. This chapter walks through the REST API layer built with Axum—the routing, request handling, error responses, and authentication that sit between all your clients and the core node logic.

- `bitcoin/src/web/server.rs` (server startup and configuration)
- `bitcoin/src/web/routes/` (endpoint paths and methods)
- `bitcoin/src/web/handlers/` (request logic and responses)
- `bitcoin/src/web/middleware/` (authentication, logging, rate limiting)
- `bitcoin/src/web/models/` (request and response types)

24.1 Introduction and Architecture Overview

The web API layer follows a modular architecture that cleanly separates concerns. Each component has a well-defined responsibility, making the codebase maintainable and testable.

Directory Structure

```
bitcoin/src/web/
+-- mod.rs                  # Module exports
+-- server.rs               # Server initialization
+-- routes/                 # Route definitions
|   +-- mod.rs
|   +-- api.rs              # API routes
|   +-- web.rs              # Web UI routes
+-- handlers/               # Request handlers
|   +-- mod.rs
|   +-- blockchain.rs       # Blockchain endpoints
|   +-- wallet.rs           # Wallet operations
|   +-- transaction.rs      # Transaction management
|   +-- mining.rs           # Mining operations
|   +-- health.rs           # Health checks
|   +-- validation.rs       # Request validation
+-- middleware/             # HTTP middleware
|   +-- mod.rs
|   +-- auth.rs             # Authentication
|   +-- cors.rs             # CORS configuration
|   +-- logging.rs          # Logging
|   +-- rate_limit.rs       # Rate limiting
+-- models/                 # Data models
|   +-- mod.rs
|   +-- requests.rs         # Request structures
|   +-- responses.rs        # Response structures
|   +-- errors.rs           # Error models
+-- openapi.rs              # OpenAPI specification
```

Component Responsibilities

> **i Routes**
>
> Routes define endpoint paths and HTTP methods, connecting URLs to handler functions. Routes are organized by functionality (API routes, web routes) and can be nested or merged.

> **i Handlers**
>
> Handlers contain the business logic for processing requests. Each handler is an async function that extracts data from requests, performs operations using the blockchain node context, and returns structured responses.

> **i Middleware**
>
> Middleware provides cross-cutting concerns like authentication, CORS, logging, and error handling. Middleware wraps handlers, processing requests before they reach handlers and responses after handlers complete.

> **i Models**
>
> Models define the structure of requests and responses using Rust types. Models provide type safety, automatic serialization/deserialization, and validation.

> **i Server**
>
> The server orchestrates the entire web layer, combining routes, middleware, and state into a complete application. It handles server lifecycle, graceful shutdown, and configuration management.

Design Principles

The web API architecture follows five key principles:

1. Separation of Concerns Each component has a single, well-defined responsibility. Routes define endpoints, not business logic. Handlers contain business logic, not routing details. Middleware handles cross-cutting concerns, not domain logic. This separation makes the codebase easier to understand, test, and maintain.

2. Type Safety Rust's type system ensures compile-time validation of requests and responses. Type mismatches are caught during compilation, not at runtime. This includes request extraction, response construction, and state sharing.

3. Async-First Design The entire web layer is built on async/await, enabling efficient concurrent request handling. All handlers are async functions, and the server uses Tokio's async runtime to manage concurrency.

4. Security by Default Security measures are built into the architecture from the ground up: API key-based authentication protects sensitive endpoints, CORS is configured appropriately, internal errors don't leak sensitive information, and request data is validated before processing.

5. Automatic Documentation OpenAPI/Swagger documentation is automatically generated from code, ensuring documentation stays synchronized with implementation.

Request Flow

The diagram above shows the complete request pipeline. We now examine how each stage is implemented, starting with server configuration. Understanding how requests flow through the system is crucial for debugging and extending the API:

Figure 24.1: HTTP Request Processing Pipeline

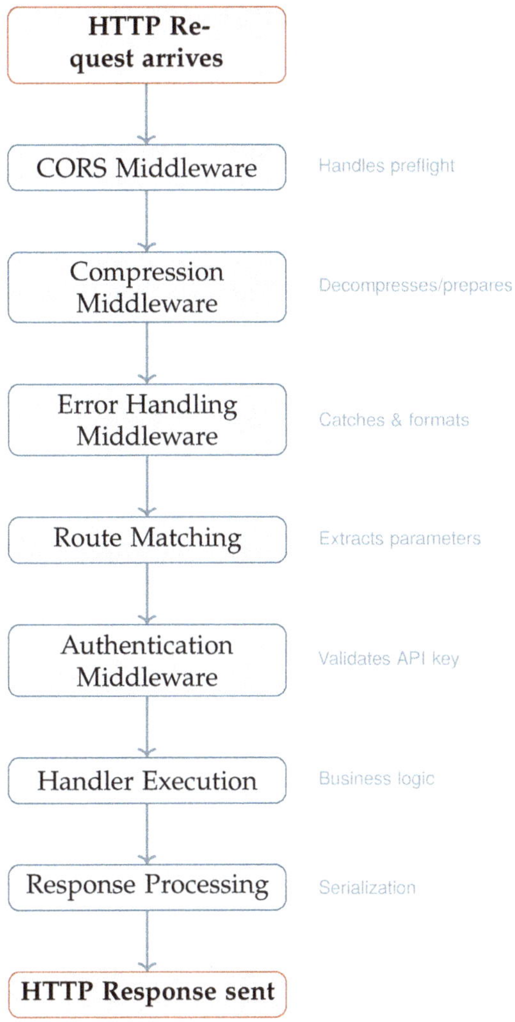

Technology Stack

Axum A modern, ergonomic web framework built on Tokio and Tower that leverages Rust's type system for compile-time safety and excellent performance.

Tokio Powers all async operations, providing the runtime for concurrent request handling.

Tower Provides middleware abstractions and HTTP-specific components like CORS and compression.

Serde Handles JSON serialization and deserialization for request/response bodies.

Utoipa Generates OpenAPI documentation from Rust types.

Tracing Provides structured logging and diagnostics for monitoring and debugging.

24.2 Server Setup and Configuration

The web server is the entry point for all HTTP requests. We explore how it is structured and configured below.

WebServer Structure

The server configuration and node context are encapsulated in the `WebServer` struct:

```rust
pub struct WebServer {
    config: WebServerConfig,
    node: Arc<NodeContext>,
}
```

Listing 237: WebServer struct with configuration

The server holds two key components:

- **Configuration**: Server settings like host, port, CORS, and rate limiting
- **Node Context**: A shared reference to the blockchain node, allowing handlers to access blockchain data

Configuration

All configurable aspects of the server are defined in the `WebServerConfig` struct:

```rust
#[derive(Debug, Clone)]
pub struct WebServerConfig {
    pub host: String,
    pub port: u16,
    pub enable_cors: bool,
    pub enable_rate_limiting: bool,
    pub rate_limit_requests_per_second: u32,
    pub rate_limit_burst_size: u32,
}
```

Listing 238: WebServerConfig struct with sensible defaults

Default Configuration Sensible defaults are provided through the `Default` implementation: Host `0.0.0.0` listens on all network interfaces, which is necessary when running inside Docker or Kubernetes. Port `8080` is a conventional development default. The rate limiter is set conservatively at 10 requests per second for the teaching environment. These defaults work well for development; in production, configuration is done based on specific needs.

Creating the Application Router

The complete application router is built by combining routes and middleware in the `create_app()` method:

```rust
pub fn create_app(
    &self,
) -> Result<Router, Box<dyn std::error::Error + Send + Sync>> {
    let app = Router::new()
        .merge(create_all_api_routes())
        .merge(create_wallet_only_routes())
        .merge(create_web_routes())
        .with_state(self.node.clone());
    // The state is applied after all routes are merged, making the NodeContext
    // available to every handler via Axum's State extractor.

    // Add middleware layers
    let mut app = app;

    // Rate limiting middleware
    if self.config.enable_rate_limiting {
        let rl_config = RateLimitConfig::default();
        if let Some(manager) = build_rate_limiter_manager(&rl_config)? {
            app = app.layer(from_fn_with_state(
                manager,
                axum_rate_limiter::limiter::middleware,
            ));
        }
    }

    // CORS middleware
    if self.config.enable_cors {
        app = app.layer(cors::create_cors_layer());
    }
```

Listing 239: Building the application router with routes and state (part 1)

Once the primary middleware layers are configured, we apply compression and error handling to complete the middleware stack. These final layers wrap the entire request processing pipeline.

```
    // Compression middleware
    app = app.layer(CompressionLayer::new());

    // Error handling middleware
    app =
app.layer(axum::middleware::from_fn(handle_errors));

    Ok(app)
}
```

Listing 240: Adding compression and error handling middleware (part 2)

Router Construction The router is built in several steps:

1. **Route Merging**: Three sets of routes are merged:
   - `create_all_api_routes()` — Main API endpoints including admin routes and health checks
   - `create_wallet_only_routes()` — Wallet-specific endpoints with authentication
   - `create_web_routes()` — Web UI serving and Swagger documentation
2. **State Injection**: The `.with_state(self.node.clone())` call makes the `NodeContext` available to all handlers through Axum's state extraction.
3. **Middleware Layers**: Middleware is applied in order using `.layer()`. Each layer wraps the previous one, creating a request processing pipeline.

Starting the Server

The server is started with graceful shutdown support:

```
pub async fn start_with_shutdown(
    &self,
) -> Result<(), Box<dyn std::error::Error + Send + Sync>> {
    let app = self.create_app()?;

    let addr = SocketAddr::from(([0, 0, 0, 0], self.config.port));

    tracing::info!("Starting web server on {} with graceful shutdown",
                   addr);

    let listener = tokio::net::TcpListener::bind(addr).await?;

    // Handle shutdown signal
    let shutdown_signal = async {
        tokio::signal::ctrl_c()
            .await
            .expect("Failed to install CTRL+C signal handler");
        tracing::info!("Shutdown signal received");
    };

    axum::serve(
        listener,
        app.into_make_service_with_connect_info::<SocketAddr>(),
    )
    .with_graceful_shutdown(shutdown_signal)
    .await?;

    Ok(())
}
```

Listing 241: Server startup with graceful shutdown

Graceful Shutdown The server listens for `CTRL+C` signals and shuts down gracefully. This means in-flight requests are allowed to complete, new connections are rejected, and the server exits cleanly. This is crucial for production deployments where we need to update the server without dropping active requests.

24.3 Routing System

The routing system organizes endpoints into logical groups and applies appropriate middleware.

Route Organization

Routes are organized into four main categories:

1. **Public API Routes** (`/api/v1/*`): Main API endpoints
2. **Admin Routes** (`/api/admin/*`): Admin-only endpoints with authentication
3. **Wallet Routes** (`/api/wallet/*`): Wallet operations with authentication
4. **Web Routes** (/): Web UI and documentation

API Route Structure

The main API endpoints are defined as follows:

```
pub fn create_api_routes() -> Router<Arc<NodeContext>> {
    Router::new()
        // Blockchain endpoints
        .route("/blockchain", get(blockchain::get_blockchain_info))
        .route("/blockchain/blocks", get(blockchain::get_blocks))
        .route("/blockchain/blocks/latest",
               get(blockchain::get_latest_blocks))
        .route("/blockchain/blocks/{hash}",
               get(blockchain::get_block_by_hash))

        // Wallet endpoints
        .route("/wallet", post(wallet::create_wallet))
        .route("/wallet/addresses", get(wallet::get_addresses))
        .route("/wallet/{address}", get(wallet::get_wallet_info))
        .route("/wallet/{address}/balance",
               get(wallet::get_balance))

        // Transaction endpoints
        .route("/transactions", post(transaction::send_transaction))
        .route("/transactions", get(transaction::get_transactions))
        .route("/transactions/mempool",
               get(transaction::get_mempool))
```

Listing 242: Main API route definitions: blockchain and wallet (part 1)

The transaction and mining endpoints complete the set of core API routes. These provide access to mempool transactions and mining operations:

```
        .route("/transactions/mempool/{txid}",

get(transaction::get_mempool_transaction))
        .route("/transactions/address/{address}",

get(transaction::get_address_transactions))

        // Mining endpoints
        .route("/mining/info",
get(mining::get_mining_info))
        .route("/mining/generatetoaddress",
                post(mining::generate_to_address))
}
```

Listing 243: Main API route definitions: transactions and mining (part 2)

Route Patterns Routes are defined using handler functions from the `handlers/` directory:

- **GET routes**: Retrieve data using handlers like `blockchain::get_blockchain_info`
- **POST routes**: Create resources using handlers like `wallet::create_wallet`
- **Path parameters**: `{hash}`, `{address}`, `{txid}` extract values from the URL
- **Query parameters**: Handled through Axum's `Query` extractor in handlers

Admin Routes

The API routes are wrapped with authentication middleware:

```
pub fn create_admin_api_routes() -> Router<Arc<NodeContext>> {
    Router::new()
        .nest("/api/admin", create_api_routes())
        .nest("/api/admin", create_monitor_api_routes())
        .layer(axum::middleware::from_fn(require_admin))
}
```

Listing 244: Admin routes with authentication

Nesting Routes Axum's `.nest()` method allows us to prefix routes. Here, we nest all API routes under `/api/admin`, and the `require_admin` middleware ensures only authenticated admin users can access them.

Wallet-Only Routes

A subset of endpoints for wallet operations is provided:

```
pub fn create_wallet_only_routes() -> Router<Arc<NodeContext>> {
    let wallet_only = Router::new()
        .route("/wallet", post(wallet::create_wallet))
        .route("/transactions", post(transaction::send_transaction));

    Router::new()
        .nest("/api/wallet", wallet_only)
        .layer(axum::middleware::from_fn(require_wallet))
}
```

Listing 245: Wallet-only routes with separate authentication

Why Separate Wallet Routes? Wallet routes use a different authentication key (`BITCOIN_API_WALLET_KEY`) than admin routes. This approach allows us to: give wallet applications limited access (create wallets, send transactions), keep admin operations separate and more secure, and support different use cases (user wallets vs. administrative tools).

Health Check Routes

Health check routes that are public and don't require authentication are defined as follows:

```
pub fn create_monitor_api_routes() ->
Router<Arc<NodeContext>> {
    Router::new()
        .route("/health", get(health::health_check))
        .route("/health/live", get(health::liveness))
        .route("/health/ready",
get(health::readiness))
}
```

Listing 246: Public health check endpoints

These endpoints are essential for container orchestration (Kubernetes and Docker use these for health checks), monitoring (external systems can check service health), and load balancers (can route traffic based on readiness status).

24.4 Request Handlers

Handlers contain the business logic for processing requests. Each handler is an async function that extracts data from the request, processes the data, and returns a response.

Handler Pattern

All handlers follow a consistent pattern:

```
pub async fn handler_name(
    State(node): State<Arc<NodeContext>>,
    // ... other extractors (Path, Query, Json)
) -> Result<Json<ApiResponse<T>>, StatusCode> {
    // 1. Extract and validate input
    // 2. Process the request using NodeContext
    // 3. Build response
    // 4. Return success or error
}
```

Listing 247: Standard handler pattern

Key Components

1. **State Extraction**: `State(node)` gives us access to the blockchain node
2. **Input Extraction**: `Path`, `Query`, `Json` extract data from the request
3. **Return Type**: `Result<Json<ApiResponse<T», StatusCode>` provides type-safe responses
4. **Error Handling**: We convert errors to appropriate HTTP status codes
5. **Async/Await**: All handlers are async functions

Blockchain Handlers

Get Blockchain Info Access to blockchain data is implemented as follows:

```
pub async fn get_blockchain_info(
    State(node): State<Arc<NodeContext>>,
) -> Result<Json<ApiResponse<BlockchainInfoResponse>>,
          StatusCode> {
    let height = node.get_blockchain_height().await
        .map_err(|_| StatusCode::INTERNAL_SERVER_ERROR)?;

    let last_block = node.blockchain().get_last_block().await
        .map_err(|_| StatusCode::INTERNAL_SERVER_ERROR)?;

    let mempool_size = node.get_mempool_size()
        .map_err(|_| StatusCode::INTERNAL_SERVER_ERROR)?;

    let info = BlockchainInfoResponse {
        height,
        difficulty: 1,
        total_blocks: height,
        total_transactions: /* ... */,
        mempool_size,
        last_block_hash: /* ... */,
        last_block_timestamp: chrono::Utc::now(),
    };

    Ok(Json(ApiResponse::success(info)))
}
```

Listing 248: Get blockchain info handler

Get Block by Hash Block lookup by hash is implemented as follows:

```
pub async fn get_block_by_hash(
    State(node): State<Arc<NodeContext>>,
    Path(hash): Path<String>,
) -> Result<Json<ApiResponse<BlockResponse>>, StatusCode> {
    let block = node.get_block_by_hash(&hash).await
        .map_err(|_| StatusCode::INTERNAL_SERVER_ERROR)?;

    match block {
        Some(block) => {
            let response = BlockResponse {
                hash: block.get_hash().to_string(),
                previous_hash: block.get_previous_hash().to_string(),
                // ... other fields
            };
            Ok(Json(ApiResponse::success(response)))
        }
        None => Err(StatusCode::NOT_FOUND),
    }
}
```

Listing 249: Get block by hash handler with path extraction

The `Path(hash)` extractor automatically extracts the `{hash}` parameter from the URL. Axum handles the parsing and validation for us.

Wallet Handlers

Create Wallet Wallet creation is implemented as follows:

```
pub async fn create_wallet(
    State(_node): State<Arc<NodeContext>>,
    Json(_request): Json<CreateWalletRequest>,
) -> Result<Json<ApiResponse<WalletResponse>>, StatusCode> {
    let mut wallet_service = WalletService::new()
        .map_err(|_| StatusCode::INTERNAL_SERVER_ERROR)?;

    let address = wallet_service.create_wallet()
        .map_err(|_| StatusCode::INTERNAL_SERVER_ERROR)?;

    let wallet = wallet_service.get_wallet(&address)
        .ok_or(StatusCode::INTERNAL_SERVER_ERROR)?;

    let response = WalletResponse {
        address: address.as_string(),
        public_key: HEXLOWER.encode(wallet.get_public_key()),
        // (HEXLOWER is provided by the data-encoding crate and encodes bytes as
        // a lowercase hexadecimal string.)
        // In this teaching implementation, WalletService is instantiated per request
        // for clarity. A production system would inject a shared instance via
        // application state to avoid per-request disk I/O.
        created_at: chrono::Utc::now(),
    };

    Ok(Json(ApiResponse::success(response)))
}
```

Listing 250: Create wallet handler

Get Balance Balance queries with type-safe path extraction are implemented as follows:

```
pub async fn get_balance(
    State(node): State<Arc<NodeContext>>,
    Path(address): Path<WalletAddress>,
) -> Result<Json<ApiResponse<BalanceResponse>>, StatusCode> {
    let balance = node.get_balance(&address).await
        .map_err(|_| StatusCode::INTERNAL_SERVER_ERROR)?;

    let utxo_set = UTXOSet::new(node.blockchain().clone());
    let utxo_count = utxo_set.utxo_count(&address).await
        .map_err(|_| StatusCode::INTERNAL_SERVER_ERROR)?;

    let response = BalanceResponse {
        address: address.as_string(),
        balance,
        utxo_count,
        updated_at: chrono::Utc::now(),
    };

    Ok(Json(ApiResponse::success(response)))
}
```

Listing 251: Get balance handler with typed path parameter

Notice that `Path(address)` extracts a `WalletAddress` directly, not a `String`. Axum can deserialize path parameters into custom types, providing compile-time type safety.

Transaction Handlers

Send Transaction Transaction submission is implemented as follows:

```
pub async fn send_transaction(
    State(node): State<Arc<NodeContext>>,
    Json(request): Json<SendTransactionRequest>,
) -> Result<Json<ApiResponse<SendBitCoinResponse>>,
            StatusCode> {
    let txid = node.btc_transaction(
        &request.from_address,
        &request.to_address,
        request.amount
    ).await.map_err(|e| {
        error!("Failed to create transaction: {}", e);
        StatusCode::BAD_REQUEST
    })?;

    info!("Transaction {} submitted successfully", txid);

    let response = SendBitCoinResponse {
        txid,
        timestamp: chrono::Utc::now(),
    };

    Ok(Json(ApiResponse::success(response)))
}
```

Listing 252: Send transaction handler with error mapping

When `btc_transaction` fails, we log the error, map it to `BAD_REQUEST`, and return early. `BAD_REQUEST` is HTTP status `400` and means "the request itself is malformed — something on your end, not ours." Other status codes used elsewhere in this chapter follow the same convention: `401 UNAUTHORIZED` (the request lacks valid credentials), `404 NOT_FOUND` (the addressed resource does not exist), `429 TOO_MANY_REQUESTS` (rate limit exceeded), `500 INTERNAL_SERVER_ERROR` (the node itself failed while handling the request), and `503 SERVICE_UNAVAILABLE` (the node is up but temporarily refusing work). Mapping every error path to the right code is what lets a client tell "I sent the wrong thing" from "the server is broken."

Mining Handlers

Get Mining Info Mining status is provided as follows:

```
pub async fn get_mining_info(
    State(node): State<Arc<NodeContext>>,
) -> Result<Json<ApiResponse<MiningInfoResponse>>,
            StatusCode> {
    let height = node.get_blockchain_height().await
        .map_err(|_|
StatusCode::INTERNAL_SERVER_ERROR)?;

    let mempool_size = node.get_mempool_size()
        .map_err(|_|
StatusCode::INTERNAL_SERVER_ERROR)?;

    let response = MiningInfoResponse {
        blocks: height as u64,
        currentblocksize: 0,
        currentblocktx: mempool_size as u32,
        difficulty: 1.0,
        networkhashps: 0.0,
        pooledtx: mempool_size as u32,
    };

    Ok(Json(ApiResponse::success(response)))
}
```

Listing 253: Get mining info handler

Generate to Address Block generation is implemented as follows:

```
pub async fn generate_to_address(
    State(node): State<Arc<NodeContext>>,
    Json(request): Json<GenerateToAddressRequest>,
) -> Result<Json<ApiResponse<GenerateToAddressResponse>>,
            StatusCode> {
    // Validate address
    let address = WalletAddress::from_string(&request.address)
        .map_err(|_| StatusCode::BAD_REQUEST)?;

    // Generate blocks
    let block_hashes = (0..request.nblocks)
        .map(|_| {
            broadcast_new_block(&node, &address).await
        })
        .collect::<Result<Vec<_>, _>>()
        .map_err(|_| StatusCode::INTERNAL_SERVER_ERROR)?;

    let response = GenerateToAddressResponse {
        block_hashes,
    };

    Ok(Json(ApiResponse::success(response)))
}
```

Listing 254: Generate to address handler

Health Check Handlers

Health Check Comprehensive system status is provided as follows:

```
pub async fn health_check(
    State(node): State<Arc<NodeContext>>,
) -> Result<Json<ApiResponse<HealthResponse>>, StatusCode> {
    let height = node.get_blockchain_height().await
        .map_err(|_| StatusCode::INTERNAL_SERVER_ERROR)?;

    let connected_peers = node.get_peer_count().unwrap_or(0);

    let health_response = HealthResponse {
        status: "healthy".to_string(),
        version: env!("CARGO_PKG_VERSION").to_string(),
        uptime_seconds: /* ... */,
        blockchain_height: height,
        connected_peers,
        memory_usage_mb: 0.0,
    };

    Ok(Json(ApiResponse::success(health_response)))
}
```

Listing 255: Health check handler with full metrics

Liveness Probe A simple liveness check is provided as follows:

```
pub async fn liveness() -> Result<Json<ApiResponse<String>>,
                                  StatusCode> {
    Ok(Json(ApiResponse::success("alive".to_string())))
}
```

Listing 256: Liveness probe handler

Readiness Probe We check if the service is ready to handle requests:

```
pub async fn readiness(
    State(node): State<Arc<NodeContext>>,
) -> Result<Json<ApiResponse<String>>, StatusCode> {
    match node.get_blockchain_height().await {
        Ok(_) =>
Ok(Json(ApiResponse::success("ready".to_string()))),
        Err(_) =>
Err(StatusCode::SERVICE_UNAVAILABLE),
    }
}
```

Listing 257: Readiness probe handler

Why Three Health Endpoints?

- `/health` : Comprehensive health check with detailed metrics
- `/health/live` : Simple liveness check (is the process running?)
- `/health/ready` : Readiness check (can the service handle requests?)

Kubernetes uses `/health/live` to determine if a pod should be restarted and `/health/ready` to determine if traffic should be routed to the pod.

24.5 Middleware Layer

Middleware provides cross-cutting concerns like authentication, CORS, logging, and error handling.

Authentication Middleware

Routes are protected by checking API keys in authentication middleware:

```
pub async fn require_role(
    mut req: axum::http::Request<axum::body::Body>,
    required: Role,
    next: axum::middleware::Next,
) -> Result<axum::response::Response, StatusCode> {
    let key = req.headers().get("X-API-Key")
        .and_then(|h| h.to_str().ok());

    let caller_role = match key {
        Some(k) if is_admin_key(k) => Role::Admin,
        Some(k) if is_wallet_key(k) => Role::Wallet,
        _ => return Err(StatusCode::UNAUTHORIZED),
    };

    // Admin can access wallet routes too
    let allowed = caller_role == required
        || (caller_role == Role::Admin
            && required == Role::Wallet);
```

Listing 258: Role extraction in authentication middleware (part 1)

After determining whether the caller has sufficient privilege, we reject unauthorized requests and attach the role to the request for use by downstream handlers.

```
    if !allowed {
        return Err(StatusCode::FORBIDDEN);
    }

    // Attach role to extensions for handlers
    req.extensions_mut().insert(caller_role);

    Ok(next.run(req).await)
}
```

Listing 259: Authorization and role attachment (part 2)

How Authentication Works

1. Extract API Key from the `X-API-Key` header
2. Determine Role by checking if the key matches admin or wallet keys
3. Check Authorization to verify the role has permission for the route
4. Attach Role to request extensions for handlers to use
5. Continue or Reject the request

Role Hierarchy Admin users can access both admin and wallet routes, but wallet users can only access wallet routes. This provides a clear security model.

Convenience Functions Convenience wrappers are provided as follows:

```rust
pub async fn require_admin(
    req: axum::http::Request<axum::body::Body>,
    next: axum::middleware::Next,
) -> Result<axum::response::Response, StatusCode> {
    require_role(req, Role::Admin, next).await
}

pub async fn require_wallet(
    req: axum::http::Request<axum::body::Body>,
    next: axum::middleware::Next,
) -> Result<axum::response::Response, StatusCode> {
    require_role(req, Role::Wallet, next).await
}
```

Listing 260: Authentication middleware convenience functions

Key Validation API keys are validated from environment variables as follows:

```
fn is_admin_key(k: &str) -> bool {
    let expected = std::env::var("BITCOIN_API_ADMIN_KEY")
        .unwrap_or_else(|_| "admin-secret".to_string());
    k == expected
}

fn is_wallet_key(k: &str) -> bool {
    let expected = std::env::var("BITCOIN_API_WALLET_KEY")
        .unwrap_or_else(|_| "wallet-secret".to_string());
    k == expected
}
```

Listing 261: API key validation from environment

> ⚠ Security Note
>
> In production, always set strong keys via environment variables. Consider using a key management service for production deployments.

CORS Middleware

Web browsers are allowed to make requests from different origins through CORS (Cross-Origin Resource Sharing). By default, a browser will refuse to let JavaScript loaded from `https://app.example.com` make a `fetch()` call to `https://api.example.com`, because the origins differ. CORS is the mechanism the server uses to opt in: before the real request, the browser sends a small "preflight" `OPTIONS` request asking "are you willing to accept a cross-origin call from this origin, with this method, with these headers?" If the server's response says yes, the actual request follows. The middleware below answers that preflight.

```
pub fn create_cors_layer() -> CorsLayer {
    CorsLayer::new()
        .allow_origin(Any)
        .allow_methods(Any)
        .allow_headers(Any)
        .expose_headers(Any)
        .max_age(std::time::Duration::from_secs(86400))
}
```

Listing 262: CORS middleware configuration

CORS Configuration

- `allow_origin(Any)` : Allows requests from any origin (development only)
- `allow_methods(Any)` : Allows all HTTP methods (GET, POST, etc.)
- `allow_headers(Any)` : Allows all request headers
- `expose_headers(Any)` : Exposes all response headers to JavaScript
- `max_age` : Caches the preflight result for `86400` seconds (24 hours), so the browser does not need to re-ask the server's permission on every subsequent cross-origin call.

Production CORS For production, we use a restricted version:

```
pub fn create_cors_layer_with_origins(
    origins: Vec<String>,
) -> CorsLayer {
    let mut cors = CorsLayer::new()
        .allow_methods(Any)
        .allow_headers(Any)
        .expose_headers(Any)
.max_age(std::time::Duration::from_secs(86400));

    for origin in origins {
        if let Ok(parsed_origin) =
origin.parse::<axum::http::HeaderValue>() {
            cors = cors.allow_origin(parsed_origin);
        }
    }

    cors
}
```

Listing 263: Production CORS with restricted origins

Rate Limiting Middleware

We prevent abuse by limiting the number of requests clients can make within a specified time window.

```
pub struct RateLimitConfig {
    pub requests_per_second: u32,
    pub burst_size: u32,
}

pub fn create_rate_limit_layer(
    config: RateLimitConfig,
) -> impl tower::Layer<axum::Router> + Clone {
    // Returns rate limiting layer
}
```

Listing 264: Rate limiting configuration

Rate Limiting Features

- **Token Bucket Algorithm**: Allows bursts up to `burst_size` while maintaining average rate
- **Per-IP Limiting**: Tracks requests by client IP address
- **Per-API-Key Limiting**: Supports API key-based rate limiting
- **Automatic Cleanup**: Removes inactive entries to manage memory
- **Standard Headers**: Returns `X-RateLimit-Limit`, `X-RateLimit-Remaining`
- **429 Response**: Returns `429 Too Many Requests` when limits exceeded

Error Handling Middleware

Errors are caught and formatted through error handling middleware:

```
async fn handle_errors(
    request: axum::http::Request<axum::body::Body>,
    next: axum::middleware::Next,
) -> Result<axum::response::Response, StatusCode> {
    let response = next.run(request).await;

    // Log error response body if status indicates error
    let is_error = response.status().is_server_error()
        || response.status().is_client_error();
    if is_error {
        let (parts, body) = response.into_parts();
        let body_bytes = axum::body::to_bytes(body, usize::MAX)
            .await
            .unwrap_or_default();
        let body_str = String::from_utf8_lossy(&body_bytes);

        tracing::error!(
            "[handle_errors]: Error response ({}): {}",
            parts.status,
            body_str
        );
```

Listing 265: Error handling middleware: error detection and logging

After detecting and logging the error, internal server errors are sanitized before being sent to the client:

```
            // Format internal server errors safely
            if parts.status == StatusCode::INTERNAL_SERVER_ERROR {
                let error_response = ErrorResponse {
                    error: "Internal Server Error".to_string(),
                    message:
                        "An unexpected error occurred".to_string(),
                    status_code: 500,
                    timestamp: chrono::Utc::now(),
                };

                return Ok(Json(ApiResponse::<()>::error(
                    serde_json::to_string(&error_response)
                        .unwrap_or_else(|_|
                            "Unknown error".to_string()),
                )).into_response());
            }

            Ok(response)
        } else {
            Ok(response)
        }
}
```

Listing 266: Error handling middleware: sanitized error response

Error Handling Flow

1. Run Next Middleware to process the request
2. Check Status to determine if the response indicates an error
3. Log Errors for debugging
4. Format Errors by converting internal server errors to user-friendly responses
5. Preserve Errors by allowing other errors to pass through unchanged

i Error Sanitization

Internal server errors are sanitized before being sent to clients. This prevents leaking sensitive information like stack traces or internal paths.

24.6 Data Models

Data models define the structure of requests and responses. They provide type safety and automatic serialization/deserialization using Serde and Utoipa.

Response Models

Generic API Response All API responses use a consistent wrapper:

```rust
#[derive(Debug, Serialize, Deserialize, ToSchema)]
pub struct ApiResponse<T> {
    pub success: bool,
    pub data: Option<T>,
    pub error: Option<String>,
    pub timestamp: DateTime<Utc>,
}

impl<T> ApiResponse<T> {
    pub fn success(data: T) -> Self {
        Self {
            success: true,
            data: Some(data),
            error: None,
            timestamp: Utc::now(),
        }
    }

    pub fn error(error: String) -> Self {
        Self {
            success: false,
            data: None,
            error: Some(error),
            timestamp: Utc::now(),
        }
    }
}
```

Listing 267: Generic API response wrapper

Why This Structure?

- **Consistent Format**: All responses follow the same structure
- **Type Safety**: Generic `T` ensures compile-time type checking
- **Error Handling**: Errors are clearly distinguished from success
- **Timestamps**: Every response includes a timestamp for debugging

```
#[derive(Debug, Serialize, Deserialize, ToSchema)]
pub struct BlockchainInfoResponse {
    pub height: usize,
    pub difficulty: u32,
    pub total_blocks: usize,
    pub total_transactions: usize,
    pub mempool_size: usize,
    pub last_block_hash: String,
    pub last_block_timestamp: DateTime<Utc>,
}
```

Listing 268: Blockchain information response model

```
#[derive(Debug, Serialize, Deserialize, ToSchema)]
pub struct BlockResponse {
    pub hash: String,
    pub previous_hash: String,
    pub timestamp: DateTime<Utc>,
    pub height: usize,
    pub nonce: u64,
    pub difficulty: u32,
    pub transaction_count: usize,
    pub merkle_root: String,
    pub size_bytes: usize,
}
```

Listing 269: Block response model

```
#[derive(Debug, Serialize, Deserialize, ToSchema)]
pub struct TransactionResponse {
    pub txid: String,
    pub is_coinbase: bool,
    pub input_count: usize,
    pub output_count: usize,
    pub total_input_value: i32,
    pub total_output_value: i32,
    pub fee: i32,
    pub timestamp: DateTime<Utc>,
    pub size_bytes: usize,
}
```

Listing 270: Transaction response model

```
#[derive(Debug, Serialize, Deserialize, ToSchema)]
pub struct WalletResponse {
    pub address: String,
    pub public_key: String,
    pub created_at: DateTime<Utc>,
}
```

Listing 271: Wallet response model

```
#[derive(Debug, Serialize, Deserialize, ToSchema)]
pub struct BalanceResponse {
    pub address: String,
    pub balance: i32,
    pub unconfirmed_balance: i32,
    pub utxo_count: usize,
    pub last_updated: DateTime<Utc>,
}
```

Listing 272: Balance response model

Request Models

Request models define the structure of incoming requests and include validation:

```
#[derive(Debug, Serialize, Deserialize, Validate,
         ToSchema)]
pub struct CreateWalletRequest {
    #[validate(length(
        min = 1,
        max = 100,
        message = "Wallet name must be 1-100
characters"
    ))]
    pub name: Option<String>,
}
```

Listing 273: Create wallet request with validation

```
#[derive(Debug, Serialize, Deserialize, Validate,
         ToSchema)]
pub struct SendTransactionRequest {
    pub from_address: WalletAddress,
    pub to_address: WalletAddress,
    #[validate(range(
        min = 1,
        message = "Amount must be greater than 0"
    ))]
    pub amount: i32,
}
```

Listing 274: Send transaction request with validation

```rust
#[derive(Debug, Serialize, Deserialize, Validate,
         ToSchema)]
pub struct BlockQuery {
    #[validate(range(
        min = 0,
        message = "Page must be 0 or greater"
    ))]
    pub page: Option<u32>,

    #[validate(range(
        min = 1,
        max = 100,
        message = "Limit must be 1-100"
    ))]
    pub limit: Option<u32>,

    pub hash: Option<String>,
}
```

Listing 275: Block query parameters with validation

Validation The `validator` crate provides compile-time and runtime validation:

- **Length validation**: Ensures strings are within bounds
- **Range validation**: Ensures numbers are within bounds
- **Custom validation**: Can be added for complex rules

Error Models

Error models provide structured error responses:

```
#[derive(Debug, Serialize, Deserialize, ToSchema)]
pub struct ErrorResponse {
    pub error: String,
    pub message: String,
    pub status_code: u16,
    pub timestamp: DateTime<Utc>,
}
```

Listing 276: Error response model

```
#[derive(Debug, Serialize, Deserialize)]
pub enum WebError {
    ValidationError(String),
    NotFound(String),
    InternalError(String),
    Unauthorized(String),
    RateLimitExceeded,
    InvalidRequest(String),
    ServiceUnavailable(String),
}
```

Listing 277: Web error enumeration

```
impl WebError {
    pub fn status_code(&self) -> u16 {
        match self {
            WebError::ValidationError(_) => 400,
            WebError::NotFound(_) => 404,
            WebError::InternalError(_) => 500,
            WebError::Unauthorized(_) => 401,
            WebError::RateLimitExceeded => 429,
            WebError::InvalidRequest(_) => 400,
            WebError::ServiceUnavailable(_) => 503,
        }
    }
}
```

Listing 278: Error to HTTP status code mapping

24.7 Error Handling

Error handling in the web layer follows a consistent pattern that provides clear feedback to clients while maintaining security.

Error Flow

1. **Handler Error**: Handler encounters an error
2. **Status Code Mapping**: Error is mapped to appropriate HTTP status code
3. **Error Response**: Error is formatted into `ErrorResponse`
4. **Logging**: Error is logged for debugging
5. **Client Response**: Formatted error is sent to client

Common Error Patterns

```
match block {
    Some(block) => Ok(Json(ApiResponse::success(response))),
    None => Err(StatusCode::NOT_FOUND),
}
```

Listing 279: Not found error pattern

```
if !request.validate().is_ok() {
    return Err(StatusCode::BAD_REQUEST);
}
```

Listing 280: Validation error pattern

```
let result = operation().await
    .map_err(|e| {
        error!("Operation failed: {}", e);
        StatusCode::INTERNAL_SERVER_ERROR
    })?;
```

Listing 281: Internal server error pattern

Error Middleware

The `handle_errors()` function in `server.rs` catches unhandled errors and formats them. Internal server errors are sanitized before being sent to clients. This prevents leaking sensitive information like stack traces or internal paths.

24.8 Rate Limiting Implementation

We prevent abuse by limiting the number of requests clients can make within a specified time window.

Why Rate Limiting Matters

Blockchains are resource-heavy systems: even "simple" endpoints might touch storage, validate objects, or query UTXO state. A web API without protections is easy to overload intentionally (DoS) or accidentally (misconfigured clients). Rate limiting gives us a predictable upper bound on request volume per client and per endpoint.

Implementation Overview

We implemented rate limiting as Axum middleware using the `axum_rate_limiter` crate. The middleware:

- Uses a **Redis-backed token bucket** to track limits across server instances
- Supports multiple strategies (IP, URL, header, query, body)
- Allows an **IP whitelist** to bypass rate limiting for trusted sources
- Adds response headers: `X-RateLimit-Limit` , `X-RateLimit-Remaining`
- Rejects requests with **HTTP 429** when limits are exceeded

Token Bucket Algorithm

Think of every bucket as a small wallet of tokens:

- **Capacity** (`tokens_count`): Maximum tokens the bucket can hold (burst allowance)
- **Refill interval** (`add_tokens_every` seconds): How often a token is added back
- Every request **spends 1 token**
- If bucket has **0 tokens**, the request is rejected (429)

Settings File (TOML) Schema

The limiter reads configuration from a TOML file. Set the path using the `RL_SETTINGS_PATH` environment variable (default: `./Settings.toml`).

```
[rate_limiter]
redis_addr = "127.0.0.1:6379"
ip_whitelist = ["127.0.0.1"]
```

Listing 282: Rate limiter TOML configuration

```
[rate_limiter]
redis_addr = "127.0.0.1:6379"
ip_whitelist = ["127.0.0.1"]

# Per-IP limit: bursts of 20, refill 1 token per 6
sec
[[rate_limiter.limiter]]
strategy = "ip"
global_bucket = { tokens_count = 20,
add_tokens_every = 6 }

# Tighten specific expensive endpoints
[[rate_limiter.limiter]]
strategy = "url"
global_bucket = { tokens_count = 60,
add_tokens_every = 1 }
buckets_per_value = [
  { value = "/api/mining/generate",
    tokens_count = 2, add_tokens_every = 60 },
]
```

Listing 283: Complete rate limiter configuration

24.9 OpenAPI Documentation

The web layer includes automatic OpenAPI/Swagger documentation generation using the `utoipa` crate.

OpenAPI Definition

```
#[derive(OpenApi)]
#[openapi(
    paths(
        health::health_check,
        blockchain::get_blockchain_info,
        wallet::create_wallet,
        // ... all endpoints
    ),
    components(
        schemas(
            BlockchainInfoResponse,
            WalletResponse,
            // ... all models
        )
    ),
    tags(
        (name = "Health",
         description = "Health check endpoints"),
        (name = "Blockchain",
         description = "Blockchain data and information"),
        // ... all tags
    ),
```

Listing 284: OpenAPI definition with paths and schemas (part 1)

The metadata section completes the OpenAPI specification by defining service information and server configuration. Swagger UI uses this information to display the API details and determine where requests should be directed.

```
    info(
        title = "Blockchain API",
        version = "0.1.0",
        description = "A comprehensive blockchain
API"
    ),
    servers(
        (
            url = "http://localhost:8080",
            description = "Local development server"
        )
    )
)]
pub struct ApiDoc;
```

Listing 285: OpenAPI metadata and server configuration (part 2)

Swagger UI

The `create_swagger_ui()` function serves Swagger UI automatically:

```
pub fn create_swagger_ui() -> SwaggerUi {
    SwaggerUi::new("/swagger-ui")
        .url("/api-docs/openapi.json",
ApiDoc::openapi())
}
```

Listing 286: Swagger UI creation

Benefits

- **Interactive Documentation**: Test endpoints directly from browser
- **Automatic Updates**: Documentation stays in sync with code
- **Type Safety**: OpenAPI schema generated from Rust types
- **Client Generation**: Generate client libraries from schema

How Data Models Generate OpenAPI Schemas

When a data model has the `ToSchema` derive macro, Utoipa automatically generates an OpenAPI schema. Example:

```
#[derive(Debug, Serialize, Deserialize, ToSchema)]
pub struct WalletResponse {
    pub address: String,
    pub public_key: String,
    pub created_at: DateTime<Utc>,
}
```

Listing 287: Data model with OpenAPI schema generation

Generates OpenAPI schema:

```
{
  "WalletResponse": {
    "type": "object",
    "required": ["address", "public_key",
"created_at"],
    "properties": {
      "address": { "type": "string" },
      "public_key": { "type": "string" },
      "created_at": {
        "type": "string",
        "format": "date-time"
      }
    }
  }
}
```

Listing 288: Generated OpenAPI schema from model

Accessing Documentation

Once the server is running:

- **Swagger UI**: `http://localhost:8080/swagger-ui` — Interactive documentation
- **OpenAPI JSON**: `http://localhost:8080/api-docs/openapi.json` — Raw specification

24.10 Security Architecture

Security is built into the web layer from the ground up.

Authentication

API Key Authentication

- Keys are passed via `X-API-Key` header
- Admin and wallet keys are separate
- Keys are validated against environment variables
- Default keys are provided for development only

Role-Based Access Control

- **Admin role**: Full access to all endpoints
- **Wallet role**: Limited access to wallet operations
- **Unauthenticated**: Only health check endpoints

CORS Configuration

Development Allows all origins (for local development), all methods and headers.

Production

- Restrict to specific origins
- Limit methods and headers
- Set appropriate cache times

Error Handling Security

Error Sanitization

- Internal errors don't leak stack traces
- Sensitive information is filtered
- Generic error messages for clients
- Detailed errors in logs only

Rate Limiting

- Per-IP rate limiting
- Per-API-key rate limiting
- Configurable limits
- Burst handling

24.11 Best Practices and Patterns

Throughout the web layer, we follow several best practices.

Type Safety

- Use Rust's type system for compile-time safety
- Custom types for domain concepts (`WalletAddress` , etc.)
- Strong typing prevents many runtime errors

Async-First Design

- All handlers are async
- Non-blocking I/O throughout
- Efficient concurrent request handling

Consistent Error Handling

- All errors return appropriate HTTP status codes
- Structured error responses
- Comprehensive error logging with full context

Separation of Concerns

- Routes define endpoints
- Handlers contain business logic
- Middleware handles cross-cutting concerns
- Models define data structures

Documentation

- OpenAPI documentation automatically generated
- Inline documentation for all public functions
- Examples in documentation

Structured Logging and Observability

We use structured logging with key-value pairs for queryability:

```
use tracing::{error, info};

// Good: Structured logging with context
info!(
    txid = %txid,
    from = %from_address,
    to = %to_address,
    amount = amount,
    "Transaction submitted successfully"
);

// Good: Error logging with full context
error!(
    error = %e,
    txid = %txid,
    from = %from_address,
    "Failed to process transaction"
);
```

Listing 289: Structured logging with context

```
use tracing::instrument;

#[instrument]
async fn process_transaction(txid: String) {
    // Automatic span creation with function name
    // All logs include span context
    info!("Processing transaction");
}
```

Listing 290: Spans for operation context

Log Level Guidelines

- **ERROR**: Operation failures that prevent completion
- **WARN**: Recoverable issues or deprecations
- **INFO**: Normal operation events (request/response, state changes)
- **DEBUG**: Detailed diagnostics (disabled in production)
- **TRACE**: Very detailed tracing (disabled in production)

Testing Considerations

- Handlers are pure functions (easy to test)
- State is injected (easy to mock)
- Error cases are explicit

24.12 Framework Reference: Axum

▷ Deep Dive: Axum Framework Reference

This section provides a detailed reference to Axum framework features used in our blockchain API.

State Injection

State injection makes data available to all handlers without global variables, with compile-time type safety.

```rust
// Create router with state
let app = Router::new()
    .merge(routes)
    .with_state(self.node.clone());

// Extract in handlers
pub async fn get_blockchain_info(
    State(node): State<Arc<NodeContext>>,
) -> Result<Json<ApiResponse<BlockchainInfoResponse>>,
                StatusCode> {
    let height = node.get_blockchain_height().await?;
    Ok(Json(ApiResponse::success(response)))
}
```

Listing 291: State injection pattern

Key Concepts

1. Type must match between `.with_state()` and `State()` extractor
2. Use `Arc<T>` for shared ownership without cloning
3. State is typically immutable; use interior mutability if needed

Middleware Layers

Middleware processes requests in order and provides cross-cutting concerns.

Middleware Execution Order Layers wrap each other; order matters:

```
let mut app =
Router::new().with_state(self.node.clone());

// 1. CORS (outermost - handles preflight first)
app = app.layer(cors_layer());

// 2. Compression
app = app.layer(CompressionLayer::new());

// 3. Error handling (innermost - catches
handler errors)
app = app.layer(axum::middleware::from_fn(handl
e_errors));

// Request flow: CORS -> Compression -> Error
Handler -> Handler
```

Listing 292: Middleware layer order

```
async fn my_middleware(
    request: Request<Body>,
    next: Next,
) -> Result<Response, StatusCode> {
    // Pre-processing
    let response = next.run(request).await;
    // Post-processing
    Ok(response)
}

// Apply with from_fn
.layer(axum::middleware::from_fn(my_middleware))
```

Listing 293: Custom middleware pattern

Tower Layers and Services Axum is built on Tower, which provides:

- **Services**: Async functions that take requests and return responses
- **Layers**: Middleware that wraps services to add functionality
- **Composability**: Middleware can be stacked and combined

```
use tower_http::cors::CorsLayer;
use tower_http::compression::CompressionLayer;
use tower_http::trace::TraceLayer;
use tower_http::services::ServeDir;

.layer(CorsLayer::new().allow_origin(Any))
.layer(CompressionLayer::new())
.layer(TraceLayer::new_for_http())
.nest_service("/assets",
ServeDir::new("/path/to/assets"))
```

Listing 294: Tower HTTP middleware components

Request Extractors

Extractors pull data from HTTP requests and make it available to handlers.

```
// Route: "/blockchain/blocks/{hash}"
pub async fn get_block_by_hash(
    State(node): State<Arc<NodeContext>>,
    Path(hash): Path<String>,
) -> Result<Json<ApiResponse<BlockResponse>>,
            StatusCode> {
    let block =
node.get_block_by_hash(&hash).await?;
    Ok(Json(ApiResponse::success(block)))
}
```

Listing 295: Path parameter extraction

Type-Safe Path Extraction Axum deserializes path parameters into custom types:

```
pub async fn get_balance(
    State(node): State<Arc<NodeContext>>,
    Path(address): Path<WalletAddress>,  // Custom type
) -> Result<Json<ApiResponse<BalanceResponse>>,
            StatusCode> {
    let balance = node.get_balance(&address).await?;
    Ok(Json(ApiResponse::success(balance)))
}
```

Listing 296: Custom type path extraction

Query Extractor Query parameters are extracted and deserialized:

```
pub async fn get_blocks(
    State(node): State<Arc<NodeContext>>,
    Query(params): Query<BlockQuery>,
) -> Result<Json<ApiResponse<Vec<BlockResponse>>>,
            StatusCode> {
    let page = params.page.unwrap_or(0);
    let limit = params.limit.unwrap_or(10).min(100);
    // ... fetch and return blocks
}
```

Listing 297: Query parameter extraction

JSON Extractor JSON request bodies are automatically deserialized:

```
pub async fn send_transaction(
    State(node): State<Arc<NodeContext>>,
    Json(request): Json<SendTransactionRequest>,
) -> Result<Json<ApiResponse<SendBitCoinResponse>>,
            StatusCode> {
    // request is automatically deserialized
    // Validation via validator crate happens here
}
```

Listing 298: JSON body extraction

Routing

Routes organize endpoints and HTTP methods.

```
Router::new()
    .route("/path", get(handler1))
    .route("/path", post(handler2))
    .route("/path/:id", get(handler3))
```

Listing 299: Basic route definitions

```
let admin_routes = Router::new()
    .route("/users", get(list_users))
    .route("/users/:id", delete(delete_user));

Router::new()
    .nest("/api/admin", admin_routes)
    .route("/health", get(health))
```

Listing 300: Route nesting and merging

Response Types

Handlers return different response types depending on the situation.

```rust
pub async fn handler() -> Result<Json<MyResponse>,
                                  StatusCode> {
    Ok(Json(MyResponse { /* ... */ }))
}
```

Listing 301: JSON response type

```rust
pub async fn handler() -> Result<StatusCode, StatusCode> {
    // Return success (no body)
    Ok(StatusCode::OK)

    // Return error
    Err(StatusCode::NOT_FOUND)
}
```

Listing 302: Status code response

IntoResponse Trait Axum uses the `IntoResponse` trait to convert handler return types into HTTP responses. Any type implementing `IntoResponse` can be returned from a handler:

```
impl<T: Serialize> IntoResponse for Json<T> {
    fn into_response(self) -> Response {
        // Serializes T to JSON
        // Sets Content-Type header
        // Returns Response
    }
}

// Handlers return values that implement IntoResponse
pub async fn handler()
    -> impl IntoResponse
{
    Json(response)  // Implements IntoResponse
}
```

Listing 303: IntoResponse trait implementation

Error Handling

Axum provides error handling through extractors and middleware.

```
pub async fn handler(
    Path(id): Path<u64>,
) -> Result<Json<MyResponse>, StatusCode> {
    let item = database.get(id)
        .ok_or(StatusCode::NOT_FOUND)?;

    Ok(Json(response))
}
```

Listing 304: Error response pattern

CORS Configuration

```
use tower_http::cors::{CorsLayer, Any};

let cors = CorsLayer::new()
    .allow_origin(Any)
    .allow_methods(Any)
    .allow_headers(Any);

app = app.layer(cors);
```

Listing 305: Axum CORS setup

Compression

```
use tower_http::compression::CompressionLayer;

app = app.layer(CompressionLayer::new());
```

Listing 306: Axum compression setup

Async/Await

All Axum handlers are async, enabling concurrent request handling:

```
pub async fn handler(
    State(node): State<Arc<NodeContext>>,
) -> Result<Json<ApiResponse<T>>, StatusCode> {
    // Can use .await on async operations
    let data = node.get_data().await?;
    Ok(Json(ApiResponse::success(data)))
}
```

Listing 307: Async handler pattern

Key Takeaways

- ✓ A complete REST API using Axum with type-safe routing, handlers, and extractors was built
- ✓ Authentication and authorization middleware with role-based access control was implemented
- ✓ CORS, compression, and rate limiting were configured for production readiness
- ✓ Data models with validation for request and response structures were designed
- ✓ Comprehensive error handling with appropriate HTTP status codes was established
- ✓ Automatic OpenAPI/Swagger documentation is generated from Rust types
- ✓ Async-first design patterns enable efficient concurrent request handling
- ✓ Security best practices are followed: sanitized error responses, API key validation, input validation
- ✓ Structured logging with tracing provides observability and debugging
- ✓ Separation of concerns is demonstrated through distinct modules: routes, handlers, middleware, and models

25

Desktop Admin Interface (Iced)

▷ **What you will learn in this chapter**

- Build a desktop admin interface using the Iced framework's Model-View-Update pattern
- Implement state management, async API calls, and UI event handling in pure Rust
- Design modular UI components with styling and layout
- Integrate with the bitcoin-api crate for blockchain communication

You want a native desktop admin panel for your blockchain node—one that shows live block height, peer count, and mempool status, written entirely in Rust with no JavaScript. This chapter builds that panel using Iced, a cross-platform GUI framework inspired by Elm. It uses a Model-View-Update architecture: your state lives in a struct, user clicks produce messages (enum variants), and an `update` function mutates state in response. This chapter explains the `bitcoin-desktop-ui` crate—how the MVU loop boots, how messages dispatch to handlers, and how the UI makes async HTTP calls to the node's REST API.

25.1 What This UI Is (In One Sentence)

The desktop admin UI is a **thin MVU shell**: it renders state (`view.rs`), mutates state in response to messages (`update.rs`), and performs async admin calls (`api.rs`) on a Tokio runtime (`runtime.rs`).

The methods involved in this architecture are: `main` (boot + theme + app start), `init_runtime` and `spawn_on_tokio` (async boundary), `AdminApp::{new, clear_related_data}` (state and screen cleanup), `update` (message dispatcher), and `view` and `view_*` helpers (rendering).

25.2 Diagram: MVU Event Loop (Iced)

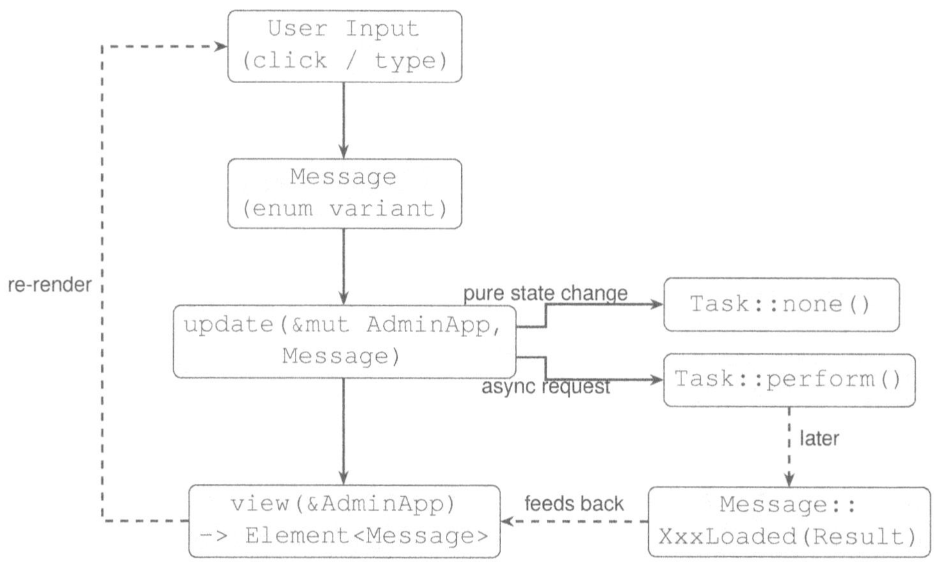

Figure 25.1: MVU event loop in Iced: input → message → update → view cycle

In Iced, side effects are represented as `Task` values — `Task::none()` for pure state updates with no I/O, and `Task::perform()` for async operations that return a result later.

25.3 Diagram: Async Boundary (HTTP Requests)

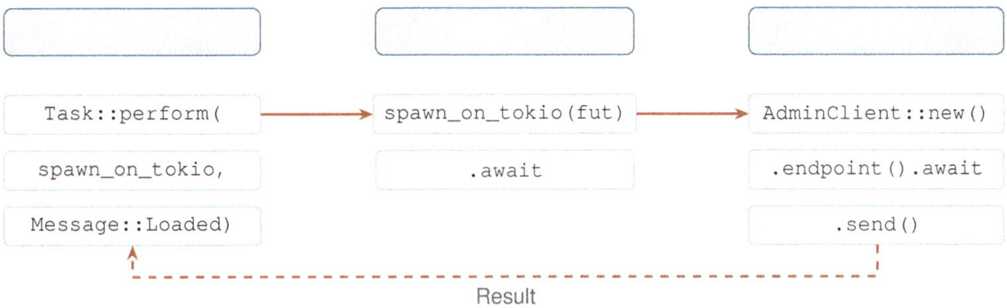

Figure 25.2: Async boundary: synchronous update dispatches to Tokio runtime, which calls the API

25.4 File Organization

Together, these chapters walk through implementation in:

- `bitcoin-desktop-ui-iced/src/main.rs`
- `bitcoin-desktop-ui-iced/src/runtime.rs`
- `bitcoin-desktop-ui-iced/src/types.rs`
- `bitcoin-desktop-ui-iced/src/app.rs`
- `bitcoin-desktop-ui-iced/src/api.rs`
- `bitcoin-desktop-ui-iced/src/update.rs`
- `bitcoin-desktop-ui-iced/src/view.rs`

25.5 Application Entrypoint

```
mod api;
mod app;
mod runtime;
mod types;
mod update;
mod view;

use app::AdminApp;
use iced::{Theme, application};
use runtime::init_runtime;
use update::update;
use view::view;
```

Listing 308: App entrypoint (part 1: module declarations) (`bitcoin-desktop-ui-iced/src/main.rs`)

The `main` function is where the MVU event loop begins. It initializes the Tokio runtime, configures logging, and enters the Iced application loop.

```
fn main() -> iced::Result {
    // Initialize tracing subscriber for logging
    tracing_subscriber::fmt()
        .with_env_filter(tracing_subscriber::EnvFilter::from_default_env())
        .with_target(false)
        .init();

    // Initialize Tokio runtime for async operations
    init_runtime();

    // Run the application
    application(AdminApp::new, update, view)
        .title(title)
        .theme(theme)
        .run()
}
```

Listing 309: App entrypoint (part 2: main loop) (`bitcoin-desktop-ui-iced/src/main.rs`)

Walkthrough: what `main` wires together:

- **Modules**: `update` and `view` are the MVU "engine"; everything else exists to support them.
- **`init_runtime()`** : starts an async executor so later HTTP tasks don't block the UI thread.
- **`application(AdminApp::new, update, view).run()`** : creates initial state once, then enters the event loop:
  - `view(&AdminApp)` draws the UI
  - user interaction emits `Message`
  - `update(&mut AdminApp, Message)` mutates state and optionally schedules work

25.6 Tokio Runtime Bridge

```rust
use std::sync::OnceLock;

// Store the Tokio runtime handle globally so tasks can access it
static TOKIO_HANDLE: OnceLock<tokio::runtime::Handle> = OnceLock::new();

pub fn init_runtime() {
    // Create a Tokio runtime for async operations
    // This must outlive the application to keep the reactor running
    let rt = tokio::runtime::Runtime::new()
        .expect("Failed to create Tokio runtime");

    // Store the handle globally so it can be accessed from any thread
    TOKIO_HANDLE
        .set(rt.handle().clone())
        .expect("Failed to set Tokio handle");

    // Keep the runtime alive in a background thread
    std::thread::spawn(move || {
        rt.block_on(async {
            // Keep the runtime alive indefinitely
            std::future::pending::<()>().await;
        });
    });
}
```

Listing 310: Tokio runtime bridge: initialization (`bitcoin-desktop-ui-iced/src/runtime.rs`, part 1)

The `init_runtime()` function runs once at application startup, creating a **background Tokio runtime** that persists for the entire lifetime of the UI. The global `TOKIO_HANDLE` enables any part of the UI to spawn async work without needing thread-local state.

```
// Helper function to wrap a future to ensure it runs on Tokio runtime
pub fn spawn_on_tokio<F>(fut: F)
    -> impl std::future::Future<Output = F::Output> + Send
where
    F: std::future::Future + Send + 'static,
    F::Output: Send + 'static,
{
    let handle = TOKIO_HANDLE
        .get()
        .expect("Tokio runtime not initialized")
        .clone();
    async move { handle.spawn(fut).await.unwrap() }
}
```

Listing 311: Tokio runtime bridge: async spawning (`bitcoin-desktop-ui-iced/src/runtime.rs`, part 2)

Walkthrough: why we need `spawn_on_tokio`:

Iced's update loop is **synchronous**: it runs on the main UI thread, and any function that blocks (e.g., a one-second HTTP call) freezes the window for the same duration—menus stop responding, text cursors stop blinking, the OS marks the app "Not Responding". Tokio, on a separate thread pool, has no such constraint: it is built to run thousands of concurrent futures in parallel. `spawn_on_tokio(...)` is the bridge between the two worlds, giving us a clean "async boundary":

- `update.rs` can return a `Task<Message>` immediately (UI stays responsive)
- Tokio runs the future in the background
- the result is converted into a `Message::XxxLoaded(...)` and re-enters the update loop

25.7 Navigation and Events

The `types.rs` file defines navigation enums and the `Message` enum, which is the "event vocabulary" of the UI:

```
#[derive(Debug, Clone, Copy, PartialEq, Eq)]
pub enum Menu {
    Blockchain,
    Wallet,
    Transactions,
    Mining,
    Health,
}

#[derive(Debug, Clone, Copy, PartialEq, Eq)]
pub enum WalletSection {
    GetWalletInfo,
    GetBalance,
    Create,
    Send,
    History,
    Addresses,
}
```

Listing 312: Navigation enums: menu and wallet sections (`bitcoin-desktop-ui-iced/src/types.rs`, part 1)

The `Menu` enum represents top-level navigation tabs in the interface, while `WalletSection` breaks down wallet-related operations into distinct screens within the Wallet tab.

```
#[derive(Debug, Clone, Copy, PartialEq, Eq)]
pub enum BlockchainSection {
    Info,
    LatestBlocks,
    AllBlocks,
    BlockByHash,
}
```

Listing 313: Navigation enums: blockchain section (`bitcoin-desktop-ui-iced/src/types.rs`, part 2)

The `Message` enum encodes all possible user interactions and async outcomes. It is split into three logical categories: UI navigation, input field changes, and async API results.

```
#[derive(Debug, Clone)]
pub enum Message {
    // Menu/UI navigation
    MenuChanged(Menu),
    WalletSectionChanged(WalletSection),
    BlockchainSectionChanged(BlockchainSection),

    // Configuration inputs
    BaseUrlChanged(String),
    ApiKeyChanged(String),

    // Field inputs
    BlockHashChanged(String),
    MiningAddressChanged(String),
    MiningNBlocksChanged(String),
    TxidChanged(String),
}
```

Listing 314: Message enum (part 1: navigation and inputs) (`bitcoin-desktop-ui-iced/src/types.rs`)

The request messages trigger async work in the update loop, while result messages carry the outcomes back from the Tokio runtime.

```
pub enum Message {
    // Request messages (trigger API calls)
    FetchInfo,
    FetchBlocks,
    FetchBlockByHash(String),
    GenerateToAddress {
        address: String,
        nblocks: u32,
        maxtries: Option<u32>,
    },

    // Result messages (from async API calls)
    InfoLoaded(Result<ApiResponse<BlockchainInfo>,
String>),
BlocksLoaded(Result<ApiResponse<Vec<BlockSummary>>,
String>),
    BlockByHashLoaded(Result<ApiResponse<Value>,
String>),
    GenerateToAddressDone(Result<ApiResponse<Value>,
String>),
}
```

Listing 315: Message enum (part 2: requests and results) (`bitcoin-desktop-ui-iced/src/types.rs`)

Walkthrough: `Message` is the UI's event vocabulary:

Treat `Message` as a **strict interface** between the view and the update loop:

- **Input messages** (`BaseUrlChanged` , `MiningAddressChanged` , ...): pure state changes.
- **Request messages** (`FetchInfo` , `FetchBlocks` , `CreateWalletAdmin` , ...): these trigger `Task::perform(...)` in the update loop.
- **Result messages** (`InfoLoaded` , `BlocksLoaded` , `TxSent` , ...): these store JSON into `AdminApp` and update status/editor buffers.
- **UI mechanics** (hover + section routing): `*MenuHovered(bool)` and `*SectionChanged(...)` exist to drive popups and the active panel.

This design keeps the view layer simple: it never "does" network calls—it only emits intent.

25.8 Application State

```rust
#[derive(Debug)]
pub struct AdminApp {
    pub menu: Menu,
    pub base_url: String,
    pub api_key: String,
    pub status: String,
    pub info: Option<BlockchainInfo>,
    pub blocks: Vec<BlockSummary>,
}
```

Listing 316: Application state (part 1: configuration and core data) (bitcoin-desktop-ui-iced/src/app.rs)

The struct continues with input fields for various actions, plus wallet and transaction-specific data:

```rust
pub struct AdminApp {
    // Inputs for actions
    pub block_hash_input: String,
    pub mining_address_input: String,
    pub mining_nblocks_input: String,
    pub txid_input: String,

    // Wallet admin state
    pub wallet_label_input: String,
    pub addresses: Vec<String>,
    pub wallet_info: Option<Value>,
    pub wallet_balance: Option<Value>,
    pub created_wallet_address: Option<String>,

    // Send transaction state
    pub send_from_address: String,
    pub send_to_address: String,
    pub send_amount: String,
}
```

Listing 317: Application state (part 1b: action input fields) (bitcoin-desktop-ui-iced/src/app.rs)

The struct continues with navigation state, menu hover tracking for popups, and cached response data used by different admin screens:

```
pub struct AdminApp {
    // Navigation state
    pub wallet_section: WalletSection,
    pub transaction_section: TransactionSection,
    pub blockchain_section: BlockchainSection,
    pub mining_section: MiningSection,
    pub health_section: HealthSection,

    // Menu hover state for popups
    pub blockchain_menu_hovered: bool,
    pub wallet_menu_hovered: bool,
    pub transaction_menu_hovered: bool,
    pub mining_menu_hovered: bool,
    pub health_menu_hovered: bool,

    // Response data storage
    pub blocks_all_data: Option<Value>,
    pub block_by_hash_data: Option<Value>,
    pub mining_info_data: Option<Value>,
    pub health_data: Option<Value>,
    pub mempool_data: Option<Value>,
    pub transactions_data: Option<Value>,
}
```

Listing 318: Application state (part 2a: navigation and data fields) (`bitcoin-desktop-ui-iced/src/app.rs`)

Text editor states allow users to select and copy JSON responses directly from the UI. The constructor initializes all fields with sensible defaults:

```
pub struct AdminApp {
    // Text editor states for selectable JSON display
    pub transactions_editor: iced::widget::text_editor::Content,
    pub mempool_editor: iced::widget::text_editor::Content,
    pub wallet_info_editor: iced::widget::text_editor::Content,
    pub blockchain_info_editor: iced::widget::text_editor::Content,
}

impl AdminApp {
    pub fn new() -> (Self, iced::Task<Message>) {
        (
            Self {
                menu: Menu::Blockchain,
                base_url: "http://127.0.0.1:8080".into(),
                api_key: std::env::var("BITCOIN_API_ADMIN_KEY")
                    .unwrap_or_else(|_| "admin-secret".into()),
                status: String::new(),
                // ... (remaining fields initialized)
            },
            iced::Task::none(),
        )
    }
}
```

Listing 319: Application state (part 2b: editors and constructor) (`bitcoin-desktop-ui-iced/src/app.rs`)

The `AdminApp` struct houses configuration and UI presentation state. The `new()` function initializes all fields with sensible defaults, with API credentials loaded from environment variables. A helper method manages data lifecycle by clearing stale cached responses when new API calls are made.

```rust
impl AdminApp {
    /// Clear previously loaded data for a specific section
    pub fn clear_related_data(&mut self, section: DataSection) {
        // "Hygiene rule": when we load one dataset, clear adjacent datasets
        // so the UI doesn't render stale JSON next to fresh JSON.
        match section {
            DataSection::BlockchainInfo => {
                self.blocks_all_data = None;
                self.block_by_hash_data = None;
            }
            DataSection::BlocksAll => {
                self.block_by_hash_data = None;
            }
            // ... (more cases)
        }
    }
}
```

Listing 320: Application state: data hygiene helper

Walkthrough: what lives in `AdminApp` (and why):

`AdminApp` is intentionally "wide": it contains both **domain-ish data** and **UI presentation state**.

- **Configuration**: `base_url`, `api_key` (what server we talk to).
- **Navigation**: `menu` + section enums (which panel to render).
- **Inputs**: text fields like `block_hash_input`, `send_amount` (what the user typed).
- **Responses**: `*_data: Option<Value>` are cached JSON payloads to display.
- **Editors**: `*_editor: text_editor::Content` exist so JSON can be selectable/copyable and scrollable.

The `clear_related_data(...)` helper is a small UX rule: when you fetch one dataset, clear nearby datasets so stale JSON doesn't linger on screen.

25.9 Async API Client Helpers

```rust
use bitcoin_api::{AdminClient, ApiConfig, ApiResponse, BlockchainInfo};

pub async fn fetch_info(cfg: ApiConfig)
    -> Result<ApiResponse<BlockchainInfo>, String>
{
    // A new client is constructed per call; config contains base_url + API key.
    let client = AdminClient::new(cfg).map_err(|e| e.to_string())?;
    client
        .get_blockchain_info()
        .await
        .map_err(|e| e.to_string())
}

pub async fn fetch_blocks(cfg: ApiConfig)
    -> Result<ApiResponse<Vec<BlockSummary>>, String>
{
    let client = AdminClient::new(cfg).map_err(|e| e.to_string())?;
    client.get_latest_blocks().await.map_err(|e| e.to_string())
}
```

Listing 321: Async API client helpers: blockchain queries (part 1: info and blocks) (`bitcoin-desktop-ui-iced/src/api.rs`)

The block-by-hash query and mining functions follow the same pattern. Each helper wraps the `AdminClient` error handling and async/await boundary:

```
pub async fn fetch_block_by_hash(
    cfg: ApiConfig,
    hash: String,
) -> Result<ApiResponse<Value>, String> {
    let client = AdminClient::new(cfg).map_err(|e| e.to_string())?;
    client
        .get_block_by_hash(&hash)
        .await
        .map_err(|e| e.to_string())
}
```

Listing 322: Async API client helpers: blockchain by hash (`bitcoin-desktop-ui-iced/src/api.rs`, part 1b)

These helper functions provide read-only access to blockchain state: general info, the latest block summaries, and a specific block by hash. Each constructs a fresh `AdminClient` and delegates to the corresponding API method, converting errors to strings for the UI.

```
pub async fn fetch_mining_info(cfg: ApiConfig)
    -> Result<ApiResponse<Value>, String>
{
    let client = AdminClient::new(cfg).map_err(|e| e.to_string())?;
    client.get_mining_info().await.map_err(|e| e.to_string())
}

pub async fn generate_to_address(
    cfg: ApiConfig,
    address: String,
    nblocks: u32,
    maxtries: Option<u32>,
) -> Result<ApiResponse<Value>, String> {
    let client = AdminClient::new(cfg).map_err(|e| e.to_string())?;
    client
        .generate_to_address(&address, nblocks, maxtries)
        .await
        .map_err(|e| e.to_string())
}
```

Listing 323: Async API client helpers: mining and health (`bitcoin-desktop-ui-iced/src/api.rs`, part 2)

The second set of helper functions covers wallet administration and transaction submission. These follow the same pattern: construct a fresh `AdminClient` from the configuration, call the appropriate method on the client, and propagate errors as strings for UI consumption.

```
pub async fn fetch_health(cfg: ApiConfig)
    -> Result<ApiResponse<Value>, String>
{
    let client = AdminClient::new(cfg).map_err(|e|
e.to_string())?;
    client.health().await.map_err(|e| e.to_string())
}

pub async fn fetch_mempool(cfg: ApiConfig)
    -> Result<ApiResponse<Value>, String>
{
    let client = AdminClient::new(cfg).map_err(|e|
e.to_string())?;
    client.get_mempool().await.map_err(|e|
e.to_string())
}
```

Listing 324: Async API client helpers: health and mempool queries (`bitcoin-desktop-ui-iced/src/api.rs`, part 3)

The health and mempool functions provide diagnostic endpoints. The next part covers wallet mutation operations that modify on-chain state.

```
pub async fn create_wallet_admin(
    cfg: ApiConfig,
    req: CreateWalletRequest,
) -> Result<ApiResponse<CreateWalletResponse>, String> {
    let client = AdminClient::new(cfg).map_err(|e| e.to_string())?;
    client
        .create_wallet_admin(&req)
        .await
        .map_err(|e| e.to_string())
}

pub async fn send_transaction(
    cfg: ApiConfig,
    req: SendTransactionRequest,
) -> Result<ApiResponse<SendTransactionResponse>, String> {
    let client = AdminClient::new(cfg).map_err(|e| e.to_string())?;
    client
        .send_transaction_admin(&req)
        .await
        .map_err(|e| e.to_string())
}
```

Listing 325: Async API client helpers: wallet and transaction operations (`bitcoin-desktop-ui-iced/src/api.rs`, part 4)

Walkthrough: how `api.rs` supports the update loop:

This module is intentionally boring: each function is a **single HTTP call** wrapped in an `async fn` with a UI-friendly error type.

- **Inputs**: `ApiConfig` is built from `AdminApp { base_url, api_key }` in the update function.
- **Return type**: `Result<ApiResponse<T>, String>`
  - `Err(String)` means: "we could not even complete the request" (client construction, network error, decode error, etc.).

  - `Ok(ApiResponse<T>)` means: "we got a response envelope"; it can still represent application-level failure via `api.success == false`.
- **Why build a client per call?** It keeps the UI side stateless and makes each request self-contained. In the update loop you can read each `Task::perform(spawn_on_tokio(api_call), Message::XxxLoaded)` arm as a direct mapping: *message → API call → loaded message*.

25.10 The Update Loop: Message Dispatcher

```
use crate::api::*;
use crate::app::AdminApp;
use crate::runtime::spawn_on_tokio;
use crate::types::{DataSection, Menu, Message};
use bitcoin_api::ApiConfig;
use iced::Task;

pub fn update(app: &mut AdminApp, message: Message) -> Task<Message> {
    match message {
```

Listing 326: Update loop: imports and function signature (`bitcoin-desktop-ui-iced/src/update.rs`, part 1a)

The update function is the central message dispatcher of the MVU architecture. It handles pure state mutations and returns async tasks for I/O operations.

```
        // Pure state changes (no I/O)
        Message::MenuChanged(m) => {
            app.menu = m;
            Task::none()
        }
        Message::BaseUrlChanged(v) => {
            app.base_url = v;
            Task::none()
        }
        Message::ApiKeyChanged(v) => {
            app.api_key = v;
            Task::none()
        }
        Message::BlockHashChanged(v) => {
            app.block_hash_input = v;
            Task::none()
        }
```

Listing 327: Update loop: configuration state changes (`bitcoin-desktop-ui-iced/src/update.rs`, part 1b)

Configuration changes and input field updates are handled synchronously. For API calls, the message handler constructs an async task and returns it to Iced.

```
        // Async request: spawn API call on Tokio runtime
        Message::FetchInfo => {
            let cfg = ApiConfig {
                base_url: app.base_url.clone(),
                api_key: Some(app.api_key.clone()),
            };
            Task::perform(
                spawn_on_tokio(fetch_info(cfg)),
                Message::InfoLoaded,
            )
        }
```

Listing 328: Update loop: info retrieval request (`bitcoin-desktop-ui-iced/src/update.rs`, part 1b)

The async request returns a Task that the Iced framework will handle. When the HTTP response arrives, it is converted to a `Message::InfoLoaded` and re-enters the update loop.

```
        Message::InfoLoaded(res) => {
            match res {
                Ok(api) => {
                    if api.success {
                        app.info = api.data.clone();
                        if let Some(ref data) = api.data {
                            let json_str = serde_json::to_string_pretty(data)
                                .unwrap_or_else(|_| "Error formatting".to_string());
                            app.blockchain_info_editor =
                                iced::widget::text_editor::Content::with_text(&json_str);
                        }
                        app.status = "Blockchain info loaded".into();
                    } else {
                        app.status = api.error
                            .unwrap_or_else(|| "Error loading info".into());
                        app.info = None;
                    }
                }
                Err(e) => {
                    app.status = e;
                    app.info = None;
                }
            }
            Task::none()
        }
```

Listing 329: Update loop: info result handling (`bitcoin-desktop-ui-iced/src/update.rs`, part 1c)

The block queries follow the same pattern. When the user requests blocks from the blockchain, the update function clears any previously stored data and dispatches the fetch request. The result handler populates the blocks list and displays the count in the status bar.

```
        Message::FetchBlocks => {
            app.clear_related_data(DataSection::Blocks);
            let cfg = ApiConfig {
                base_url: app.base_url.clone(),
                api_key: Some(app.api_key.clone()),
            };
            Task::perform(
                spawn_on_tokio(fetch_blocks(cfg)),
                Message::BlocksLoaded,
            )
        }
```

Listing 330: Update loop: block retrieval request (`bitcoin-desktop-ui-iced/src/update.rs`, part 2)

The result handler for blocks follows the same pattern: unwrap the response, store data in the app, format a user-facing status message, and handle errors gracefully.

```
            Message::BlocksLoaded(res) => {
                match res {
                    Ok(api) => {
                        if api.success {
                            app.blocks = api.data.unwrap_or_default();
                            app.status = format!("Loaded {} blocks", app.blocks.len());
                        } else {
                            app.status = api.error
                                .unwrap_or_else(|| "Error loading blocks".into());
                        }
                    }
                    Err(e) => {
                        app.status = e;
                    }
                }
                Task::none()
            }

            // Similar patterns for all other messages...
            _ => Task::none(),
        }
    }
```

Listing 331: Update loop: block result handling and fallback (`bitcoin-desktop-ui-iced/src/update.rs`, part 2b)

Walkthrough: the async "round-trip" pattern (UI → HTTP → UI):

The update loop follows a consistent three-step pattern for every API call:

1. **Input message arrives** (user clicks button or types).
2. **Update handler** (sync):
   - Mutates local state immediately (inputs/status/hover state).
   - Returns `Task::perform(spawn_on_tokio(async { http_call().await }), Messa`

3. **Async work happens** (on Tokio runtime, background):
   - `api.rs` → `AdminClient` → HTTP → JSON.
4. **Result message arrives** (`Message::XxxLoaded(Result<ApiResponse<T>, String`
5. **Update handler** (sync, again):
   - Stores JSON payload in `app.*_data` .
   - Updates text editor buffers (pretty JSON).
   - Updates `app.status` for UX feedback.

This separates concerns cleanly: the view never blocks, `update` remains lightweight, and I/O happens on the Tokio runtime.

25.11 The View Layer: Rendering and Dispatch

```rust
use crate::app::AdminApp;
use crate::types::{Menu, Message, BlockchainSection};
use iced::Element;
use iced::widget::{button, column, container, row, text, text_input};

pub fn view<'a>(app: &'a AdminApp) -> Element<'a, Message> {
    // The view is (mostly) pure: it reads app and returns an Element<Message>.
    // Any "actions" are triggered by Messages, handled in update.rs.

    // Toolbar: configure base_url and api_key
    let toolbar = row![
        text("Base URL:").size(12),
        text_input("http://127.0.0.1:8080", &app.base_url)
            .on_input(Message::BaseUrlChanged)
            .width(iced::Length::Fixed(250.0)),
        text("Admin Key:").size(12),
        text_input("admin-secret", &app.api_key)
            .on_input(Message::ApiKeyChanged)
            .width(iced::Length::Fixed(200.0)),
        text(format!("Status: {}", app.status))
            .size(12)
            .width(iced::Length::Fill),
    ]
    .spacing(8)
    .padding(8);
```

Listing 332: View function: toolbar and navigation assembly (part 1a: toolbar) (`bitcoin-desktop-ui-iced/src/view.rs`)

The toolbar row displays and collects configuration inputs (base URL and API key), plus a status message. The navigation menu creates five buttons corresponding to each top-level menu section:

```
    // Left navigation menu
    let nav_buttons = column![
        button("Blockchain")
.on_press(Message::MenuChanged(Menu::Blockchain)),
        button("Wallet")
.on_press(Message::MenuChanged(Menu::Wallet)),
        button("Transactions")
.on_press(Message::MenuChanged(Menu::Transactions)),
        button("Mining")
.on_press(Message::MenuChanged(Menu::Mining)),
        button("Health")
.on_press(Message::MenuChanged(Menu::Health)),
    ]
    .spacing(4)
    .padding(8);
}
```

Listing 333: View function: navigation menu (part 1b: menu buttons) (`bitcoin-desktop-ui-iced/src/view.rs`)

```
    // Main content panel: dispatch to view_* functions by menu
    let content = match app.menu {
        Menu::Blockchain => view_blockchain(app),
        Menu::Wallet => view_wallet(app),
        Menu::Transactions => view_transactions(app),
        Menu::Mining => view_mining(app),
        Menu::Health => view_health(app),
    };

    // Assemble: toolbar + (nav + content)
    container(
        column![
            toolbar,
            row![
                container(nav_buttons).width(iced::Length::Fixed(150.0)),
                container(content).width(iced::Length::Fill),
            ]
            .spacing(8)
            .height(iced::Length::Fill),
        ]
        .spacing(8)
    )
    .padding(8)
    .into()
}
```

Listing 334: View function: content dispatch and layout (`bitcoin-desktop-ui-iced/src/view.rs`, part 2)

The helper functions render section-specific content. The `view_blockchain` function demonstrates the pattern: it dispatches on the current subsection (Info or LatestBlocks) and renders either a button and editor for displaying JSON, or a button and list for showing block summaries. Similar functions exist for wallet, transaction, mining, and health sections.

```
fn view_blockchain<'a>(app: &'a AdminApp) -> Element<'a, Message> {
    match app.blockchain_section {
        BlockchainSection::Info => {
            column![
                button("Fetch Info").on_press(Message::FetchInfo),
                text_editor(&app.blockchain_info_editor)
                    .on_action(Message::BlockchainInfoEditorAction),
            ]
            .spacing(8)
            .into()
        }
```

Listing 335: View function: blockchain Info section (`bitcoin-desktop-ui-iced/src/view.rs`)

The LatestBlocks variant displays a button to fetch the latest blocks and shows the count in a text label. The catch-all branch prompts the user to select a section:

```
        BlockchainSection::LatestBlocks => {
            column![
                button("Fetch Blocks").on_press(Message::FetchBlocks),
                row![
                    text(format!("Loaded: {} blocks", app.blocks.len())),
                ]
                .spacing(8),
            ]
            .spacing(8)
            .into()
        }
        _ => container(text("Select a section")).into(),
    }
}

// Similar for view_wallet, view_transactions, view_mining, view_health...
```

Listing 336: View function: blockchain LatestBlocks and fallback (`bitcoin-desktop-ui-iced/src/view.rs`, part 2)

Walkthrough: view dispatch + popup hover model:

The view function is organized into layers:

1. **Toolbar** (top): configuration inputs (`base_url`, `api_key`) and status feedback.
2. **Navigation** (left): menu buttons dispatch `Message::MenuChanged(...)`.
3. **Main content panel** (right): matches on `app.menu` to dispatch to `view_blockchain`, `view_wallet`, etc.

Each content panel handles its own sub-sections and data display:

- Buttons emit request messages (`FetchInfo`, `FetchBlocks`, etc.).
- Text editors display and allow copying of JSON responses.
- Input fields emit change messages (`BlockHashChanged`, etc.).
- Hover states drive popup menus: when `app.blockchain_menu_hovered == true`, the UI renders a submenu; when false, it disappears.

The view layer never calls the API directly—all side effects go through messages and the update loop.

Key Takeaways

- ✓ This chapter covered Model-View-Update architecture in Iced, including state management, message dispatch, and view rendering in pure Rust.
- ✓ Complete MVU cycle implementation: Model state (`AdminApp`), Message types, Update logic (`update` function), and View rendering (`view` function).
- ✓ Async API communication with the bitcoin-api crate for real-time blockchain data via a Tokio runtime bridge.
- ✓ Modular UI components with popup menus, selectable text, and consistent styling.
- ✓ Async boundary pattern: sync MVU loop paired with Tokio-powered HTTP for responsive UI during long-running network calls.

25.12 Exercises

1. **Add a Refresh Button** — Add a "Refresh" button to the admin UI that reloads blockchain data from the API. Define a new `Message::Refresh` variant, implement the update handler to trigger an API call, and add the button to the view. Observe how the MVU cycle processes this new interaction.
2. **MVU Cycle Trace** — Pick any user interaction (e.g., clicking "Mine Block") and trace the complete MVU cycle: which `Message` variant is generated, what the `Update` function does, what side effects (API calls, state changes) occur, and how the `View` reflects the new state.

25.13 Further Reading

- **Iced Framework Documentation** — API reference for the Iced GUI framework at https://docs.rs/iced/.
- **Iced Examples Repository** — Official examples demonstrating various Iced patterns at https://github.com/iced-rs/iced/tree/master/examples.
- **The Elm Architecture** — The original MVU pattern that inspired Iced's design at https://guide.elm-lang.org/architecture/.

26

Desktop Admin Interface (Tauri)

▷ **What you will learn in this chapter**

- Build the same admin functionality using Tauri 2 with a Rust backend and React frontend
- Implement IPC commands that bridge Rust and TypeScript across the process boundary
- Compare the Tauri architecture with the Iced MVU approach from the previous chapter
- Use Zustand for state management and React Query for data fetching in the frontend

SAME admin panel, different approach. Chapter 25 built it in pure Rust with an MVU framework. This chapter builds it with a Rust backend and a React frontend, packaged into a 10MB desktop app instead of Electron's 150MB. Tauri does this by using your operating system's native webview instead of bundling Chromium. The Rust side exposes handlers via `#[tauri::command]`, which React calls over an IPC (inter-process communication) bridge — the JavaScript running inside the webview invokes a named Rust function by string, Tauri serializes the arguments, and the Rust handler returns a JSON-encoded result. This is the same mental model as a local RPC call. This chapter explains the `bitcoin-desktop-ui-tauri` crate—how the Rust backend and React frontend communicate, and how the same blockchain logic gets exposed through a different architecture.

26.1 What This UI Is (In One Sentence)

The Tauri desktop admin UI is a **two-language desktop application**: a Rust backend exposes 22 `#[tauri::command]` handlers that wrap the `bitcoin-api` crate, while a React/TypeScript frontend calls those handlers through Tauri's IPC bridge using `invoke()`.

The Tauri desktop admin UI consists of: `main` (Tauri app setup, state management, command registration), `BitcoinApiService::*` (service layer wrapping `AdminClient` HTTP calls), `commands::*` (22 Tauri command handlers across 6 modules), `commands.ts` → `invoke()` (TypeScript-to-Rust bridge), and React pages (18 views), components (14 shared), hooks (2 custom).

26.2 Why Tauri? (Iced vs. Tauri — An Architectural Comparison)

In Chapter 25 we built the same admin dashboard with Iced—a pure-Rust, single-language MVU framework. Chapter 26 builds the identical **feature set** (blockchain info, wallet management, mining controls, health checks) with Tauri, which gives us a **Rust backend paired with a web frontend**. Both approaches have real trade-offs:
The state-management row deserves a quick gloss for readers who haven't met the React ecosystem before. **Zustand** is a lightweight client-state library that holds purely local UI state (which tab is active, form field values). **React Query** fetches and caches data from the backend, handling loading states, error retries, and cache invalidation. The Iced version collapses both roles into a single `AdminApp` struct because Rust's MVU model makes no distinction between "UI state" and "cached server state"—both live in the same struct and are updated by the same `Message` handlers.

The key point: both apps call exactly the same `AdminClient` methods from the `bitcoin-api` crate. The difference is where the UI layer lives (Rust vs. browser) and how events cross the boundary (Iced `Message` vs. Tauri `invoke`).

Table 26.1: Iced vs. Tauri: Architectural comparison

Aspect	Iced (Chapter 25)	Tauri (this chapter)
Languages	Rust only	Rust backend + TypeScript/React frontend
UI paradigm	MVU (Model-View-Update)	Component-based (React) with IPC bridge
State management	Single `AdminApp` struct	Zustand (client) + React Query (server)
Async boundary	Manual Tokio runtime in background thread (`spawn_on_tokio`)	Tauri handles async natively—`#[tauri::command]` functions are async
Event vocabulary	`Message` enum with ~50 variants	React Router routes + React Query cache keys
Styling	Iced built-in widgets (programmatic)	Tailwind CSS (declarative)
Shared code	`bitcoin-api` crate (Rust)	`bitcoin-api` crate (Rust)—same crate, same API calls
Binary size	Smaller (pure Rust)	Larger (embeds Chromium webview)
Ecosystem	Iced widgets only	Full npm ecosystem (React Query, Zod, Lucide, etc.)

i Tip

Both the Iced admin (Chapter 25) and this Tauri admin consume the same `bitcoin-api` crate for blockchain communication. This means the backend API is framework-agnostic—you could add a third frontend without changing any backend code.

26.3 Diagram: Tauri IPC Architecture

Data flows from the React frontend through IPC to the Rust backend and then to the blockchain API server. IPC (inter-process communication) is how the TypeScript frontend and Rust backend exchange data: the frontend calls a named function via `invoke()`, Tauri marshals the arguments across the process boundary, and the Rust backend returns JSON.

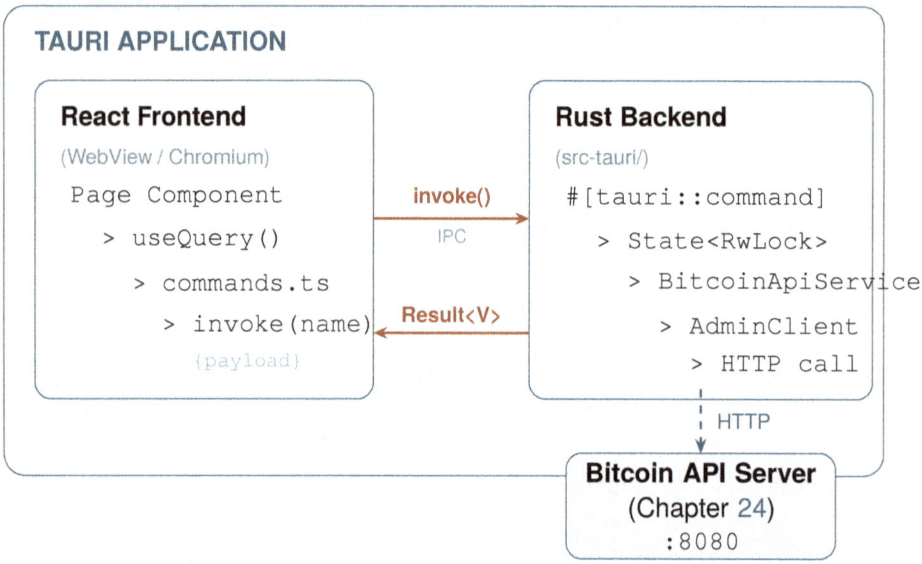

Figure 26.1: Tauri IPC Architecture: data flow from React frontend through IPC to Rust backend

26.4 File Organization

The Tauri application is split between two directories:

- **Rust backend** (`src-tauri/`):
  - `src/main.rs` (app setup, state, command registration)
  - `src/api/service.rs` (service layer wrapping `AdminClient`)
  - `src/commands/` (22 handlers across 6 modules)
- **React frontend** (`src/`):
  - `src/commands.ts` (IPC bridge via `invoke()`)
  - `src/pages/` (18 views)
  - `src/components/` (14 shared components)
  - `src/hooks/` (custom hooks for queries)

26.5 Rust Backend Architecture

The Rust backend follows a layered architecture:

1. **Tauri state** (`main.rs`): Global state managed via `State<RwLock<AppState»` . `State<T>` is Tauri's dependency-injection wrapper (it hands each command handler a reference to shared application data); the inner `RwLock` permits many concurrent readers with a single exclusive writer, so queries do not block each other but writes serialize.
2. **Service layer** (`api/service.rs`): `BitcoinApiService` wraps `AdminClient` HTTP calls with async/await.
3. **Command handlers** (`commands/*.rs`): 22 `#[tauri::command]` functions that call the service and return results over IPC.

```rust
use tauri::State;
use std::sync::RwLock;

#[derive(Clone, serde::Serialize, serde::Deserialize)]
pub struct AppState {
    pub base_url: String,
    pub api_key: String,
}

fn main() {
    tauri::Builder::default()
        // Initialize AppState with default values
        .manage(AppState {
            base_url: "http://127.0.0.1:8080".to_string(),
            api_key: std::env::var("BITCOIN_API_ADMIN_KEY")
                .unwrap_or_else(|_| "admin-secret".to_string()),
        })
```

Listing 337: Main Tauri app setup: state and initialization (`src-tauri/src/main.rs` , part 1)

The `AppState` struct holds shared configuration (base URL and admin API key), making it available to all command handlers through Tauri's dependency injection. The builder creates the state with defaults, reading the API key from the environment if available.

```
        // Register all command handlers
        .invoke_handler(tauri::generate_handler![
            cmd_get_blockchain_info,
            cmd_get_latest_blocks,
            cmd_get_blocks,
            cmd_get_block_by_hash,
            cmd_get_mining_info,
            cmd_generate_to_address,
            cmd_get_health,
            cmd_get_liveness,
            cmd_get_readiness,
            cmd_get_mempool,
            cmd_get_mempool_transaction,
            cmd_get_transactions,
            cmd_get_address_transactions,
            cmd_create_wallet_admin,
            cmd_get_addresses_admin,
            cmd_get_wallet_info_admin,
            cmd_get_balance_admin,
            cmd_send_transaction_admin,
            cmd_set_base_url,
            cmd_set_api_key,
            cmd_get_config,
            cmd_check_connection,
        ])
        .run(tauri::generate_context!())
        .expect("error while running tauri application");
}
```

Listing 338: Main Tauri app setup: command handlers (`src-tauri/src/main.rs`, part 2)

Tauri injects `State<AppState>` into each command handler automatically — every handler has access to the shared application state without explicitly passing it. The state is accessed in command handlers via the `State<AppState>` parameter injected by Tauri.

```
use bitcoin_api::{AdminClient, ApiConfig, ApiResponse, BlockchainInfo};
use serde_json::Value;

pub struct BitcoinApiService;

impl BitcoinApiService {
    pub async fn get_blockchain_info(
        base_url: String,
        api_key: String,
    ) -> Result<ApiResponse<BlockchainInfo>, String> {
        let config = ApiConfig {
            base_url,
            api_key: Some(api_key),
        };
        let client = AdminClient::new(config)
            .map_err(|e| e.to_string())?;
        client
            .get_blockchain_info()
            .await
            .map_err(|e| e.to_string())
    }
}
```

Listing 339: Service layer: read operations (`src-tauri/src/api/service.rs`, part 1)

The `BitcoinApiService` encapsulates HTTP calls to the bitcoin-api crate. Each async method constructs an `ApiConfig`, creates a client, and delegates to the corresponding API method. This service layer sits between Tauri command handlers and the blockchain API.

```rust
impl BitcoinApiService {
    pub async fn generate_to_address(
        base_url: String,
        api_key: String,
        address: String,
        nblocks: u32,
        maxtries: Option<u32>,
    ) -> Result<ApiResponse<Value>, String> {
        let config = ApiConfig {
            base_url,
            api_key: Some(api_key),
        };
        let client = AdminClient::new(config)
            .map_err(|e| e.to_string())?;
        client
            .generate_to_address(&address, nblocks, maxtries)
            .await
            .map_err(|e| e.to_string())
    }
}
```

Listing 340: Service layer: write operations (`src-tauri/src/api/service.rs`, part 2)

```rust
use crate::api::service::BitcoinApiService;
use tauri::State;
use serde_json::Value;

use crate::AppState;

#[tauri::command]
pub async fn cmd_get_blockchain_info(
    state: State<'_, AppState>,
) -> Result<Value, String> {
    let response =
BitcoinApiService::get_blockchain_info(
        state.base_url.clone(),
        state.api_key.clone(),
    )
    .await?;

    // Return the entire API response as JSON
    serde_json::to_value(&response)
        .map_err(|e| e.to_string())
}

#[tauri::command]
pub async fn cmd_generate_to_address(
    state: State<'_, AppState>,
    address: String,
    nblocks: u32,
    maxtries: Option<u32>,
) -> Result<Value, String> {
    let response =
BitcoinApiService::generate_to_address(
        state.base_url.clone(),
        state.api_key.clone(),
        address,
        nblocks,
        maxtries,
    )
    .await?;

    serde_json::to_value(&response)
        .map_err(|e| e.to_string())
}
```

Listing 341: Command handler example (`src-tauri/src/commands/blockchain.rs`)

Walkthrough: the command handler pattern:

Every command follows the same structure:

1. Receive parameters from the IPC invocation.
2. Call a corresponding `BitcoinApiService` method (which calls the bitcoin-api HTTP API).
3. Return the result as JSON over IPC.

This keeps the Rust side simple: it's a thin bridge between TypeScript and `AdminClient`.

26.6 TypeScript-to-Rust Bridge

The `commands.ts` module is the TypeScript side of the IPC bridge. Each function wraps a single `invoke()` call, mapping a Tauri command name to a typed async function that React hooks can call directly. The first group covers blockchain and mining queries:

```
import { invoke } from '@tauri-apps/api/core';
import { BlockchainInfo, BlockSummary, ApiResponse }
from './types';

export async function getBlockchainInfo():
Promise<ApiResponse<BlockchainInfo>> {
    return invoke<ApiResponse<BlockchainInfo>>('cmd_
    get_blockchain_info');
}

export async function getLatestBlocks():
Promise<ApiResponse<BlockSummary[]>> {
    return invoke<ApiResponse<BlockSummary[]>>('cmd_
    get_latest_blocks');
}

export async function getBlocks():
Promise<ApiResponse<any>> {
    return
    invoke<ApiResponse<any>>('cmd_get_blocks');
}

export async function getBlockByHash(hash: string):
Promise<ApiResponse<any>> {
    return invoke<ApiResponse<any>>('cmd_get_block_b
    y_hash', { hash
    });
}
```

Listing 342: IPC command wrappers: blockchain queries (`src/commands.ts`, part 1)

The mining and health-check wrappers follow the same one-function-per-command pattern. The `generateToAddress` function accepts optional `maxtries` to cap the mining loop:

```
export async function getMiningInfo():
Promise<ApiResponse<any>> {
    return
    invoke<ApiResponse<any>>('cmd_get_mining_info');
}

export async function generateToAddress(
    address: string,
    nblocks: number,
    maxtries?: number,
): Promise<ApiResponse<any>> {
    return invoke<ApiResponse<any>>('cmd_generate_to
    _address',
    {
        address,
        nblocks,
        maxtries,
    });
}

export async function getHealth():
Promise<ApiResponse<any>> {
    return
    invoke<ApiResponse<any>>('cmd_get_health');
}

export async function getLiveness():
Promise<ApiResponse<any>> {
    return
    invoke<ApiResponse<any>>('cmd_get_liveness');
}

export async function getReadiness():
Promise<ApiResponse<any>> {
    return
    invoke<ApiResponse<any>>('cmd_get_readiness');
}
```

Listing 343: IPC command wrappers: mining and health checks (`src/commands.ts`, part 2)

The second group wraps transaction and wallet administration commands, which allow the UI to interact with the mempool, view transaction history, and manage wallet accounts via IPC invocations.

```
export async function getMempool():
Promise<ApiResponse<any>> {
    return
    invoke<ApiResponse<any>>('cmd_get_mempool');
}

export async function getMempoolTransaction(txid:
string): Promise<ApiResponse<any>> {
    return invoke<ApiResponse<any>>('cmd_get_mempool
    _transaction', { txid
    });
}

export async function getTransactions():
Promise<ApiResponse<any>> {
    return
    invoke<ApiResponse<any>>('cmd_get_transactions');
}

export async function
getAddressTransactions(address: string):
Promise<ApiResponse<any>> {
    return invoke<ApiResponse<any>>('cmd_get_address
    _transactions', { address
    });
}
```

Listing 344: IPC command wrappers: mempool and transaction queries (`src/commands.ts`, part 3)

The wallet administration commands create wallets, query balances, and send transactions. The final three functions manage the runtime API configuration (base URL and API key):

```
export async function createWalletAdmin(label?:
string): Promise<ApiResponse<any>> {
    return invoke<ApiResponse<any>>('cmd_create_wallet_admin', { label
    });
}

export async function getAddressesAdmin():
Promise<ApiResponse<any>> {
    return invoke<ApiResponse<any>>('cmd_get_addresses_admin');
}

export async function getWalletInfoAdmin(address:
string): Promise<ApiResponse<any>> {
    return invoke<ApiResponse<any>>('cmd_get_wallet_info_admin', { address
    });
}

export async function getBalanceAdmin(address:
string): Promise<ApiResponse<any>> {
    return invoke<ApiResponse<any>>('cmd_get_balance_admin', { address
    });
}

export async function sendTransactionAdmin(
    from: string, to: string, amount: number,
): Promise<ApiResponse<any>> {
    return invoke<ApiResponse<any>>('cmd_send_transaction_admin', { from, to, amount
    });
}

export async function setBaseUrl(url: string):
Promise<void> {
    return invoke<void>('cmd_set_base_url', { url });
}

export async function setApiKey(key: string):
Promise<void> {
    return invoke<void>('cmd_set_api_key', { key });
}

export async function getConfig(): Promise<{
baseUrl: string; apiKey: string }> {
    return invoke<{ baseUrl: string; apiKey: string
    }>('cmd_get_config');
}
```

Listing 345: IPC command wrappers: wallet and config operations

Walkthrough: `invoke()` is the IPC bridge:

Each TypeScript function calls `invoke(command_name, payload?)` which:

1. Serializes the arguments to JSON.
2. Sends them across the IPC boundary to the Rust backend.
3. Waits for the command handler to finish.
4. Deserializes and returns the result.

The pattern is clean: no manual message queues or event systems—just async/await.

26.7 React Frontend Infrastructure

The frontend uses React Query (v5) for async state management:

```
import { useQuery } from '@tanstack/react-query';
import * as commands from '../commands';

export function useBlockchainInfo() {
    return useQuery({
        queryKey: ['blockchainInfo'],
        queryFn: () => commands.getBlockchainInfo(),
        staleTime: 10000, // 10 seconds
    });
}

export function useLatestBlocks() {
    return useQuery({
        queryKey: ['latestBlocks'],
        queryFn: () => commands.getLatestBlocks(),
        staleTime: 10000,
    });
}

export function useMiningInfo() {
    return useQuery({
        queryKey: ['miningInfo'],
        queryFn: () => commands.getMiningInfo(),
        staleTime: 30000, // 30 seconds
    });
}
```

Listing 346: React Query hooks (`src/hooks/useBlockchain.ts`)

Key Takeaways

- ✓ Tauri IPC architecture: desktop application with Rust backend and TypeScript/React frontend, bridged by 22 `#[tauri::command]` handlers.
- ✓ Dependency injection via Tauri's `State<AppState>` for managing shared configuration (base URL, API key) across command handlers.
- ✓ Service layer pattern: `BitcoinApiService` wrapping `AdminClient` HTTP calls, decoupling Tauri handlers from blockchain API details.
- ✓ TypeScript IPC bridge: `invoke()` wrapping all commands for type-safe async communication across the process boundary.
- ✓ React Query (v5) for server-state management (balances, transactions) with automatic caching and refetching at configurable intervals.
- ✓ Comparison with Iced MVU: both architectures call the same `bitcoin-api` crate, but Tauri separates UI concerns (React) from business logic (Rust).

27

Wallet UI (Iced)

▷ **What you will learn in this chapter**

- Build a user-facing wallet interface for managing addresses, balances, and transactions
- Implement persistent encrypted storage of wallet data using an embedded database
- Extend the Iced MVU pattern with database initialization and query semantics
- Design for real wallet workflows: address generation, sending funds, transaction history

THIS chapter returns to the Iced MVU framework from Chapter 25 but pivots audiences: Chapters 25 and 26 built an *administrative* dashboard for an operator who already runs a node, whereas this chapter builds a *user-facing* wallet for someone whose only interest is holding and spending coins. That shift reshapes every design decision — the admin UI could afford to refetch blockchain state on every open, but a wallet must remember the user's addresses across sessions, must keep private keys out of memory when not in use, and must survive an app crash without losing funds. Those requirements push this chapter past Chapter 25's pure in-memory state and into **persistent encrypted storage**.

The `bitcoin-wallet-ui` crate is a user-facing wallet interface for managing addresses, balances, and transactions. Unlike the admin UI (Chapter 25), the wallet UI prioritizes end-user workflows: creating wallets, sending transactions, viewing transaction history, and persisting encryption keys securely.

> ▷ **Focus**
>
> This chapter focuses on the wallet interface, not the wallet implementation itself. The wallet backend is explained in Chapter 23 (Wallet System). Here we build the MVU shell and persistence layer that puts that wallet to work in a user's hands.

The wallet UI uses the same Iced MVU pattern as Chapter 25 but adds **persistent encrypted storage**. An embedded database (Chapter 29) stores wallet metadata and derived data, eliminating the need to re-query the blockchain for every session.

27.1 What This UI Is (In One Sentence)

The wallet UI is a **user-facing MVU application** that adds **persistent encrypted storage**: it renders wallet state (`view.rs`), mutates state in response to user actions (`update.rs`), performs async API calls (`api.rs`), and persists balances and transaction history to an encrypted database (`database.rs`).

27.2 Architectural Map

This wallet UI is a message-driven state machine that adds persistence to the MVU pattern:

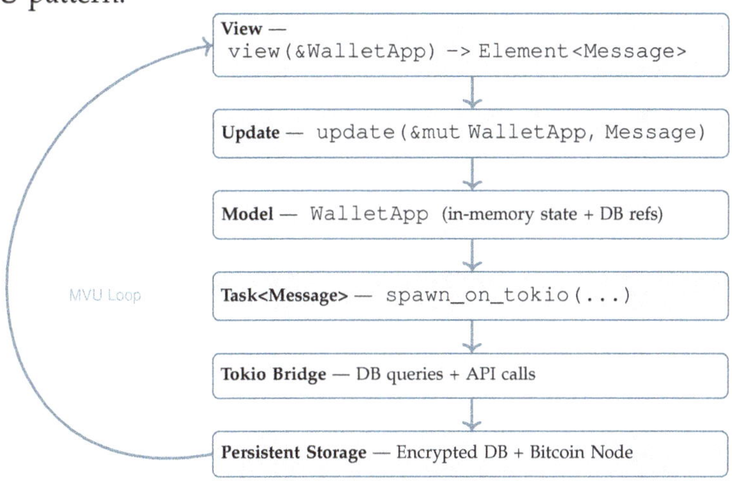

27.3 Boot Sequence and Wiring

```rust
mod api;
mod app;
mod database;
mod runtime;
mod types;
mod update;
mod view;

use app::WalletApp;
use iced::{Theme, application};
use runtime::init_runtime;
use update::update;
use view::view;
```

Listing 347: Main entrypoint: modules and imports (`bitcoin-wallet-ui/src/main.rs`, part 1)

The wallet application is organized into the same modular structure as the admin interface: state (`app`), type definitions (`types`), message handlers (`update`), rendering (`view`), API communication (`api`), async runtime support (`runtime`), and persistent storage (`database`).

```rust
fn main() -> iced::Result {
    // 1) Async precondition: initialize Tokio runtime for API calls
    init_runtime();

    // 2) Persistence precondition: generate deterministic database password
    let db_password = generate_database_password();
    if let Err(e) = database::init_database(&db_password) {
        eprintln!("Failed to initialize database: {}", e);
    }

    // 3) Enter Iced's MVU loop
    application(WalletApp::new, update, view)
        .title(title)
        .theme(theme)
        .run()
}
```

Listing 348: Main entrypoint: initialization sequence (`bitcoin-wallet-ui/src/main.rs`, part 2)

The database password is generated deterministically from the user's environment (username and home directory) so that the same user always unlocks the same encrypted database.

```
fn generate_database_password() -> String {
    use std::collections::hash_map::DefaultHasher;
    use std::hash::{Hash, Hasher};

    let mut hasher = DefaultHasher::new();

    // Deterministic password from username + home directory
    if let Ok(username) = std::env::var("USER") {
        username.hash(&mut hasher);
    } else if let Ok(username) = std::env::var("USERNAME") {
        username.hash(&mut hasher);
    }

    if let Some(home) = dirs::home_dir() {
        home.to_string_lossy().hash(&mut hasher);
    }

    // Return hex-encoded hash as password
    format!("{:x}", hasher.finish())
}
```

Listing 349: Main entrypoint — password generation

Walkthrough: three preconditions before MVU starts:

1. **Async execution**: `init_runtime()` (same as Chapter 25) creates a Tokio runtime for API calls.
2. **Persistent storage**: `init_database(password)` opens/creates an encrypted SQLite database (see Chapter 29).
3. **MVU loop**: `application(WalletApp::new, update, view).run()` starts the event loop.

The database password is generated deterministically from the user's username and home directory, so:

- Same user on same machine: same password, so the database can be reopened.
- Different user or machine: different password, so wallets are not trivially portable.

Threat model. This design assumes an attacker cannot read your home directory. If they can, the username and home path are trivially recoverable and the database key is reconstructed from those two facts alone. It is a *convenience* barrier, not a cryptographic one, and is appropriate for a local learning project. A production wallet should store the key in the operating system's secure credential store (Keychain on macOS, Credential Manager on Windows, libsecret on Linux) or require a user-entered passphrase, in both cases fed through a password-based KDF such as PBKDF2 or Argon2id before it reaches SQLCipher.

27.4 Wallet Application State

```rust
use bitcoin_api::WalletClient;

#[derive(Debug)]
pub struct WalletApp {
    // Current wallet
    pub current_wallet: Option<String>,
    pub wallets: Vec<String>,

    // Balances and transaction history
    pub balance: Option<u64>,
    pub transactions: Vec<Transaction>,
    pub unspent_outputs: Vec<UnspentOutput>,

    // UI state
    pub active_tab: Tab,
    pub selected_address: Option<String>,
    pub input_send_to: String,
    pub input_amount: String,
    pub status: String,

    // Derivation path management
    pub derivation_path: String,
    pub generated_addresses: Vec<String>,
}
```

Listing 350: Wallet application state: the main app struct (`bitcoin-wallet-ui/src/app.rs`, part 1)

The `WalletApp` struct holds the complete wallet UI state: which wallet is loaded, current balance and transaction history, active tab, and user input fields. It is organized into logical groups: wallet identity, derived data (balances and transaction history), UI state (tabs and user input), and derivation path management for address generation.

```
#[derive(Debug, Clone)]
pub struct Transaction {
    pub txid: String,
    pub timestamp: i64,
    pub amount: i64,
    pub fee: Option<i64>,
    pub from_addresses: Vec<String>,
    pub to_addresses: Vec<String>,
}
```

Listing 351: Wallet application state: transaction data type (`bitcoin-wallet-ui/src/app.rs`, part 2)

The `Transaction` struct represents a blockchain transaction with its metadata for display and analysis in the wallet UI.

```
#[derive(Debug, Clone)]
pub struct UnspentOutput {
    pub txid: String,
    pub vout: usize,
    pub amount: u64,
    pub address: String,
}

#[derive(Debug, Clone, Copy, PartialEq, Eq)]
pub enum Tab {
    Addresses,
    SendTransaction,
    History,
    Balance,
}
```

Listing 352: Wallet application state: UTXO and tab types (`bitcoin-wallet-ui/src/app.rs`, part 3)

The wallet application consists of a main state struct alongside several supporting types. The `WalletApp` manages wallet identity, balances, and transaction data, while `Transaction` and `UnspentOutput` represent blockchain state. The `Tab` enum drives navigation between UI sections.

```
impl Default for WalletApp {
    fn default() -> Self {
        Self {
            current_wallet: None,
            wallets: Vec::new(),
            balance: None,
            transactions: Vec::new(),
            unspent_outputs: Vec::new(),
            active_tab: Tab::Addresses,
            selected_address: None,
            input_send_to: String::new(),
            input_amount: String::new(),
            status: String::from("Ready"),
            derivation_path: "m/44'/0'/0'/0".to_string(),
            generated_addresses: Vec::new(),
        }
    }
}
```

Listing 353: Wallet application state: initialization and defaults (part 1)

The `Default` trait provides sensible initial values for all fields. The wallet starts with no active wallet, empty balances and transaction history, and the first address tab selected. The `derivation_path` default, `"m/44'/0'/0'/0"`, is a **BIP44** path — a widely adopted convention for deriving many addresses from one seed. Reading left to right: `m` is the master key, `44'` selects the BIP44 standard (the trailing apostrophe means *hardened* derivation, which breaks parent-to-child key leakage), `0'` is the coin type (0 = Bitcoin), the next `0'` is the account index, and the trailing `0` is the external chain (receive addresses; `1` would be change). Each address generated by this wallet extends the path with one more index (`/0`, `/1`, ...), giving the wallet a fresh address per request while keeping all of them recoverable from the single seed.

```
impl WalletApp {
    pub fn new() -> (Self, iced::Task<Message>) {
        (Self::default(), iced::Task::none())
    }
}
```

Listing 354: Wallet application state: initialization and defaults (part 2)

Walkthrough: wallet state design:

`WalletApp` groups state into three categories:

- **Wallet identity**: `current_wallet` (active wallet address), `wallets` (list of known wallets).
- **Derived data**: `balance`, `transactions`, `unspent_outputs` (cached from API or database).
- **UI state**: `active_tab`, `input_*` (user inputs), `status` (feedback message).

Unlike the admin UI, the wallet UI is designed around a **single active wallet**—the user selects one wallet to manage at a time.

27.5 Message Types

```
#[derive(Debug, Clone)]
pub enum Message {
    // Wallet selection
    SelectWallet(String),
    FetchWalletList,
    WalletListLoaded(Result<Vec<String>, String>),

    // Balance and transaction history
    FetchBalance(String),
    BalanceLoaded(Result<BalanceResponse, String>),

    FetchTransactionHistory(String),
    HistoryLoaded(Result<Vec<Transaction>, String>),

    FetchUnspentOutputs(String),
    UnspentLoaded(Result<Vec<UnspentOutput>, String>),

    // Address generation
    GenerateAddress,
    AddressGenerated(Result<String, String>),
```

Listing 355: Message enum: wallet and data queries (`bitcoin-wallet-ui/src/types.rs`, part 1)

The first group of messages handles wallet selection (which wallet to operate on) and fetching blockchain data (balances, transaction history, unspent outputs, addresses). Each fetch message has a corresponding loaded message that carries the result.

```
    // Sending transactions
    SendToChanged(String),
    AmountChanged(String),
    SendTransaction,
    TransactionSent(Result<String, String>),

    // Navigation
    TabChanged(Tab),

    // Persistence
    SaveToDatabaseRequested,
    SaveToDatabase(Result<(), String>),
}
```

Listing 356: Message enum: user input and persistence (`bitcoin-wallet-ui/src/types.rs`, part 2)

Messages fall into four categories:

- **Wallet operations**: select wallet, fetch wallets, generate addresses.
- **Balance/history queries**: fetch balance, transaction history, unspent outputs.
- **Transactions**: send Bitcoin (user inputs and submission).
- **Persistence**: save and load from encrypted database.

27.6 Update Loop

```rust
use crate::api;
use crate::app::WalletApp;
use crate::database;
use crate::runtime::spawn_on_tokio;
use crate::types::Message;
use iced::Task;

pub fn update(app: &mut WalletApp, message: Message) -> Task<Message> {
    match message {
        Message::TabChanged(tab) => {
            app.active_tab = tab;
            Task::none()
        }

        Message::SelectWallet(wallet) => {
            app.current_wallet = Some(wallet.clone());
            app.status = format!("Selected wallet: {}", wallet);
            // Automatically fetch balance for the selected wallet
            let task_fetch_balance = Task::perform(
                spawn_on_tokio(api::fetch_balance(wallet.clone())),
                Message::BalanceLoaded,
            );
            task_fetch_balance
        }
```

Listing 357: Update loop: setup and navigation handlers (`bitcoin-wallet-ui/src/update.rs`, part 1)

The update function begins by dispatching on the message type. Navigation changes (tab selection) are handled immediately, while wallet selection triggers an asynchronous balance fetch.

```
        Message::FetchBalance(wallet_addr) => {
            Task::perform(
                spawn_on_tokio(api::fetch_balance(wallet_addr)),
                Message::BalanceLoaded,
            )
        }
```

Listing 358: Update loop: balance fetch trigger (`bitcoin-wallet-ui/src/update.rs`, part 2)

The `FetchBalance` message spawns an async task to retrieve the current balance from the Bitcoin API. Once the API responds, the result is wrapped in a `BalanceLoaded` message.

```
        Message::BalanceLoaded(result) => match result {
            Ok(response) => {
                app.balance = Some(response.balance);
                // All monetary values are in satoshis (1~BTC = 100{,}000{,}000 satoshis), following Bitcoin convention.
                app.status = format!(
                    "Balance: {} satoshis",
                    response.balance
                );
                if let Some(ref w) = app.current_wallet {
                    Task::perform(
                        spawn_on_tokio(async move {
                            database::save_balance(
                                &w.clone(), response.balance
                            ).await
                        }),
                        |r| Message::SaveToDatabase(r),
                    )
                } else {
                    Task::none()
                }
            }
```

Listing 359: Update loop: balance result handler - success case (part 2b)

When the balance fetch succeeds, the app updates the balance field and sends an async message to persist it to the database.

```
            Err(e) => {
                app.status = format!(
                    "Error fetching balance: {}", e
                );
                Task::none()
            }
        }
```

Listing 360: Update loop: balance result handler - error case (part 2c)

The first group of message handlers manages tab navigation and wallet selection. When a wallet is selected, the update function automatically fetches its balance, demonstrating the pattern of triggering follow-up API calls in response to user actions.

```
        Message::SendToChanged(address) => {
            app.input_send_to = address;
            Task::none()
        }

        Message::AmountChanged(amount) => {
            app.input_amount = amount;
            Task::none()
        }
```

Listing 361: Update loop: transaction input and submission (`bitcoin-wallet-ui/src/update.rs`, part 2)

The next part handles the transaction submission workflow. When the user clicks "Send", the update function validates inputs and submits a transaction request to the Bitcoin API. Once the remote API responds, the result handler clears input fields and updates the status message.

```
        Message::SendTransaction => {
            if let Some(ref wallet) = app.current_wallet {
                if app.input_send_to.is_empty() ||
                   app.input_amount.is_empty() {
                    app.status =
                        "Recipient and amount required".into();
                    return Task::none();
                }
                let amount: u64 =
                    match app.input_amount.parse() {
                        Ok(a) => a,
                        Err(_) => {
                            app.status =
                                "Invalid amount".into();
                            return Task::none();
                        }
                    };
                let from = wallet.clone();
                let to = app.input_send_to.clone();
                // Dispatch to send_transaction
```

Listing 362: Update loop: transaction validation (part 3)

The validation extracts the wallet address, checks that both recipient and amount are provided, and parses the amount as a 64-bit unsigned integer. If any check fails, an error message is set and the function returns immediately without dispatching.

```
                    Task::perform(
                        spawn_on_tokio(api::send_transaction(
                            from, to, amount
                        )),
                        Message::TransactionSent,
                    )
                } else {
                    app.status = "No wallet selected".into();
                    Task::none()
                }
            }
```

Listing 363: Update loop: transaction dispatch (part 3b)

The SendTransaction handler validates that a wallet is selected, both the recipient address and amount are provided, and the amount parses to a valid integer. If validation passes, it spawns an async API call; otherwise it sets an error status.

```
        Message::TransactionSent(result) => {
            match result {
                Ok(txid) => {
                    app.status = format!("Transaction sent: {}", txid);
                    app.input_send_to.clear();
                    app.input_amount.clear();
                }
                Err(e) => {
                    app.status = format!("Error sending transaction: {}", e);
                }
            }
            Task::none()
        }

        _ => Task::none(),
    }
}
```

Listing 364: Update loop: transaction result handling and catch-all (`bitcoin-wallet-ui/src/update.rs`, part 4)

Key Takeaways

- ✓ Wallet UI extending Iced's MVU pattern with persistent encrypted storage via an embedded database.
- ✓ Boot sequence: Tokio runtime initialization, deterministic password generation from environment, database creation, then MVU loop startup.
- ✓ Wallet application state: identity (current wallet, wallet list), derived data (balance, transactions, UTXOs), and UI state (tabs, input fields).
- ✓ Message-driven state machine: fetch operations (wallet selection, balance, transaction history) paired with result handlers that update state and trigger persistence.
- ✓ Update loop pattern: immediate state updates for UI actions, async delegation to API calls via `spawn_on_tokio`, and follow-up persistence tasks triggered by successful fetches.
- ✓ User workflows: wallet selection, address generation, transaction validation/submission, and automatic caching of balance and transaction history to the database.

28

Wallet UI (Tauri)

▷ **What you will learn in this chapter**

- Build a user-facing wallet interface using Tauri 2 (Rust backend + React frontend)
- Implement secure persistent storage for wallet keys and transaction history
- Design a modern React UI for real wallet workflows with transaction signing
- Integrate Tauri commands for database operations and transaction broadcast

SAME wallet, different framework. Chapter 27 built it in pure Rust with Iced. This chapter rebuilds it with Tauri 2—a Rust backend that holds keys and signs transactions, paired with a React frontend that provides the user interface. You get React's rich ecosystem of UI libraries while keeping crypto-sensitive operations in Rust. In Tauri, the two halves talk over **IPC** (*inter-process communication*): the frontend calls a named Rust function by string, and Tauri marshals the arguments across the process boundary, runs the function, and returns the result as JSON—private keys never leave the Rust side. This chapter explains the `bitcoin-wallet-ui-tauri` crate—how the backend persists encrypted keys, how the frontend calls signing commands, and how a single transaction signing request flows from UI, through the IPC boundary, into Rust, and back as a signed hash.

28.1 What This UI Is (In One Sentence)

The Tauri wallet UI is a **two-language user-facing application** that adds **secure key storage**: a Rust backend exposes 18 `#[tauri::command]` handlers for wallet operations (address generation, balance queries, transaction signing and broadcast), while a React frontend provides a modern dashboard for managing addresses, sending transactions, and viewing history.

28.2 Architectural Differences: Iced vs. Tauri Wallet

Both the Iced (Chapter 27) and Tauri (this chapter) wallet implementations expose the same operations:

Table 28.1: Wallet UI: Iced vs. Tauri

Aspect	Iced Wallet (Ch. 18)	Tauri Wallet (Ch. 19)
Languages	Rust only	Rust backend + React/-TypeScript
State persistence	SQLite with encrypted password	SQLite via Rust backend, React state (Zustand)
Key storage	In-memory + database	In Rust backend (`State<RwLock>`), never exposed to JS
Transaction signing	Rust (sync)	Rust backend via command, never touches frontend
Event handling	`Message` enum	React Router + React Query
UI styling	Iced widgets (programmatic)	Tailwind CSS + React components

> **i Security Note**
>
> Both implementations follow the same security principle: **private keys stay in Rust**. In Iced, keys are in memory and encrypted at rest in SQLite. In Tauri, keys are in Rust backend state and never serialized to JSON/-JavaScript. Transaction signing happens in Rust; the frontend only receives the signed transaction hash.

28.3 Rust Backend Architecture

```
use tauri::State;
use std::sync::RwLock;

#[derive(Clone, serde::Serialize, serde::Deserialize)]
pub struct WalletState {
    pub current_wallet: Option<String>,
    pub wallets: Vec<String>,
    pub database_password: String,
}

#[derive(Clone)]
pub struct AppState {
    pub wallet: RwLock<WalletState>,
    pub base_url: String,
}
```

Listing 365: Tauri wallet main — state structures (`src-tauri/src/main.rs`)

The `AppState` wraps the wallet in an `RwLock` for thread-safe, interior-mutable access. The `main` function constructs this state and passes it to the Tauri builder:

```
fn main() {
    let app_state = AppState {
        wallet: RwLock::new(WalletState {
            current_wallet: None,
            wallets: Vec::new(),
            database_password: generate_database_password(),
        }),
        base_url: "http://127.0.0.1:8080".to_string(),
    };
```

Listing 366: Tauri wallet main (part 1a: state initialization)

The Tauri builder then registers all 18 command handlers and launches the application. Each handler name maps directly to a `#[tauri::command]` function in the Rust backend:

```
    tauri::Builder::default()
        .manage(app_state)
        .invoke_handler(tauri::generate_handler![
            cmd_list_wallets,
            cmd_create_wallet,
            cmd_select_wallet,
            cmd_get_balance,
            cmd_get_addresses,
            cmd_generate_address,
            cmd_get_transaction_history,
            cmd_get_unspent_outputs,
            cmd_send_transaction,
            cmd_sign_transaction,
            cmd_get_tx_status,
            cmd_export_wallet,
            cmd_import_wallet,
            cmd_backup_wallet,
            cmd_set_passphrase,
            cmd_unlock_wallet,
            cmd_get_wallet_info,
            cmd_cancel_transaction,
        ])
        .run(tauri::generate_context!())
        .expect("error while running tauri application");
}
```

Listing 367: Tauri wallet main (part 1b: builder and command registration)

The password for the encrypted wallet database is generated deterministically from the user's environment, so the same user on the same machine always unlocks the same database:

```rust
fn generate_database_password() -> String {
    use std::collections::hash_map::DefaultHasher;
    use std::hash::{Hash, Hasher};

    let mut hasher = DefaultHasher::new();
    if let Ok(username) = std::env::var("USER") {
        username.hash(&mut hasher);
    }
    if let Some(home) = dirs::home_dir() {
        home.to_string_lossy().hash(&mut hasher);
    }
    format!("{:x}", hasher.finish())
}
```

Listing 368: Tauri wallet main — builder and command registration (part 2: password generation)

Walkthrough: the command handler pattern:

Every command follows the same structure:

1. Extract `State<AppState>` parameter injected by Tauri.
2. Call a corresponding `WalletClient` method from the bitcoin-api crate.
3. Return the result (or error) as JSON over IPC.

Crucially, transaction signing and key management happen in the Rust backend—the frontend never touches private keys.

28.4 React Frontend: State Management and Commands

The React frontend uses the same patterns as the admin Tauri UI (Chapter 26): React Query for async data fetching and Zustand for local UI state. Custom hooks wrap the IPC `invoke()` calls so that components never call commands directly. Tauri's `invoke(name, args)` is an async JavaScript function: it sends the command name and a JSON payload across the IPC boundary, awaits the Rust handler's return value, and resolves a Promise with the result—so hooks built on top of it compose with any async-aware state library (React Query here, but also SWR or plain `async/await`).

React Query divides work by direction: `useQuery` wraps *reads* (balance, transaction history) and gives them automatic caching, deduplication, and background refetching, while `useMutation` wraps *writes* (create wallet, send transaction) and exposes success/error callbacks for invalidating cached reads once the server-side state has changed. The numeric `staleTime` option in the listings below is measured in *milliseconds*: `staleTime: 30000` marks data fresh for 30 seconds (wallet list changes rarely), while `staleTime: 10000` marks balances fresh for 10 seconds (they change more often). A value of `0` would mean "refetch on every access."

```
import { useQuery, useMutation } from
'@tanstack/react-query';
import * as commands from '../commands';

export function useWalletList() {
    return useQuery({
        queryKey: ['wallets'],
        queryFn: () => commands.listWallets(),
        staleTime: 30000,
    });
}

export function useBalance(address: string | null) {
    return useQuery({
        queryKey: ['balance', address],
        queryFn: () => address ?
        commands.getBalance(address) :
        Promise.resolve(0),
        enabled: !!address,
        staleTime: 10000,   // 10 seconds
    });
}

\needspace{4\baselineskip}
\code{staleTime} is specified in milliseconds:
30{,}000\,ms = 30 seconds (appropriate for wallet
lists that change infrequently) and 10{,}000\,ms =
10 seconds (for balances that update more often).
```

Listing 369: React Query hooks — data fetching (`src/hooks/useWallet.ts`, part 1)

The `useQuery` hooks handle reads with automatic caching and refetching. The mutation hooks below handle writes—creating wallets and sending transactions:

```
export function useSendTransaction() {
    return useMutation({
        mutationFn: (params: { from: string; to:
        string; amount: number }) =>
            commands.sendTransaction(params.from,
            params.to, params.amount),
    });
}

export function useCreateWallet() {
    return useMutation({
        mutationFn: (label?: string) =>
        commands.createWallet(label),
        onSuccess: () => {
            queryClient.invalidateQueries(['wallet',
            'addresses'])
            // Show toast success
        },
    });
}

\needspace{4\baselineskip}
When a new wallet is created, the wallet-addresses
cache becomes stale, so \code{onSuccess} calls
\code{invalidateQueries} to trigger a refetch of the
updated list.
```

Listing 370: React Query hooks — mutations (`src/hooks/useWallet.ts` , part 2)

React Query manages server state (data from the Bitcoin API), while local component state handles UI (forms, modals, etc.):

1. **useQuery**: automatic caching and refetching for reads (balance, transaction history).
2. **useMutation**: explicit side effects for writes (create wallet, send transaction).

Each query/mutation calls the corresponding function in `commands.ts` , which uses Tauri's `invoke()` .

When the user submits a transaction, `mutate()` fires the backend request. On success, `onSuccess` invalidates the balance and transaction-history caches, causing React Query to refetch them automatically — so the UI reflects the new state without a manual refresh.

28.5 Persistent Database Layer

Both Iced (Chapter 27) and Tauri (this chapter) wallets use the same encrypted SQLite database (Chapter 29) for persistence. The difference is where the encryption happens:

- **Iced**: database initialization happens in `main.rs` before MVU starts.
- **Tauri**: database initialization happens in a startup command; the frontend can choose when to unlock it (e.g., with a passphrase).

```rust
use crate::AppState;
use tauri::State;

#[tauri::command]
pub async fn cmd_init_database(
    state: State<'_, AppState>,
    password: Option<String>,
) -> Result<(), String> {
    let wallet_state = state.wallet.read()
        .map_err(|e| format!("Failed to read state:
{}", e))?;

    // Use provided password or deterministic
password
    let pwd = password.unwrap_or_else(|| {
        wallet_state.database_password.clone()
    });

    // Initialize SQLite with encryption (XChaCha20
via sqlcipher or similar)
    database::init_with_password(&pwd)
        .await
        .map_err(|e| e.to_string())
}
```

Listing 371: Database initialization command (`src-tauri/src/commands/database.rs`)

After initializing the database, the next two commands handle persistence of wallet data: saving the wallet state and loading it back on application restart.

```
#[tauri::command]
pub async fn cmd_save_wallet(
    wallet_address: String,
    wallet_data: serde_json::Value,
) -> Result<(), String> {
    database::save_wallet(&wallet_address, &wallet_data)
        .await
        .map_err(|e| e.to_string())
}

#[tauri::command]
pub async fn cmd_load_wallet(
    wallet_address: String,
) -> Result<serde_json::Value, String> {
    database::load_wallet(&wallet_address)
        .await
        .map_err(|e| e.to_string())
}
```

Listing 372: Database persistence commands (part 2)

The database persists:

- Wallet metadata (addresses, labels).
- Transaction history (cached from the blockchain node).
- Encrypted key material (never directly accessed by the frontend).

Key Takeaways

- ✓ This chapter covered a user-facing Tauri wallet with Rust backend and React frontend, paralleling the Iced wallet from Chapter 27.
- ✓ Command handlers exposing 18 wallet operations (create, balance, send, history, etc.), with transaction signing performed in Rust.
- ✓ React Query managing server state (balances, transactions) and integrating with Tauri's IPC via `invoke()` .
- ✓ Encrypted database persistence for wallet metadata and transaction history (Chapter 29 details the database design).
- ✓ Security model with private keys maintained in Rust backend state, never reaching the JavaScript/React frontend.

28.6 Exercises

1. **Add a Transaction Confirmation Dialog** — Modify the "Send" command to return a transaction preview (recipients, amounts, fees) to the frontend. Add a React modal that displays this preview and requires explicit confirmation before broadcasting. Trace the IPC round-trip: React → Tauri command → Bitcoin API → JSON response → modal display.
2. **Implement Wallet Recovery** — Add a "Restore Wallet" feature: allow the user to input a seed phrase, call a backend command to derive addresses from the seed, and persist them to the database. Compare this with the "Create Wallet" flow.

28.7 Further Reading

- **Tauri Documentation** — API reference and examples at `https://tauri.app/docs/`.
- **React Query Documentation** — Server state management at `https://tanstack.com/query/`.
- **Chapter 23: Wallet System** — The wallet implementation that both UIs consume.
- **Chapter 29: Embedded Database** — SQLite encryption and persistence layer.

29

Embedded Database & Persistence

▷ **What you will learn in this chapter**

- Integrate SQLCipher for encrypted wallet storage across both Iced and Tauri frontends
- Design database schemas and implement migrations using the table-recreation technique
- Handle thread safety with `OnceLock<Mutex<Connection»` and the singleton table pattern
- Implement deterministic password generation so both wallet UIs share one encrypted database file

BOTH wallet applications in this project—the Iced wallet (Chapter 27) and the Tauri wallet (Chapter 28)—persist user configuration and wallet addresses in an encrypted SQLite database built via SQLCipher. This chapter covers the shared persistence layer used by both, explaining the patterns once so that neither wallet chapter needs to repeat the material.

This section focuses on two reader-facing goals:

- **Security**: sensitive values (like API keys) are stored encrypted at rest, without requiring the user to type a passphrase.
- **Continuity**: wallet addresses and settings survive process restarts, so the wallet list is stable and the node connection is remembered.

▲ SQLCipher encryption and key strength

SQLCipher encryption is only as strong as the password. The deterministic password used here is a 64-bit non-cryptographic hash of the username and home directory—below the modern brute-force threshold. This trades key-derivation strength for the convenience of sharing one database between both wallet UIs without a passphrase prompt. In a production system, replace this with Argon2id-based key derivation (see Section 29.5 for details).

▷ Note

Both the Iced and Tauri wallets share the same encrypted database file. Changes made in one wallet are immediately visible in the other — there is no synchronization delay because they operate on the same SQLite file.

—

29.1 What is SQLCipher?

SQLCipher is a fork of SQLite that adds transparent 256-bit AES encryption to the entire database file. From Rust, we interact with it through the `rusqlite` crate (with the `bundled-sqlcipher` feature flag), which compiles SQLCipher from source and links it statically — no system library installation required. The API is identical to regular SQLite; the only difference is that you supply an encryption key via `PRAGMA key` before any other operation. This gives us encrypted-at-rest storage with zero additional infrastructure.

The database code in both apps is nearly identical. The Iced wallet stores it in a single file (`src/database.rs`), while the Tauri wallet organizes it into a module directory (`src-tauri/src/database/mod.rs` + `tests.rs`). The schema, key derivation, initialization sequence, and CRUD operations are the same. Differences will be noted as they arise.

To keep this chapter readable without a repository open, the complete, verbatim source files are provided in the companion code listings appendix.

29.2 Database Schema

This persistence layer is intentionally small and pragmatic. Four tables store the essential wallet data:

- **`settings`**: `base_url`, `api_key` — required so the UI can reconnect to the node without retyping configuration each time.
- **`wallet_addresses`**: `address`, optional `label`, `created_at` — required so the wallet list is stable and selectable after restart.
- **`schema_version`**: `version` — required so the database can evolve safely over time via migrations.
- **`users`**: `first_name`, `last_name`, `profile_picture` (BLOB) — present to support future UI work; in the current code the persistence primitives exist (schema + migrations), even if UI integration is minimal.

Database Schema

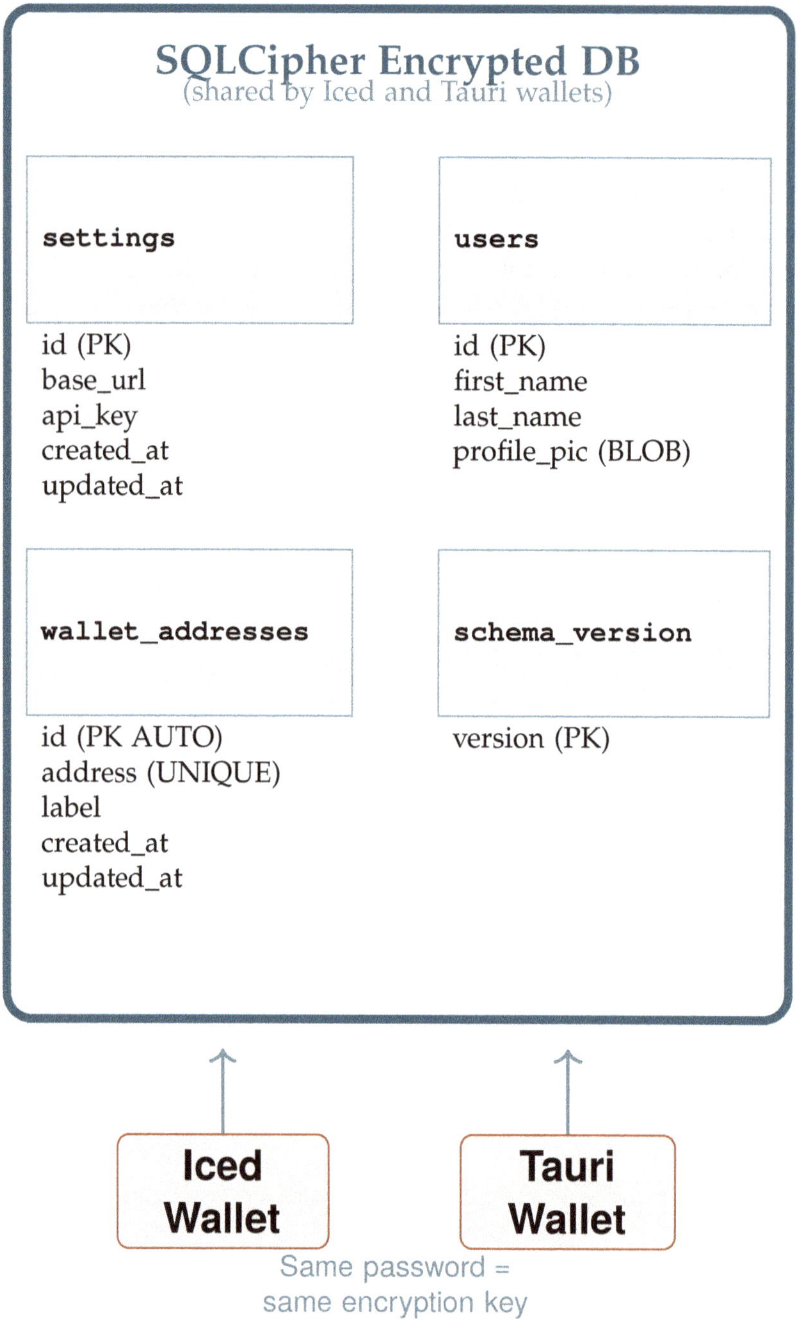
SQLCipher Encrypted DB
(shared by Iced and Tauri wallets)
settings
id (PK)
base_url
api_key
created_at
updated_at
users
id (PK)
first_name
last_name
profile_pic (BLOB)
wallet_addresses
id (PK AUTO)
address (UNIQUE)
label
created_at
updated_at
schema_version
version (PK)
Iced Wallet
Tauri Wallet
Same password =
same encryption key

29.3 Architecture: a single encrypted database + a single guarded connection

A single global connection is used in both wallets:

```
static DB_CONN: OnceLock<Mutex<Connection>> =
OnceLock::new();
```

This is a deliberate trade-off suitable for a GUI application:

- it avoids passing a connection through every call,
- it ensures access is serialized (SQLite `Connection` is not safe to share without synchronization),
- and it keeps the API of the module simple — any function in the module can call `get_connection()` to get a `MutexGuard<Connection>`.

`OnceLock` is a standard-library primitive that can be written to exactly once and then read forever—like a global variable that is initialized lazily on first use and is immutable afterward. Combined with `Mutex`, it gives us a connection that is created once at startup and safely shared across threads. The `OnceLock` guarantees that `init_database` can only succeed once per process. After that, `get_connection()` serves as the narrow waist: every read/write operation acquires the mutex, executes its query, and releases the lock when the guard drops.

29.4 Cargo dependency: `rusqlite` with `bundled-sqlcipher`

Both wallets declare the same dependency:

```
rusqlite = { version = "0.39", features =
["bundled-sqlcipher"] }
dirs = "6.0"
```

The `bundled-sqlcipher` feature compiles SQLCipher from source during `cargo build`, so no external SQLCipher library installation is needed. The `dirs` crate provides cross-platform data directory resolution (e.g., `/Library/Application Support` on macOS, `/.local/share` on Linux, `%APPDATA%` on Windows).

29.5 Key derivation: deterministic password generation

The database password is generated without user interaction. Both wallets use an identical `generate_database_password` function—in fact, the Tauri version includes the comment "EXACT replica from bitcoin-wallet-ui-iced":

```
fn generate_database_password() -> String {
    use std::collections::hash_map::DefaultHasher;
    use std::hash::{Hash, Hasher};

    let mut hasher = DefaultHasher::new();

    // Use username
    if let Ok(username) = std::env::var("USER") {
        username.hash(&mut hasher);
    } else if let Ok(username) = std::env::var("USERNAME") {
        username.hash(&mut hasher);
    }

    // Use home directory
    if let Some(home) = dirs::home_dir() {
        home.to_string_lossy().hash(&mut hasher);
    }

    // Use application name
    "bitcoin-wallet-ui".hash(&mut hasher);

    // Convert to hex string
    format!("{:x}", hasher.finish())
}
```

Listing 373: Deterministic password generation (identical in both wallets)

This design emphasizes **zero-interaction UX**: the user is never prompted for a passphrase, but the file is still encrypted at rest. The password is deterministic—the same user on the same machine always produces the same key—which means both the Iced and Tauri wallets can open the same database file.

Three inputs feed the hash:

1. **Username**: from `$USER` (Unix/macOS) or `$USERNAME` (Windows).
2. **Home directory**: via `dirs::home_dir()`, which resolves platform-specific paths.
3. **Application name**: the literal string `"bitcoin-wallet-ui"`.

`DefaultHasher` produces a 64-bit hash, which is converted to a hex string. Two things about this are deliberately weaker than production practice. First, 64 bits is below the modern brute-force threshold — 2^{64} operations is tractable for a well-funded attacker, whereas PBKDF2 or Argon2 produce 128- to 256-bit keys that are not. Second, `DefaultHasher` is a *non-cryptographic* hash tuned for speed, not resistance: given any candidate password guess, verifying it against the hash is essentially free, so an attacker with the encrypted database file can try millions of guesses per second. Password-based key derivation functions like PBKDF2 and Argon2 deliberately burn CPU and memory per guess to make that economics backwards. For a local development/learning tool the trade-off is acceptable: the encryption prevents casual file inspection, and the determinism avoids lockout. For a production wallet, replace this function with an Argon2id-based derivation that includes a per-install salt and tune the work factor to take roughly a second on the target hardware.

> ▷ **Note**
>
> Because the application name `"bitcoin-wallet-ui"` is the same in both Iced and Tauri wallets, and because both store the file at the same path (<data_dir>/bitcoin-wallet-ui/bitcoin-wallet.db), the two wallet apps share the same database. This is intentional — a user who switches between the two frontends sees the same wallets and settings.

29.6 Database initialization

The initialization sequence is identical in both wallets. The caller generates the password and passes it in:

```
// In main() --- identical in both wallets
let db_password = generate_database_password();
if let Err(e) = database::init_database(&db_password) {
    eprintln!("Failed to initialize database: {}", e);
    // Continue anyway - settings will use defaults
}
```

Annotated listing: `init_database`

```
pub fn init_database(password: &str) -> SqliteResult<()> {
    let db_path = get_database_path();

    // 1) Ensure the parent directory exists. This makes the module robust on
    // first run.
    if let Some(parent) = db_path.parent() {
        std::fs::create_dir_all(parent).map_err(|e| {
            // Map an I/O error into a rusqlite error so we keep one error
            // domain.
            rusqlite::Error::SqliteFailure(
                rusqlite::ffi::Error::new(rusqlite::ffi::SQLITE_CANTOPEN),
                Some(format!("Failed to create database directory: {}", e)),
            )
        })?;
    }

    // 2) Open (or create) the SQLite file.
    let conn = Connection::open(&db_path)?;

    // 3) Critical SQLCipher step: set the encryption key *immediately* after
    // opening, before ANY other SQL statement (even a SELECT).
    conn.pragma_update(None, "key", password)?;

    // SQLCipher reads the database file header on the first SQL operation. If an unencrypted query runs before \code{PRAGMA key} is set, SQLCipher concludes the file is plaintext, and subsequent encryption operations fail.
```

Listing 374: `init_database` : establishing the encrypted connection (part 1)

The next critical step enables foreign keys and applies schema initialization. This separation demonstrates the order-dependent nature of database setup: the encryption key must be set before reading any user data, and the schema must exist before any application logic touches the connection.

```
    // 4) Enable foreign keys (good SQLite hygiene; harmless if unused).
    conn.pragma_update(None, "foreign_keys", "ON")?;

    // 5) Create base schema + apply migrations before the connection is
    // exposed.
    create_tables(&conn)?;
    run_migrations(&conn)?;

    // 6) Store the connection globally for the rest of the process lifetime.
    DB_CONN.set(Mutex::new(conn)).map_err(|_| {
        rusqlite::Error::SqliteFailure(
            rusqlite::ffi::Error::new(rusqlite::ffi::SQLITE_MISUSE),
            Some("Database already initialized".to_string()),
        )
    })?;

    Ok(())
}
```

Listing 375: `init_database` : establishing the encrypted connection (part 2)

This six-step sequence embodies a reusable pattern:

1. **Ensure directories exist** — `create_dir_all` is idempotent.
2. **Open the file** — `Connection::open` creates the file if it doesn't exist.
3. **Set the encryption key** — this must be the very first pragma. If we ran any other SQL first, SQLCipher would treat the database as unencrypted.
4. **Enable foreign keys** — SQLite disables them by default.
5. **Create tables and run migrations** — before exposing the connection to any caller.

6. **Store globally** — `OnceLock::set` fails if already initialized, which we surface as a `SQLITE_MISUSE` error.

`get_database_path`

The database file location is resolved via the `dirs` crate:

```
fn get_database_path() -> PathBuf {
    let mut path = dirs::data_dir().unwrap_or_else(|| PathBuf::from("."));
    path.push("bitcoin-wallet-ui");
    path.push(DB_FILENAME);
    path
}
```

This resolves to platform-specific paths:

Platform	Path
macOS	`~/Library/Application Support/bitcoin-wallet-ui/bitcoin-wal`
Linux	`~/.local/share/bitcoin-wallet-ui/bitcoin-wallet.db`
Windows	`%APPDATA%/bitcoin-wallet-ui/bitcoin-wallet.db`

29.7 Connection acquisition: `get_connection`

`get_connection` is the narrow waist of the module: every read/write operation goes through it. It ensures the database was initialized and acquires the global mutex:

```
fn get_connection() -> SqliteResult<
    std::sync::MutexGuard<'static, Connection>
> {
    DB_CONN
        .get()
        .ok_or_else(|| {
            // The database was never initialized
            // --- UI must call init_database at startup.
            rusqlite::Error::SqliteFailure(
                rusqlite::ffi::Error::new(
                    rusqlite::ffi::SQLITE_MISUSE
                ),
                Some("Database not initialized".to_string()),
            )
        })?
```

Listing 376: `get_connection` : the singleton access point (part 1)

Once the `OnceLock` is retrieved, the next step acquires the mutex lock to synchronize access to the underlying connection.

```
            .lock()
            .map_err(|_| {
                // Poisoned mutex implies a panic
                // while holding the lock.
                rusqlite::Error::SqliteFailure(
                    rusqlite::ffi::Error::new(
                        rusqlite::ffi::SQLITE_MISUSE
                    ),
                    Some("Failed to acquire lock".to_string()),
                )
            })
}
```

Listing 377: `get_connection` : the singleton access point (part 2)

Two things can go wrong: `OnceLock::get()` returns `None` if `init_database` was never called, and `Mutex::lock()` returns `Err` if a previous caller panicked while holding the lock (poisoning the mutex). Both are mapped into the `rusqlite::Error` domain so every database function has a uniform error type.

`OnceLock` guarantees the database connection is initialized exactly once; subsequent `.get()` calls return the cached connection without locking overhead.

29.8 Schema and defaults: `create_tables`

`create_tables` can be understood through three lenses:

- **Singleton settings**: `settings.id` has `CHECK (id = 1)` so there can be only one row.
- **Uniqueness**: `wallet_addresses.address` is `UNIQUE` to prevent duplicates.
- **Schema versioning**: `schema_version` is created and initialized to `SCHEMA_VERSION` (currently 2).

Settings and wallet addresses tables

```
fn create_tables(conn: &Connection) -> SqliteResult<()> {
    // -- Settings table --
    // The \code{CHECK (id = 1)} constraint ensures at most one row can exist in the table \textemdash\ any attempt to insert a row with a different \code{id} fails, making this table behave as a singleton key-value store.
    conn.execute(
        "CREATE TABLE IF NOT EXISTS settings (
            id INTEGER PRIMARY KEY CHECK (id = 1),
            base_url TEXT NOT NULL DEFAULT '...',
            api_key TEXT NOT NULL DEFAULT '',
            created_at TEXT NOT NULL DEFAULT (datetime('now')),
            updated_at TEXT NOT NULL DEFAULT (datetime('now'))
        )",
        [],
    )?;
```

Listing 378: `create_tables` : settings table (part 1)

After creating the settings table, we populate its singleton row if it does not already exist, reading the API key from an environment variable with a fallback default.

```
    // Populate singleton row on first run.
    let count: i64 = conn.query_row(
        "SELECT COUNT(*) FROM settings",
        [],
        |row| row.get(0)
    )?;
    if count == 0 {
        conn.execute(
            "INSERT INTO settings (id, base_url, api_key) \
             VALUES (1, 'http://127.0.0.1:8080', ?)",
            params![
                std::env::var("BITCOIN_API_WALLET_KEY")
                    .unwrap_or_else(|_| "wallet-secret".to_string())
            ],
        )?;
    }
```

Listing 379: `create_tables` : populate settings (part 2)

After populating the singleton settings row, we create the wallet addresses table, which stores user-generated wallet addresses with optional labels and timestamps.

```
    // -- Wallet addresses table --
    conn.execute(
        "CREATE TABLE IF NOT EXISTS wallet_addresses
(
            id INTEGER PRIMARY KEY AUTOINCREMENT,
            address TEXT NOT NULL UNIQUE,
            label TEXT,
            created_at TEXT NOT NULL DEFAULT
(datetime('now')),
            updated_at TEXT NOT NULL DEFAULT
(datetime('now'))
        )",
        [],
    )?;
```

Listing 380: `create_tables` : wallet address table (part 3)

```
    conn.execute(
        "CREATE INDEX IF NOT EXISTS \
         idx_wallet_addresses_address \
         ON wallet_addresses(address)",
        [],
    )?;
```

Listing 381: `create_tables` : wallet address index (part 4)

The index on the address column enables efficient lookups when checking for duplicates or updating a wallet's label.

```
    // -- User profile table --
    conn.execute(
        "CREATE TABLE IF NOT EXISTS users (
            id INTEGER PRIMARY KEY CHECK (id = 1),
            first_name TEXT,
            last_name TEXT,
            profile_picture BLOB,
            created_at TEXT NOT NULL DEFAULT (datetime('now')),
            updated_at TEXT NOT NULL DEFAULT (datetime('now'))
        )",
        [],
    )?;

    // -- Schema version table --
    conn.execute(
        "CREATE TABLE IF NOT EXISTS schema_version (
            version INTEGER PRIMARY KEY
        )",
        [],
    )?;
```

Listing 382: `create_tables` : user profile and schema tables (part 5)

The user profile table follows the singleton pattern (like settings), while the schema version table stores only a single integer to track database migrations.

```
    let version_count: i64 = conn.query_row(
        "SELECT COUNT(*) FROM schema_version",
        [],
        |row| row.get(0)
    )?;
    if version_count == 0 {
        conn.execute(
            "INSERT INTO schema_version (version) VALUES (?)",
            params![SCHEMA_VERSION],
        )?;
    }

    Ok(())
}
```

Listing 383: `create_tables` : schema version initialization (part 6)

A pattern called the **singleton table** uses `CHECK (id = 1)` on both `settings` and `users` to prevent more than one row. This is a simple and effective alternative to a key-value store when a fixed set of fields is required.

29.9 Migrations: evolving the database safely

Migrations address one of the most common real-world problems: shipping a new binary against a database created by an older version.

The current code includes one migration, from schema version 1 to version 2:

- **Change**: `users.profile_picture_path` (TEXT) ~ `users.profile_picture` (BLOB).
- **Challenge**: SQLite does not support `ALTER COLUMN` to change a column type, nor does it support `DROP COLUMN` prior to version 3.35. PostgreSQL and MySQL let you change a column in place; SQLite does not, because its storage format packs rows tightly and rewriting one column requires rewriting every row anyway.

- **Solution**: Recreate the table via `execute_batch` within a transaction. The canonical recipe is: (1) create a new table with the desired schema under a temporary name, (2) copy rows from the old table, converting each column's data as needed, (3) drop the old table, (4) rename the new table to the original name. Wrapping all four steps in `BEGIN TRANSACTION` / `COMMIT` makes the migration atomic—if any step fails, the database is left untouched.

`run_migrations`

```
fn run_migrations(conn: &Connection) -> SqliteResult<()> {
    let current_version: i32 = conn
        .query_row("SELECT version FROM schema_version LIMIT 1", [], |row| {
            row.get(0)
        })
        .unwrap_or(0);

    // Migration 1 -> 2: detect old column and recreate table
    if current_version < 2 {
        let table_info = conn.prepare("PRAGMA table_info(users)")?;
        let has_old_column = table_info.exists()?;

        if has_old_column {
            conn.execute_batch(
                "BEGIN TRANSACTION;
                 CREATE TABLE users_new (
                     id INTEGER PRIMARY KEY CHECK (id = 1),
```

Listing 384: Migration from schema v1 to v2: read version (part 1)

The first part reads the current schema version and checks whether the v1 to v2 migration is needed. If the table has the old column structure, we proceed with the atomic table recreation.

```
                        first_name TEXT,
                        last_name TEXT,
                        profile_picture BLOB,
                        created_at TEXT NOT NULL,
                        updated_at TEXT NOT NULL
                    );
                    INSERT INTO users_new
                      SELECT id, first_name, last_name, NULL,
                             created_at, updated_at FROM users;
                    DROP TABLE users;
                    ALTER TABLE users_new RENAME TO users;
                    COMMIT;"
                )?;
            }

            conn.execute("UPDATE schema_version SET version = ?", params![2])?;
        }
```

Listing 385: Migration from schema v1 to v2: execute migration (part 2)

After the table is recreated with the new column types, we update the version to 2 so this migration never runs again.

```
    if current_version < SCHEMA_VERSION {
        conn.execute(
            "UPDATE schema_version SET version = ?",
            params![SCHEMA_VERSION]
        )?;
    }

    Ok(())
}
```

Listing 386: Migration from schema v1 to v2: update version (part 3)

SQLite's `PRAGMA table_info()` introspects the current schema before making changes. This makes the migration idempotent: running it against a database that has already been migrated is a no-op. The "recreate table" technique—create a new table with the desired schema, copy the data, drop the old table, rename the new table—is the standard approach for SQLite schema changes that go beyond what `ALTER TABLE` can express.

29.10 Data types

The same two public types are defined in both wallets. The only difference is that the Tauri wallet adds `Serialize` and `Deserialize` derives (required for Tauri IPC serialization):

```
// Iced wallet
#[derive(Debug, Clone)]
pub struct Settings {
    pub base_url: String,
    pub api_key: String,
}

#[derive(Debug, Clone)]
pub struct WalletAddress {
    pub address: String,
    pub label: Option<String>,
    pub created_at: String,
}
```

Listing 387: Public data types: Iced wallet (part 1)

The Iced wallet uses these types directly with `Debug` and `Clone` derives, since it doesn't require serialization for IPC. The Tauri wallet, however, must serialize across the command bridge.

```rust
// Tauri wallet (adds Serialize/Deserialize)
#[derive(Debug, Clone, Serialize, Deserialize)]
pub struct Settings {
    pub base_url: String,
    pub api_key: String,
}

impl WalletAddress {
    pub fn new(address: String, label: Option<String>) -> Self {
        Self {
            address,
            label,
            created_at: String::new(), // Set by database
        }
    }
}
```

Listing 388: Public data types: Tauri wallet and helper methods (part 2)

`created_at` is intentionally left empty; the database's `DEFAULT (datetime('now'))` clause assigns the timestamp on insert.

29.11 Settings persistence: load and save

`load_settings`

```
pub fn load_settings() -> SqliteResult<Settings> {
    let conn = get_connection()?;

    conn.query_row(
        "SELECT base_url, api_key FROM settings WHERE id = 1",
        [],
        |row| {
            Ok(Settings {
                base_url: row.get(0)?,
                api_key: row.get(1)?,
            })
        },
    )
}
```

Listing 389: Reading settings from the singleton row

`save_settings`

```
pub fn save_settings(settings: &Settings) -> SqliteResult<()> {
    let conn = get_connection()?;

    conn.execute(
        "UPDATE settings SET base_url = ?, \
         api_key = ?, \
         updated_at = datetime('now') WHERE id = 1",
        params![settings.base_url, settings.api_key],
    )?;

    Ok(())
}
```

Listing 390: Updating settings

29.12 Wallet address persistence: insert-or-update

The wallet list must be stable under these operations:

- creating a new wallet (insert),
- creating another wallet with the same address (update label; should not duplicate),
- loading all wallets (display list, newest first).

save_wallet_address — upsert pattern

```
pub fn save_wallet_address(wallet: &WalletAddress)
    -> SqliteResult<WalletAddress>
{
    let conn = get_connection()?;
    // This is an ``upsert by error recovery'' pattern: optimistically attempt \code{INSERT}, and if it fails due to a unique-constraint violation, fall back to \code{UPDATE}. This is simpler than checking whether the row exists before writing.
    match conn.execute(
        "INSERT INTO wallet_addresses \
         (address, label, updated_at) \
         VALUES (?, ?, datetime('now'))",
        params![wallet.address, wallet.label],
    ) {
        Ok(_) => fetch_wallet(&conn, &wallet.address),
        Err(rusqlite::Error::SqliteFailure(err, _))
            if err.code == rusqlite::ErrorCode::ConstraintViolation =>
        {
            conn.execute(
                "UPDATE wallet_addresses SET \
                 label = ?, updated_at = \
                 datetime('now') WHERE address = ?",
                params![wallet.label, wallet.address],
            )?;
            fetch_wallet(&conn, &wallet.address)
        }
        Err(e) => Err(e),
    }
}
```

Listing 391: Insert or update a wallet address (part 1)

This function attempts to insert the wallet address. If the insert succeeds, it retrieves the complete record. If a constraint violation occurs (address already exists), it updates the label and retrieves the record again. A helper function eliminates duplicate query logic.

This is an **upsert by error recovery**: rather than first running a `SELECT` to check for existence and then choosing `INSERT` or `UPDATE`, we optimistically attempt the `INSERT` and treat the unique-constraint failure as a signal to fall through to the `UPDATE`. The advantage is atomicity—between a separate `SELECT` and the subsequent write, another writer could slip in and change what we just read, but the single `INSERT` either succeeds or fails as a single database operation. SQLite's native `INSERT OR REPLACE` or `ON CONFLICT DO UPDATE` syntax achieves the same result in one statement; the match-on-error form is kept here because it surfaces the control flow explicitly and lets us handle the two paths (new record vs. existing record) with clear, distinct code.

```
fn fetch_wallet(
    conn: &Connection,
    address: &str
) -> SqliteResult<WalletAddress> {
    conn.query_row(
        "SELECT address, label, created_at \
         FROM wallet_addresses \
         WHERE address = ?",
        params![address],
        |row| {
            Ok(WalletAddress {
                address: row.get(0)?,
                label: row.get(1)?,
                created_at: row.get(2)?,
            })
        },
    )
}
```

Listing 392: Helper to fetch wallet by address (part 2)

This provides a stable call pattern: the caller always gets a complete `WalletAddress` back, regardless of whether the operation was insert or update. The `ConstraintViolation` match arm is the key—it converts what would normally be an error into a fallback update.

`load_wallet_addresses`

```
pub fn load_wallet_addresses() -> SqliteResult<Vec<WalletAddress>> {
    let conn = get_connection()?;
    let mut stmt = conn.prepare(
        "SELECT address, label, created_at \
         FROM wallet_addresses \
         ORDER BY created_at DESC"
    )?;

    let addresses = stmt.query_map([], |row| {
        Ok(WalletAddress {
            address: row.get(0)?,
            label: row.get(1)?,
            created_at: row.get(2)?,
        })
    })?;

    addresses.collect::<Result<Vec<_>, _>>()
}
```

Listing 393: Loading the entire wallet list

29.13 Additional Tauri operations

The Tauri wallet adds two CRUD operations not in Iced:

29.14 Iced vs. Tauri: comparison

The database layer is the most shared code between the two wallet frontends. Here is a precise comparison:
The takeaway is that the schema and initialization are identical. The Tauri wallet adds `Serialize` / `Deserialize` (needed for IPC), renames one function to avoid command-layer naming conflicts, and adds delete + label update operations.

```rust
pub fn delete_wallet_address_db(address: &str) -> SqliteResult<()> {
    get_connection()?.execute(
        "DELETE FROM wallet_addresses WHERE address = ?",
        params![address]
    )?;
    Ok(())
}

pub fn update_wallet_label_db(
    address: &str,
    label: &str
) -> SqliteResult<()> {
    get_connection()?.execute(
        "UPDATE wallet_addresses SET \
         label = ?, \
         updated_at = datetime('now') \
         WHERE address = ?",
        params![label, address],
    )?;
    Ok(())
}
```

Listing 394: Tauri-specific deletion and label updates

Aspect	Iced Wallet	Tauri Wallet
File location	`src/database.rs`	`src-tauri/src/database/mod.rs`
Schema	4 tables, v2	4 tables, v2 (identical)
`init_database`	Identical	Identical
`create_tables`	Identical	Identical
`run_migrations`	Identical	Identical
Types	`Debug, Clone`	`Debug, Clone, Serialize, Deserializ`
Save settings	`save_settings`	`save_settings_db`
Delete wallet	Not implemented	`delete_wallet_address_db`
Update label	Not implemented	`update_wallet_label_db`
Unit tests	None	7 tests in `tests.rs`

29.15 Integration points in the wallet UIs

This database layer is integrated at three points in each wallet, though the specific mechanism differs.

Iced wallet integration

1. **Startup** (`main.rs`): generates a database password, then calls `init_database(..)` .
2. **Initial model** (`WalletApp::new`): populates the Iced model by calling `load_settings()` and `load_wallet_addresses()` .
3. **Update loop** (`update.rs`): `Message::SaveSettings` calls `save_settings()` ; `Message::WalletCreated` calls `save_wallet_address()` .

Persistence is a side effect in the state machine (`update`), not in the view.

Tauri wallet integration

1. **Startup** (`main.rs`): generates a database password, then calls `init_database(..)` .
2. **AppState initialization** (`config/mod.rs`): `AppState::default()` calls `load_settings()` to populate initial state from the database with env var fallback.
3. **Tauri commands** (`commands/settings.rs` , `commands/wallet.rs`): each `#[tauri::command]` handler calls the appropriate database function. For example, `create_wallet` calls the remote API then `save_wallet_address()` to persist locally.

The Tauri integration is more fine-grained because each command handler is an independent async function, rather than a single `update` state machine.

Test	What it validates
`test_schema_creation`	All four tables exist after setup
`test_settings_crud`	Read defaults, update, verify changes
`test_wallet_address_crud`	Insert, read, update label, delete
`test_wallet_address_uniqueness`	Duplicate address insert fails
`test_wallet_list_ordering`	`ORDER BY created_at DESC` returns newest first
`test_schema_version`	Version table contains expected value (2)
`test_settings_singleton_constraint`	`CHECK(id = 1)` rejects `id = 2`

29.16 Unit tests (Tauri wallet)

The Tauri wallet includes a test suite that validates the database layer without SQLCipher encryption (using in-memory SQLite). The test helper `setup_test_db()` creates the same schema in memory, then each test exercises a specific aspect:

`Connection::open_in_memory()` is used without encryption, isolating the database logic from SQLCipher's key management. This is a practical testing pattern: the SQL schema and CRUD logic are the same whether or not the file is encrypted, so in-memory tests cover the logic without the complexity of key setup.

29.17 Summary

Key Takeaways

- ✓ This chapter covered SQLCipher integration for encrypted wallet storage across both Iced and Tauri frontends.
- ✓ Database schemas designed with migrations implemented using the table-recreation technique.
- ✓ Thread safety handled with `OnceLock<Mutex<Connection>>` and the singleton table pattern.
- ✓ Deterministic password generation enabling both wallet UIs to share one encrypted database file.

In the next chapter, we build the web admin interface — a React/TypeScript application that provides browser-based access to the blockchain.

i Companion Chapter

Complete source code including both Iced and Tauri implementations, tests, and the shared password generation function is available in the companion code listings appendix. In the print edition, these listings appear in the Appendix: Source Reference.

—

29.18 Exercises

1. **Add a New Table** — Create a new `transaction_memos` table in the SQLCipher database for storing user-provided notes on transactions. Write the migration using the table-recreation technique, implement insert and query functions, and write a test that stores and retrieves a memo.
2. **Thread Safety Verification** — Write a test that spawns two threads, each attempting to write to the database simultaneously through the `OnceLock<Mutex<Connection>>` singleton. Verify that both writes succeed without data corruption and that the mutex correctly serializes access.

30

Web Admin Interface

▷ **What you will learn in this chapter**

- Build a React/TypeScript web admin interface with modern component architecture
- Implement state management with React Query and authentication patterns
- Structure the frontend build process and deployment pipeline
- Apply TypeScript type safety to API integration and response handling

THE desktop admin interfaces (Chapters 25 and 26) run on a single operator's machine. For teams or remote monitoring, a browser-based dashboard is more practical—it requires no installation and can be accessed from any device on the network. This chapter builds a React admin interface that visualizes blocks, peers, mempool activity, and wallet operations in real time, talking to the same REST API the desktop UIs use (Chapter 24). It's deployed as a static website that talks to the node over HTTP, so you can run it anywhere—on the same machine as the node, on a different server, even in the cloud. This chapter explains the `bitcoin-web-ui/` codebase: React component architecture, data fetching patterns with React Query, TypeScript types for API responses, and routing between dashboard pages.

30.1 Overview and architectural spine

To understand the entire application quickly, read the code in this order:

1. **`src/main.tsx`** : bootstraps React into the DOM.
2. **`src/App.tsx`** : composes providers + routes + layout.
3. **`src/contexts/ApiConfigContext.tsx`** : the "global config" for base URL and API key.
4. **`src/services/api.ts`** : the HTTP boundary (one method per endpoint).
5. **`src/hooks/useApi.ts`** : the "query/mutation surface" used by components.
6. **Feature components** (Dashboard, Blockchain screens, Wallet screens): each is a thin layer that calls hooks and renders results.

30.2 Layer boundaries diagram

```
UI layer: routes + components
+- App.tsx
|  +- routes + providers
|  +- Screens
|     +- Dashboard / Wallet / Mining / ...
|
Data layer: React Query hooks
+- useApi.ts
|  +- useQuery / useMutation
|  +- cache keys + invalidation
|
HTTP boundary
+- ApiClient (Axios)
|  +- one method per endpoint
|
Rust node
+- /api/admin/* endpoints
```

The payoff of this structure is local reasoning: each layer has a single responsibility, and we can understand each without reading the others.

- A component answers: "what do we render?"
- A hook answers: "how do we fetch/cache/invalidate?"
- The API client answers: "what URL, what HTTP verb, what headers, what types?"

30.3 End-to-end data flow

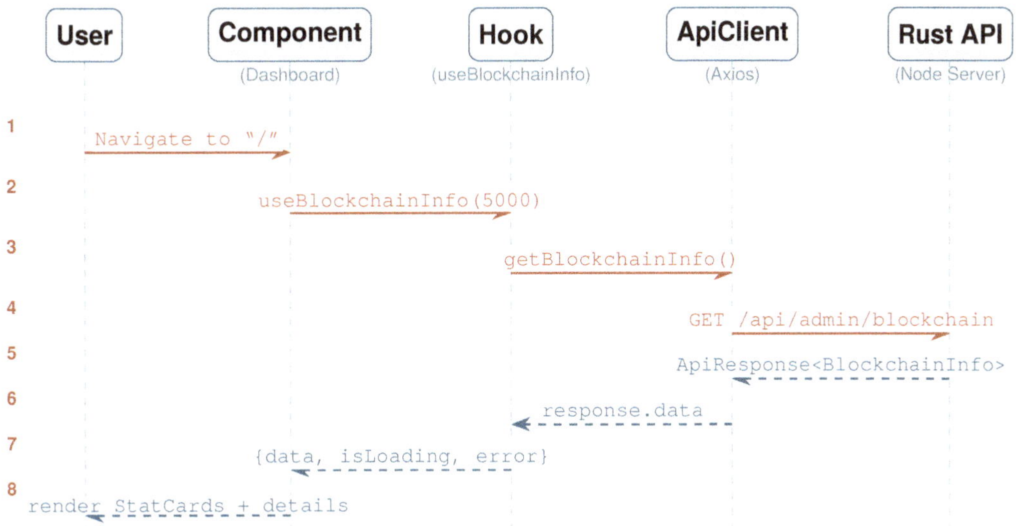

Figure 30.1: End-to-end data flow: from user navigation to rendered dashboard

The key design decision is separation of concerns:

- **Components** render UI and own local form state.
- **Hooks** define cache keys, enablement, invalidation, and mutation feedback.
- **ApiClient** performs the HTTP requests and returns typed responses.

30.4 Entry point: `src/main.tsx`

`main.tsx` is intentionally minimal: it mounts the app and imports global CSS. The architectural advantage is a single composition root (`App`) and a single place where all providers and routing are defined.

```
import React from 'react'
import ReactDOM from 'react-dom/client'
import App from './App.tsx'
import './index.css'

ReactDOM.createRoot(document.getElementById('root')!)
  .render(
    <React.StrictMode>
      <App />
    </React.StrictMode>,
  )
```

Listing 395: Browser entry point — mounting React

30.5 Composition root: providers + routes

`App.tsx` is the most important file for "what exists" in the UI:

- It defines the global **React Query client** (retry policy, focus refetch behavior).
- It enables global **API configuration** via `ApiConfigProvider`.
- It creates the **routing table** for all screens.
- It mounts the `Layout`, which provides the consistent navbar + sidebar.

```
import { QueryClient, QueryClientProvider } from
'react-query'
import { BrowserRouter as Router, Routes, Route }
from 'react-router-dom'
import { ApiConfigProvider } from
'./contexts/ApiConfigContext'
import Layout from './components/Layout'
import Dashboard from './pages/Dashboard'
// ... other page imports

const queryClient = new QueryClient({
  defaultOptions: {
    queries: {
      retry: 1,
      staleTime: 5 * 60 * 1000, // 5 min
    },
  },
})

export default function App() {
  return (
    <QueryClientProvider client={queryClient}>
      <ApiConfigProvider>
        <Router>
          <Layout>
            <Routes>
              <Route path="/" element={<Dashboard
              />} />
              <Route path="/blockchain"
              element={<BlockchainScreen />} />
              <Route path="/wallet"
              element={<WalletScreen />} />
              {/* ... more routes */}
            </Routes>
          </Layout>
        </Router>
      </ApiConfigProvider>
    </QueryClientProvider>
  )
}
```

Listing 396: Application root with providers and routing

30.6 Global configuration: API settings

The web UI cannot assume a fixed backend address or key in all deployments. The solution is:

- store `baseURL` and `apiKey` in **React Context** (a React feature that makes a value available to every descendant component without threading it through props at each level; it solves the "prop drilling" problem when a setting is read deep in the tree),
- persist them to **localStorage** (a browser-level key/value store scoped to the origin; values survive page reloads and tab closures, so the user does not re-enter settings on every visit),
- and update the API client singleton when they change.

This yields a simple rule for the rest of the codebase:

- Components do **not** pass `baseURL` / `apiKey` around as props.
- API calls always go through `getApiClient()` and therefore always use the latest config.

```
import React, { createContext, useState, useEffect,
ReactNode } from 'react'

interface ApiConfig {
  baseURL: string
  apiKey: string
}

export const ApiConfigContext = createContext<{
  config: ApiConfig
  setConfig: (config: ApiConfig) => void
} | undefined>(undefined)

export function ApiConfigProvider({ children }: {
children: ReactNode }) {
  const [config, setConfig] = useState<ApiConfig>(()
  => {
    const saved = localStorage.getItem('apiConfig')
    return saved
      ? JSON.parse(saved)
      : { baseURL: 'http://127.0.0.1:8080', apiKey:
      '' }
  })

  useEffect(() => {
    localStorage.setItem('apiConfig',
    JSON.stringify(config))
  }, [config])

  return (
    <ApiConfigContext.Provider value={{ config,
    setConfig }}>
      {children}
    </ApiConfigContext.Provider>
  )
}

export function useApiConfig() {
  const context = React.useContext(ApiConfigContext)
  if (!context) {
    throw new Error('useApiConfig must be used
    within ApiConfigProvider')
  }
  return context
}
```

Listing 397: API configuration context and persistence

▲ Security — what belongs in `localStorage`

`localStorage` is fully readable by any JavaScript running on the page, so an XSS vulnerability would expose everything stored in it. This is acceptable for admin API keys to a local endpoint but unsuitable for private keys or seed phrases. It is **not** safe for private keys, seed phrases, user passwords, or any credential whose compromise cannot be trivially rotated. For higher-sensitivity material use an HTTP-only cookie (browser cannot read it from JavaScript), a session-scoped in-memory variable, or — for wallet-class secrets — a native desktop wallet like the Tauri wallet in Chapter 28.

30.7 The HTTP boundary: `ApiClient`

This module is the only place that "knows" about:

- endpoint paths (`/api/admin/...`),
- request shape (GET vs POST),
- and authentication header injection (`X-API-Key`).

Everything above it (hooks/components) is *business/UI logic*; everything below it is *HTTP transport*.

```
import axios, { AxiosInstance } from 'axios'
import { useApiConfig } from
'../contexts/ApiConfigContext'

interface ApiResponse<T> {
  success: boolean
  data?: T
  error?: string
}

class ApiClient {
  private instance: AxiosInstance

  constructor(baseURL: string =
  'http://127.0.0.1:8080',
              apiKey: string = '') {
    this.instance = axios.create({
      baseURL,
      timeout: 10000,
      headers: {
        'Content-Type': 'application/json',
      },
    })

    if (apiKey) {
      this.instance.defaults.headers.common['X-API-K
      ey'] =
      apiKey
    }
  }

  async getBlockchainInfo() {
    const res = await
    this.instance.get<ApiResponse<BlockchainInfo>>(
      '/api/admin/blockchain'
    )
    return res.data
  }

  async getAllBlocks(limit?: number, offset?:
  number) {
    const res = await
    this.instance.get<ApiResponse<BlockList>>(
      '/api/admin/blocks',
      { params: { limit, offset } }
    )
    return res.data
  }

  async createWallet(label?: string) {
    const res = await this.instance.post<ApiResponse
    <CreateWalletResponse>>(
```

▲ Security note

The default web admin configuration does not include rate limiting or CSRF protection. Before deploying to a production environment, add these middleware layers to the API gateway. See Chapter 24 for details on the middleware stack.

30.8 The data-access surface: React Query hooks

Each hook defines the UI's public "data layer." Key components include:

- a **query key** for cache identity,
- a **query function** to call an ApiClient method,
- optional behavior like:
  - `enabled` to gate requests until input exists,
  - `refetchInterval` for auto-refresh,
  - `onSuccess` to invalidate caches and trigger feedback toast messages for mutations.

The most important hooks to understand first are:

- `useBlockchainInfo(refetchInterval?)` for dashboards and global status.
- `useCreateWallet`, `useSendTransaction`, `useGenerateBlocks` for mutations.
- `useAllBlocks` and `useAllTransactions` for on-demand "bulk" screens (`enabled: false`).

Cache keys use a hierarchical tuple structure — for example, `['blockchain', 'info']` — so that `invalidateQueries(['blockchain'])` invalidates all blockchain-scoped queries without affecting wallet queries.

```
import { useQuery, useMutation, useQueryClient }
from 'react-query'
import { getApiClient } from '../services/api'
import { useApiConfig } from
'../contexts/ApiConfigContext'

export function useBlockchainInfo(refetchInterval?:
number) {
  const { config } = useApiConfig()
  const client = getApiClient(config.baseURL,
  config.apiKey)

  return useQuery({
    queryKey: ['blockchain', 'info'],
    queryFn: () => client.getBlockchainInfo(),
    staleTime: 5 * 60 * 1000,  // 5 minutes
    refetchInterval,
  })
}

\needspace{4\baselineskip}
Blockchain state changes relatively slowly (a new
block approximately every ten minutes), so a
five-minute stale time is reasonable before forcing
a refetch.

export function useCreateWallet() {
  const queryClient = useQueryClient()
  const { config } = useApiConfig()
  const client = getApiClient(config.baseURL,
  config.apiKey)

  return useMutation(
    async (label?: string) =>
    client.createWallet(label),
    {
      onSuccess: () => {
        queryClient.invalidateQueries(['wallet',
        'addresses'])
        // Show toast success
      },
      onError: (error: any) => {
        // Show toast error
      },
    }
  )
}

export function useSendTransaction() {
  const queryClient = useQueryClient()
  const { config } = useApiConfig()
  const client = getApiClient(config.baseURL,
  config.apiKey)
```

30.9 The UI shell: layout + navigation

The UI shell lets the rest of the code stay "page focused." Two aspects matter most:

- **API configuration UX** is concentrated in the navbar. That means any page can assume the API client is configured; it does not need its own base-url inputs.
- **Sidebar state tracks the current route**, so deep links keep the correct menu open (`openMenuPath` is derived from `location.pathname`).

```
import { useState } from 'react'
import { useLocation } from 'react-router-dom'
import Navbar from './Navbar'
import Sidebar from './Sidebar'

export default function Layout({ children }: {
children: React.ReactNode }) {
  const location = useLocation()
  const [sidebarOpen, setSidebarOpen] =
  useState(true)

  return (
    <div className="flex h-screen">
      {sidebarOpen && <Sidebar
      currentPath={location.pathname} />}
      <div className="flex-1 flex flex-col">
        <Navbar
          onToggleSidebar={() =>
          setSidebarOpen(!sidebarOpen)}
        />
        <main className="flex-1 overflow-auto p-6">
          {children}
        </main>
      </div>
    </div>
  )
}
```

Listing 400: Layout component with navbar and sidebar

30.10 A representative query screen: Dashboard

The dashboard is the simplest example of the project's standard query flow:

1. Call a hook.
2. If loading, render `LoadingSpinner`.
3. If error, render `ErrorMessage`.
4. If data, render a UI view that mixes:
   - "human-friendly" components (`StatCard`),
   - and exact values (formatted timestamps, hashes, etc.).

```
import { useBlockchainInfo } from '../hooks/useApi'
import StatCard from '../components/StatCard'
import LoadingSpinner from
'../components/LoadingSpinner'
import ErrorMessage from '../components/ErrorMessage'

export default function Dashboard() {
  const { data, isLoading, error } =
  useBlockchainInfo(5000)

  if (isLoading) return <LoadingSpinner />
  if (error) return <ErrorMessage error={error} />
  if (!data?.data) return <div>No data</div>

  const info = data.data

  return (
    <div className="grid grid-cols-1 md:grid-cols-4
    gap-4">
      <StatCard
        title="Block Height"
        value={info.height}
        description={`${info.total_transactions}
        txs`}
      />
      <StatCard
        title="Pending Transactions"
        value={info.pending_transaction_count}
        description="in mempool"
      />
      <StatCard
        title="Difficulty"
        value={info.difficulty.toFixed(4)}
        description="current target"
      />
      <StatCard
        title="Total Supply"
        value={`${(info.total_supply /
        1e8).toFixed(4)} BTC`}
        description="all time"
      />
    </div>
  )
}
```

Listing 401: Dashboard — the standard query pattern

30.11 A representative mutation screen: Create Wallet

The "create wallet" screen demonstrates the project's mutation conventions:

- UI handles local form state (`label`).
- Hook handles mutation lifecycle + user feedback:
  - success toast,
  - cache invalidation (`wallet/addresses`).

```
import { useState } from 'react'
import { useCreateWallet } from '../hooks/useApi'
import Button from '../components/Button'
import JsonViewer from '../components/JsonViewer'

export default function CreateWallet() {
  const [label, setLabel] = useState('')
  const { mutate, isLoading, data, error } =
  useCreateWallet()

  const handleCreate = () => {
    if (!label.trim()) {
      alert('Please enter a label')
      return
    }
    mutate(label)
  }

  return (
    <div className="max-w-2xl">
      <h2 className="text-2xl font-bold mb-4">Create
      Wallet</h2>

      <div className="mb-4">
        <label className="block text-sm font-medium
        mb-2">
          Wallet Label
        </label>
        <input
          type="text"
          value={label}
          onChange={(e) => setLabel(e.target.value)}
          className="w-full px-3 py-2 border rounded"
          placeholder="My Wallet"
        />
      </div>

      <Button
        onClick={handleCreate}
        disabled={isLoading}
        className="mb-6"
      >
        {isLoading ? 'Creating...' : 'Create Wallet'}
      </Button>

      {error && (
        <div className="bg-red-50 text-red-700 p-4
        rounded mb-4">
          Error: {error instanceof Error ?
          error.message : 'Unknown error'}
        </div>
      )}
```

30.12 Mutation flow diagram

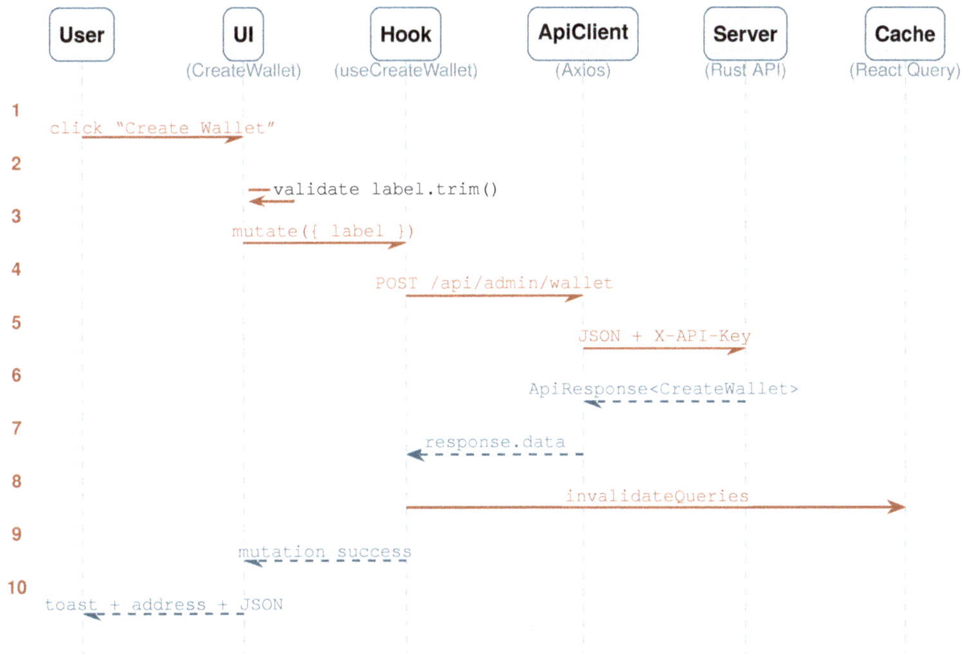

Figure 30.2: Mutation flow: creating a wallet from user click to cache invalidation

30.13 Screens mixing UI state and bulk loading

These screens show the project's "bulk load escape hatch" pattern:

- React Query hooks are configured with `enabled: false` to avoid auto-fetching.
- The component triggers fetches on-demand via `refetch()`.
- When loading "all pages," the component uses the API client directly in a loop.

This is a pragmatic compromise: React Query is excellent for caching and typical screen loads, while an explicit loop is simpler for "load everything" workflows.

```
import { useState } from 'react'
import { useAllBlocks } from '../hooks/useApi'
import { getApiClient } from '../services/api'
import { useApiConfig } from
'../contexts/ApiConfigContext'

export default function AllBlocks() {
  const { config } = useApiConfig()
  const [allBlocks, setAllBlocks] = useState([])
  const [loadingAll, setLoadingAll] = useState(false)

  const handleLoadAll = async () => {
    setLoadingAll(true)
    const client = getApiClient(config.baseURL,
    config.apiKey)
    const blocks = []
    let offset = 0
    const limit = 100

    while (true) {
      const result = await
      client.getAllBlocks(limit, offset)
      if (!result.data || result.data.items.length
      === 0) break
      blocks.push(...result.data.items)
      offset += limit
    }

    setAllBlocks(blocks)
    setLoadingAll(false)
  }

  return (
    <div>
      <h2 className="text-2xl font-bold mb-4">All
      Blocks</h2>
      <button
        onClick={handleLoadAll}
        disabled={loadingAll}
        className="px-4 py-2 bg-blue-600 text-white
        rounded"
      >
        {loadingAll ? 'Loading...' : 'Load All
        Blocks'}
      </button>

      {allBlocks.length > 0 && (
        <div className="mt-6">
          <p className="text-gray-600 mb-4">
            Loaded {allBlocks.length} blocks
          </p>
          <table className="w-full border">
            <thead>
```

30.14 Summary

Key Takeaways

- ✓ This chapter covered building a React/TypeScript web admin interface with modern component architecture.
- ✓ State management implementation using React Query and authentication patterns.
- ✓ Frontend build process and deployment pipeline structure.
- ✓ TypeScript type safety applied to API integration and response handling.

The Web Admin UI follows a clean layering approach:

- **Routes and providers** are composed in `App.tsx` .
- **Global configuration** is managed by `ApiConfigContext` .
- **HTTP transport** is isolated in `ApiClient` .
- **Caching + async lifecycle** are expressed in React Query hooks.
- **Components** remain thin and predictable: render based on `data/isLoading/error` .

i Companion Chapter

Complete React component source code is available in the companion code listings appendix. In the print edition, these listings appear in the Appendix: Source Reference.

30.15 Exercises

1. **Add a Dashboard Widget** — Create a new React component that displays the current block height, pending transaction count, and connected peer count. Use React Query to fetch the data and implement auto-refresh every 10 seconds.
2. **Authentication Flow Analysis** — Trace the authentication flow from login form submission through API call, token storage, and authenticated request headers. Identify what happens when a token expires mid-session and how the UI handles the 401 response.

30.16 Further Reading

- **React Documentation** — https://react.dev/ — Official React guides and API reference.
- **TypeScript Handbook** — https://www.typescriptlang.org/docs/handbook/ — TypeScript language features and best practices.
- **TanStack Query (React Query)** — https://tanstack.com/query/ — Data fetching and caching for the web UI.

Part II

Deployment & Operations

Chapters 31–32 take your blockchain from a single binary to a production-ready distributed system—first with Docker Compose for local multi-node testing, then with Kubernetes for scalable cloud deployment.

31

Deployment: Docker Compose

▷ **What you will learn in this chapter**

- Deploy a multi-node blockchain network using Docker Compose
- Configure container networking, port mapping, and volume management
- Scale services and manage deployment topologies for development and testing
- Troubleshoot common Docker Compose deployment issues
- Understand container naming, instance identification, and execution flow
- Implement sequential startup coordination for reliable node formation

Up to this point in the book, we have been running a single node from `cargo run`. But Bitcoin is a distributed system—you need multiple nodes to test peer discovery, block propagation, and chain synchronization. Docker Compose lets you spin up a configurable number of interconnected nodes with a single command, each with its own storage volume, while sharing a common network. This chapter bridges the gap between "the code compiles" and "the system actually works as a network."

i

Scope This chapter covers local development and small-scale Docker Compose deployments. For production-grade orchestration with autoscaling and high availability, see Chapter 32 (Kubernetes).

31.1 Overview and Quick Start

Docker Compose deployment is **code-driven**: the `docker-compose.yml` file describes the container topology, while orchestration logic (instance numbering, port selection, sequential startup, hostname resolution) lives in the **entrypoint and helper scripts**. We will start with the network topology—how containers find and talk to each other—then build up to scaling, debugging, and managing script changes.

Container Topology

Figure 31.1 shows the typical multi-node layout:

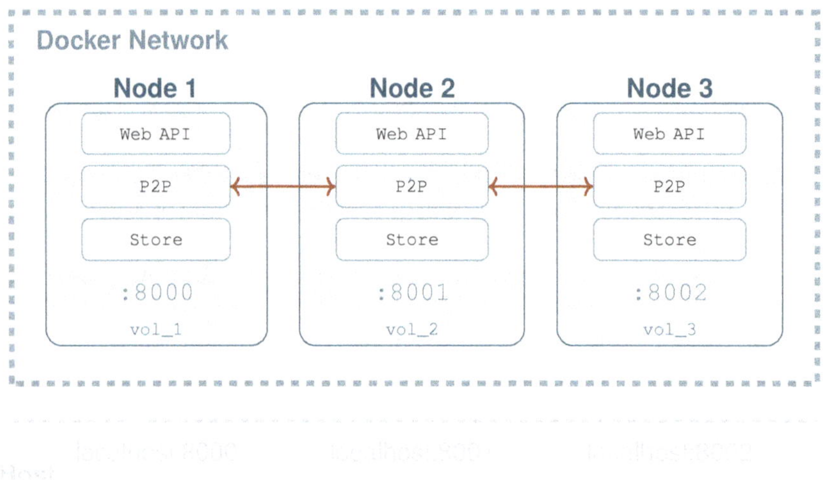

Figure 31.1: Docker Compose Deployment Topology: Multi-Node Network with Storage Volumes

Quick Start: Single Miner and Webserver

Before starting, set up wallet addresses. Use either address pool (recommended) or direct assignment:

```
cd ci/docker-compose/configs

# Set up address pool
export WALLET_ADDRESS_POOL="addr1,addr2"

# Start services
docker compose up -d

# Result:
# - redis (rate limiting backend)
# - miner_1 (P2P port 2001, uses addr1)
# - webserver_1 (Web 8080, P2P 2101, uses addr2)
```

Listing 404: Quick Start: Address Pool Method

Alternative: direct assignment:

```
cd ci/docker-compose/configs
export NODE_MINING_ADDRESS=3npBNyKSEwhCQWTXHFjwR8Rb6
6kjq6khfZSdmLPm8Gde9XoTwW
docker compose up -d
```

Listing 405: Quick Start: Direct Assignment

Access webserver at `http://localhost:8080`.

Scaling to Multiple Instances

Once comfortable with basic setup, scale to multiple instances:

```
cd ci/docker-compose/configs

# Set up address pool (at least 5 addresses)
export
WALLET_ADDRESS_POOL="addr1,addr2,addr3,addr4,addr5"

# Scale to 3 miners and 2 webservers
./docker-compose.scale.sh 3 2

# Results:
# - miner_1 -> addr1 (port 2001)
# - miner_2 -> addr2 (port 2002)
# - miner_3 -> addr3 (port 2003)
# - webserver_1 -> addr4 (port 8080, P2P 2101)
# - webserver_2 -> addr5 (port 8081, P2P 2102)
```

Listing 406: Scale to Multiple Miners and Webservers

> ▷ **Note**
>
> Always use the helper script `./docker-compose.scale.sh` to ensure **ALL instances** have ports accessible externally. Using `docker compose -scale` directly only maps ports for the first instance.

31.2 Architecture and Execution Flow

Container Naming and Instance Identification

Docker Compose names containers using the pattern:

$$\text{<project>\_<service>\_<instance>} \tag{31.1}$$

Examples:

- `blockchain_miner_1` (first miner instance)
- `blockchain_miner_2` (second miner instance)
- `blockchain_webserver_1` (first webserver instance)

The entrypoint script extracts container identity from Docker's `HOSTNAME` environment variable and normalizes it into `CONTAINER_NAME`. It then extracts the instance number using a regex pattern:

```
CONTAINER_NAME="${HOSTNAME:-}"  # e.g.
"blockchain_miner_1"

# Extract instance number from container name
if [[ "${CONTAINER_NAME}" =~ _([0-9]+)$ ]]; then
    INSTANCE_NUMBER="${BASH_REMATCH[1]}"  # e.g. 1
fi
```

Listing 407: Instance Number Extraction

Port Calculation

Each service has a *base port* (the port assigned to instance 1), and each additional instance adds 1 to it. The formula is **port = base_port + (instance_number − 1)** — the subtraction is what makes instance 1 map to the base port itself rather than base + 1. Miner base port is 2001; webserver HTTP base is 8080; webserver P2P base is 2101. This keeps instances numbered 1, 2, 3, ... while their ports increment naturally.

Table 31.1: Port Calculation Formula

Service	Instance	Formula	Port
Miner	1	$2001 + 1 - 1$	2001
Miner	2	$2001 + 2 - 1$	2002
Miner	3	$2001 + 3 - 1$	2003
Webserver (Web)	1	$8080 + 1 - 1$	8080
Webserver (Web)	2	$8080 + 2 - 1$	8081
Webserver (P2P)	1	$2101 + 1 - 1$	2101
Webserver (P2P)	2	$2101 + 2 - 1$	2102

Data Directory Isolation

Each instance uses an isolated data directory:

```
# Per-instance data directories
DATA_DIR="data${INSTANCE_NUMBER}"
BLOCKS_TREE="blocks${INSTANCE_NUMBER}"

# Examples:
# Instance 1: data1/, blocks1/
# Instance 2: data2/, blocks2/
# Instance 3: data3/, blocks3/
```

Listing 408: Data Directory Naming

Data is persisted in Docker volumes:

- Miners: `miner-data` and `miner-wallets`
- Webservers: `webserver-data` and `webserver-wallets`

Docker volumes persist data across container restarts, ensuring that blockchain state and wallet files survive when containers are stopped and recreated.

Execution Timeline

The startup flow progresses through these phases:

Figure 31.2: Docker Compose Startup Order

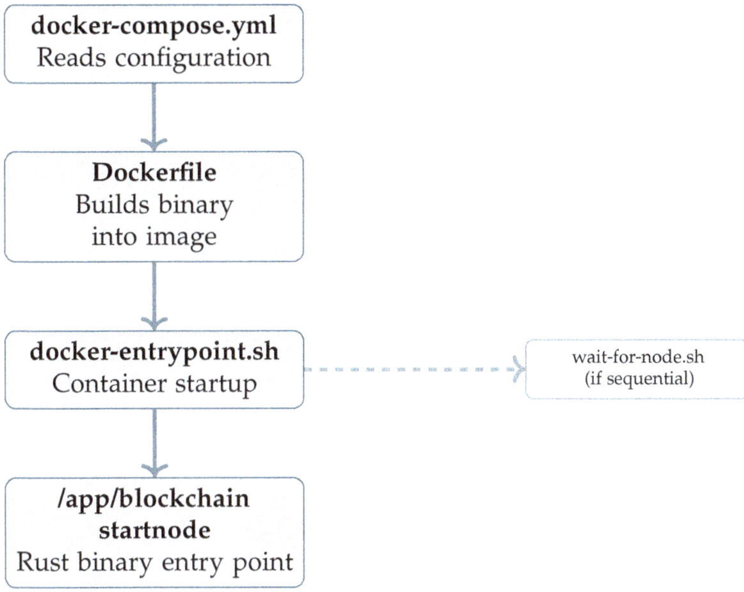

31.3 Deployment Topology and Networking

Miner Connection Chain

When scaling miners, they form a sequential chain:

Webserver Connections

Important: Webservers **always** connect to miners, never to other webservers.

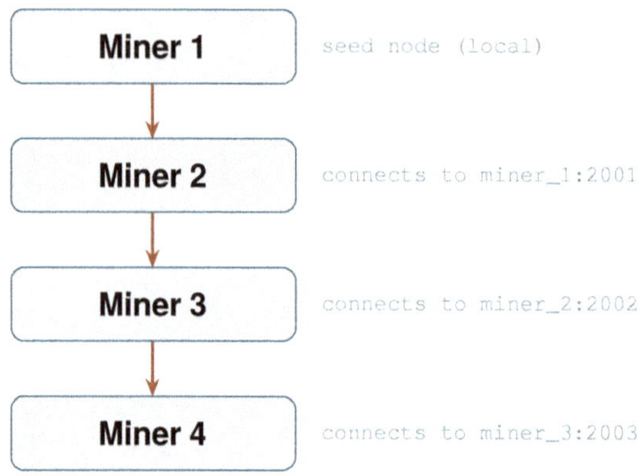

Figure 31.3: Miner connection chain: each miner connects to its predecessor

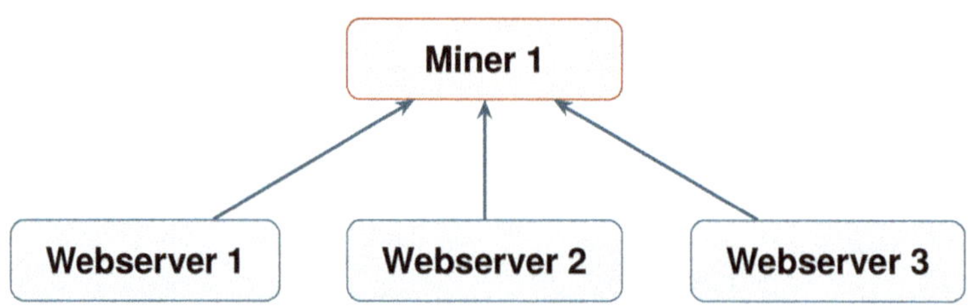

Figure 31.4: Webserver topology: all webservers connect to the first miner, never to each other

Network Topologies

Single Miner + Multiple Webservers (Star)

All webservers connect to the single miner:

```
./docker-compose.scale.sh 1 3
```

Listing 409: Star Topology: One Miner, Multiple Webservers

Multiple Miners (Chain)

Miners form a linear chain:

```
./docker-compose.scale.sh 3 1
```

Listing 410: Chain Topology: Multiple Miners

Multiple Miners + Multiple Webservers (Hybrid)

Miners form a chain; webservers star around the first miner:

```
./docker-compose.scale.sh 3 2
```

Listing 411: Hybrid Topology: Multiple Miners and Webservers

Sequential Startup Coordination

Nodes start one at a time rather than all at once because each node needs to discover at least one already-running peer before it can join the network. If all nodes started simultaneously, they would all broadcast discovery requests into an empty network and none of them would find anyone. When `SEQUENTIAL_STARTUP=yes` (default), nodes start in sequence:

1. Instance 1 starts immediately (no wait needed)
2. Instance 2 waits for Instance 1 to be ready, then connects to it
3. Instance 3 waits for Instance 2 to be ready, then connects to it
4. And so on...

Without sequential startup, `miner_2` might attempt to connect to `miner_1` before it is ready, causing connection timeouts. The wait script ensures each instance is accepting connections before the next one starts. For miners, it waits for the previous miner. For webservers, it always waits for miners.

```
# Enable sequential startup (default)
export SEQUENTIAL_STARTUP=yes
./docker-compose.scale.sh 3 2

# Or disable for simultaneous startup
export SEQUENTIAL_STARTUP=no
./docker-compose.scale.sh 3 2
```

Listing 412: Sequential Startup Configuration

31.4 Port Mapping and External Access

The Port Mapping Challenge

Docker Compose only maps ports for the first instance when using `-scale`. Additional instances created by scaling do NOT get ports mapped to the host.

Table 31.2: Port Mapping Limitation

Instance	Internal	External	Accessible?
miner_1	2001	2001	Yes
miner_2	2002	—	No
miner_3	2003	—	No

Solution: Use Helper Script

The `./docker-compose.scale.sh` script automatically generates port mappings for all instances:

```
cd ci/docker-compose/configs
./docker-compose.scale.sh 3 2

# This script:
# 1. Generates docker-compose.override.yml with port
mappings
# 2. Scales services with all ports accessible
externally
# 3. All instances have ports mapped to host
```

Listing 413: Using the Helper Script for Scaling

Alternative: Manual Override File

If you prefer to generate the override file manually:

```
cd ci/docker-compose/configs

# Step 1: Generate override file
./generate-compose-ports.sh 3 2

# Step 2: Start services
docker compose up -d --scale miner=3 --scale
webserver=2
```

Listing 414: Manual Port Override Generation

31.5 DNS Resolution Mechanism

Understanding Docker Compose DNS

Docker Compose creates an internal DNS system that resolves **service names** (defined in `docker-compose.yml`), but **NOT instance names**. A service name like `miner` round-robins across all currently running miner replicas; there is no DNS name that reaches a specific instance. This is fine for client-to-server traffic (any miner will do), but wrong for peer-to-peer traffic where each node must address its peers individually. The entrypoint script therefore translates an instance reference like `miner_2:PORT` into a service reference like `miner:PORT` and then distinguishes which instance it actually wanted by selecting a different `PORT` for each replica—DNS picks *a* miner, the port picks *which* one.

Table 31.3: Docker Compose DNS Resolution

Hostname	Type	Resolves?	Result
`miner`	Service name	Yes	172.19.0.2
`miner_1`	Instance name	No	Error
`miner_2`	Instance name	No	Error

The Conversion Mechanism

Docker's internal DNS resolver returns all IP addresses registered for a service name. The connecting client picks one — typically round-robin — so traffic distributes automatically across replicas. The entrypoint script converts instance names to service names for DNS resolution:

```
# Input from wait script
PREV_ADDR="miner_1:2001"

# Initialize resolution address
RESOLVE_ADDR="${PREV_ADDR}"

# Pattern match: miner_N:PORT
if [[ "${PREV_ADDR}" =~ ^miner_([0-9]+): ]]; then
    # Extract port and convert to service name
    PORT_PART="${PREV_ADDR##*:}"          # Extract
    port
    RESOLVE_ADDR="miner:${PORT_PART}"     # Use
    service name
fi

# Now resolve using Docker DNS
PREV_ADDR_RESOLVED=$(resolve_hostname_to_ip
"${RESOLVE_ADDR}")
# Result: PREV_ADDR_RESOLVED="172.19.0.2:2001"
```

Listing 415: Instance Name to Service Name Conversion

Why this works: `miner` (the service name) resolves in Docker Compose DNS, but `miner_1` (the instance name) does not.

31.6 Deployment Scenarios and Operations

Scenario 1: Development Setup

Single miner and webserver for local development:

```
cd ci/docker-compose/configs

export WALLET_ADDRESS_POOL="addr1,addr2"
docker compose up -d

# Accessible at:
# - Miner P2P: localhost:2001
# - Webserver Web: http://localhost:8080
# - Webserver P2P: localhost:2101
```

Listing 416: Single Miner + Webserver Deployment

Scenario 2: Multiple Mining Nodes

Test distributed mining with three miners:

```
cd ci/docker-compose/configs

export WALLET_ADDRESS_POOL="addr1,addr2,addr3,addr4"
./docker-compose.scale.sh 3 1

# Topology:
# miner_1 <- miner_2 <- miner_3
# ^
# webserver_1 (accesses all blocks via miner network)
```

Listing 417: Three Miners + One Webserver

Scenario 3: High Availability Web Access

Multiple webservers for redundancy:

```
cd ci/docker-compose/configs

export WALLET_ADDRESS_POOL="addr1,addr2,addr3,addr4"
./docker-compose.scale.sh 1 3

# Result:
# - miner_1 (port 2001)
# - webserver_1 (port 8080)
# - webserver_2 (port 8081)
# - webserver_3 (port 8082)
# All webservers connect to miner_1
```

Listing 418: One Miner + Three Webservers

Scenario 4: Production-like Configuration

Multiple miners and webservers:

```
cd ci/docker-compose/configs

export
WALLET_ADDRESS_POOL="addr1,addr2,addr3,addr4,addr5"
./docker-compose.scale.sh 3 2
```

Listing 419: Three Miners + Two Webservers

31.7 Managing Script Changes

Important: Rebuild Docker Image

The `docker-entrypoint.sh` and `wait-for-node.sh` scripts are copied into the Docker image during build. To deploy changes, you **MUST rebuild** the Docker image—Docker will use cached layers otherwise.

```
# CRITICAL: Use --no-cache for script changes
cd ci/docker-compose/configs

# Stop existing containers
docker compose down

# Rebuild with no cache
docker compose build --no-cache

# Start fresh
docker compose up -d
```

Listing 420: Deploying Script Changes

> **▲ Caching Pitfall**
>
> Using `docker compose build` alone may use cached layers. For script changes, always use `-no-cache` .

31.8 Environment Variables and Configuration

Wallet Address Distribution

Method 1: Address Pool (Recommended)

Each node automatically selects an address by index:

```
# Create pool with at least one address per instance
export
WALLET_ADDRESS_POOL="addr1,addr2,addr3,addr4,addr5"

# Start with automatic selection
docker compose up -d --scale miner=3 --scale
webserver=2

# Result:
# miner_1 -> addr1
# miner_2 -> addr2
# miner_3 -> addr3
# webserver_1 -> addr4
# webserver_2 -> addr5
```

Listing 421: Address Pool Configuration

Method 2: Direct Assignment

Use the same address for all instances:

```
export NODE_MINING_ADDRESS=3npBNyKSEwhCQWTXHFjwR8Rb6
6kjq6khfZSdmLPm8Gde9XoTwW
docker compose up -d --scale miner=3
```

Listing 422: Direct Address Assignment

Rate Limiting Configuration

The webserver loads `axum_rate_limiter` settings from the file `ci/docker-compose/configs/Settings.toml`:

```
# Compose mounts Settings.toml -> /app/Settings.toml
# Environment variable:
RL_SETTINGS_PATH=/app/Settings.toml

# To change limits:
# 1. Edit configs/Settings.toml
# 2. Restart webserver
docker compose restart webserver
```

Listing 423: Rate Limiting Setup

31.9 Monitoring and Troubleshooting

View Running Containers

```
docker compose ps
```

Listing 424: Check Container Status

View Logs

```
# All miner logs
docker compose logs -f miner

# All webserver logs
docker compose logs -f webserver

# Specific instance
docker compose logs -f miner_1
```

Listing 425: Monitor Container Logs

Common Issues

This section covers the most frequent problems encountered when running the multi-node Docker environment and how to diagnose them quickly.

Port Conflicts

```
docker compose ps
netstat -tulpn | grep -E '2001|8080|2101'
```

Listing 426: Diagnose Port Conflicts

Data Persistence

```
# List volumes
docker volume ls | grep blockchain

# Inspect volume
docker volume inspect blockchain_miner-data

# Remove volumes (WARNING: deletes data)
docker compose down -v
```

Listing 427: Check Data Persistence

Nodes Not Connecting

```
# Check if target node is ready
docker compose exec miner_2 nc -zv miner_1 2001

# Check connection environment variable
docker compose exec miner_2 env | grep
NODE_CONNECT_NODES

# View connection errors in logs
docker compose logs miner_2 | grep -i connect
```

Listing 428: Troubleshoot Node Connectivity

31.10 Accessing the Webserver

Health Checks

```
# Liveness probe
curl -f http://localhost:8080/api/health/live

# Readiness probe
curl -f http://localhost:8080/api/health/ready
```

Listing 429: Webserver Health Endpoints

Swagger UI

Access interactive API documentation at:

`http://localhost:8080/swagger-ui/` (31.2)

API Authentication

All API endpoints require the `X-API-Key` header. Default keys:

- Admin API: `admin-secret`
- Wallet API: `wallet-secret`

```
# Get blockchain info
curl -H "X-API-Key: admin-secret" \
  http://localhost:8080/api/admin/blockchain

# Get latest blocks
curl -H "X-API-Key: admin-secret" \
  http://localhost:8080/api/admin/blockchain/blocks/
  latest

# Create wallet
curl -X POST \
  -H "X-API-Key: wallet-secret" \
  -H "Content-Type: application/json" \
  http://localhost:8080/api/wallet/wallet
```

Listing 430: API Call Examples

31.11 Cleanup

Stop Services

```
# Stop all services (keeps volumes)
docker compose down

# Stop and remove volumes (deletes all data)
docker compose down -v

# View volumes before deletion
docker volume ls | grep blockchain
```

Listing 431: Stopping Docker Compose Services

Key Takeaways

- ✓ This chapter covered deploying a multi-node blockchain network using Docker Compose with configurable topologies.
- ✓ Container networking, port mapping via helper scripts, and volume management for data persistence.
- ✓ Instance identification, port calculation, and data directory isolation patterns.
- ✓ Sequential startup coordination to ensure reliable node formation.
- ✓ DNS resolution management by converting instance names to service names for Docker's internal DNS.
- ✓ Script change deployment through rebuilding Docker images without cache.
- ✓ Monitoring and troubleshooting common deployment issues with logging and health checks.

32

Deployment: Kubernetes

▷ **What you will learn in this chapter**

- Deploy the blockchain network on Kubernetes for production-grade orchestration
- Configure StatefulSets with per-pod storage for stateful blockchain nodes
- Understand service discovery, DNS, and networking in Kubernetes
- Implement horizontal pod autoscaling and high availability
- Migrate from Docker Compose to Kubernetes manifests
- Troubleshoot and operate Kubernetes deployments

Docker Compose excels for local development, but Kubernetes is built for long-running systems in production. If a blockchain node crashes, Kubernetes restarts it automatically. If you need more nodes, you change a replica count. If you push a new image, Kubernetes rolls it out without downtime. This chapter shows how the same Docker images from Chapter 31 are deployed into a system that can run reliably in production.

i

Prerequisites This chapter assumes you have read Chapter 31 (Docker Compose) and have basic familiarity with Kubernetes concepts. A local cluster like Minikube or kind is recommended for following along.

32.1 Introduction and Architecture

Why Kubernetes After Docker Compose

Table 32.1: Docker Compose vs. Kubernetes

Feature	Docker Compose	Kubernetes
Self-healing	Limited	✓Restarts and reschedules
Rolling updates	Manual	✓Built-in rollout/rollback
Service discovery	Docker DNS	✓Cluster DNS + Services
Autoscaling	Manual	✓HPA
Stateful workloads	Possible	✓First-class StatefulSets
Multi-node	No	✓Native

In this repo, Kubernetes matters because **miners and webservers are stateful** (disk-backed databases and wallets), and Kubernetes provides StatefulSets with per-pod PersistentVolumeClaims—the right primitive to manage this cleanly. A **StatefulSet** differs from a **Deployment** in two ways that matter here: it assigns each pod a stable, predictable name (`miner-0`, `miner-1`, ...) rather than a random suffix, and it binds each pod to its own persistent volume that follows the pod across restarts. Deployments treat pods as interchangeable cattle; StatefulSets treat them as named pets. For a database-backed peer-to-peer node, where every pod has its own chain state and its peers need to address it by name, the named-pet model is the only one that works.

What You'll Build

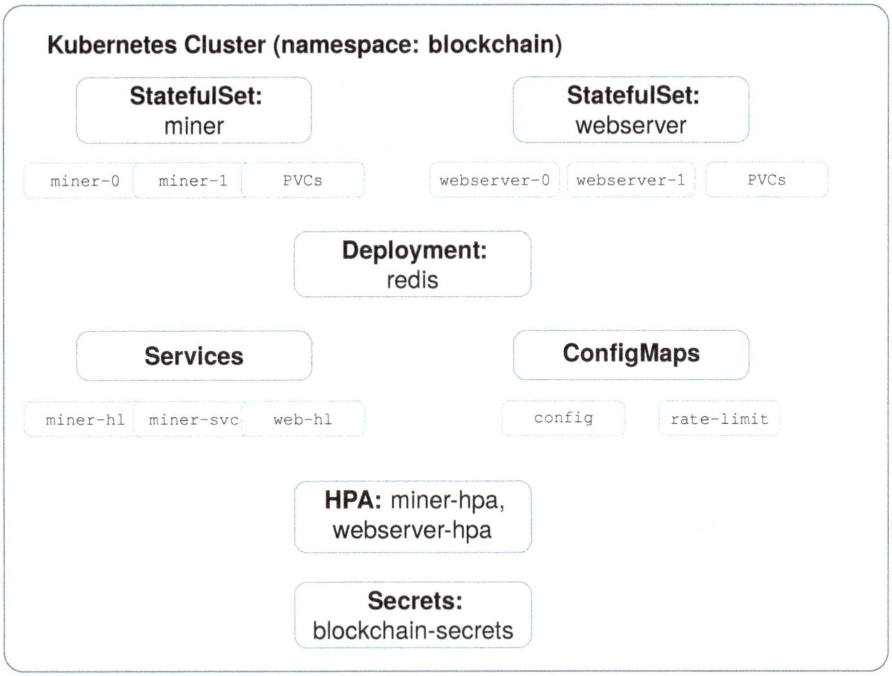

Figure 32.1: Kubernetes Deployment Architecture: StatefulSets, Services, and Configuration

32.2 Core Kubernetes Concepts

Namespace

A Namespace provides resource isolation and scoping. All resources in this repo live in the `blockchain` namespace.

```yaml
apiVersion: v1
kind: Namespace
metadata:
  name: blockchain
  labels:
    name: blockchain
    environment: production
```

Listing 432: Namespace Definition

ConfigMap

ConfigMaps store non-sensitive configuration data. In this repo, two ConfigMaps are used:

- `blockchain-config`: General node settings (as env vars)
- `rate-limit-settings`: `Settings.toml` (mounted as file)

```yaml
apiVersion: v1
kind: ConfigMap
metadata:
  name: blockchain-config
  namespace: blockchain
data:
  MINER_NODE_IS_MINER: "yes"
  MINER_NODE_CONNECT_NODES: "local"
  WEBSERVER_NODE_IS_WEB_SERVER: "yes"
  WEBSERVER_NODE_CONNECT_NODES: >-
    miner-service.blockchain.svc.cluster.local:2001
  SEQUENTIAL_STARTUP: "no"
  WALLET_FILE: "wallets/wallets.dat"
```

Listing 433: ConfigMap for Node Settings

Secret

Secrets store sensitive data like API keys. Values are base64-encoded (not encrypted by default).

```
apiVersion: v1
kind: Secret
metadata:
  name: blockchain-secrets
  namespace: blockchain
type: Opaque
stringData:
  BITCOIN_API_ADMIN_KEY: "admin-secret"
  BITCOIN_API_WALLET_KEY: "wallet-secret"
  # Optional: if omitted, entrypoint auto-creates
and persists
  # MINER_ADDRESS: ""
```

Listing 434: Secret for API Keys

StatefulSet vs. Deployment

A StatefulSet manages **stateful pods** with:

- Stable pod identity (`miner-0` , `miner-1` ,...)
- Stable per-pod storage via `volumeClaimTemplates`
- Stable per-pod DNS identity when used with a headless Service

A regular `Deployment` assigns random pod names that change on restart; StatefulSets give each pod a stable, predictable name (`miner-0` , `miner-1` , ...) that persists across restarts — essential for peer-to-peer systems where nodes must address each other by name. In this repo, both miners and webservers are stateful (disk-backed chain DB and wallets), so both run as StatefulSets.

```yaml
apiVersion: apps/v1
kind: StatefulSet
metadata:
  name: webserver
  namespace: blockchain
spec:
  serviceName: webserver-headless
  replicas: 2
  selector:
    matchLabels:
      app: webserver
  template:
    metadata:
      labels:
        app: webserver
    spec:
      containers:
      - name: blockchain-node
        image: blockchain-node:latest
        ports:
        - name: web
          containerPort: 8080
        - name: p2p
          containerPort: 2001
        volumeMounts:
        - name: webserver-data
          mountPath: /app/data
        - name: webserver-wallets
          mountPath: /app/wallets
  volumeClaimTemplates:
  - metadata:
      name: webserver-data
    spec:
      accessModes: ["ReadWriteOnce"]
      resources:
        requests:
          storage: 50Gi
  - metadata:
      name: webserver-wallets
    spec:
      accessModes: ["ReadWriteOnce"]
      resources:
        requests:
          storage: 1Gi
```

Listing 435: StatefulSet for Webservers

The `volumeClaimTemplates` section creates **one PVC per pod**, ensuring each webserver/miner has isolated disk storage. This avoids shared-disk locking issues (e.g., Sled DB lock contention) that would occur if multiple replicas shared the same storage path.

Service: Normal and Headless

In Kubernetes, it is common to have **two Services** for the same application:

1. A **headless Service** (`clusterIP: None`) for stable **per-pod identity** (DNS)
2. A **normal Service** (ClusterIP/NodePort/LoadBalancer) for stable **load-balanced access**

A headless Service publishes one DNS record per pod, enabling direct peer-to-peer communication. A normal (ClusterIP) Service provides a single virtual IP that load-balances across replicas, suitable for client traffic that does not need to target a specific pod. The two Service types solve complementary problems. A headless Service skips the virtual cluster IP entirely and publishes one DNS record per pod (`miner-0.miner-headless.default.svc.cluster.local` , `miner-1....` , `...`); peer-to-peer traffic needs this so each node can reach a specific other node. A normal Service allocates one virtual IP and load-balances incoming traffic across all ready pods; web-browser traffic needs this because the client does not care which webserver handles the request. `ClusterIP` exposes the Service only inside the cluster; `NodePort` also opens a port on every node's external IP; `LoadBalancer` additionally provisions a cloud-provider load balancer with a public IP. This repo uses a headless Service for node-to-node traffic and a normal Service (type depends on your cluster) for the admin and wallet frontends.

```yaml
apiVersion: v1
kind: Service
metadata:
  name: webserver-headless
  namespace: blockchain
spec:
  clusterIP: None  # Headless service
  selector:
    app: webserver
  ports:
  - name: web
    port: 8080
    targetPort: 8080
  - name: p2p
    port: 2001
    targetPort: 2001
```

Listing 436: Headless Service (Per-Pod DNS Identity)

A headless Service enables stable DNS names like:

$$\texttt{webserver-0.webserver-headless.blockchain.svc.cluster.local} \tag{32.1}$$

```yaml
apiVersion: v1
kind: Service
metadata:
  name: webserver-service
  namespace: blockchain
spec:
  type: LoadBalancer
  selector:
    app: webserver
  ports:
  - name: web
    port: 8080
    targetPort: 8080
```

Listing 437: Normal Service (Load-Balanced Access)

Service Discovery

In Kubernetes, pods connect using Service DNS names:

$$\texttt{<service-name>.<namespace>.svc.cluster.local} \tag{32.2}$$

Example: A webserver connecting to a miner:

```
# Docker Compose
NODE_CONNECT_NODES=miner_1:2001

# Kubernetes
NODE_CONNECT_NODES=miner-service.blockchain.svc.clus⌋
ter.local:2001
```

Listing 438: Service Discovery: Webserver to Miner

32.3 Setup and Quick Start

Prerequisites

Install the required tools:

```
brew install kubectl
brew install minikube
brew install docker
```

Listing 439: Install Kubernetes Tools (macOS)

Start Minikube Cluster

```
cd ci/kubernetes

# Start cluster with metrics-server addon (required
for HPA)
minikube start --cpus=4 --memory=3072mb \
  --addons=metrics-server
```

Listing 440: Start Local Kubernetes Cluster

Build and Load Docker Image

```
# Use Minikube's Docker daemon
eval $(minikube docker-env)

# Build from repository root
cd ../../  # (where Dockerfile is)
docker build -t blockchain-node:latest -f Dockerfile
.

# Restore normal Docker
eval $(minikube docker-env -u)
```

Listing 441: Build Image into Minikube

Deploy Using Script

```
cd ci/kubernetes/manifests
./deploy.sh
```

Listing 442: Deploy All Kubernetes Resources

The deployment script applies manifests in dependency order:

1. Namespace
2. ConfigMaps and Secrets
3. PersistentVolumeClaims
4. Redis (rate limiting backend)
5. StatefulSets (miners and webservers)
6. Services
7. HPA configurations
8. Pod Disruption Budgets

Verify Deployment

```
# Check pod status
kubectl get pods -n blockchain

# Wait for all pods to be ready
kubectl wait --for=condition=ready pod \
  -l app=miner -n blockchain --timeout=300s
kubectl wait --for=condition=ready pod \
  -l app=webserver -n blockchain --timeout=300s

# View all resources
kubectl get all -n blockchain
```

Listing 443: Verify Pods Are Running

Access Webserver (Port Forward)

```
kubectl port-forward -n blockchain \
  svc/webserver-service 8080:8080

# Then access at http://localhost:8080
```

Listing 444: Port-Forward to Webserver Service

32.4 Migration from Docker Compose

Step 1: Build and Push Image

For local Minikube: use the image loaded in the "Build and Load Docker Image" section above.

For cloud: tag and push to your registry:

```
docker build -t blockchain-node:latest -f Dockerfile
.
docker tag blockchain-node:latest
your-registry/blockchain-node:v1.0.0
docker push your-registry/blockchain-node:v1.0.0
```

Listing 445: Push to Container Registry

Step 2: Create Namespace

```
kubectl apply -f 01-namespace.yaml
```

Listing 446: Create Blockchain Namespace

Step 3: Create ConfigMaps and Secrets

```
kubectl apply -f 02-configmap.yaml
kubectl apply -f 03-secrets.yaml
kubectl apply -f 14-configmap-rate-limit.yaml
```

Listing 447: Apply Configuration and Secrets

Step 4: Create StatefulSets

StatefulSets automatically create per-pod PVCs based on `volumeClaimTemplates`:

```
kubectl apply -f 15-redis.yaml
kubectl apply -f 06-statefulset-miner.yaml
kubectl apply -f 07-deployment-webserver.yaml
```

Listing 448: Deploy StatefulSets

Step 5: Create Services

```
kubectl apply -f 08-service-miner-headless.yaml
kubectl apply -f 08-service-miner.yaml
kubectl apply -f 09-service-webserver-headless.yaml
kubectl apply -f 09-service-webserver.yaml
```

Listing 449: Deploy Services for Networking

Step 6: Configure HPA (Autoscaling)

```
kubectl apply -f 10-hpa-webserver.yaml
kubectl apply -f 11-hpa-miner.yaml
```

Listing 450: Deploy Horizontal Pod Autoscalers

Key Differences from Docker Compose

Table 32.2: Migration: Docker Compose to Kubernetes

Aspect	Docker Compose	Kubernetes
Service discovery	`miner_1:2001`	`miner-service...:2001`
Scaling	`-scale miner=3`	`kubectl scale statefulset miner ...`
Port mapping	Manual in compose	Service types (ClusterIP, LB)
Storage	Docker volumes	PersistentVolumeClaims
Configuration	Env vars	ConfigMaps + Secrets
Rolling updates	Manual	`kubectl rollout`

32.5 Operations and Scaling

Manual Scaling

Scale StatefulSets by changing replica count:

```
# Scale webservers to 5 replicas
kubectl scale statefulset webserver -n blockchain \
  --replicas=5

# Scale miners to 3
kubectl scale statefulset miner -n blockchain \
  --replicas=3
```

Listing 451: Manual Pod Scaling

Viewing Logs

```
# All miner logs
kubectl logs -n blockchain -l app=miner -f

# Specific pod
kubectl logs -n blockchain miner-0 -f

# Show previous container logs (for crashes)
kubectl logs -n blockchain miner-0 --previous
```

Listing 452: Stream Container Logs

Update Configuration

```
# Edit ConfigMap
kubectl edit configmap blockchain-config -n
blockchain

# Restart pods to pick up changes
kubectl rollout restart statefulset/webserver \
  -n blockchain
kubectl rollout restart statefulset/miner -n
blockchain
```

Listing 453: Update and Rollout Configuration

Rolling Updates

```
# Update image
kubectl set image statefulset/webserver \
  blockchain-node=blockchain-node:v1.1.0 \
  -n blockchain

# Watch rollout progress
kubectl rollout status statefulset/webserver \
  -n blockchain

# Rollback if needed
kubectl rollout undo statefulset/webserver -n
blockchain
```

Listing 454: Rolling Update Strategy

32.6 Horizontal Pod Autoscaling (HPA)

HPA automatically adjusts replica counts based on CPU and memory metrics. The Horizontal Pod Autoscaler monitors CPU and memory usage reported by the metrics server. When usage exceeds the configured threshold, the HPA increases the replica count; when it drops below, replicas are scaled down.

```
apiVersion: autoscaling/v2
kind: HorizontalPodAutoscaler
metadata:
  name: webserver-hpa
  namespace: blockchain
spec:
  scaleTargetRef:
    apiVersion: apps/v1
    kind: StatefulSet
    name: webserver
  minReplicas: 1
  maxReplicas: 10
  metrics:
  - type: Resource
    resource:
      name: cpu
      target:
        type: Utilization
        averageUtilization: 70
```

Listing 455: HPA Configuration

Verify HPA Status

```
# View HPA status
kubectl describe hpa webserver-hpa -n blockchain

# Check current resource usage
kubectl top pods -n blockchain

# If \`kubectl top\` fails, enable metrics-server:
minikube addons enable metrics-server

# Verify Metrics API is available
kubectl get apiservices | grep metrics
```

Listing 456: Check Autoscaling Status

32.7 Troubleshooting

Symptom: CrashLoopBackOff

Container starts and immediately exits, then Kubernetes restarts it in a loop.

```
# View logs from crashed container
kubectl logs -n blockchain miner-0 --previous \
  --tail 200

# Describe pod for events and probe failures
kubectl describe pod miner-0 -n blockchain

# Common cause: invalid MINER\_ADDRESS
# Fix: remove placeholder or set real address
```

Listing 457: Debug CrashLoopBackOff

Symptom: Pod Running but Not Ready

Container is running, but readiness probes fail.

```
# Describe pod to see probe failures
kubectl describe pod miner-0 -n blockchain

# Common causes:
# - Port mismatches between container and probe
# - Process not listening on expected port
# - Application startup delay
```

Listing 458: Debug Readiness Issues

Symptom: Storage Lock Errors

Multiple webserver pods trying to open same Sled database simultaneously.

```
# Verify each webserver has its own PVC
kubectl get pvc -n blockchain | grep webserver

# If sharing storage, ensure StatefulSet with
# volumeClaimTemplates is used (not Deployment)
# with shared PVC
```

Listing 459: Debug Storage Lock Errors

Symptom: HPA Not Working

```
# Check HPA status
kubectl describe hpa webserver-hpa -n blockchain

# Check if metrics are available
kubectl top pods -n blockchain

# If metrics unavailable, enable metrics-server:
minikube addons enable metrics-server

# Verify the Metrics API is registered:
kubectl get apiservices | grep metrics
```

Listing 460: Debug HPA Issues

32.8 Cleanup

```
cd ci/kubernetes/manifests
./undeploy.sh

# Or delete namespace (removes all resources)
kubectl delete namespace blockchain

# Stop local cluster (keeps cluster on disk)
minikube stop

# Remove local cluster completely
minikube delete
```

Listing 461: Delete Kubernetes Deployment

32.9 Production Considerations

Persistent Storage

In production:

- Use cloud-provided storage classes (AWS EBS, Google Persistent Disks, Azure Disks)
- Ensure PVCs are backed by reliable block storage with snapshots/backups
- StatefulSets with per-pod PVCs prevent shared-disk locking

Resource Requests and Limits

Set appropriate CPU and memory requests/limits to:

- Enable proper scheduling
- Prevent resource starvation
- Trigger autoscaling based on actual usage

```
resources:
  requests:
    cpu: "500m"
    memory: "512Mi"
  limits:
    cpu: "2000m"
    memory: "2Gi"
```

Listing 462: Resource Configuration

Network Policies

In production, restrict network traffic using Kubernetes NetworkPolicies to limit which pods can communicate.

Secrets Management

For production, use proper secret management:

- Sealed Secrets (automatic encryption)
- External Secrets Operator (integrate with Vault, AWS Secrets Manager)
- Avoid base64-encoding as security (not encryption)

Key Takeaways

- ✓ This chapter covered deploying the blockchain network on Kubernetes using StatefulSets for stateful miners and webservers.
- ✓ StatefulSets with per-pod PersistentVolumeClaims as the right primitive for disk-backed databases.
- ✓ Service discovery implementation using normal and headless Services for load-balanced and per-pod DNS access.
- ✓ Horizontal Pod Autoscaling configured to automatically adjust replica counts based on CPU/memory metrics.
- ✓ Migration path from Docker Compose to Kubernetes through building images, creating manifests, and applying resources in dependency order.
- ✓ Deployment scaling both manually using `kubectl scale` and automatically using HPA.
- ✓ Common issue troubleshooting: CrashLoopBackOff, readiness failures, storage locks, and HPA misconfiguration.
- ✓ Production best practices: persistent storage, resource management, network policies, and secrets management.

—

Part III

Language Reference

Chapter 33 is a self-contained Rust language reference covering every feature used in the implementation chapters—from ownership and traits through async/await and concurrency—so you can read it before or alongside the main text.

33

Rust Language Guide

> ▷ **What you will learn in this chapter**
>
> - Understand Rust's ownership and borrowing system for memory safety
> - Apply traits, generics, and lifetimes to write flexible code
> - Handle errors idiomatically with `Result`, `Option`, and the `?` operator
> - Write async code with Tokio and manage concurrency with channels and synchronization primitives
> - Test Rust code at unit and integration levels using the built-in test framework
> - Apply best practices and idioms for production-grade systems programming

If you can write Python or JavaScript but have never touched Rust, this chapter is your bridge into the implementation chapters. Rust looks unfamiliar at first—*borrow checkers* (a compile-time pass that proves every reference points at still-live data), *lifetimes* (annotations that name how long a reference is valid so the borrow checker can verify it), *pattern matching* (case analysis on enum variants and struct fields that the compiler forces to be exhaustive)—but these features directly prevent entire categories of bugs that plague C++ and even Go. This chapter covers what you need to read the rest of this book: ownership (how Rust tracks who owns each piece of memory), borrowing (how you can temporarily use someone else's data), traits (Rust's way of saying "any type that implements this interface"), and async (how to write concurrent code without callbacks or promises). We anchor every concept to examples from the blockchain codebase.

33.1 Installation and Setup

Install Rust using rustup, the official toolchain manager:

```
# macOS / Linux
curl --proto '=https' --tlsv2 -sSf
https://sh.rustup.rs | sh
source "$HOME/.cargo/env"

# Windows (PowerShell)
winget install --id Rustlang.Rustup -e

# Verify installation
rustc --version
cargo --version
```

Essential tools:

- `cargo build` (compile), `cargo test` (test), `cargo run` (execute)
- `cargo fmt` (format code)
- `cargo clippy` (lint and flag mistakes)

Install components if missing:

```
rustup component add rustfmt clippy
```

For IDE support, install rust-analyzer: VS Code extension or IntelliJ/CLion plugin.

33.2 Introduction to Rust

Rust's core principles center on three seemingly contradictory goals:

1. **Safety**: The compiler prevents memory safety bugs and data races at compile time
2. **Performance**: Zero-cost abstractions mean high-level features compile to efficient machine code
3. **Concurrency**: The type system enables "fearless concurrency"—safe concurrent code without data races

These principles aren't trade-offs. Rust achieves all three through careful language design and compile-time analysis. In blockchain systems where a single bug can compromise the entire system, Rust's compile-time safety is a strategic advantage.

Why Rust for Blockchain?

Blockchain systems have unique requirements making Rust particularly well-suited:

- **Security**: Process untrusted input safely; compile-time checks catch many bugs before production
- **Performance**: Transaction processing requires low latency; Rust's zero-cost abstractions ensure performance
- **Concurrency**: Nodes handle many concurrent operations (network, transactions, mining); Rust's type system ensures thread safety
- **Reliability**: Continuous operation requires memory safety; Rust's ownership system prevents crashes from memory errors

33.3 Ownership and Borrowing

Ownership is Rust's distinctive feature—a compile-time system that tracks data ownership and ensures memory is freed exactly once, automatically. These three rules solve a fundamental problem: traditional languages use either garbage collection (runtime overhead, latency spikes) or manual memory management (use-after-free bugs, memory leaks). Rust checks ownership at compile time, guaranteeing memory safety with zero runtime cost. Three rules govern it:

1. **Each value has one owner**: Only one variable owns each value at any time
2. **Only one mutable borrow at a time**: Prevents data races
3. **Values drop when owner goes out of scope**: Automatic cleanup without garbage collection

Ownership in Practice

From the blockchain implementation (`bitcoin/src/primitives/transaction.rs`):

```
impl TXInput {
    pub fn new(txid: &[u8], vout: usize) -> TXInput {
        TXInput {
            txid: txid.to_vec(),   // Takes ownership of new Vec
            vout,
        }
    }
    pub fn get_txid(&self) -> &[u8] {   // Returns borrowed ref
        self.txid.as_slice()
    }
}
```

Listing 463: Ownership example in TXInput implementation

The `new` function receives a borrowed slice but creates a new `Vec<u8>` that the `TXInput` owns. The `to_vec()` method creates owned data; the `get_txid()` method returns a borrowed reference.

Borrowing

Immutable borrows (`&T`): Multiple readers, no modifications.

```
pub fn uses_key(&self, pub_key_hash: &[u8]) -> bool {
    hash_pub_key(self.pub_key.as_slice()).eq(pub_key_hash)
}
```

Listing 464: Immutable borrowing

Mutable borrows (`&mut T`): One exclusive writer.

```
fn set_key(&mut self, key: Vec<u8>) {
    self.pub_key = key;   // Exclusive mutable access
}
```

Listing 465: Mutable borrowing

The borrow checker enforces these rules at compile time, preventing data races without runtime overhead.

Ownership Transfer (Moves)

When ownership transfers between variables, it's zero-cost—just pointer transfer:

```
pub fn new(blockchain: BlockchainService) ->
NodeContext {
    NodeContext { blockchain }  // Move, not copy
}
```

Listing 466: Ownership move

In the blockchain implementation, borrowing is used for reads (efficient), while moves are used for isolation (transactional safety).

33.4 Data Structures: Structs and Enums

Structs and enums are Rust's primary mechanisms for modeling domain concepts.

Structs

Structs group related data with named fields. From the blockchain implementation (`bitcoin/src/primitives/block.rs`):

```rust
#[derive(Clone, Serialize, Deserialize)]
pub struct BlockHeader {
    timestamp: i64,
    pre_block_hash: String,
    hash: String,
    nonce: i64,
    height: usize,
}

#[derive(Clone, Serialize, Deserialize)]
pub struct Block {
    header: BlockHeader,
    transactions: Vec<Transaction>,
}
```

Listing 467: Struct definitions for blocks

Structs compose data hierarchically, make the domain model self-documenting, and allow implementing methods in `impl` blocks.

Enums

Enums represent values that are one of several variants. From `bitcoin/src/error.rs`:

```
#[derive(Clone, Error, Debug)]
pub enum BtcError {
    #[error("Blockchain not found: {0}")]
    BlockchainNotFoundError(String),
    #[error("Invalid transaction")]
    InvalidTransaction,
    #[error("Not enough funds")]
    NotEnoughFunds,
}
```

Listing 468: Error enum with variants

Enums can carry data (unit, tuple, or struct variants) and are exhaustively pattern-matched by the compiler.

33.5 Traits: Polymorphism and Code Reuse

Traits define shared behavior that types can implement. They enable polymorphism and code reuse.

Defining and Implementing Traits

Traits specify a contract. From `bitcoin/src/node/peers.rs`:

```
#[derive(Clone, Debug, Eq, PartialEq, Hash)]
pub struct Node {
    addr: SocketAddr,
}

impl Node {
    fn new(addr: SocketAddr) -> Node {
        Node { addr }
    }
    pub fn get_addr(&self) -> SocketAddr {
        self.addr
    }
}

impl Default for Node {
    fn default() -> Self {
        Self::new(/* ... */)
    }
}
```

Listing 469: Trait implementation example

Trait Bounds

Trait bounds constrain generic types. From `bitcoin/src/chain/chainstate.rs`:

```
async fn read<F, Fut, T>(&self, f: F) -> Result<T>
where
    F: FnOnce(BlockchainFileSystem) -> Fut + Send,
    Fut: Future<Output = Result<T>> + Send,
    T: Send + 'static,
{
    let blockchain_guard = self.0.read().await;
    f(blockchain_guard.clone()).await
}
```

Listing 470: Trait bounds in generic functions

Bounds like `F: FnOnce(...) + Send` ensure `F` can be called once and is safe to send between threads.

33.6 Error Handling

Error handling is explicit and type-safe in Rust. `Result<T, E>` represents operations that can fail; `Option<T>` represents values that might not exist.

Result Type

The `Result<T, E>` type represents outcomes of operations that can succeed or fail. Example from `bitcoin/src/primitives/transaction.rs`:

```
impl TXOutput {
    pub fn new(value: i32, address: &WalletAddress) -> Result<TXOutput> {
        let mut output = TXOutput {
            value,
            in_global_mem_pool: false,
            pub_key_hash: vec![],
        };
        output.lock(address)?;  // ? operator propagates errors
        Ok(output)
    }

    fn lock(&mut self, address: &WalletAddress) -> Result<()> {
        let pub_key_hash = get_pub_key_hash(address)?;
        self.pub_key_hash = pub_key_hash;
        Ok(())
    }
}
```

Listing 471: Result type in transaction output creation

This example shows how `Result` types flow through code. The `?` operator automatically propagates errors—if `lock()` returns an error, the function immediately returns that error.

Rust provides several methods for working with `Result` types:

- **? operator**: Most common; unwraps `Ok` or returns error immediately
- **`unwrap()`** : Unwraps `Ok` or panics; useful in tests
- **`expect()`** : Like `unwrap()` , with custom panic message
- **`map()`** : Transforms `Ok` value if present
- **`map_err()`** : Transforms `Err` value if present

Option Type

`Option<T>` represents values that might not exist, replacing null pointers with explicit handling. Example from `bitcoin/src/node/peers.rs`:

```rust
pub fn first(&self) -> Result<Option<Node>> {
    let inner = self
        .inner
        .read()
        .map_err(|e| BtcError::NodesInnerPoisonedLockError(e.to_string()))?;
    Ok(inner.iter().next().cloned())  // Returns Option<Node>
}
```

Listing 472: Option type in peer management

The `first()` method returns `Result<Option<Node»`, showing how `Result` and `Option` combine. The outer `Result` represents potential errors, while the inner `Option` represents whether a node was found.

Working with `Option` requires explicit handling:

- **`unwrap_or()`** : Provides default if `None`
- **`unwrap_or_else()`** : Computes default lazily if `None`
- **`map()`** : Transforms `Some` value if present
- **`and_then()`** : Chains operations returning `Option`
- **`match`** : Exhaustive pattern matching for both `Some` and `None`

The ? Operator

The ? operator is syntactic sugar for early return: if the expression evaluates to Err , ? immediately returns that error from the enclosing function; if Ok , it unwraps the inner value and execution continues. Example from bitcoin/src/primitives/block.rs:

```
pub fn deserialize(bytes: &[u8]) -> Result<Block> {
    bincode::serde::decode_from_slice(bytes, bincode::config::standard())
        .map_err(|e| BtcError::BlockDeserializationError(e.to_string()))
        .map(|(block, _)| block)
}
```

Listing 473: Error propagation with the ? operator

The ? operator checks if the operation succeeded. If it returned Ok , it unwraps the value. If it returned Err , it immediately returns that error from the function. This is equivalent to a match statement with early return but much more concise.

33.7 Generics: Type Parameters and Code Reuse

Rust generics have zero runtime overhead. The compiler generates a specialized copy of the function for each concrete type used (a process called monomorphization), so generic code runs exactly as fast as hand-written type-specific code. From `bitcoin/src/web/models/responses.rs`:

```
#[derive(Debug, Serialize, Deserialize)]
pub struct ApiResponse<T> {
    pub success: bool,
    pub data: Option<T>,
    pub error: Option<String>,
}

impl<T> ApiResponse<T> {
    pub fn success(data: T) -> Self {
        Self { success: true, data: Some(data), error: None }
    }
}
```

Listing 474: Generic struct for API responses

Generic structs wrap any type. `ApiResponse<T>` enables consistent response formats for all endpoints.

Monomorphization

The compiler generates separate code for each concrete type:

```
// Generic function
fn process<T: Serialize>(item: T) -> Vec<u8> { ... }

// Compiler generates:
// fn process_Transaction(...) { ... }
// fn process_Block(...) { ... }
```

Zero runtime overhead; each monomorphized function is optimized for its type.

33.8 Lifetimes: Managing Reference Validity

A **lifetime** is Rust's way of tracking how long a reference is valid. Without lifetimes, the compiler could not prevent you from holding a pointer to data that has already been freed—the classic "use after free" bug that causes crashes and security vulnerabilities in C and C++. Rust makes you annotate lifetimes so the compiler can prove, at compile time, that every reference outlives its data. Most of the time, Rust can infer lifetimes automatically through lifetime elision rules.

The `'static` Lifetime

The `'static` lifetime represents data that lives for the entire program duration. Example from `bitcoin/src/web/routes/web.rs`:

```
async fn react_app_not_built() -> Html<&'static str>
{
    Html(
        r#"
        <!DOCTYPE html>
        ...
        "#
    )
}
```

Listing 475: Static lifetime for string literals

String literals have the `'static` lifetime because they're compiled into the binary and exist for the program's entire execution.

Lifetime Elision

Writing explicit lifetime annotations for every function would be verbose. Rust infers lifetimes automatically through elision rules. Rust applies three elision rules automatically: (1) each input reference gets its own lifetime parameter, (2) if there is exactly one input lifetime, the output gets that lifetime, and (3) if one of the inputs is `&self` or `&mut self`, the output gets self's lifetime.

```
// Lifetime elided - compiler infers automatically
pub fn get_txid(&self) -> &[u8] {
    self.txid.as_slice()
}

// Equivalent explicit version (what compiler infers)
pub fn get_txid<'a>(&'a self) -> &'a [u8] {
    self.txid.as_slice()
}
```

Listing 476: Lifetime elision example

Examples of these three rules follow:

33.9 Smart Pointers: Shared Ownership

Smart pointers enable shared ownership when single ownership isn't sufficient. `Arc` provides thread-safe shared ownership; `Rc` provides single-threaded shared ownership.

Arc: Atomic Reference Counting

Without `Arc`, you cannot pass the same data to two threads — each `move` tries to take exclusive ownership. `Arc` (Atomic Reference Counting) lets multiple threads share ownership; the data is freed only when the last `Arc` clone is dropped. Example from `bitcoin/src/chain/chainstate.rs`:

```rust
use std::sync::Arc;
use tokio::sync::RwLock as TokioRwLock;

#[derive(Debug)]
pub struct BlockchainService(Arc<TokioRwLock<BlockchainFileSystem>>);

impl Clone for BlockchainService {
    fn clone(&self) -> Self {
        BlockchainService(self.0.clone())  // Clones Arc, not data
    }
}
```

Listing 477: Arc for thread-safe shared ownership

The `BlockchainService` wraps blockchain data in `Arc<TokioRwLock<BlockchainFileSystem>>`. When we clone a `BlockchainService`, we're cloning the `Arc`, which just increments a reference counter. The actual blockchain data isn't copied, making cloning efficient.

`Arc` provides:

- **Thread Safety**: Uses atomic operations for reference counting
- **Reference Counting**: Tracks references; frees data when last reference drops
- **Immutable by Default**: Data inside `Arc` is immutable; wrap in `Mutex` or `RwLock` to modify

The immutability rule is a direct consequence of sharing: once two threads hold the same `Arc`, one thread mutating the inner value while the other reads would be a data race, which Rust forbids at compile time. `Mutex` and `RwLock` lift the restriction by serializing access—a thread that wants to mutate acquires the lock, does its work, and releases it, so there is never a reader and a writer on the same data at the same instant. This is the "interior mutability" pattern: the `Arc` itself is immutable (you cannot reassign its contents), but the lock inside grants controlled, synchronized mutation to whoever holds it.

33.10 Pattern Matching

Pattern matching enables exhaustive case handling. From `bitcoin/src/node/server.rs`:

```
match listener.accept() {
    Ok((stream, _peer)) => {
        tokio::spawn(async move { /* process stream */ });
    }
    Err(e) => error!("accept error: {}", e),
}
```

Listing 478: Match expression for error handling

The compiler enforces exhaustiveness—all variants must be handled.

if let

`if let` concisely handles one pattern:

```
let tip_hash = if let Some(data) = data {
    process(data)
} else {
    default_value()
};
```

Less verbose than `match` when handling one case.

33.11 Derive Macros

Derive macros automatically generate trait implementations. From `bitcoin/src/primitives/transaction.rs`:

```rust
#[derive(Clone, Default, Serialize, Deserialize)]
pub struct TXInput {
    txid: Vec<u8>,
    vout: usize,
    signature: Vec<u8>,
    pub_key: Vec<u8>,
}
```

Listing 479: Derive macro for automatic implementations

Four traits generated from one line: reduces boilerplate, ensures correctness, handles field additions automatically.

Common derives:

- **`Clone`** : Explicit copying via `.clone()`
- **`Debug`** : Format with `{:?}` and `{:#?}`
- **`PartialEq`** / **`Eq`** : Equality comparison
- **`Hash`** : Use as HashMap/HashSet keys
- **`Serialize`** / **`Deserialize`** : Convert to/from JSON or binary

33.12 Async/Await: Asynchronous Programming

Async/await enables writing asynchronous code that looks synchronous but doesn't block threads. Async functions return `Future` types; `.await` suspends execution until futures complete.

Async Functions

Example from `bitcoin/src/web/handlers/blockchain.rs`:

```rust
pub async fn get_blockchain_info(
    State(node): State<Arc<NodeContext>>,
) -> Result<Json<ApiResponse<BlockchainInfoResponse>>, StatusCode> {
    let height = node
        .get_blockchain_height()
        .await // Yields control, resumes when ready
        .map_err(|_| StatusCode::INTERNAL_SERVER_ERROR)?;

    // ... rest of handler
}
```

Listing 480: Async function for blockchain info retrieval

This handler is marked `async`, returning a `Future` that produces the `Result` when awaited. Inside, we call `.await` on `get_blockchain_height()`, yielding control. While waiting, the async runtime can process other requests, enabling high concurrency.

Async Patterns

Pattern 1: Concurrent Operations

```rust
use tokio::join;

let (blocks, transactions) = join!(
    get_blocks(),
    get_transactions()
).await;
```

Pattern 2: Timeout Handling

```
use tokio::time::{timeout, Duration};

match timeout(Duration::from_secs(5), operation()).await {
    Ok(result) => result?,
    Err(_) => Err(BtcError::Timeout),
}
```

33.13 Concurrency: Thread Safety

Rust's type system ensures thread safety through `Send` and `Sync` marker traits. These traits don't have methods—they indicate whether types can be safely used across thread boundaries.

Send and Sync Traits

`Send` indicates a type can be safely transferred between threads. `Sync` indicates a type can be safely shared between threads via references.

Example from `bitcoin/src/chain/chainstate.rs`:

```
async fn read<F, Fut, T>(&self, f: F) -> Result<T>
where
    F: FnOnce(BlockchainFileSystem) -> Fut + Send,  // Must be Send
    Fut: Future<Output = Result<T>> + Send,  // Must be Send
    T: Send + 'static,  // Must be Send
{
    // ...
}
```

Listing 481: Send and Sync trait bounds

These bounds ensure thread safety. Most Rust types implement `Send` and `Sync` automatically.

Mutex and RwLock

`Mutex` and `RwLock` provide thread-safe interior mutability. Example from `bitcoin/src/node/peers.rs`:

```
use std::sync::RwLock;

pub struct Nodes {
    inner: RwLock<HashSet<Node>>,
}

impl Nodes {
    pub fn add_node(&self, addr: SocketAddr) -> Result<()> {
        let mut inner = self
            .inner
            .write()   // Acquires write lock
            .map_err(|e| BtcError::NodesInnerPoisonedLockError(e.to_string()))?;
        inner.insert(Node::new(addr));
        Ok(())
    }
}
```

Listing 482: RwLock for thread-safe shared state

`RwLock` allows multiple readers or one writer. For write-heavy workloads, use `Mutex`. For async code, use `TokioRwLock<T>` or `TokioMutex<T>`.

33.14 Modules: Code Organization

Modules organize code hierarchically and control visibility. Example from `bitcoin/src/wallet/mod.rs`:

```
pub mod wallet_impl;
pub mod wallet_service;

pub use wallet_impl::{
    Wallet, WalletAddress, convert_address, hash_pub_key,
};

pub use wallet_service::{WalletService};
```

Listing 483: Module organization with re-exports

Declare sub-modules with `pub mod`. Use `pub use` to re-export items, creating convenient public APIs while keeping internal structure flexible.

Visibility levels:

- **`pub`** : Public, accessible from anywhere
- **(no modifier)**: Private, within same module only
- **`pub(crate)`** : Public within crate only
- **`pub(super)`** : Public to parent module

33.15 Iterators and Closures

Iterators and closures enable functional programming patterns with zero runtime overhead.

Iterators

Iterators are lazy—operations don't execute until consumed. From `bitcoin/src/net/net_processing.rs`:

```
nodes_to_add.iter().for_each(|node| {
    let node_addr = *node;
    tokio::spawn(async move {
        send_known_nodes(&node_addr,
all_nodes).await;
    });
});
```

Listing 484: Iterator with for_each

Common iterator methods:

- **`iter()`** : Immutable references
- **`iter_mut()`** : Mutable references
- **`into_iter()`** : Takes ownership
- **`map()`**, **`filter()`** : Transform and filter lazily
- **`collect()`** : Consume and collect into collection
- **`for_each()`** : Execute closure for each item

Closures

Closures are anonymous functions with capture. Three closure traits based on capture:

- **`FnOnce`** : Called once; takes ownership of captured variables
- **`FnMut`** : Multiple calls; requires mutable borrow
- **`Fn`** : Multiple calls; requires immutable borrow

Example from `bitcoin/src/chain/chainstate.rs`:

```
async fn read<F, Fut, T>(&self, f: F) -> Result<T>
where
    F: FnOnce(BlockchainFileSystem) -> Fut + Send,
    Fut: Future<Output = Result<T>> + Send,
    T: Send + 'static,
{
    let blockchain_guard = self.0.read().await;
    f(blockchain_guard.clone()).await
}
```

Listing 485: Closure traits in generic function

33.16 Type Conversions

Type conversion traits define how types convert to/from other types.

From and Into

`From<T>` converts `T` to `Self` (infallible). `Into<T>` is auto-implemented; implement `From` and get `Into` free. Example from `bitcoin/src/node/server.rs`:

```
impl FromStr for ConnectNode {
    type Err = std::net::AddrParseError;

    fn from_str(s: &str) -> Result<Self, Self::Err> {
        if s == "local" {
            Ok(ConnectNode::Local)
        } else {
            let ip_addr = s.parse()?;
            Ok(ConnectNode::Remote(ip_addr))
        }
    }
}
```

Listing 486: FromStr implementation

TryFrom and TryInto

`TryFrom<T>` converts `T` to `Self` (fallible, returns `Result`). `TryInto<T>` is auto-implemented. Example from `bitcoin/src/primitives/block.rs`:

```
impl TryFrom<Block> for IVec {
    type Error = BtcError;

    fn try_from(block: Block) -> Result<Self, Self::Error> {
        let serialized = block.serialize()?;
        Ok(IVec::from(serialized))
    }
}
```

Listing 487: TryFrom for fallible conversion

33.17 Testing

Testing is fundamental to building reliable blockchain software. Rust's type system catches many errors at compile time, but comprehensive testing ensures code behaves correctly at runtime.

Basic Test Structure

```rust
#[test]
fn test_transaction_creation() {
    let tx = Transaction::new();
    assert!(tx.is_valid());
}

#[test]
fn test_transaction_id_generation() {
    let tx = create_test_transaction();
    let id = tx.get_id();

    assert_eq!(id.len(), 32);
    assert!(!id.is_empty());
}
```

Listing 488: Simple unit test

Async Tests

For testing async code, use `#[tokio::test]`:

```rust
#[tokio::test]
async fn test_blockchain_operation() {
    let blockchain = create_test_blockchain().await;
    let result =
blockchain.process_transaction(tx).await;
    assert!(result.is_ok());
}
```

Listing 489: Async test with tokio

Test Modules

Tests are organized in modules only compiled in test mode:

```rust
#[cfg(test)]
mod tests {
    use super::*;

    mod creation {
        use super::*;
        #[test] fn test_new_transaction() { }
    }

    mod validation {
        use super::*;
        #[test] fn test_valid_transaction() { }
    }

    mod serialization {
        use super::*;
        #[test] fn test_serialize() { }
    }
}
```

Listing 490: Test module organization

Test Helpers and Fixtures

Use Rust's ownership system for automatic cleanup via the `Drop` trait:

```rust
struct TestDatabaseGuard {
    db_path: String,
}

impl Drop for TestDatabaseGuard {
    fn drop(&mut self) {
        let _ = std::fs::remove_dir_all(&self.db_path);
    }
}

#[test]
fn test_with_database() {
    let _guard = TestDatabaseGuard::new();
    // Guard automatically cleans up when test ends
}
```

Listing 491: RAII-based test fixture

Running Tests

```bash
# Run all tests
cargo test

# Run tests with output
cargo test -- --nocapture

# Run a specific test
cargo test test_transaction_creation

# Run tests sequentially (for file-based databases)
cargo test -- --test-threads=1
```

33.18 Best Practices

Error Handling

Use `Result` over panicking: Return `Result` for recoverable errors, panic only for unrecoverable errors.

```
// Good: Returns Result
pub fn new(value: i32, address: &WalletAddress) ->
Result<TXOutput> {
    if value < 0 {
        return Err(TransactionError::InvalidAmount);
    }
    Ok(TXOutput { value, address: address.clone() })
}

// Bad: Panics on error
pub fn new(value: i32, address: &WalletAddress) ->
TXOutput {
    assert!(value >= 0, "Value must be
non-negative");
    TXOutput { value, address: address.clone() }
}
```

Listing 492: Error handling best practice

Use `?` for error propagation: Concise and readable.

```
// Good: Use ? operator
pub fn process_transaction(&self, tx: Transaction)
-> Result<()> {
    validate_transaction(&tx)?;
    add_to_mempool(tx)?;
    Ok(())
}
```

Listing 493: Error propagation best practice

Memory Management

Use `Arc` for shared ownership:

```rust
// Good: Arc for shared ownership
let shared: Arc<NodeContext> = Arc::new(node);
let clone1 = Arc::clone(&shared);  // Cheap

// Bad: Cloning entire struct
let shared = node.clone();  // Expensive
```

Listing 494: Arc for shared ownership

Prefer borrowing over ownership: When only reading data, borrowing is more efficient.

```rust
// Good: Borrows reference
pub fn get_txid(&self) -> &[u8] {
    &self.txid
}

// Bad: Unnecessary clone
pub fn get_txid(&self) -> Vec<u8> {
    self.txid.clone()
}
```

Listing 495: Borrowing best practice

Type System

Leverage the type system for compile-time safety:

```rust
// Good: Type-safe wrappers prevent mixing up types
pub struct WalletAddress(String);
pub struct TransactionId(Vec<u8>);
pub struct BlockHash(Vec<u8>);

// Bad: Raw types can be confused
fn process_tx(id: Vec<u8>) { }
fn process_block(hash: Vec<u8>) { }
```

Listing 496: Type-safe wrappers

Concurrency

Use `RwLock` for read-heavy workloads: Multiple readers or one writer.

Prefer message passing over shared state: Use channels instead of locks when possible.

Use `Arc<T>` for thread-safe shared ownership.

Testing

Test both success and error cases: Don't just test the happy path.

Use descriptive test names: Clearly state what is being tested.

Follow Arrange-Act-Assert pattern: Structure tests clearly.

Use test helpers to reduce duplication: Create reusable test utilities.

Key Takeaways

- ✓ Rust's ownership system ensures memory safety and enables fine-grained control over resource management
- ✓ Borrowing and moving are compile-time decisions that lead to safer code without runtime overhead
- ✓ Traits define shared behavior and enable polymorphism with zero-cost abstractions
- ✓ Generics and monomorphization provide type safety without performance penalties
- ✓ Lifetimes ensure references remain valid; most of the time they're inferred automatically
- ✓ Smart pointers like `Arc` enable shared ownership while maintaining safety
- ✓ Error handling with `Result` and `Option` is explicit and type-safe
- ✓ Pattern matching enables exhaustive case handling with compile-time verification
- ✓ Async/await enables efficient concurrent I/O without blocking threads
- ✓ The type system prevents Send and Sync violations at compile time
- ✓ Modules organize code hierarchically while controlling visibility
- ✓ Iterators and closures provide functional patterns with zero overhead
- ✓ Type conversions are explicit and type-safe via `From`, `Into`, `TryFrom`, `TryInto`
- ✓ Comprehensive testing with unit, integration, and async tests ensures reliability
- ✓ Best practices emphasize explicit error handling, type safety, and leveraging the compiler
- ✓ Rust's combination of safety, performance, and concurrency makes it ideal for blockchain systems

Index

Colophon

This book was typeset using LaTeX with the `memoir` document class, configured for Crown Quarto format (7.44 × 9.69 inches).

Typography

The body text is set in *TeX Gyre Pagella* (a Palatino revival) at 11 pt with 1.05× leading. Section headings and navigational elements use *TeX Gyre Heros* (Helvetica family). Code listings and inline code use *TeX Gyre Cursor* (Courier family). Mathematical notation uses *Palatino Math* via the `mathpazo` package. Microtypographic refinements—character protrusion, font expansion, and tracking—are provided by the `microtype` package.

Color system

The book's visual identity is built around Rust Orange (`#B7410E`) for accent elements and Dark Teal (`#2C5F7C`) for structural headings. Eleven callout box families provide instant visual classification of notes, tips, warnings, checkpoints, and code references.

Code presentation

Source code is syntax-highlighted using the `minted` package with Pygments. Rust listings include line numbers and support inline LaTeX annotations via escape sequences. Numbered annotation circles connect code lines to explanatory notes below each listing.

Production tools

The PDF was produced with pdfLaTeX and `latexmk`. Diagrams were created with Ti*k*Z. The index was generated with `makeindex` and the glossary with `glossaries-extra`. Version control was managed with Git.

First Edition — 2026

www.ingramcontent.com/pod-product-compliance
Lightning Source LLC
LaVergne TN
LVHW060008210926
848481LV00013B/3672
9798995431114